PROPERTY LAW AND SOCIAL MORALITY

Property Law and Social Morality develops a theory of property that highlights the social construction of obligations that individuals owe each other. By viewing property law through the lens of obligations rather than through the lens of rights, the author affirms the existence of important property rights (when no obligation to another exists) and defines the scope of those rights (when an obligation to another does exist). By describing the scope of the decisions that individuals are permitted to make and the requirements of other-regarding decisions, the author develops a single theory to explain the dynamics of private and common property, including exclusion, nuisance, shared decision making, and decision making over time. By developing a theory of social recognition, the author adds to our understanding of property evolution and the principle of equal freedom that helps us chart the scope of property rights and the limits on government interference with those rights.

Professor Peter M. Gerhart has been a dean; a legal scholar in antitrust, regulated industries, international trade, international transactions, international intellectual property law, torts, and property; and a scholar of globalization. A graduate of Columbia Law School, he has taught at the law schools of The Ohio State University and Case Western Reserve University, and, as a visiting professor, at the law schools of Georgetown and the University of Texas, the Central European University in Budapest, and the Weatherhead School of Business. He is the author of *Tort Law and Social Morality* (Cambridge University Press, 2010) and has published articles in a wide variety of fields.

Property Law and Social Morality

PETER M. GERHART
Case Western Reserve University School of Law

CAMBRIDGE
UNIVERSITY PRESS

32 Avenue of the Americas, New York NY 10013-2473, USA

Cambridge University Press is part of the University of Cambridge.

It furthers the University's mission by disseminating knowledge in the pursuit of education, learning, and research at the highest international levels of excellence.

www.cambridge.org
Information on this title: www.cambridge.org/9781107006454

© Peter M. Gerhart 2014

This publication is in copyright. Subject to statutory exception and to the provisions of relevant collective licensing agreements, no reproduction of any part may take place without the written permission of Cambridge University Press.

First published 2014

A catalog record for this publication is available from the British Library.

Library of Congress Cataloging in Publication Data
Gerhart, Peter M.
Property law and social morality / Peter M. Gerhart, Case Western Reserve University School of Law.
    pages cm
Includes bibliographical references and index.
ISBN 978-1-107-00645-4 (hardback)
1. Right of property – Social aspects.   I. Title.
K721.5.G47   2014
346.04–dc23   2013027357

ISBN 978-1-107-00645-4 Hardback

Cambridge University Press has no responsibility for the persistence or accuracy of URLs for external or third-party Internet Web sites referred to in this publication and does not guarantee that any content on such Web sites is, or will remain, accurate or appropriate.

Dr. Louise F. Westfall: great human being, inspiring leader, believer

Contents

Preface		*page* ix
Acknowledgments		xiii
PART I	**A UNIFIED THEORY**	1
1	Property's Values	3
2	An Overview of the Theory	46
3	Owner as Decision Maker	62
4	Ownership and Social Recognition	73
5	Other-Regarding Decision Making	109
6	Assigning Burdens and Benefits	129
PART II	**APPLICATIONS**	159
7	Exclusion	161
8	Nuisance: Spatial Coordination	185
9	Concurrent Decision Makers	212
10	Temporal Coordination	227
PART III	**LEGISLATIVE REGULATION AND SOCIAL MORALITY**	247
11	A Theory of Legislative Regulation	249
12	The Takings Power	274
13	Legislative Regulation and Assigning Burdens	290
14	The Promise of Unity	311
References		317
Index		329

Preface

Property makes people's blood boil, although in different ways for people with property and people without it. Property law makes people's eyes glaze over, for property is encrusted with ancient formalities and arcane language. Property is at once a red-hot topic and a sleeper, a subject central to our political and social lives and Exhibit I in the pantheon of legal formalism.

When asked several years ago to teach the first-year Property Law course, I readily agreed. I wanted to see whether the ideas I had developed over a dozen years of teaching Tort Law would help remove property's political patina and the shroud of legal formalism. In the torts course, I had developed a way of thinking about one individual's responsibility for the well-being of others – a theory of private law that might be of value in understanding property law. Indeed, the more I read and taught, the more I realized that the way to defang and demystify property law was to reorient the field to understand it as one about how individuals ought to treat one another if they are to form an authentic community. Just as tort law is often (but not exclusively) about the rules of the road (and therefore about the rules governing open access property), property law concerns the rules governing the allocation and governance of resources in other ownership forms. I also realized that, unlike in tort law, I had to develop a theory of how individuals in a community, functioning as a group of individuals through their state, ought to think about their individual well-being in light of their collective well-being. Although tort law, drawn as it is from interpersonal relationships, rarely raises issues of collective well-being and collective will, property law must confront the relationship between the individual and the society in which individuals interact.

This book results from that exploration. Starting from the well-grounded notion that property law is about the relationship between individuals regarding things, whether owned privately or in common, I offer this account of how we might think about and justify what the law expects of individuals and a community of individuals in property relationships. My account is based on a theory of social morality, by which I mean the way individuals interact when they would act morally, private owner to nonowner, private owner to private owner, among common owners, and between the community (represented by its state) and a private owner. It is a theory of ownership because it is a theory about which decisions of owners are worthy of respect by the community and which decisions by the community are worthy of respect by individuals. It is a theory of responsibility with respect to resources because it reveals how individuals ought to think about each other's well-being when they, and their community, have conflicts over resources.

The book has three parts. Part I presents a theory of private law as it pertains to property – a theory about what each individual can expect from other individuals when disputes arise over resources. I lay out four propositions that, taken together, provide a framework for addressing conflicts over property in private law and for determining when individuals are acting morally as they work out resource conflicts. In Part II, I apply that framework to suggest how we might think differently about the central areas of the private law of property: exclusion, nuisance, concurrent decision making, and temporal coordination.

The theory developed in Parts I and II is a theory of the obligations of one individual to other individuals. It is a theory of responsibility because it identifies the obligations that are categorical as between free and equal individuals. It is also a consequential theory because it acknowledges that individuals must take into account some (but not all) consequences when deciding how to fulfill their responsibilities. This integration of the deontic and the consequential relies on a distinction between the methodology an individual who would act morally would use to think about his or her relationships with other individuals (the deontic) and the kinds of considerations that are relevant when the individual employs that method (the consequential). The categorical obligation is the obligation to act as one would if one had used a method of making decisions that is agnostic as to the decision maker's ends. The method itself determines which consequences the ideal decision maker may not take into account and the weight to be given the factors the ideal decision maker must take into account. I also show how individuals ought to reconcile their responsibilities to others with the consequences of their decisions when the two appear to conflict.

Part III focuses on the relationship between the individual and the community of individuals as represented by their state. Property is a part of a complex and evolving social and political system that shapes the rights and limitations of ownership and the relationship between ownership and the well-being of

Preface

the community. Whereas Parts I and II model the proper social relationship between individuals, Part III models the proper social relationship between the individual and the community of individuals acting through their state. Like its earlier counterparts, Part III is also a theory of bilateral relationships, for it models the relationship between the individual and the community as one of bilateral responsibility. It too is a theory of moral decision making, for it too describes the kind of considerations that govern decision making about resources when the individual and the community interact, including both limitations on owners (imposed by the state) and limitations on the state (imposed by the concept of property). Just as Parts I and II chart the content and limits of property rights in private law, Part III charts the content and limits of property rights when subjected to the will of the community through the state's legislative power.

Acknowledgments

The book has benefited from comments by colleagues who have taken the time to set me straight or encourage me, or both, including colleagues at Case Western Reserve – Jonathan Adler, Juliet Kostritsky, and Catherine LaCroix (who tutored me on land use planning) – and by colleagues elsewhere – Jim Krier (whose careful reading helped me avoid mistakes), Paul Malloy, Douglas North (for portions of the manuscript), and Joseph Singer. None of them, of course, is responsible for what I have written, nor do they necessarily share my views. Teaching is about learning, and I have learned from my students at Case Western Reserve and as a visiting professor at the University of Texas. Students in my seminar on Theories of Property Law at Case Western Reserve read drafts of various chapters and did their own research in the shadow of these ideas, helping sharpen many and modify some. The book has also benefited from the efforts of splendid research assistants who have worked with me over the past four years; Andrea Lee worked with me on a sustained and supportive basis, and Benjamin Galea, Zachary Smigiel, Andrew Webman, Seth Corthell, and Alexander Ahern have done smaller, but significant, stints along the way. Lingyu Jia volunteered her time for several projects that found their way into these pages, and, at the University of Texas, Elizabeth Nguyen took the manuscript from almost done to completion. Bobby Cheren, who was instrumental in helping me develop a casebook to reflect the ideas here, shaped many of the ideas in this book through our many fruitful discussions and our collaboration on the casebook.

The manuscript was overseen in various drafts by Catherine Adkins and Iwona Hrelja at Case Western Reserve and by Angel Leffingwell and Penny Tillman at the University of Texas. To all of these individuals, I express my deep gratitude.

PART I

A UNIFIED THEORY

This part develops a theory of social morality and property. Chapter 1 describes my project, outlines four propositions that constitute the core of the theory, and relates the theory to existing literature. Chapter 2 summarizes the four propositions and shows the relationship between then. Chapters 3 through 6 support the four propositions in greater detail; one proposition is discussed in each chapter.

The theory developed in this part is one of private law – the theory encompasses claims that one individual can justly make against other individuals. Part II then applies the theory to four central issues of the private law of property: exclusion, nuisance, concurrent decision making, and temporal coordination. Part III applies the theory to understand the justification for, and limits on, state regulation of property uses.

1 Property's Values

A society is known by its property system because a society's property system expresses society's values about the distribution and use of its resources. Yet a theory of property that is also a social theory is difficult to develop because it requires a theory of social cooperation that understands rights and responsibilities over resources to reflect the values that support social cohesion. What is it about the concept of property that supplies the social glue necessary to ensure security to private owners while recognizing the legitimate interests of nonowners, and how does a society envision a property system that dissuades individuals from using lawlessness to get their way and yet allows the property system to evolve in response to technological and social changes?

This book offers such a theory. It differs from existing theory in its search for unity along the many dimensions that now create cleavages in property theory,[1] including the distinction between philosophical and economic justice,[2] between a private owner's rights and a private owner's responsibilities, between

[1] Unification theories are not new in law. See, e.g., Calabresi and Melamed (1972). A notable philosophical approach that examines the unity of private law is in Brudner (1995). Generally, however, unification theories tend to be advanced by scholars who take an economic approach to law, whereas classification theories – those that conquer by dividing – tend to be advanced by scholars who take a philosophical approach to law. The theory here attempts to unify these two methodologies. Beyond the legal literature, this work seeks to build on a growing body of work from the social sciences and philosophy that seeks to unify, across traditional divides, our understanding of the world. See, e.g., from the social sciences, Gintis (2009) and Binmore (2006), and from philosophy, Parfit (2011).

[2] The theory here is thus distinct from theories that seek unification in either welfare maximization or in unified legal or philosophical principles. In particular, the unification theory here is distinguished from the elegant unification thesis of Alan Brudner (1995) in two primary ways. The theory here distinguishes between the function of the law in mediating between individual interests and the goals of the law in maximizing something. The failure to make that distinction, and the associated conflation of goal-oriented and functional theories, creates an unnecessary dichotomy between philosophical approaches (which are fully consistent with the law's mediation function) and welfare-enhancing theories (if they are thought to assume

private and non-private property, between the individual and the state, between private and public law, and between obligations accepted voluntarily (as in contract law) and obligations undertaken as a member of a community (as in tort and property law). The demands of the unification project are stringent.

- The unification of philosophical and economic justice requires a theory that is attuned to the requirements of obligations and corrective justice while taking consequences seriously.
- The unification of rights and responsibilities requires a theory that justifies both the existence and the scope of rights, so that rights and their limitations can be understood to emanate from a single set of values.
- A unified view of the individual and the state requires a theory that situates each individual as a participant in forming the policies of the state, while protecting the individual from overreaching by the state.
- The unified view of various forms of private and non-private property (including property owned by the state) requires a unified concept of property that explains both property's essentialism and its diversity.[3]
- The unification of private and public law requires us to view the two by understanding the relationship between individuals acting as individuals and individuals acting as participants in a community.
- Finally, the unification of obligations taken on voluntarily and obligations imposed by law requires a theory of obligations that emanates from decisions individuals make, so that all obligations are in some sense self-imposed, even if their existence and scope depend on their legal recognition.

To unify property theory across these dimensions, I focus on the values that shape a system of property and that allow the law to claim to reflect a system of moral action. By identifying a structured framework for organizing our thought about the values used to resolve disparate interests and claims, we unify our understanding across what otherwise appear to be large chasms of

---

that the end to be achieved determines the content of the law). In fact, welfare enhancement may be the law's function without being the law's goal because the mediating function of the law can, as I describe here, be understood to mediate between the well-being of free and equal individuals. This allows philosophical and welfare-enhancing theories to be unified. A second distinction between Brudner's unification theory and the theory here is my insistence that theory reflect basic principles but also explain and justify the outcome of cases.

[3] Most theories of property are, in fact, theories of private property and do not account for common property or the many mixed forms of property (*see*, e.g., Merrill 2012). This is a mistake. Common property employs a different concept of ownership but not a different concept of property, and the choice between various forms of private and common property is a social choice that seeks to align form and function. Only a theory that is unified across property forms provides a comprehensive theory.

conflicting ideas, while providing a structured basis for assessing the morality of the law.[4]

As has been recognized at least since the time of Hume, the concept of property (in any of its forms) addresses an inescapable issue every society faces: Who ought to make decisions about resources and how ought those decisions to be made? By focusing on ownership as a system by which a society allocates and recognizes decision-making authority, and by understanding how decisions about resources ought to be made, we can develop a unified view that sees the concept of property as a social response to society's need for an institutional framework for peaceably addressing disputes over resources.

The theory here displays several characteristics. It is unlike other theories of property because it seeks to understand how rights and responsibilities over resources flow from a single set of values. Many theories explain and justify the existence of private property, including theories of autonomy, personhood, incentives, and so forth.[5] But those theories generally fail to explain the limitations on an owner's rights in the same terms that justify the rights in the first place. In other words, property theory justifies the existence, but not the scope, of various forms of property rights. I am interested not only in the values that give rise to property but in how those same values limit property rights. What is it about autonomy, personhood, or incentives that also justify the law in limiting property rights? Rights theories generally provide no basis for understanding the scope of rights in the same terms that justify the existence of the rights; a theory of responsibility does.

Under the presentation here, property rights arise when an individual has no responsibilities to look out for the well-being of other individuals, and it understands limitations on property rights to arise when an owner does have responsibilities to other individuals. The theory seeks to unify private law by focusing on the circumstances that require one individual to take into account the well-being of other individuals and that, because of that obligation, give the other a legal claim against the individual. In this view, property law, like tort and contract law, responds to the question of what we owe each other.

---

[4] From one perspective, the theory builds on pluralist theories in that it accepts the assertion that various values underlie property law and that any account of property must take that plurality of values into account (*see generally* Dagan 2011). From another perspective, the theory developed here seeks to provide what pluralist theory denies: a unified way of thinking about the values that animate a property system. My claim is not that theory provides answers to issues raised by property law. My claim is that theory provides a unified way of thinking about the values underlying the property system so that analysis proceeds in an orderly, structured way and so that debates about the just resolution of property issues are about how best to implement a unified methodology rather than how to "balance" disparate values.

[5] For a recent, excellent overview of existing theory, *see* Alexander and Peñalver (2012).

Although what property owners owe each other and nonowners may be less expansive than in torts and contracts (for reasons that will be discussed), the responsibility of an individual for the well-being of others is nonetheless the key to understanding the scope of property rights.

Natural law influences the theory here because it presupposes that the law arises from human interaction and from the need for humans to develop institutions, social and legal, that limit conflict and enhance cooperation. The theory is both descriptive and justificatory. It purports to describe the pattern of social and legal relationships that determine the forms and uses of property and also to understand those patterns in the context of a theory of the values that give the patterns their normative force. By proposing a theory that identifies the factors society uses, and ought to use, to institutionalize structured decisions about the society's resources, the theory provides a framework for understanding and comparing property systems in different societies.

Law and economics analysis intersects with the theory here because both understand property law to function to maximize individual well-being.[6] Unlike most economic approaches, however, the theory does not assume that the maximizing process is either value-free or self-defining. Instead, the theory faces directly, as many economic theories do not, the question of whose well-being matters and how we determine whose well-being must be sacrificed so that another's well-being may increase. The theory can also be considered to be a philosophical approach in that it accepts the equal freedom of individuals, understands that individuals have categorical obligations toward one another, and posits that moral action can be articulated in a way that ensures that human behavior reflects those obligations. Unlike most philosophical approaches, however, the theory is not afraid to understand obligation by evaluating the consequences of not following the obligations, and it understands categorical imperatives in terms that are not hypothetical or conditional but that also take context into account. The theory integrates economic and philosophical approaches by understanding the maximization of well-being and the principle of equal respect for the freedom of individuals to be two ways of expressing the same thought.[7]

---

[6] Economic theory has evolved from a focus on wealth maximization to a focus on welfare maximization, and then (in some quarters) to an emphasis on well-being maximization. I use the term "well-being" because it conveys the notion that an individual may determine what he or she values and because it focuses on emotional as well as material personal health.

[7] The theory is resonant with Jedediah Purdy's claim that "visions of the economic order – particularly those derived from the Scottish Enlightenment – were attempts to integrate multiple dimensions of freedom within a legal regime," including negative freedom, a range of meaningful alternatives, and the capacity to choose among those alternatives. Purdy (2010) at 44.

Values as Inputs 7

The theory advances its unification goal by addressing four dichotomies that divide theorists into various camps: the dichotomy between essentialist and bundle-of-sticks approaches to property, the dichotomy between rights-based theories and assent-based theories, the dichotomy between individual interests and social interests, and the dichotomy between values as inputs and values as outputs. Each of these dichotomies is addressed by advancing a proposition that makes the dichotomy disappear. Collectively, the four propositions form a coherent and complete theory of property as an institution of social organization.

In this chapter, I present an overview of the theory and explain how readers might understand the theory in the context of contemporary ideas about property. Section 1.1 describes the kind of theory I am advancing, explaining the difference between a theory that focuses on outputs (what individuals can do with property) and a theory, such as the one here, that focuses on inputs (what values are relevant when society and individuals make decisions about property). Section 1.2 introduces the four propositions that make up the core of the theory. Section 1.3 then situates the theory in the context of contemporary theories of property.

1.1 VALUES AS INPUTS

Scholars use the term "values" in two quite distinct senses. We talk about the value of something, which uses the term "value" as a measure of output, a measure of what people get out of something. Property is valuable, of course. That is why we spend so much time debating about, and sometimes fighting over, property. We want a system of property to provide value to society and we want owners to get as must value out of the property as possible. We worry if the state takes away too much value from our property. Adding value to our resources makes us all better off because we all benefit from that value in some way; property values enhance one another. Each of these senses of the word "value" focuses on value as an output – a measure of what we get out of something.

But we also use the term "value" as a measure of the input into something – an aspect of our decision that impels the direction and content of our choice because it gives us satisfaction. The statement "I like ice cream" is a statement of values that are inputs into an individual's decision about what to consume. The statement "You may not come on my property" is a statement about the values an owner uses when deciding whether to exercise her right to exclude.

The values we care about in developing a theory of property are not what we get out of a resource but what values a community expects an individual to use in making decisions about resources. A system of law is a reflection of the values a society uses, and expects an individual to use, to make judgments about which of various positions the law might take on issues it confronts. A system of property law is a statement about what a society values when it must choose between various ways of shaping systems for making decisions about resources.

We can fruitfully explore the significance of the different meanings of the term "value" by reexamining the fundamental question: What is property? The conventional idea of property as a "thing" is obviously correct as far as it goes. Property consists of things external to people, over which one or more persons is allowed to claim dominion.[8] But the view of property-as-thing does not reveal the relationship between the thing and an individual claiming dominion over the thing. It therefore gives no sense of the values that people use to determine which things to claim or what to do with the things they rightfully claim. As an object, the thing has no value in itself. The thing as an object is given social value because of the values individuals use to make decisions about the thing. Rather than thinking of property as a thing, we can think of property as a resource, which conveys some sense that the thing has value to a person. The thing that is property-as-a-resource forms the identity of the individual claiming dominion – the personhood theory of property of Hegel and Radin[9] – and is an expression of individual purposive action – the Kantian theory of property.[10] The thing that we call property is a resource that embodies core values that are worthy of recognition.

Others have broadened the property-as-thing idea by suggesting that property law is really about relationships between individuals over things.[11] What one individual values and owns privately another individual may not own, and ownership therefore excludes what another would value about the resource. This view does not deny the property-as-thing notion; it just highlights the fact that ownership is not a value-neutral word and that in any value-oriented approach the relationship between owner and nonowner is relevant. The relationship-between-people view, however, can be understood in two quite

---

[8] Blackstone (1765–69), Book II at 2. Not surprisingly, this view is prominent among those who emphasize the right to exclude as property's primary characteristic. Merrill (1998), Merrill and Smith (2010); Smith (2004), Penner (2006), Penner (1997).
[9] Hegel (1942), Radin (1982).
[10] Ripstein (2009) at 91.
[11] The notion that property is about relationships between individuals over things reflects the legal realist's observation that ownership both empowers owners and excludes nonowners and therefore is about the relationship between them. *See, e.g.*, Cohen (1935).

Values as Inputs

distinct ways. It might focus on the relationship between individuals over things they value, or it might focus on the values that people bring to their relationships with others when making decision about resources.

The first, and conventional, way of understanding the relationship-over-things notion is to see a resource as defining the relationship between two or more individuals. A fox is subject to ownership and ownership is determined by the relative strength of two conflicting claimants, one of whom will get the value of the fox.[12] The disposition of the claims governs the relationship between the claimants with respect to that resource: one gets it and the other does not, and that determination governs the relationship between the claimants and the value of the fox. Or, we can think of the relationship between owner and nonowner with respect to a resource – say, a dock. The owner has certain rights – to exclude, for example – and the nonowner has certain rights – say, to take refuge at the dock from a dangerous storm.[13] Again, the law is determining the relationship between individuals with respect to that thing. The law does not change the resource; it simply awards the resource's value (as an output) to one individual over another, determining who gets the value as an output.

The relationship-over-things view can be interpreted in another way, which is the one I endorse. We can understand property by the values that serve as inputs into determining the relationship between individuals. The award of the resource or access to the resource is itself value-based. If we understand the values that go into determining the relationship between individuals (the values we use to determine who gets the value of the thing), we understand property in a different way. That is, if we look at property not as a resource to be assigned but as society's expression of social values that are important in making the assignment, we begin to see the normative content of the notion of property – its ability to express values and its role as a device for mediating relationships between people. What is important is not that things have value; it is that things *express* value, particularly the values that determine how individuals ought to treat each other with respect to that resource and how the state ought to treat individuals. Accordingly, we can see property as the expression of social values, not as the award of value to one individual or another. Such a theory understands the law to be mediating between the diverse interests of owners and nonowners based on values that ought to be accounted for in making decisions about resources. And such a theory identifies the values that

[12] Pierson v. Post, 3 Cai R. 175 (1805).
[13] Ploof v. Putnam, 71 A. 188 (1908).

owners and nonowners have in common, so that property relationships arise from shared, rather than opposing, values.[14]

With this perspective, the heart of the book's unification goal is to break methodological and justificatory ground by providing a new way of thinking about property relationships. Property theory is not lacking in ideas that depict the values (as inputs) that support theories of private property.[15] Nor, for that matter, is property theory lacking in values that support the rights of nonowners or the rights or owners against other owners.[16] Property theory is, however, significantly dichotomous; as Larry Lessig has said, "property is binary at its core."[17] Whether we view property from the standpoint of clashing interests, clashing rights, or clashing values, property theory emphasizes competing, rather than unified, positions and therefore requires a balancing methodology. This book seeks to provide a corrective by developing a justification for the content of property law that sees the rights of owners and nonowners to grow from a set of shared values rather than from a set of conflicting interests. A theory of an owner's rights is a theory of property (by definition) but not a theory of property law because it does not account for an owner's responsibilities except by balancing. And a theory of an owner's social responsibility is a theory of access to property but not a theory of property law because it represents interests that are opposed to, rather than unified with, the rights of owners. The theory I seek accounts *simultaneously* for rights and their limitations based on shared values so that the law need not balance diverse interests.

---

[14] The distinction between values as inputs and values as outputs can be captured as follows: individuals put a value on things in terms of what they are willing to give up to obtain those things; that is value as a measure of output. But the factors that determine how much a person is willing to give up depend on the strength of an individual's attachment to the thing, and that attachment may be deeper or more integral to that person's identity than his or her willingness to pay. That is value as an input. That is the sense of attachment that Margaret Jane Radin (1982) described in her theory of property as personhood. *See also* Madison (1961) ("The protection of the [diversity of faculties of men] if the first object of government."). The distinction between value as an input and value as an output partly reflects an individual's wealth, of course, but it also reflects the distinction between various measures of wants and needs. The factors that determine how much a person would give up to acquire something and how much a person would demand to give up something often differs. This is the endowment effect, which suggests that individuals value what they have more than what they do not have. Either way, what is important analytically is the value-determinants of a resource.

[15] The tendency for theory to concentrate on rights rather than their limitations or the responsibilities of ownership is common to economic and philosophical approaches. Representative economic approaches are Shavell (2004) and Posner (2011). Representative philosophical approaches are Waldron (1988) and Penner (1997).

[16] Alexander (2009), Dagan (2011), Rose (1986), Singer (1988).

[17] Lessig (2006) at *81. For a historical review of the thought that has supported the dichotomy between the rights of owners and the rights of the community, see Alexander (1997).

To the extent that it exists, the unity of property law is thought to come from a methodology that balances rights, interests, or values. The methodological pattern of property theory is this: identify the clashing rights, interests, or values and find a way to "balance" them in order to determine the content of property law.[18] Often this boils down to a theory that either starts with the rights of owners and understands the rights of nonowners to be exceptions to those rights (often begrudged exceptions),[19] or that starts with the rights of nonowners or of the community and understands property theory to be derived from those rights, limited only by the weight given to owners' rights.

A methodology of balancing conflicting rights, interests, and values has familiar problems: the problem of comparing incommensurables (an owner's interest in keeping someone out; an outsider's interest in access), the problem of agreeing on weights to be assigned to incommensurables (should the owner's interest be given added weight in recognition of her ownership?), and the problem of defining the borders between the various rights, interests, or values that individuals advance.[20] No matter how finely or eloquently one articulates the test, a balancing methodology seems always to reduce itself to a statement of the following kind: an owner has the right to exclude a nonowner except when the owner does not. If one's goal is to understand the substantive content of the law, that approach is ineffective, for it provides no basis for understanding the normative values that would induce the law to draw the line between rights and responsibilities in one place rather than another. The rights are clear; their scope is opaque.

Instead of a balancing theory that defines, and tries to reconcile, opposing interests, the theory here suggests that rights and responsibilities over resources emanate from shared values, not from opposing forces. To be sure, people have different interests, and the interests clash, but a unification theory suggests that the reconciliation of conflicting interests comes not from their differences but from the values that individuals share. Underlying most values that are thought to support a system of property law are other values – values about the way individuals treat each other when they interrelate and how individuals account for the values that are important to one another. These are values that integrate interests between individuals and that individuals use to coordinate their activities. If incentives (or autonomy or personhood) are

---

[18] *See, e.g.*, Underkuffler (2003) (developing a theory of core rights with presumptive power that can then be evaluated in the light of conflicting interests).
[19] *See, e.g.*, Smith (2009) at 964 ("when the issue is important enough and bargains will not or should not happen, then owner's rights must give way to larger societal interests").
[20] *See, e.g.*, Singer (2009), Aleinikoff (1987), Mcfadden (1988) at 636.

important both to owners and nonowners, then we reconcile the conflicting interests in the incentive value (or the autonomy value or the personhood value) of any property regime by finding out how individuals ought to view an incentive claim (or an autonomy claim or a personhood claim) made by another. The reconciliation of conflicting claims to incentives, autonomy, or personhood must come from an underlying system of values about how those claims ought to be judged by individuals in the society.

Accordingly, I seek a theory of property that sees an owner's obligations and disabilities to flow from the same source that gave rise to the rights in the first place, so that one theory explains both the origin and the scope of the rights.[21] Under this approach, the values that give rise to the right to exclude are also the source of limitations on the right to exclude; the right to exclude and the responsibility to provide access flow from a single set of social values. And the values that allow one to be free from interference by a neighbor are the same values that restrict an owner's use of her property, so that we understand the clash of interests as working out the implication of a single obligation – the obligation to be neighborly[22] – that is shared by the creator and the recipient of a nuisance.

I am looking for a theory of the following type: A has the right to exclude for any or no reason if, but only if, X is true, where X is the value that both defines the right to exclude and provides a measure of its limitations. As long as X is well specified, this kind of theory overcomes the indeterminacy of the balancing approach and provides us with a single reference value for understanding both rights and responsibilities. With regard to nuisance law, I am looking for a theory of the following type: A has the right to use her property in any way she wants, if, but only if, she follows a decisional process of X, where X justifies her decisions about how she will use her property and (because other owners must also use process X) affirms her right to be free of unnecessary interference.

This approach is especially relevant when considering the interface between state action and property rights. Property law presents a well-known and fundamental conundrum: How can the state both protect and regulate property if there is no single set of values that the state is trying to promote in its

---

[21] The property theory propounded by Jeremy Waldron (1988) provides an example. Although his theory of private property is distinct from that provided here, it has the characteristics I am seeking. From the theory that private property enables human flourishing, he derived the obligation of a community to redistribute property to achieve human flourishing for all members of the community. In this approach, rights and obligation are supported by a single core value.

[22] Ellickson (1973).

protection and regulation? If state regulation is simply "in the public interest" and the "public interest" is not defined in terms that simultaneously authorize and limit state action, is there anything worth calling property? Moreover, if the only constraint on state regulation is to say that it cannot "go too far," by what baseline are we measuring the deviation when determining how far the regulation has gone?[23] The theory in this book develops a concept of property that understands the Constitution to both authorize and limit state regulation of property on the basis of a core concept of property, a concept that allows us to chart the border between state power and its limitations.

The four propositions I advance suggest an approach to property law that unifies ideas concerning the disparate interests of owners and nonowners into a framework that shows how each individual is charged with responsibility to account for the interests of others in a morally appropriate way. This theory avoids the problem of balancing clashing interests through an external metric by showing how each person in a property relationship must make context-appropriate decisions that are grounded on values that are themselves morally justified. When each individual makes morally justified decisions about resources based on shared values, rights in property flow from a unifying, not a dividing, source, and property binds rather than divides society.

The four propositions that make up the theory provide a framework for understanding property's values. I outline the four propositions in Section 1.2 and situate these propositions in the context of contemporary property theory in Section 1.3.

1.2 THE THEORY SUMMARIZED

The theory defended here rests on four propositions about ownership, the origin of property, human interaction, and the law's role in mediating between individual interests. Each proposition supports the others. Each proposition is found in the literature, although none is prominent. Each of the four propositions addresses one of the dichotomies that now haunt property theory. Together, the propositions provide a coherent and unified way of looking at social relationships over property.

In this introductory section, I present the four propositions in their most abstract form, along with a brief overview of their implications for private and public law. In the next section, I relate these propositions to existing property theory and to the goals of this book. In Chapter 2, I discuss the four propositions in greater detail, presenting a conceptual map of each proposition and

---

[23] Fee (2002), Lisker (1996), Rose (1988), Wenar (1997), Stein (2002).

the role that I conceive for it in the overall theory. Chapters 3 through 6 then justify each of the propositions in greater detail, one proposition per chapter.

One of the significant dichotomies of property theory is the dichotomy between essentialist theories and bundle-of-sticks theories,[24] a dichotomy that can be understood as a debate about starting points. Should we understand property by the rights it gives (albeit with exceptions) or as a system of engineering that views rights to be socially and politically constructed from various options that can be assembled and reassembled as the context dictates? The theory here bridges that dichotomy by suggesting that the essence of property is that owners have the right to make decisions about the resources entrusted to them, but their decisions are constrained because owners must take into account values that are appropriate, from a social perspective, to the decisions they are making. This theory explains how property rights can have an essence that can vary with the context (the right to make a decision). This is the proposition that the essence of property is constrained decision making (Chapter 3).

A second dichotomy in property theory is the distinction between rights-based theories and assent-based theories.[25] Rights theories suffer from under-specified descriptions of the origin of rights. Assent-based theories suffer from an underspecified description of the causal mechanism of consent. The theory proposed here, the theory of social recognition, seeks to supply what is missing from rights and assent theories and to show how they might be reconciled. When assent is given because the non–rights-holder feels that the merits of the rights claim are worthy of her recognition, then assent-based rights are also natural rights and the rights-based view explains why the rights are worthy of moral respect. The concept of social recognition supplies the second proposition supporting the theory here. Owners' decisions are constrained because an owner's rights depend on the community's acceptance of the claims, and acceptance is conditioned on owners meeting socially valued norms of behavior. Ownership rights can arise either from a sovereign with authority over the resource or from the state of nature. When ownership arises from the sovereign, property rights flow from, and are determined by, the community's recognition of the authority of the sovereign. When ownership arises from the state of nature, rights arise from the implicit recognition of the ownership

---

[24] For additional discussion, see notes 78 to 80 to this chapter.
[25] The distinction goes back at least to Blackstone (1765–69), Book II, at 8, who noted that Grotius and Puffendorf "insist that this right of occupancy is founded on a tacit and implied assent of all mankind," whereas Locke, Barbeyrac, and Titius deny the theory of assent, claiming that "the very act of occupancy, alone, being a degree of bodily labor, is, from a principle of natural justice, without any consent or compact, sufficient of itself to gain title."

claims by those who would be excluded if the claims were accepted. Either way, the rights of ownership are validated by the community – giving rights their moral force – while social recognition provides an implicit constraint on the owner's scope of decisions. This is the proposition that, at their core, property rights are socially recognized, and that the recognition comes with implicit constraints on the owner's decision-making authority (Chapter 4).

The social recognition proposition and the constrained decision-making proposition together suggest that the owner, by making decisions subject to the constraints recognized by the community, serves to mediate between the rights and responsibilities of himself and others. These propositions raise the question of how decisions about property ought to be made, which is the subject of propositions three and four.

A third dichotomy that divides property theory is the distinction between individual interests and social interests: Ought we to envision property theory to describe a process of aggregating individual interests into a social system, or ought we to understand social interests (the "public good") to be defined independently of individual interests? Is defining the social interest an aggregative process or an independent process? We know that healthy property systems account for the great disparity of individual interests while allowing resources to be used in a way that can be considered to be socially beneficial, but how ought we to understand the relationship between the individual and the collective? This dichotomy is addressed by proposition three. An owner has authority to make a wide variety of decisions about a resource, but only if her behavior reflects decisions that take into account, in an appropriate way, the interest and well-being of individuals toward whom the owner has an obligation. Similarly, nonowners and other owners must behave as if they have made decisions that appropriately consider the rights of owners (for example, the obligation to respect the owner's boundaries); they too must act as if they have made decisions that give due regard to the interests of others. The behavior of owners and nonowners that is appropriately other-regarding becomes the device that coordinates resource use between individuals and allows the law simultaneously to advance individual and social interests. This is the proposition that the law requires individuals who make decisions about resources to act as the ideal, other-regarding decision maker would act (Chapter 5).

A final dichotomy that inhabits property theory is, as I have already explained, the dichotomy between values as inputs and values as outputs. Should we understand property as a reflection of what people value (the economic view) or as a reflection of the social values that give property its ability to coordinate decisions about resources among individuals (the philosophical view)? This dichotomy is addressed in the fourth proposition. In order to account for the well-being of others, each decision maker must act in a way that appropriately assigns the burdens and benefits of decisions about resource use (the economic view), taking into account the values the community has developed to determine how to assign burdens and benefits (the philosophical view). This is the proposition that property law aims to appropriately assign the burdens and benefits of decision making over resources (Chapter 6). Once each decision maker acts as an ideal decision maker would act by appropriately assigning the burdens and benefits of decisions about resources, the property system has achieved an equilibrium that guarantees the equal freedom of each individual in the community given the existing distribution of resources. Each individual has used the appropriate cost-benefit analysis using values that are socially recognized.

These four abstract propositions are easily understood in the concept of nuisance (Chapter 8). Each owner may make decisions about how to use her property; that is what ownership is. Yet, the decisions are constrained by the obligation of each owner to think reasonably about how his or her decisions might affect other owners (private nuisance) and nonowners (public nuisance). The source of that constraint is an implicit condition put on an owner's decisions when the community recognized the owner's right to make decisions about a resource (the right to be an owner) – the condition that the owner successfully coordinate her decisions with the decisions of other owners and with nonowners. That requires that each owner act as an ideal owner, behaving as one would if one had thought appropriately about the well-being of his neighbors, which is the requirement to act as an other-regarding person would. That in turn, requires the owner to act as if she had appropriately (reasonably) balanced the burdens and benefits of the owner's use decisions, using values that reflect community values relevant to the trade-offs involved in that decision. The values that are important in this system are the values that allow an other-regarding individual to appropriately assign the burdens and benefits of decisions about resources.

Thus far, I have presented the four propositions as a matter of private law. However, the four propositions also support a vision of the role of private and public law in regulating relationships between individuals over resources and in mediating between the interests of owners and the interests of the community. Under this vision, the function of private law is to determine how and when each individual should take into account the well-being of other individuals, such that if those interests are not taken into account, another person has a claim against the decision maker. This requires the court to determine how each individual ought appropriately to assign the burdens and benefits of his decisions about the resource. In this way, private law develops concepts of interpersonal morality that determine how people ought to treat each other.

Public law has two functions: (1) it allows the state to take property (under the takings power)[26] when decisions of private owners, as mediated by the market and regulation, cannot achieve public goals; and (2) it allows the state to mediate between the private interest and the interests of the community as a whole in ways that private law cannot mediate, so that owners, when they make decisions, take a wider range of values into account, including values that are held collectively rather than individually (Chapter 11). In both functions, the state authority to act also provides limitations on the state's power over property. Under the Takings Clause the state can act if, but only if, it identifies a market failure that keeps the well-regulated market from effectively coordinating private decisions (Chapter 12). Under its public law regulatory power, the state can act if, but only if, it can achieve a more appropriate balance of the burdens and benefits of ownership than is available through private law, and it may act only if it avoids undue burdens on owners (Chapter 13).

This book elaborates on each of these propositions and provides a way of thinking about the values that must be taken into account in determining whether an individual or the community acting through its state has behaved appropriately.

1.3 CONTEMPORARY PROPERTY THEORY

We can understand the theory here in terms of the broader evolution of legal thought.[27] In the nineteenth century, law, and especially property law, was highly formalistic, built on rules and broad moral principles from which it was thought that lawmakers could derive decisions governing property conflicts. Later, legal realists challenged the law's formalism by pointing out the hazards of reasoning from rules and vacuous moralisms about justice when deciding how to resolve concrete conflicts.[28] However, they did not have a methodology to fill the substantive vacuum that their challenges identified. Over the ensuing decades, that vacuum was filled in two ways. First, the legal process school sought to understand law by understanding the process by which the law is made, implicitly suggesting that we can justify the content of the law if we could justify as legitimate the process that led to law.[29] Then, law and

---

[26] U.S. Constitution, Amendment V: "[n]or shall private property be taken for public use without just compensation." This limitation is applied to the states through the Due Process Clause of the Fourteenth Amendment. Chicago, Burlington & Quincy R.R. Co. v. Chicago, 166 U.S. 226 (1897). The takings power is discussed in Chapter 12.
[27] The rendition here follows Rubin (1996).
[28] See, e.g., Cohen (1935) and Frank (1930).
[29] See, e.g., Fuller (1964), Hart and Sacks (1994), Fuller (1978).

economics filled the vacuum by creating a goal-oriented view of law and positing welfare maximization as the law's goal.[30] Both attempts to fill the legal realist vacuum provided important insights, but neither has garnered universal support. The legal process school reached its limit with the realization, drawn from the theory of public choice,[31] that process could be subverted by individual interests, which suggested that a theory of the law's substantive validity was a necessary adjunct to any assessment of legal process. The goal-oriented view of law and economics ran into the anti-utilitarian objection that, to be useful in deciding concrete disputes, welfare maximization must assume an unrevealed idea about comparing human well-being that the economic approach could not capture.

New modes of thought about property have emerged as a reaction to law and economics and the legal process school.[32] Corrective justice theories emphasize the relational aspects of the application of law to human interaction and therefore the idea that one individual may be responsible for the wrongs that affect another individual,[33] implying that wealth maximization does not mean maximizing each individual's self-regarding interest. Institutional analysis has focused on the evolution of the institution of property, markets, and the state to determine the origins and impact of institutions, providing a way of thinking about the evolution of the relationship between the individual and the institution. More recently, as part of institutional analysis, what can be thought of as a new formalism seeks to understand law in terms of the form that legal rules take, this time understanding the law's form in terms of the costs of the information that is needed to develop and enforce the law.[34] Under this view, the law makes choices between various possible formal expressions by paying attention to the costs and benefits of acquiring the information needed to link the law with an individual's behavior.

---

[30] *See generally* Posner (2003), Shavell (2004), and Kaplow and Shavell (2002).

[31] *See generally* Farber and Frickey (1991).

[32] The critical legal studies movement reacted against the legal process school by echoing legal realists' claims about the indeterminacy of law and by borrowing from public choice theory the notion that the law reflects the social status and interests of lawmakers. The critical legal studies movement reacted against the law and economics approach by pointing out that the goal of wealth maximization entrenches existing disparities in economic and social class. *See generally* Unger (1983), Kennedy (1979) (as to property law), and Horkheimer and Adorno (1972).

[33] *See generally* Weinrib (1995) and Coleman (1992).

[34] In property law, the new formalism is represented by Henry Smith and Tom Merrill (*see, e.g.*, Merrill and Smith 2000, 2007, and Smith 2004). In contracts, the new formalism is represented by Robert Scott and Alan Schwartz (*see, e.g.*, Schwartz and Scott 2003). In tort law, the new formalism is represented by John C. P. Goldberg and Benjamin Zipursky. *See, e.g.*, Goldberg (2012), Zipursky (2012).

Although each of these approaches adds to our understanding of the substantive and normative content of property law, none of them alone has a monopoly on helping us understand the factors that lawmakers take into account, and ought to take into account, when they decide what the law should be. This book attempts to fill the substantive vacuum that the legal realists identified by drawing together several strands of thought to suggest a unified and integrated way of thinking about the factors that ought to be considered, and the weight they ought to be given, when evaluating property law. Under the view presented here, the law functions to coordinate the decisions of independent and equal individuals to address conflicting claims to resources.[35] Because property, in conjunction with other institutions (including the state and markets),[36] coordinates a society's decisions about resources, we are asking: What mix of rights and responsibilities has a community established to make sure that it gets the most out of its resources consistent with each individual's right to equal respect, as determined in accordance with the social values established by the community? This is a form of social problem solving, which the law carries out by ensuring that individual decisions are based on social-value criteria that respond appropriately to conflicting interests. The law mediates between the diverse interests of a heterogeneous community by determining which decisions of individuals have been made in accordance with values that the community endorses.[37]

The four propositions that ground the theory here reflect existing theory in manifold ways.

---

[35] A functional view differs from a goal-oriented view in a fundamental way. A goal-oriented view assumes that the end is specified before, and is external to, the law. A functional view assumes that the goal of the law is derived from the way the law functions to guide human interaction. The objection to utilitarianism is that it assumes a predefined goal, not that it focuses on the goal of human happiness. A goal-oriented theory requires an external measure of the goal, while a functional view allows the measure of well-being (including human happiness) to be defined as part of working out the law's function.

[36] See, e.g., Dagan and Heller (2001) at 577 ("an efficient liberal regime of private property is itself, oddly, a type of commons held together by virtue of the law's facilitation"); Krier (1992) at 336–338, and Rose (1990) at 37.

[37] In this regard, I am working out the details of theory advanced by others. See, e.g., Coleman (1994) at 137–38 ("The norms, and the rights [enforceable by duties in corrective justice], however, must be central to individual autonomy and well-being. The roles norms play in this regard are complex and connected. First, they create a framework within which individuals formulate and pursue their projects and plans. Second, they provide part of the wherewithal necessary to formulate and pursue those plans. Thus, any distribution sustainable by corrective justice must be stable and facilitate coordination, and it must provide the ingredients required by the liberal conception of autonomy)." Many other theories of property emphasize property's mediating role (see, e.g., Dagan and Heller 2005) (viewing property to be working out conflicts of interest between owners and others).

1.3.1 Corrective Justice

The theory here draws on existing theories of justice in straightforward ways, which is especially important in understanding the fourth proposition – that property law aims to appropriately assign the burdens and benefits of decision making over resources (Chapter 6).

1.3.1.1 The Principle of Equality. The foundational principle animating the theory here, as is true for most moral theory,[38] is the principle of equal freedom: in all dealings between individuals or between individuals and the state, each individual is entitled to respect equal to the respect given to every other individual. The equality principle, which can be stated in terms of each person's right to equal freedom consistent with the right of every other individual to equal freedom, follows Immanuel Kant's statement that "I say that man, and in general every rational being, exists as an end in himself, not merely as a means for arbitrary use by this or that will."[39] That principle led Kant to his second formulation of the Categorical Imperative: "Act in such a way that you always treat humanity, whether in your own person or in the person of any other, never simply as a means, but always at the same time as an end."[40] This is the obligation of equal treatment of the dignity and self-rule of every individual. The principle of equality imposes obligations on individuals and on the community, whether acting through judges or legislatures. As recently interpreted by Ronald Dworkin, the state "must show equal concern for the fate of every person over whom it claims dominion....[and] must respect fully the responsibility and the right of each person to decide for himself how to make something valuable of his life."[41] As a result, the state, acting as lawgiver, must "respect ... two fundamental principles of equal concern for fate and full respect for responsibility."[42]

The theory here builds on the equality principle by suggesting that what individuals expect of their state, they expect of each other. Each individual, in order to implement the equality principle, ought to take full responsibility for her decisions, while respecting the right of other individuals to express their individuality and will by the decisions they make. Each individual must act as he would if he made decisions that treated other individuals with equal

---

[38] Sandel (2009).
[39] Kant (1785) at 428. Because readers will use various editions of Kant's *Groundwork*, I cite the standard page numbers, from the edition of the *Groundwork* published by the Royal Prussian Academy in Berlin, which are included in most editions.
[40] Kant (1785) at 429.
[41] Dworkin (2011) at 55.
[42] Dworkin (2011) at 55.

freedom, allowing each individual to flourish in the way each sees fit.[43] That is why the theory focuses on an individual's decisions as the mechanism for mediating between the rights of free and equal individuals. This is hardly a self-executing principle, but it finds expression in the theory here by requiring individuals, when they make decisions, to be appropriately other-regarding (Chapter 5) and to appropriately assign the burdens and benefits of decision making over resources (Chapter 6).

The theory gives content to the principle of equality by relying on the veil of ignorance as a methodology for determining what assignment of burdens and benefits can be called moral.[44] Behind the veil of ignorance, each individual is required to reason toward a decision without knowing how he or she will be affected by the decision; each individual will therefore assign the burdens and benefits of the decision using neutral values that are common to the community and eschewing values that advance only an individual's personal agenda.[45] The resulting decision will be one that the community as a whole would endorse and that we can view to be both fair and efficient.[46]

[43] The theory here resembles the theory of human flourishing advanced recently by Gregory Alexander and Eduardo Peñalver, although it is distinct in several respects. Like the theory of human flourishing, the theory here focuses on human well-being and virtue (Alexander and Peñalver, 2012, at 87); in my theory it focuses on the virtue of looking out for the well-being of others. Both theories are grounded on the principle of equality (*Id.* at 85) and emphasize the importance of cooperation and coordinating human activity (*Id.*). The theories are distinct in that the theory of human flourishing seems to encompass both corrective justice and distributive justice, without delineating between them, whereas the theory here sharply delineates between the two forms of justice, as is discussed in the next section. Moreover, the theory of human flourishing does not attempt to sharply define the border between exclusion and access and relies on the general concept of necessity as the main normative value that gives rights to nonowners. Unlike the theory here, the authors do not seek to apply the theory to explain, justify, or reconcile seemingly conflicting strands of case law.

[44] Although the veil of ignorance was prominent in the philosophy of John Rawls (*see* Rawls, 1971) at 11–22 and 136–140, it had been used in moral theory before. John Rawls used the veil of ignorance (and its antecedent "original position") in the service of distributive justice, but it appears to be equally applicable in the context of corrective, interactive justice (*see* Gerhart, 2010, at 91–101).

[45] Binmore (2005, at 129–30) notes the similarity between the original position and a modified Golden Rule: "Do unto others as you would be done by – if you were the person to whom something would be done." (The Christian Golden Rule – do unto others as you would have them do unto you – does not account for the fact that people have different preferences and therefore do not want to be treated the same). He also points out that a version of the Golden Rule is prevalent among the major cultures and religions of the world.

[46] I use the term "efficiency" to mean Pareto efficiency: the ability of a different social arrangement to make one individual better off without making any other individual worse off. I avoid general discussions of concepts such as fairness and efficiency because, on the view presented here, the concepts can be defined only as they arise from social interaction. Under this view, concepts of fairness and efficiency do not come with predetermined definitions (except in the limited Pareto sense) and they do not serve as inputs into legal analysis. We do not ask what is

1.3.1.2 Equality in Corrective and Distributive Justice. Although both distributive and corrective justice are based on the principle of equality, their implementation requirements and content are distinct.

The relationship between individuals over resources raises two separate foundational issues. A society must determine whether the basic distribution of aggregate resources is just, as measured against a normative standard of what is deserved and needed. This is the realm of distributive justice, which asks whether the pie is fairly divided given the contributions of each individual to the size of the pie and the claims that each individual makes to secure the opportunities that the pie affords. Separately, society must determine, for any given distribution of resources, how the rights and responsibilities of owners and nonowners, now and in the future, ought to be distributed among individuals. This is the realm of corrective justice: given the distribution of resources, what is the just or morally right way for individuals to interact with other individuals over claims about resources? Private law works out the contours of corrective justice because it asks the following basic question: What claims can one individual make against another individual? This book addresses only the corrective justice aspects of property law, although it does so in both private and public law.[47]

The distinction between distributive and corrective justice is not always honored in property theory[48] but the two concepts have distinct qualities

> the most efficient way or the fairest way of organizing decisions about resources, as if there were some preexisting definition of those terms that allows us to set up social arrangements. Rather, concepts of fairness and efficiency are the outputs of the analysis. We are asking: What social arrangements does a community recognize as a way of making decisions about resources? Once we have identified those arrangements, we label them as fair and efficient in the sense that, for a particular community at a particular time, the arrangement leads to a stable social system. Whether those social systems also meet the standards of social morality depends on whether the community has met the equality principle.

[47] This is not to say that the distributive justice aspects of property law are unimportant. To the contrary, the institution of property raises issues about the distribution of resources within a society that have profound implications for the economic and social health of the society (*see, e.g.,* Singer 2011). However, those issues must be addressed by different theories of justice, political morality, and institutional decision making than the corrective justice theory developed here.

[48] In particular Hanoch Dagan uses the term "distributive justice" to refer to the division of burdens and benefits between owners and the community (Dagan 1999). I agree with him that appropriately dividing burdens and benefits between the individual and the community is the heart of understanding the scope of state power, but I do not refer to that as distributive justice in the Aristotelian sense. The division of burdens and benefits between an owner and the community is, for me, akin to the division of burdens and benefits between individuals, the central concern of corrective justice. The distinction is not merely verbal, for my reading of Aristotle's notion of distributive justice distinguishes between the claims of an individual to avoid interference by others (including the community) – what Aristotle called corrective justice – and the

and meanings. Both distributive and corrective justice "distribute" rights and responsibilities, of course, but they are fundamentally different theories of justice.[49] Most important, they address fundamentally different questions. Distributive justice is about the responsibilities that the community owes to individuals; corrective justice is about the responsibilities that each member of a community owes to other individuals and to the community. Under distributive justice, one individual makes a claim against the community that she is disserving of the community's support for her well-being; under corrective justice, an individual makes a claim against another individual or the community makes a claim against an individual. Accordingly, the responsibility of one person to contribute to another person's well-being or to the community's well-being is fundamentally different under distributive and corrective justice. Distributive justice asks what one individual owes others in the community because they are related as members of the community. It asks: What should each individual contribute to the community so that the community can fulfill its obligations to individual members of the community? Corrective justice asks: What commitments should an individual make to take into account the well-being of another individual or the community of individuals in order to meet the demands of corrective justice?[50]

Accordingly, distributive and corrective justice differ in the institutional setting for making the decision to distribute rights and responsibilities in one way rather than another. Distributive justice is the realm of the collective, acting through its legislature, and can only be carried out through public law; corrective justice is within the realm of private law, which makes decisions based on notions of corrective, interpersonal morality, not the obligations of the collective. Private law involves a claim by one individual that another individual has

claims an individual can justly make against the community for more resources. Nonetheless, there is substantial overlap between our views on the scope of state regulation. Other authors who refer to the distribution of rights and responsibilities between individuals as distributive justice include Lucy (2007) and Cane (2002).

[49] I rely on the Aristotelian distinction between distributive and corrective justice. (Aristotle, Nicomachean Ethics, Book 5). Under this conception, corrective justice "focuses on whether one party has committed and the other has suffered a transactional justice. Distributive justice deals with the distribution of whatever is divisible (Aristotle mentions honours and goods) among the participants in a political community.... Distributive justice, therefore, embodies a proportional equality, in which all participants in the distribution receive their shares according to their respective merits under the criterion in question.... Corrective justice, in contrast, features the maintenance and restoration of the notional equality with which the parties enter the transaction." (Weinrib 2002 at 350).

[50] Robert Nozick distinguishes between the type of reasons for an arrangement and the type of arrangement itself. The reasons for corrective justice and the allocations it makes are to correct a wrong in order to restore a preexisting balance. The reasons for redistribution not connected to correction are to change the preexisting balance. Nozick (1974) at 26.

wronged him; in our subject, it involves the claim by an owner that another has trespassed, or a claim by a nonowner that the owner may not deny access to the resource, or a claim by a co-owner that another co-owner owes her this or that duty.

Although property institutions obviously invoke important questions of distributive justice, "property law" as we understand it is about relations between individuals with respect to resources or between the community (acting through their state) and owners over the rights and responsibilities of private owners. To be sure, nominally property law is about the distribution of rights and responsibilities of owners and nonowners, but those rights and responsibilities are governed only by the obligations that each owes the other under principles of corrective justice and interpersonal morality. Property law is not about distributive justice, which is about the distribution of wealth, not the distribution of rights and responsibilities with respect to wealth. Distributive justice is the realm of tax and social welfare law, but not of the private law of property. The right of the richest individual in the country to enforce the law against trespass is no less than the right of the poorest individual; rights and responsibilities depend on ownership, not on ownership that is fair from the standpoint of distributive justice. Accordingly, I will refer to the allocation of rights and responsibilities when referring to private law and corrective justice, and will refer to distributive justice issues by referring to the distribution of wealth that property allows individuals to accumulate.[51]

The distinction between corrective and distributive justice raises two important subsidiary issues. First, what justifies a court in awarding damages to an individual if the award of damages restores a distribution of resources that is already unjust under the standards of distributive justice? If a person is destitute and steals from a rich person, why should not the injustice of stealing (a matter of corrective justice) be offset by the injustice of the existing distribution of resources, so that the property stays with the thief or is turned over to the state? Jules Coleman has supplied a cogent response.[52] The equality

---

[51] Although it is not necessary to the theory presented here, I side with Steven Walt (Walt 2006) on the debate about whether John Rawls's theory of justice subsumes corrective justice within distributive justice, a position taken in Kordana and Tabachnick (2006). My reliance on the veil of ignorance as the thought experiment that gives content to the requirements of corrective justice is not to the contrary because I put the veil of ignorance to work in a different context than Rawls does.

[52] Coleman (1994). Stephen Perry provides his own defense of corrective justice as conceptually distinct from distributive justice (Perry 2000). For a contrary argument, see Bagchi (2008). Correcting wrongs that restore unjust distribution of property is intuitional; laboratory experiments show that participants endorse corrective justice solutions even when they lead to results that appear to be inconsistent with distributive justice (Mitchell and Tetlock, 2006).

principle in distributive justice distributes the burdens of achieving distributive justice among individuals in the community based on the idea of equality. Individuals are asked to contribute to the redistribution in relation to their circumstances, and each individual is treated equally with respect to every other individual in the same circumstances. That notion of equality would be violated if, in implementing the dictates of corrective justice, some people were required to bear an extra portion of the burdens of distributive justice by giving up their rights to corrective justice. Principles of distributive justice determine how much a person in the situation of Bill Gates is to contribute to the required community support for individuals, and it would violate the equality of that determination if Bill Gates were also disabled from enforcing his rights under corrective justice; doing so would upset the equality of the determination made in the name of distributive justice.

The second subsidiary issue arising from the distinction between corrective and distributive justice is to locate the realm of each in judge-made law and in legislation. Judge-made law (outside of statutory or constitutional interpretation) concerns itself only with corrective justice. When the legislature acts, in what circumstances is the legislature acting out of the needs of corrective justice, and in what circumstances is it acting out of the needs of distributive justice? Although the border between distributive and corrective justice may be more difficult to draw in public law then in private law, the border is definable conceptually. When the legislature is arranging the rights and responsibilities of owners and nonowners with respect to resources, or articulating responsibilities that the owner owes the community, it is engaging in legislative implementation of principles of corrective justice and is therefore in the realm of private law.[53] It may be adjusting the rights and responsibilities determined under the common law, which it does when the legislature disagrees with the judgment of judges in private law cases. The legislature is simply taking a different view of the requirements of corrective justice. Or, it may be adjusting the rights and responsibilities as between owners and the community as a group, taking into account community interests that are not accounted for in private law. In that case, the legislature is mediating between the community as an entity and the individual, and this too is a form of corrective justice because it is defining responsibilities of owners to the community. Under this

---

[53] Goldberg (2012) at 1640 (private law defines rights and duties of individuals as they relate to one another and the rights and duties of public entities insofar as they act in a private capacity). The notion that the rights of the community against an individual are also a part of private law is controversial but serves to reinforce the relationship between land use regulation through judge-made law and through legislation. This connection is drawn in Chapter 13.

view, land use regulation is a form of corrective justice that determines the relationship between an individual and the community.

Theories of corrective justice knit individual rights and community rights together because corrective justice understands the correlativity of rights and duties and therefore the obligations that each individual in a community owes to every other individual, and to the community, when individuals interact. Under corrective justice, the concept of interpersonal wrong links the rights and obligations of people in a community. Interestingly, the corrective justice and economic agendas are similar in an important respect. Like economists, corrective justice theorists are engaged in a maximization process; they seek a balance (or equilibrium) between the way that rights and responsibilities are divided among free and equal people. Because they seek an appropriate balance between rights and responsibilities, they understand that outside of exchange relationships one person's loss will be reflected in another person's gain – that one person's right reflects another person's duty. By appropriately matching rights and duties, burdens and benefits, they seek, as economists do, to maximize the surplus in interpersonal interactions by requiring each person to appropriately treat all others.

1.3.1.3 Unity of Private Law through Burdens and Benefits. This book seeks to unify theory across the silos of property, contract, tort, and unjust enrichment, each of which implements the requirements of corrective justice. This is a controversial move. The prevailing style in academic matters is to deliberately mark the boundaries between private law topics, perhaps to give a sense of mastery of each domain. That style comes at a cost, however; by emphasizing differences, it precludes insights gained from similarities. A simple intuition ought to drive a norm of unification rather than separation: private law deals with claims that one individual may make against another individual, claims that the defendant has committed a wrong that ought to be redressed or that the defendant ought to pay compensation because the failure to compensate for harm would be a wrong. Because private law is centered on a theory of redress, a theory of wrongful decision making concerning the well-being of others must justify the redress and lie at the heart of private law. The right to demand redress then unites our understanding of property, contracts, tort, and unjust enrichment, and illuminates the overlap among them.

None of the traditional boundary markers between common law topics withstand scrutiny. Sometimes private claims are made in the context of a relationship between individuals (as in contracts and nuisance); sometimes outside of a relationship (as in negligence and trespass). The claims are sometimes about a resource that is privately owned (as in property law) and sometimes about a resource held in common (such as the highway or navigable waters). The distinctions between relational/non-relational claims and between private and common property do not "map" the domains of property, contract, tort, and unjust enrichment. Some relational claims between individuals are dealt with as torts (which, for example, govern claims for property damage against neighbors or claims by consumers against manufacturers or suppliers). Some relational and contract claims are based in property; for example, relational claims are found in servitudes, co-ownership, and common interest communities, while contract claims are addressed in landlord–tenant disputes, land contracts, and promises between landowners. Unjust enrichment spans contracts and property and contract law deals with the division of gains of trade, which can be understood as the question of how property (the gains of trade) ought to be divided.[54]

As a result, the four "disciplines" continually overlap. Property is about ownership, but if we focus on the ownership of gains of trade, so too is contract law. Tort law is often about relationships between strangers, but so too is property law (in much of nuisance law, for example).[55] Contracts are about property (there must be something to contract over) and many property relations are essentially contractual. All private law disciplines are grounded on the fundamental question of what obligations one individual in a community owes to others and the scope of those obligations. Property law is about the obligations that owners owe to nonowners and other owners, as well as the obligations that nonowners have to owners. Contract law is about the obligations that parties exploring a relationship have to each other. Tort law is about the obligations that one individual has to those who might be harmed by the individual. Unjust enrichment is about the obligation to return gains that it would be unjust to keep. The four areas are united because they are about claims by one person against another, and thus, I maintain, about how one person ought to think about the well-being of others.

It is sometimes thought that what divides torts, property, contract, and unjust enrichment is the source of an individual's obligations to others, because in contract law obligations are assent-based while (it is commonly believed) obligations in property, torts, and unjust enrichment are not. But this view can be

---

[54] Parties to a contract seek simultaneously to maximize gains from trade and capture as much of the gain as they can for themselves. They act like two prospectors who jointly look for gold. I argue in Chapter 4 that this involves not only cooperative norms that generate gains of trade but also cooperative norms that divide the gains of trade.

[55] The high transaction costs of bargaining make dispersed neighbors around a cement plant more like drivers on a highway then neighbors who negotiate about the appropriate location of a lot line.

held only by those who think that obligations are created by courts, and they have not thought enough about the basis on which courts create obligations. On the view presented here, obligations arise from decisions an individual makes, reflecting choices that fairly imply that the individual has accepted the obligation to attend to the well-being of others.[56] Obligations are not imposed on individuals; obligations arise from choices an individual makes, and are then recognized by courts. The source of obligations connects, not divides, torts, contracts, property, and unjust enrichment.

1.3.2 The Role of Law and Economics

When Learned Hand propounded the now-famous Hand formula as a way of understanding the requirements of the reasonable person, he was explaining a simple truth at the heart of private law: sometimes individuals ought to take pains so that other individuals do not suffer harms.[57] This is a description of other-regarding behavior: a basic moral requirement is that one take into account the impact of one's actions on others and absorb, in an appropriate way, the burden of reducing that harm. In the theory I advance, I seek to generalize other-regarding behavior as a morally sound way of making decisions when a person has an obligation to consider the well-being of others as the person makes decisions. This is the central core of the third proposition, the proposition that the law requires individuals who make decisions about resources to act as the ideal, other-regarding decision maker would act (Chapter 5).

Because economists have claimed the Hand formula as an economic explanation for the law,[58] and because the Hand formula is about the requirements of other-regarding behavior, property theory necessarily confronts the role of economic analysis in law. And because many people have rejected the Hand formula as a workable way of implementing a theory of morality,[59] I necessarily must confront the role of economic analysis in any theory of morality. To do that, it helps to unpack the Hand formula into separate insights about how people ought to view the obligations they owe each other.

The foundational intuition of the Hand formula (the intuition of the negligence regime) is that individuals need not eliminate or be responsible for

---

[56] Chapter 5. This theory of duty is advanced in a torts context in Gerhart (2010) at 105.
[57] United States v. Carroll Towing Co., 159 F.2d 169 (1947). Judge Hand pointed out that a reasonable person will take on burdens when those burdens are less than the probable harm to another that can be avoided by the burdens. In other words, reasonable people take on burdens for another person's benefit.
[58] Posner (1972).
[59] Weinrib (1995) at 148.

all harm from their activity. A corollary notion is that when harm results from carefully done activities, the victim bears the harm without compensation, except in those circumstances where an individual may undertake the activity only if she is prepared to compensate the victim for the harm the activity causes (strict liability). I believe that each of these propositions correctly states the requirements of justice, as I will make clear in Chapter 6. Another facet of the Hand formula is that when deciding what appropriate other-regarding behavior is, the actor must account appropriately for his own well-being and the well-being of the other, as required by the equality principle. What is at issue in applying the equality principle and the economic interpretation of the Hand formula is the basis on which an individual takes into account the well-being of another individual. This is a question of which values an individual should use in comparing one's own well-being with the well-being of another. On that issue, I believe that the economic view cannot prevail because the methods of valuation that economists have suggested are morally deficient, a point made by many. Valuing two people's well-being on the basis of revealed preferences, or by imagining hypothetical preferences that would prevail if wealth were equally distributed, misses the point that interpersonal comparisons ought to be made using social values developed through social interaction, not personal valuations. Here, the idea of values as inputs rather than as outputs clarifies the issues. What matters is the values people ought to use to shape their decisions, not how much they would pay to avoid the cost in question. In Chapter 6, I propose a method of interpersonal comparisons of well-being – the veil of ignorance – that, I believe, more closely meets the requirements of the equality principle.

This is not, however, an abandonment of the Hand formula; it is an articulation of how we ought to view the values to be used when we determine what burdens one person must accept for the benefit of another person. The Hand formula I depict is therefore not so much a formula – a word Learned Hand never used – as it is a framework for integrating various considerations that are relevant to determining when one person must sacrifice her well-being in order to protect the well-being of others, and I argue that economic analysis has a great deal to offer to that determination.

Law and economics has made two abiding contributions to legal theory: first, it has presented a vision of law as a socially constructed method of solving social problems, which allows us to get beneath the doctrinal understanding of law to articulate how the doctrine reflects the law's unique approach to addressing social issues. Economics, at bottom, is the study of relationships and it has developed refined tools for that study by understanding that any relationship (between supply and demand or between two interacting individuals) depends on the trade-offs that influence the movement of that relationship toward some form of equilibrium (which makes the relationship stable). The economic profession has added exceptional rigor and discipline to understanding the trade-offs that humans engage in as they make interdependent decisions.

Not surprisingly, law and economics covers a broad range of approaches that differ from one another in details. I embrace law and economics from two general perspectives. First, economics has no monopoly on studying relationships; all social sciences study relationships between individuals, and behavioral sciences study how individuals form belief systems that govern their interaction with others. The tools developed by economics to understand markets (impersonal relationships) can be, and are being, integrated with the tools of other social and behavioral sciences so that our understanding of relationships is subjected to a systematic and orderly analysis of how individuals form belief systems that govern their interactions with other individuals. In particular, the development of game theory has given rise to models of human interaction and decision making that are especially valuable in thinking about the relationship between cooperation and conflict.[60] One does not have to be an expert in game theory to understand its relationship to private property. As I develop the evolutionary story in Chapter 4, one individual makes a claim to a resource. Other individuals must react to that claim by either recognizing it or challenging it. The claim can lead to cooperation or conflict, and the choice between the two shapes the entire property system. Game theory provides a methodology for integrating knowledge across social science disciplines that helps us understand that interaction, because games can be played with a number of behavioral assumptions. For this reason, there are signs that we are at the beginning of a large transdisciplinary movement, with cross-disciplinary scholarship allowing us to understand human behavior from a unified social, cultural, economic, and political perspective.

Accordingly, as the behavioral sciences and philosophy cross-pollinate, economists might want to declare a cease-fire in their war to determine the relative importance of welfare and fairness in interpersonal relationships. I argue in this book that individuals interact against the background of socially constructed values about acceptable cooperative behavior – belief systems about how one ought to act when interacting with another – and that these values play a crucial role in explaining human behavior when humans interact (inside, as well as outside, of explicit markets). I also argue, from a legal perspective,

---

[60] Foundational writings on which I rely are Gintis (2009) and Binmore (2006).

Contemporary Property Theory

that cooperation depends on each cooperating individual's perception that the terms of cooperation enhance well-being and provide an acceptable division of well-being, so that cooperation depends on norms for enhancing well-being and norms for appropriately dividing well-being between individuals. The unification of the behavioral sciences in a way that shows how value formation can develop into norms of acceptable cooperative behavior should hasten our understanding that efficiency and fairness concepts are coevolving as interdependent variables.

1.3.2.1 The Coasian Revolution.
It will not surprise anyone, economist or not, that Ronald Coase makes an important appearance on these pages. I accept, without challenge, the theorems that have been developed in his name:

> **Theorem One**: If there are no transaction costs, the parties affected by interference in their activities will arrive at a mutually beneficial outcome if one is possible.[61]
>
> **Theorem Two**: That the assignment of a legal entitlement to one party or the other will not block the socially desired outcome (on efficiency grounds) when transactions costs are zero and the entitlement is well-specified.[62]

Although the theory here is sensitive to the wisdom of the theorems, the theory does not accept the further claim – sometimes made in Coase's name – that the theorems also help us determine how the law ought to award entitlements in the first place. To be sure, Coase posited that the goal in working out the problem of social cost ought to be to maximize the value of productive activity,[63] but that goal depends on how we measure and compare the value of productive activity, something that Coase did not try to specify. If the conflict is between an individual who needs a quiet environment to do her work in advanced mathematics and a professional jazz trumpeter who needs to practice, what values are in play and how ought we compare their well-being in order to maximize productive activity?

A conventional view of transaction-cost economics is that the law ought to assign entitlements by determining which party would pay the most for the entitlement, so that the law would mimic the market that would occur in a

---

[61] Shavell (2004) at 84. Sometimes the second theorem is posited to say that the parties will always arrive at a mutually beneficial outcome, but that need not be true.
[62] Shavell (2004) at 102.
[63] Coase (1960) at 15. Later he recommended that courts "understand the economic consequences of their decisions, and should, insofar as is possible ... take those consequences into account when making their decisions." Id. at 19.

frictionless world after entitlements are assigned.[64] This view, however, suggests that entitlements ought to be auctioned off to the highest bidder, and it is not clear why the law would set up an auction for assigning entitlements, a point that many economists understand.[65] Indeed, in view of the effects of the assignment of entitlements on wealth (who is required to pay to avoid the harm), the influence of preexisting wealth (who has the lowest opportunity cost of any given expenditure), and on endowment effects (owners demand more to sell than buyers are willing to pay to buy),[66] assigning entitlements by auction seems undesirable. I seek to address the question of entitlement assignment by developing a theory of interpersonal cooperation that identifies why individuals fail to reach agreements, the range of outcomes over which individuals bargain, and how bargaining individuals would pick an outcome that they can call reasonable. Chapter 4 articulates a theory of cooperation that meets those specifications, and Chapter 8 develops a way of understanding how bargaining individuals ought to value and compare their own well-being with the well-being of another in order to reach a socially appropriate entitlement.

I rely on Ronald Coase's thought in the spirit in which he wrote, which was to identify the problem of social cost, not to identify the solution to the problem of social cost. Coase's great insight is that the problem of social costs is created because two individuals make decisions that are interrelated in the sense that each imposes costs only because of the decision made by the other individual. Because that is true, the solution to the problem of social costs is to identify the individual who should have made a different decision in light of the probable decisions of others and to induce that individual to change his decision. Viewing the problem of social cost in that way allows us to solve the problem at its source: to identify which individual should have made a different decision in the context in which she was operating and to create incentives that induce her to make that decision.[67]

---

[64] Posner (2003) at 24. This is sometimes posited as a third Coase theorem. But not all economists attribute this to Coase. See Shavell (2004) at 77–109.

[65] See Shavell (2004) at 77–79 (noting that an externality can be identified only with respect to a reference point; my making noise is an externality only if the reference point is quiet; Chapter 8 argues that reference points and entitlements ought not be determined through an auction system).

[66] Baker (1975), Baker (1980), Craswell (1991), Kennedy (1981), Kelman (1975).

[67] I do not directly engage the theoretical literature sometimes associated with the law and economics movement discussing property rules, liability rules, and alienability, although my ideas are informed by it. See Calabresi and Melamed (1972) and Kaplow and Shavell (1996). I avoid engaging that body of theory to avoid an ambiguity embedded in it. That ambiguity can be described as the distinction between guidance rules (the law's commands to individuals who are inclined to obey the law even if the law provides no sanction) and enforcement rules

1.3.2.2 Externalities and Transaction Costs.

I join Ronald Coase in another internecine dispute.[68] I avoid using the term "externality" except in its narrow transactional sense.[69] The term has no stable meaning either in law[70] or in economics.[71] It is a technical term that, in some definitions, assumes that efficiency is the only value in determining when a harm ought to be internalized. It is better just to talk about social costs and the harm that one person imposes on another. As for transaction costs, they are hardly identified by name here, although they are omnipresent. The problem, as recently argued by Lee Ann Fennell, is that transaction costs identify the problem but not the solution.[72] If by transaction costs we mean impediments that keep individuals from cooperating, they are the subject of the entire book. Property and property law help society find cooperative solutions to the problem of making decisions about resources, which is done by reducing transaction

---

(the law's commands to those who would not obey the law in the absence of a sanction) (Nance, 1997). The distinction can also be described as the distinction between transactional structures – the way in which entitlements are arranged and their normative content – and enforcement (Coleman and Kraus 1986), and as the difference between the "ownership structure" of entitlements and their "degree of protection" (Ayres and Talley 1995). *See also,* Simpson (2009) at 39 (distinguishing the statement of the entitlement from the mechanism by which the entitlement is protected, which is "usually complex.") My primary interest is in how the law fashions property entitlements. I view enforcement rules to flow from, and to be responsive to, the normative theory of entitlements (*see* Nance 1997 at 837 and Nance 1985). I therefore present a theory of how the law assigns entitlements – a theory that also establishes the basis for determining the scope of an entitlement and the rules protecting it. This is especially relevant in three chapters: Chapter 6, where I address why an individual might have the obligation to compensate another even if the individual has not behaved wrongfully (in which event, the obligation to compensate another arises from the other's entitlement); Chapter 7, where I explain why trespass is sometimes protected only by a liability rule; and Chapter 8, where I explain the assignment of entitlements and the scope of protection in nuisance law.

[68] Coase (1990).
[69] Demsetz (1967)
[70] It would be possible to develop an analytical structure that gives the term "externality" a non-economic meaning. Under this alternative view, individuals impose costs on each other and the law functions to determine how we ought to view such costs. All such costs are external in the sense that the costs are ones the decision maker does not bear and are therefore external to the decision maker's decision. The law then would have three choices: to tell the decision maker to stop imposing the costs, to require that the costs be internalized by making the decision maker compensate the person bearing the cost, or to let the cost lie where it falls. That approach, like the approach in this book, would require the law to focus on how individuals ought to make decisions and what costs they should take into account when doing so. But economists have used the term "externality" for only a subset of the external costs I just described and have therefore rendered that term useful for only a part of the work of the law.
[71] Coase (1960).
[72] Fennell (2013) at 1473–74. ("Isolating and addressing transaction costs turns out to be a slippery business that can interfere with the goal of structuring resource access optimally. For property theorists it is the wrong enterprise" (footnote omitted)).

costs – that is, by overcoming the barriers that keep people from cooperating. In terms of this definition, the law functions to reduce transaction costs or, if that cannot be done, to affirm a set of norms that the community would have arrived at if there were no impediments to bargaining. This is a version of one of the Coase theorems, but identifying the problem does not simultaneously identify the solution. Nor, for the reasons just given, does it necessarily imply that the efficient solution is to assign entitlements to the highest bidder. The solution presented here to the problem of transaction costs is to overcome them by recognizing a broader set of relational norms than some economists seem willing to adopt.

1.3.3 The Evolution of Property and State

A central preoccupation of property theory explores the relationship between property and the state, a preoccupation that turns on theories of the evolution of property rights in the context of the state, and the associated relationship between property owners and other individuals in the community. A theory of the evolution of property, markets, and the state supports the second proposition – at their core, property rights are socially recognized, and the recognition places implicit constraints on the owner's decision-making authority (Chapter 4).

1.3.3.1 The Polar Positions. Political theory tends to group around one of two poles. Libertarian political thought tends to assume that rights just exist, arise spontaneously from the state of nature, or are subject to voluntary agreements that ought to be accepted because they reflect consent. Scholars of this type spend relatively little attention on the origin of rights, but ask instead about the role of the state given the preexistence of rights.[73] Their theories produce a vision of a limited state because the state arose from the need to protect rights; the rights did not arise from the state. This is the strategy of scholars such as Robert Nozick and Richard Epstein. For scholars such as these, rights

---

[73] Nozick (1974). The first sentence of the preface is: "Citizens have rights, and there are things no person or group may do to them (without violating their rights)." As a famous example, he addresses distributive justice by positing a just original acquisition or a just transfer of a holding (*Id.* at 151), but does not supply a theory of justice of acquisition or of transfer. Richard Epstein repeats this approach and avoids developing a theory of the origin of rights in property. In Epstein (2009), for example, he posits the need for a theory of the origin of property but then moves quickly to the question of what focal point people would use if they wanted to recognize rights in property. This is a theory about how a community assigns private property once it decided to allow a resource to be owned privately, but not a theory about why the community recognizes private property in the first place.

preexist the state and we ought to understand the state's function to be defined by, and limited by, those rights. These scholars do not try to account for the development of property rights from the sovereign, for example from feudal England, because they do not recognize the legitimacy of the sovereign. Accordingly, these writers find the meaning of rights to be those that arose in a state of nature, and not those that were granted by a sovereign.

Other political theory starts with the proposition that the state exists to define as well as to protect rights; it sees the state as the progenitor, as well as the protector of, rights. Theorists of this persuasion are likely to understand states to develop through an evolutionary process in which hierarchical command systems were gradually eroded as rights were wrested away from the sovereign authority and claimed by individuals. Under this view, rights are far more contingent than under libertarian approaches. Because rights were created in the light of the conflict between individuals and the state, it is hard to understand rights except insofar as they are the creations of the state. This view is not likely to pay much attention to the origin of rights from the state of nature and might even question whether there can be pre-political rights. For scholars who take this position, rights recognition and governance go hand in hand.

I adopt a centrist position. The theory here does not start with rights in a pre-social world or with human interaction that is only political. Instead, it explains how rights arise from the co-evolution of rights and the state. Chapter 4 explains that rights do not arise from the state of nature unless the community recognizes them, and that community recognition serves as political recognition. It also explains that rights emanating from the sovereign are subject to recognition by the community, making community recognition of the sovereign a prerequisite for recognition of the property rights created by the sovereign. A single theory of the origin of rights and the state explains the close association between rights and the community. This is at once a natural law theory that explains the origin of rights and a political theory that explains the origin and evolution of the state.

1.3.3.2 Communitarian Theory. Communitarian theories contribute to political theory and our understanding of the values that animate property law by focusing on the interdependence of individuals and the importance of community in facilitating individual freedom.[74] I build on the observation that "[c]ommunities, including but not limited to the state, are the mediating vehicles through which we come to acquire the resources we need

---

[74] See generally Alexander (2009) and Alexander and Peñalver (2009), Alexander (1997).

to flourish and to become fully socialized"[75] by showing, in Chapter 4, how social recognition shapes property rights and obligations.[76] And I show how obligations to others arise from the constraints implicit in the conception of property that the community has recognized. My conception of communitarian theory, however, unifies communitarian theory with theories of corrective and distributive justice, rather than suggesting that community values exert some independent influence on the law. Under my conception, the community consists of individuals who collectively, as members of a community, make three kinds of claims against owners: claims to resources as a matter of distributive justice, claims to resources as a matter of corrective justice under private law, and claims to resources under corrective justice through legislation, The resolution of those claims *is* the resolution of the relationship between individuals and the community, and if the resolution reflects the values of individuals who make up the community, the community will be stable and successful.

Distributive justice creates a community by recognizing claims of individuals to a greater share of the resources of the community and by satisfying those claims in a way that respects the equal freedom of each individual. Corrective justice in its private law setting adjusts the rights and obligations between individuals as members of, and proxies for, the community, by relying on values that the community has developed as it works out relationships between individuals. Because the property law I portray is based on morally appropriate choices between interacting individuals, I deny that in the realm of corrective justice under private law there is some community value that sits above or outside of the sum of individual well-being. The theory is grounded on the values of individual responsibility and equal respect for individuals that assures that (given the existing distribution of resources) humans will have maximum liberty (freedom consistent with the freedom of all other individuals) and the opportunity to flourish, but does not otherwise posit community values as independent forces.

Finally, the community, acting through its political processes, makes claims on owners to adjust the rights and obligation in order to take into account values that are not appropriately accounted for in private law settings. Here community values – protection of historical landmarks, spatial separation of interfering uses, and preservation of wetland, for example – influence the

---

[75] Alexander and Peñalver (2009) at 139.
[76] The concept of social recognition is, I believe, another way of expressing the fact that individuals approach the market with an interpretation of exchange that transcends their self-interest. It therefore leads to conclusions similar to the work on the market economy by Paul Malloy, albeit from a far different perspective (*see* Malloy (2000) and Malloy (2004)).

shape of property law by aggregating the burdens and benefits of ownership through the legislative process.

1.3.4 Institutional Analysis

Communities need mechanisms for coordinating decisions between individuals if they are to allow individuals to flourish within the community of individuals. Institutions serve that function. An institution is an arrangement devised by humans that constrains and organizes human behavior.[77] Under this conception, communities develop institutions such as private property, markets, systems of governance, norms, and law as coordinating devices that help mediate between the interests of individuals in the community and avoid needless conflict.

The decision-making focus of the theory here, which is developed in Chapter 3 and applied to institutional analysis in Chapter 4, unifies our understanding of institutions by allowing us to understand and evaluate institutions on the basis of the impact that institutions and individual decision making have on each other. Under this view, institutions provide the framework within which individuals make decisions; they channel decisions in a way that reduces the divergence between individual interests and collective interests. By understanding whether institutions channel decisions to meet the requirements of social morality, the theory allows us to evaluate and compare the efficacy of various institutional arrangements. Under this view, what is essential about property is the decision-making function of ownership, but we are able to understand decision making not as an unbounded right but as a contextual right that, because of institutional constraints, responds to the setting in which the decision is made. This, in turn, allows us to understand property law in terms of comparative institutional analysis and the kinds of information requirements that shape institutional arrangements.

1.3.4.1 The Essentialism Debate. Property theory is preoccupied with a debate about whether property has an essence (and, if so, what its essence is) or whether property is simply a bundle of sticks.[78] I seek to untangle this

---

[77] North (1990) at 3, Dagan (2011) at 3–4 and 28–31 (characterizing his use of the term "institution" as slightly narrower). The idea that an institution is a human arrangement that channels human decision making has spawned the New Institutional Economics as a field for organizing our understanding of the choices a community makes to constrain its decision making. For a particularly penetrating review of various features of institutional analysis, see Grief (2006).

[78] The literature is large. A recent online symposium summarizes many of the contending positions. See Economic Watch (2011). For essentialist views, see Penner (1997); for bundle-of-sticks views, see Grey (1980).

For theories that refute both positions and state a new one under the notion of institutions, see Dagan (2011) at 40.

debate by focusing, in Chapter 3, on what essentialists and bundle-of-stick advocates have in common.[79]

The bundle-of-sticks vision was developed to counter the excessive formalism of law in general and property law in particular and carries a singular message: the contours of the law need to be understood in terms of a normative theory of justice if they are to align with human behavior.[80] The fundamental call of the legal realists was not to disaggregate law for its own sake, but to build our understanding of law around the justifications for the law that explain why the law should take one shape rather than another. Once we view the bundle-of-sticks vision of property as the call for a normative basis for providing (and limiting) rights of ownership, we can understand property rights as having both in rem power and value-laden pull. Essentialism is important for the same reason. Essentialism allows us to identify the values that animate a system of practice, for it is the values that ultimately chart the course the system will take and therefore ground the practice. What is essential about a practice ought to be something that is not merely necessary and sufficient, but also a feature of the practice that is invariant. Essentialism ought to point to a feature of the practice that helps us understand the normative forces that shape the practice; essentialism ought to be justificatory, not conceptual.

The synthesis I propose is straightforward. What is essential about ownership is the right to make a decision, a feature that is consistent with all forms of property and with all major theories of the rights of ownership, including autonomy theories, incentive theories, personhood theories, and self-actualization theories. However, because the right to make decisions is constrained, the scope of this essential right takes on different contours in different contexts (and therefore assumes the shape of a bundle of sticks). This unified approach understands property law as a value-laden, but contextual, practice.

1.3.4.2 Comparative Institutional Analysis. Institutional analysis is never a unilateral question of the strengths and weaknesses of a particular institution, for any institution's strengths and weaknesses must be evaluated in light of alternative institutional arrangements.[81] Moreover, institutions

---

[79] This may be responsive to the call for a metaphor that will "resonate with existing property debates while it better describes new possibilities" (Heller 2001, at 94).

[80] *See, e.g.*, Cohen (1935) at 814 (decrying the "divorce of legal reasoning from questions of social fact and ethical value") and Holmes (1920) at 184 (formalism serves "as a cover up for consideration of social advantage" that are "the very ground and foundation of judgments").

[81] Komesar (2001), Komesar (1994).

are interdependent and co-evolving. Private property depends on markets to coordinate decisions among private owners[82]; state property relies on state processes to coordinate decisions about resources. Each institution must be compared with other institutions as an alternative way of addressing the social problem of decision making about resources, but the strength of each institution, including the institution of property itself, must be understood in conjunction with the strength of allied institutions. A theory of property-as-decision-making unifies our understanding of institutional analysis by focusing on the following question: which institutional form, along with allied institutional forms, best ensures that decisions about resources will take into account the values that society endorses?

Accordingly, property law raises two sets of institutional questions. First, a resource can be put in various institutional packages that reflect variations on ideal types of private and non-private property. Second, the law chooses between various kinds of coordinating institutions: the market, state regulation, private law, social norms, and private arrangements. The choice between institutional forms and coordinating institutions requires a theory that explains comparative institutional choice of both kinds.[83]

---

[82] The tragedy of the anticommons arises when rights over resources are so atomized and fragmented that decisions about the resource by any rights-holder can be negated by other rights-holders. As Michael Heller has written, the tragedy of the commons arises from too much use, the tragedy of the anticommons from too much exclusion (Heller 1998) at 87. His sustained analysis of the tragedy of the anticommons has revealed a surprising range of applications of a straightforward concept (*see*, Heller 1998 and Heller 2008). Two antidotes for this tragedy suggest themselves. One is to reorganize the way rights are assigned, and this is a function of both the market (by inducing someone to buy up rights and repackage them), of private governance regimes, and of the state (by exercising its powers of eminent domain or regulation). In addition, the law contains legal doctrines – boundary principles – that are intended to prevent over-fragmentation (*see* Heller 1999).

[83] No scholar has done more in recent years than Michael Heller to explore the archeology of institutional forms of property. His consistent theme – that institutional form demands attention to how decisions about resources are structured so that they allow socially responsible decisions about resources – is a major theme of the theory presented here. His theory of the anticommons, summarized in the previous note, demands that we pay attention to how decisions of separate owners become coordinated, which is influential in explaining the co-evolution of property and markets (Chapter 4) and also in the state's exercise of eminent domain power (Chapter 12). His idea that property's ideal types come in a wide variety of variations (Heller 2000, 2001 and 1999) is reflected here in the emphasis put on decision making as the unit of analysis of property law. His work, along with Hanoch Dagan, on governing the commons (Dagan and Heller 2001) provides a broader palette for addressing the tragedy of the commons and for understanding the impact of exit on decision making. In addition, Heller's notion that decision making over resources can be allocated to individuals, to governance regimes, or to cooperation induced by the possibility of exit, allows us to envision different methods of decision making over a common resource (*see* Heller 2005).

Institutional forms respond to three basic questions: First, who should make decisions about resources; second, how should those decisions be constrained so that individual and social interests are aligned; and, third, what mechanism coordinates that institutional form with those making decisions in other institutional forms? For some resources, say, public parks, the best decision maker is the state, and state decisions are constrained by the processes to which the state is subject. Or the state may want to retain ownership but privatize the management of the resource.[84] Other resources are best left to common ownership – such as highways, waterways, or open ranges – in which case the collective makes decisions about the resource and must either develop decision-making processes to govern the commons (by developing self-enforcing norms) or rely on state regulation to do so (as in the case of rules of the road). Although much of property law is about private property, we ought to understand private property as it compares to other institutional packages for resources.

Choices of institutional form and coordinating devices tend to be correlated: decisions about private property are generally coordinated through markets; decisions about state property are generally coordinated through political procedures. But that is not inevitable. State ownership can be combined with auction-like markets (as in privatization through auctions) and private property can be so highly regulated as to remove most discretion from the owner (as in the gaming industry). For each type of institutional comparison, the institutional choices a society makes reflects the relative costs and benefits of making decisions through one institutional form or another. Taking the form of property as an example, a society is likely to treat a resource as common property when the exclusion costs of private property (in terms of deprivation) are thought to be large and the costs of regulating the commons through informal sanctions are thought to be small.[85] Regulating private property through private law has comparative advantages when the dispute between two individuals raises all the relevant issues, but regulation through legislation is better when private disputes cannot adequately represent the relevant interests that are important to members of the community. The focus on decision making requires our theory to account for the comparative costs and benefits of various institutional means of making resource decisions.

Comparative institutional analysis must specify what counts as a cost and what as a benefit in evaluating various institutional arrangements. Two

---

[84] Subject, of course, to the public trust doctrine. Ill. Central. Ry. Co. v. State of Illinois, 146 U.S. 387 (1992) (navigable waters and shorelines are held by the government in trust for the general population).

[85] Ostrom (1990), Ostrom (2010), Ostrom (2011), Fennell (2011).

approaches to comparative institutional analysis are prominent in the literature: the transaction cost approach and the participatory approach. I extend these approaches by identifying the values that help us determine which transaction costs and what kinds of participation matter in constraining and shaping decisions about resources. Under the transaction-cost approach, we favor the institutional form that best reduces transaction costs, thus reducing the barriers to private cooperative arrangements. Although facilitating private coordination is a worthwhile goal, this approach requires a theory of why and when people cooperate, and this requires that we specify, as the theory here does, the values that individuals ought to take into account when coordinating their activities. For example, we choose private property if the risks of detrimental exclusion are minimal compared with the advantages of decentralized decisions coordinated through the market. But we choose common property if the risks of detrimental exclusion are greater than the benefits of decentralized, market-coordinated decisions and if externalities can be addressed successfully in governance regimes. The institutional form that best reduces transaction costs depends on how we identify and weigh the various costs and benefits.

Comparative institutional analysis that focuses on participation costs requires us to articulate who participates in each institutional form and how we value that participation, which requires that we specify the kind of participation that will best represent the values that the institution in question is designed to address. Private property excludes participation by nonowners except insofar as participation in an owner's decision-making is governed by norms, private agreements, or private law. Common property is a sensible property form only if participation is effective in addressing the tragedy of the commons, and state property has its own unique set of participation requirements. The theory developed here allows us to analyze whose participation matters and why it matters.

1.3.4.3 Information Cost Theory. The decision-making focus accepts the importance of information costs in setting up institutions to coordinate decisions among individuals. The quality of a decision – whether by an individual or by an institution – depends on the quality of information the decision maker has and can reasonably obtain. There is, however, a trade-off between the value of new information and the cost of getting that information; any institutional arrangement must account for the costs and benefits of additional information. Institutions economize on information costs by making judgments about the optimal degree of uncertainty, and they economize on the cost of information that individuals need by sending signals that decrease the information costs for those who make decisions in the face of uncertainty. In adjudication and rule-making, lawmakers must decide whether the benefits of additional information are worth the cost.[86] In crafting a legal intervention, courts and legislatures must take into account the impact of information costs on the form of intervention, and also the information requirements for those who must comply with the legal rule.

As developed by Henry Smith and Thomas Merrill, the contours of property law recognize that the law operates by creating categories or modules that serve to minimize the information costs of those who apply, and comply with, the law.[87] The law of trespass constitutes a broad category that enforces the right to exclude by minimizing the information that courts and third parties need in order to work with legal doctrine. If the property is privately owned, the boundary knowable, and access is not privileged, no individual needs to invest in information to understand that the law is "stay out."[88] Neither court nor a third party needs to get information about the use to which the property is put or the comparative value of exclusion (to the owner) and access (to the nonowner). Understanding the rules/standards debate as one about information costs allows us to understand the formal requirements of property law in a way that focuses on values important to the property system.

I build on the information cost theory of institutions by recognizing that information has benefits as well as costs, so that property theory needs to figure out when the benefits of more information outweigh its costs. Information cost theory explains why courts rely on broad rules to articulate property law – rules that allow cases to be classified in one way rather than another. But property theory must also account for the cost of deciding into which category or module any particular case should be placed. A judge must decide, for example, whether to apply the law against trespass (the exclusion strategy) or the law designating an incursion as potentially privileged (the governance strategy). Once we pay attention to the costs of categorization, we see a complex picture in which the cost of getting additional information must be measured against the benefits of a more just and refined outcome. The decision to call an

---

[86] For the role of information costs in adjudication, see Nance (2008); for the role of information costs in administrative rule-making, see Wagner (2012).

[87] Smith (2012)

[88] Thus, "under an exclusion regime, the law uses a rough informational variable or signal – such as entry – to define the right, and thus bunches together a range of uses that juries, judges, and other officials need never measure directly" (Smith 2004 at 972). The exclusion regime does this by delegating decision making to the owner and protecting that decision from judicial intervention. As Henry Smith says, this involves "a strategy of delegating information questions to owners by delineating exclusive rights to a thing enforceable against all others" (Id. at 975). The governance regime, on the other hand, involves judges, juries, and third parties in considering information about the interest of both owners and nonowners and therefore imposes additional costs on the system of determining rights and responsibilities.

incursion on an owner's property a trespass is the decision that more information about the owner and the intruder would not lead to a more normatively attractive result (or, conversely, that justice does not demand more information to resolve the dispute). Because I intend my account of property to be normative (by identifying the values that shape the law), my account adds to the understanding of the costs and benefits of the modular approach and the relationship between the costs of information and the values of property law.

The cost of categorization recognizes that it takes information to determine whether to put a case in one category or another. Consider two types of categorization costs: the costs a judge incurs in determining in which category to put a case (determination costs)[89] and the costs of enforcing the right to exclude when categories are in doubt (enforcement costs). Determination costs are the costs incurred by anyone who needs to determine whether a case falls in the exclusion category or the governance category. A judge gets a case and must determine whether to apply the rule against trespass (the exclusion strategy) or to apply (or create) a privilege to enter another's property (the governance strategy). Often that is easy and takes little information; at other times, it takes a great deal of information and thought. A judge putting a case in the exclusion category minimizes information costs by doing that, but deciding whether to put a case in that category imposes information costs not yet accounted for in existing information cost models. This is the costs of determining the boundary between exclusion and governance.

The second category of categorization costs is enforcement costs. If the categorization methodology is to reduce information costs, individuals subject to the law need to be able to identify the boundary between exclusion and governance. Just as the exclusion strategy depends on simple proxies (a boundary and entry) to reduce the information costs of complying with the exclusion rule, categorization needs a methodology that simplifies the cost of categorization to determine whether a particular case goes in the exclusion or the governance category. When the boundary between exclusion and governance is murky, misunderstood, or ad hoc, as it is now, the information costs of categorization go up enormously. Indeed, one of the categorization costs is the cost of litigating trespass cases (such as the airplane overflight and the migrant worker cases) that got to court only because the law could not define the exclusion category with enough specificity to reduce information costs. By identifying how to locate the boundary between exclusion and governance, as the theory here does, the information costs of categorization are reduced.

---

[89] Smith and Merrill refer to entitlement delineation costs, but I interpret that to be the cost of delineation once a case is put in a category.

It should be apparent that what I term "categorization," is a normative process; its information requirements are driven by the normative values that govern the right to exclude and its limitations. A judge or third party who is deciding in which category to put a case is asking the following kind of question: "Given the values the law is trying to advance, would the cost of acquiring additional information be offset by a better chance at a just resolution of this dispute?." When the judge puts a case in the exclusion category, the judge is effectively saying: "no amount of additional information about the interests of nonowners would bring about a more just result; the costs of particularization by getting information about the use of the property by the nonowner are not worth it in order to reach a just result." When a judge puts the case in the governance category, on the other hand, the judge is saying something like the following: "I cannot determine the just result without taking into account the uses of the nonowner in relation to the uses of the owner". That means that the judge needs to understand why information might be valuable to the just determination of the conflict. The process of categorization requires a normative justification for the right to exclude that allows the judge to determine whether the cost of additional information is worth the benefit of a more particularized outcome.

Understanding where the law locates the boundary between exclusion and governance requires that we understand the normative reason for saying that more information is not worth the cost. The theory here develops such an understanding.

1.4 CONCLUSION

Property theory is rife with dichotomies that obfuscate the unity of the idea of property, including the dichotomy between the rights and interests of owners and nonowners, between philosophical and economic approaches, between private and non-private property, between private and public law, and between the individual as an autonomous unit and the individual as a member of a community with collective aspirations. This chapter has identified the most important dichotomies and outlined the ways in which the theory here hopes to unify our understanding of property law across the dichotomies. An important perspective runs throughout the theory: the distinction between law as a system of outputs and law as a system of inputs. Most people think of law as the output of the deliberation and action of legal institutions. Under this view, we understand law by viewing precedent, doctrine, and theory to be inputs into deciding cases, advising clients, and predicting the future path of the law. This approach relies on the heroic assumption that we need not understand

Conclusion

the inputs that influenced the precedent, doctrine or theory we rely on when we consider the paths of the law. The theory here challenges that assumption. It suggests that what is important in understanding the law is not the law's output but the law's input: what it is that makes the output what it is. I have employed that perspective to suggest that property values ought to be understood as inputs into the legal process and have suggested a theory that allows us to implement that perspective. The four propositions I have outlined in this chapter, and will defend in the remainder of the book, provide a way of integrating values as inputs into our evaluation of property law, and to unify property theory across the many divisions that now divide property law into distinct domains.

2 An Overview of the Theory

This chapter explicates each of the four propositions that anchor the theory developed here and explains what each proposition contributes to a unified framework for thinking about why the law shapes property rights and responsibilities in one way rather than another. The following four chapters support each proposition on its own terms.

2.1 DECISION MAKING

I claim that the essence of ownership is the right to make decisions about a resource, but that the decisions are constrained in their scope. The vision of owner as decision maker runs throughout property theory,[1] and it is accepted that property rights – the right to use, to exclude, to transfer, and so on[2] – are constrained by the limitations on what the owner may do with his property. The theory here is unique in putting the concept of owner as constrained decision maker at the heart of a theory of property.[3] This idea is further developed in Chapter 3.

---

[1] *See, e.g.*, Heller (2006) at 45, and (2001) at 83; Waldron (1985) at 327 ("In a private property system, a rule is laid down that, *in the case of each object, the individual person whose name is attached to that object is to determine how the object shall be used and by whom. His decision is to be upheld by the society as final.*") (emphasis in original); Harris (1996) at 236 (referring to "choice" to describe Hegel's concept of freedom), and Purdy (2010). Sometimes, the relationship between property and decision making is implicit in an author's treatment of property. Michael Heller's discussion of forms of property revolves around the relationship between forms of property and sound decisions about resource use (*see* Heller (1998), (1999), (2001), and (2008)). Carol Rose's emphasis on preference choice, especially when an individual's preferences clash with those of another individual, focuses on decision making as what owners do (*see* Rose (1994) at 28).

[2] Honore (1987) at 161 (describing eleven standard incidents of ownership).

[3] The concept of owner-as-decision-maker exploits recent scholarship that identifies ownership in terms of agenda-setting (Katz, 2008, 2010, and 2011), or the right to set the normative

The vision of owner-as-constrained-decision-maker identifies both the raison d'être for property and the invariant unit of analysis for evaluating property's role in society. From the time humans began collecting in communities, they needed a method of making decisions about resources in order to avoid decision making by force. The form of decision making chosen by a community and the constraints the community puts on decisions determine the relationship between individuals and the community with respect to resources. Private property reflects the belief that decisions about many resources are best left in the hands of individuals, coordinated by the market and constrained by law. Forms of common property reflect the belief that decisions about resources are best left in the hands of individuals who share use rights, but this belief puts a burden on individuals to develop modes of decision making that are acceptable to, and productive for, the common owners. State-owned property puts property in the hands of the political process (a different form of decision making) and constrains state decisions through political forces. Whatever the institutional form property takes (and there are many variations), we understand forms of property if we identify who makes decisions and how decisions are made and constrained.

The concept of constrained decision making is important because it helps us understand the relationship between law and human behavior. The law operates to mediate between and among the interests of owners and nonowners by assessing how owners and nonowners conduct themselves and comparing that behavior with the behavior of an ideal decision maker – one who has appropriately accounted for the factors that are required for the kind of decisions being made. An owner who wants to fence in his property is required to think in a particular way about where the plot line is so that the owner avoids trespassing on his neighbor's property; the decision of where to put the fence must consider factors that a neighborly decision maker would take into account (for example, whether surveys and boundary posts are reliable). The concept of constrained decision making also illuminates the relationship between private and public law. In private law, courts assess individuals' decisions about resources by comparing an individual's behavior with the behavior of an ideal decision maker and correcting those behaviors that do not seem to embody an appropriate way of thinking about the well-being of others. In public law, the state, by prohibiting or requiring certain decisions about property, further constrains the decisions

standing of the nonowner (Dorfman, 2010), or in terms of the right to determine the use of the property (Claeys, 2011). Each of those contributions can be understood to suggest the basic distinction that I draw, which is between the right of an owner to do something (such as the right to exclude nonowners) and the right of an owner to make a decision about what to do (such as an owner's decision about whether she is authorized to exclude nonowners).

owners make, requiring an owner/decision maker to take into account a broader range of factors that align her decisions with society's values.

2.2 SOCIAL RECOGNITION

A central preoccupation of property theory is the origin of property rights. Theory is divided between statist theories – the notion that all property rights are derived from the state[4] – and state-of-nature theories – the notion that property rights arise in some natural way from the state of nature and need only be protected by the state. A great deal hangs on the distinction. If rights are creations of the state, it is not clear why the state could not rearrange or even abolish the rights. If rights arise from pre-political sources, it is unclear how the state can play any role in shaping the scope of the rights without meeting community resistance. In Chapter 4, I argue that property rights arise, and are worthy of moral respect, because they follow terms under which the community recognizes claims over resources. They function as rights because of that recognition, and social recognition determines the scope of the rights. Further, I argue that the evolutionary mechanism by which owners make claims and the community accepts or rejects the claims is at work whether we view property rights as being derived from the sovereign or as arising spontaneously from the state of nature.

Property rights arise from the state of nature as individuals either reject or accept the claims that others make; rejections lead to threats of violence and either renegotiation or actual violence, whereas acceptance leads to claims that mature into rights (by virtue of their acceptance). Over time, the pre-political community settles on the recognition of claims that can be made without the threat of renegotiation through violence. Property rights arising from the sovereign reflect acceptance of the sovereign's authority (and last only so long as that authority is accepted). They evolve as the relationship between individuals and the sovereign evolve. That relationship is subject to violent shocks and procedural evolution as the relationship between the individual and the state is renegotiated in light of threats of violence and social pressure. In either case, the scope of property rights with respect to particular resources is determined by the terms under which non–rights-holding members of the community recognize them.[5]

---

[4] A dramatic statement of this position is found in *Commonwealth of Massachusetts v. Alger*, 61 Mass. (7 Cush) 53 (1851) (expressing belief that property rights are created by the state and therefore may be limited by the state).
[5] I hope to show that rights based on recognition are rights in the sense that Waldron, following Dworkin, uses the term: "a rights-based argument is an argument which appeals to *rights*: one

Naturally, the shape and content of rights are constantly in flux because the social recognition of claims changes in response to changing power relationships or changing perceptions of the terms under which rights ought to be accepted. Because threats of violence are a substitute for social recognition, property rights develop over time subject to both implicit social negotiation and explicit violence. Moreover, because property norms, state decision making, and reliance on markets are subject to similar evolutionary forces, and because they serve as complementary institutions, the institutional mix that affects property law is continually in flux. The evolution is not over, but the rule of law is intended to subject property relationships to orderly change, without extralegal violence, as the terms under which the community recognizes property claims are reconsidered in light of changing circumstances and evolving values. Within many countries, the rule of law seems to be working tolerably well; however, between countries and between sects within countries, disputes over resources continue to fill the world with violence.

The social recognition concept is important because the scope of rights is determined by the terms under which the claims to resources are recognized; by determining the scope of the rights it recognizes, a community also determines the claims that it rejects, and the terms under which the rights may be exercised. Courts, in adjusting private disputes, are determining the rights and responsibilities of owners by determining the best way to think about claims to resources and the impact of those claims on others; the best way of thinking about those claims is derived from an understanding of the relationship between owners and others. This is a source of protection for owners because it allows courts to demark the scope of decision making that is acknowledged to be theirs and protects that scope of decision making from others' impermissible claims. And the legislature, when it regulates to reset the rights and responsibilities of owners that courts have assigned, has a basis for understanding what rights it may not infringe – the rights acceptable to the community – and what rights it may limit on behalf of the community.

The idea that property rights are socially recognized is not inimical to the concept of private property. Social recognition does not foreshadow that ownership rights are necessarily restricted or that they are restricted by some vague

---

defends a social arrangement by showing how it respects or promotes respect for the rights that people have." (Waldron 1988, at 62). Not all assent gives rise to rights, of course, for some assent may be coerced or given under mistake. For that reason, the fact of assent does not itself give rise to rights. It is the reason for the assent that gives rise to rights. When the assent is given because the non–rights-holder recognizes the merits of the rights claimant, assent-based rights are natural rights that can be defended or promoted because of the widespread respect they command – respect for the normativity of the claim.

sense of social interests. Because social recognition is the source of property rights, as well as the source of limitations on property rights, we understand the strength of property rights by understanding the values that shape their social recognition. First, we understand a right as a claim that others have a moral obligation to respect, and social recognition provides the moral basis for respecting property rights. Second, private property affords a wide swath of decision-making authority precisely because the community wants a decision maker whose decisions are not subject to review and second-guessing by the community. Third, the community also wants a decision maker whose subjective valuation of the property generally prevails over objective or community valuations. Private property allows patterns of decision making to emerge that are themselves valued by the community because decentralized and dispersed decisions provide a special place for individuality, emphasizing values of autonomy, privacy, industry, and capacity fulfillment. Finally, as I will argue in Chapter 5, an owner's obligations to the community arise only from an owner's decisions, and this means that an owner's decision-making autonomy is not compromised by the notion that constraints on an owner's rights are socially recognized. The concept of private property is strengthened because the community expects most decisions of an owner to be unquestioned by the community and therefore beyond the reach of regulation by courts or legislatures.

The concept of social recognition signifies that in a broad sense owners exercise their rights on behalf of the community, performing a function that the community asks of them (to make decisions about the resource), but subject to implicit obligations the community imposes as a condition for recognizing the rights. It utilizes a principal/agent model to link the owner to the community and to understand the relationship between owner and community. It implies that property regimes reflect an overall social compact, and that owners are agents for the community, exercising powers given by the community under constraints imposed by the community. By understanding the values that underlie the community's social recognition, we determine the scope of the rights of ownership and limitations on those rights and how those rights and obligations are connected to the interests of the community. Moreover, the social recognition concept helps us clarify the relationship between the state and its citizens. The state's power to affect property relationships through private and public law enables the community to affect the nature of the rights that the community has recognized in owners. At the same time, the social recognition concept suggests the limits of state authority with respect to property. Social recognition implies not only a legitimate function in overseeing

Social Recognition 51

the power the community has delegated to owners, but also a limitation on the right to interfere with that power when it is being exercised legitimately.

In the United States, social recognition is in the hands of courts and legislative processes. We can ground our understanding of the social recognition concept by recasting the familiar work of courts and legislatures.

2.2.1 *Judicial Recognition*

Courts, in their common law role, perform three property-related functions: they allocate resources between private property and common property, they choose owners from among various claimants to private property, and they determine the rights and responsibilities of owners and nonowners in order to justly coordinate decisions about resources. Each of these functions reflects the concept of social recognition.

Courts decide who makes decisions about resources by choosing between private and non-private ownership. In the airplane overflight cases,[6] for example, courts were asked to determine whether the owner of land controlled airspace used by commercial airlines. The issue was one of social recognition: Should courts recognize that decisions about airspace ought to be made by private landowners or by common owners of the airspace (where decisions could be made by those who used the airspace or by the state on behalf of common owners)? The choice was not difficult, and courts had a uniform response, which (although differing in their reasons) can be understood as follows: recognizing decision-making authority in individual property owners would increase burdens on commercial flights with little benefit to land owners (because coordinating permissions for flying was subject to significant bargaining cost and holdout problems). By contrast, recognizing airspace as a resource held in common would produce little burden on landowners but yield substantial benefit to airlines. Accordingly, flying over someone's land was not a trespass. The airspace would be dedicated to the public, with decision making left up to the process that most effectively coordinated conflicting use of the airspace by airlines.

Similarly, in the famous *Moore v. Regents of the University of California*,[7] the court was asked to recognize an individual's rights to control the use of his cells after his spleen was removed for medical reasons. Defendant sought the unfettered right to use the cells for research and to patent the research

---

[6] *See, e.g.*, Hinman v. Pacific Air Transport, 84 F. 2d 755 (9th Cir. 1936). *See generally* Banner (2008).
[7] 793 P.2d 479 (Cal. 1990).

results. The court ruled that although plaintiff had the right to be informed of defendant's proposed use of his cells, the plaintiff had no right to control the use of the cells after they were extracted. The court recognized the defendant's claim because the medical center would use its rights in the cell in the public interest – developing new cell lines under the incentive of the patent system and then dedicating those cell lines to the public domain when patent protection ended.

In the same vein, the right of publicity requires courts to determine which aspects of a person's fame can be claimed as private property (by the person who is famous) and which ought to be dedicated to the public domain as a resource for the community. This is social recognition of a claim of rights that determines the allocation of decision-making authority over the fame that a performer has created. Justice Kozinski framed the issue well: "The very point of intellectual property law is to protect only against certain specific kinds of appropriation";[8] courts in right-of-publicity cases necessarily focus on the division between private and non-private property.[9]

When a resource is suitable for private ownership, common law courts recognize, on behalf of the community, who the owner ought to be. Adverse possession embodies social recognition that the community, through its courts, ought to change the owner of property to recognize past mistakes or new expectations. The law of finders embodies social recognition of factors determining which claimant to lost or mislaid property ought to be recognized as the decision maker and stakeholder for the true owner. When property is abandoned or capable of being taken from the public domain, the concept of possession embodies the social recognition of which attributes of capture are most worthy of the reward of private property.

Finally, common law decisions about the permissible scope of decision making by owners embody judicial and social recognition of rights and responsibilities. The law of trespass charts the socially recognized border between exclusion and access.[10] The law of nuisance charts the socially recognized border between legitimate and illegitimate uses of property when an owner's use conflicts with a neighbor's use.[11] The law of estates and future interests, the law of servitudes, and landlord–tenant law chart the socially recognized allocation of decision-making authority over time between sequential owners.[12] The

---

[8] White v. Samsung Elecs. Am., Inc., 989 F. 2d 1512, 1514 (9th Cir. 1993) (Kozinski, J., dissenting).
[9] These are not, of course, the only instances in which courts distinguish between private and non-private property. Foxes are objects of private ownership; flowing water is not.
[10] *See* Chapter 7.
[11] *See* Chapter 8.
[12] *See* Chapter 9.

law of common owners and users charts the recognition of decision-making authority when more than one person has authority to make decisions about a resource.[13]

2.2.2 Legislative Recognition

The state power to regulate property relationships also reflects social recognition. Through the Takings Clause, the state may move property from private to public owners and, under certain conditions, from one private owner to another.[14] It exercises, in other words, the power to change the existing recognition of property rights and responsibilities in response to changing circumstances, social needs, and market failures. To be sure, the Constitution both grants and restrains state power under the Takings Clause (by requiring that the taking be for a public use and with just compensation). But that too is consistent with the social recognition concept because it implies an agency relationship between the community and the individual, and in agency relationships principals bind themselves to respect the decision-making autonomy they have given their agents. That is the social recognition purpose of the Constitution: to bind the community (the principal) by stating the circumstances under which the principal may, and may not, exercise its power. Under this view, the Constitution (on behalf of the community) limits the state so that the state's power to change property relationships depends on the valid determination that the system of coordinating private property decisions through well-regulated markets has broken down.

Similarly, the state's power to regulate property usage in the name of the health, welfare, and safety of the community gives it the power to change the terms of preexisting social recognition.[15] However, the state is circumscribed by concepts of due process, regulatory takings, equal protection, and the Contracts Clause, and this reinforces the social recognition concept by protecting owners from overbearing legislation. Finally, although it plays an uncontroversial role in mature property regimes, the doctrine of escheat reinforces the social recognition concept. Under escheat, if an individual dies without heirs, or if property is otherwise unclaimed, the property goes to the state to deal with as it will. This default reversionary interest in the state recognizes that property returns to its roots – that is, to the community as represented by its state.

---

[13] *See* Chapter 10.
[14] *See* Chapter 12.
[15] *See* Chapter 13.

2.3 OTHER-REGARDING DECISIONS

The law assesses behavior by comparing an individual's behavior with that of an ideal decision maker, one whose decision is to be considered to be moral because it appropriately accounts for the well-being of others. In a world of interacting individuals, ideal decision makers must take into account, in an appropriate way, the well- being of others if their decisions are to be considered moral. In the language of tort law, individuals must invest in reasonable precautions to prevent decreased well-being for others. In the language of economists, decision makers must account for the social cost of their decisions. In the language of moral philosophy, each individual, in the decisions she makes, must show equal respect for the freedom of every other individual. I claim that the image of the ideal decision maker is central to understanding the scope of rights over resources. The concept of appropriately other-regarding (and therefore ideal) decision making is developed in Chapter 5. The question of how the ideal decision maker appropriately thinks about her well-being in the context of due regard for the well-being of others is developed in Chapter 6.

The concept of the ideal other-regarding decision maker requires the law to evaluate individual decisions by identifying the factors that a moral decision maker would take into account if the decision maker is to appropriately reflect equal respect for each individual. Both the existence and the scope of an individual's duty are implicated. The obligation to think of how one's choices may affect others is omnipresent, but the obligation to incorporate the well-being of others – which I will call the obligation to be other-regarding – is a subset of that general obligation. As we will see, the law must first determine *when* an ideal decision maker has the obligation to make other-regarding decisions – the concept of duty. A person sitting alone in her home has no obligation to take the well-being of a neighbor down the street or others into account when deciding how to advance her own well-being; her general obligation is to think about whether she has an obligation and, having none, need not make an other-regarding decision. A person emitting dense smoke from her chimney does.[16] When an ideal decision maker has the obligation to be other-regarding, the decision maker must determine the scope of her duty by appropriately

---

[16] In terms of contemporary theory, an individual who has no duty to take into account the well-being of others may implement an exclusion strategy, relying only on her self-regarding interest to decide whether to grant another access to the property. An individual who has the obligation to take into account the well-being of others must implement a governance strategy, determining how best to integrate the interests of others with her own interest. The distinction between exclusion and governance is developed in Smith (2002) and Merrill and Smith (2001).

balancing her interest in her own well-being with the interests of the other individuals and acting accordingly.

Other-regarding decisions are a form of rational decision making that allows one person to coordinate her decisions with the decisions of others. Other-regarding decisions are distinct from altruistic decisions because other-regarding decisions are required if the individual is to act lawfully, whereas altruistic decisions are those made even in the absence of a legal duty. If there is to be coordination, it is because individuals adopt a form of rational behavior that appropriately takes the well-being of others into account, successfully melding their self-regarding and other-regarding inclinations. When the law says "make reasonable decisions," as it does in private law, the law is commanding people to act as if they had accounted for the well-being of others in an appropriate way – that is, to be appropriately other-regarding. Indeed, I will argue that all forms of responsibility for the well-being of others, including those generally thought of as implementing strict liability or unjust enrichment, are implementing the other-regarding decisions of an ideal decision maker. In the theory developed here, the community develops norms that reflect other-regarding values and those norms influence how courts evaluate decisions to make sure that they are socially moral.

2.4 APPROPRIATE ASSIGNMENT OF BURDENS AND BENEFITS

In Chapter 6, I provide a basis for thinking about what factors the individual who must be other-regarding ought to take into account when deciding how to behave. The decision maker who would be other-regarding will appropriately assign the burdens and benefits of decisions about resources. Property law assigns benefits (the right to exclude) and burdens (the obligation to respect boundaries) and seeks to have those assignments reflect social values that evolve over time through the interaction of individuals in the community. People behaving as they would if they made decisions about resources in a moral, other-regarding way will seek to appropriately assign the burdens and benefits of decisions about resources so that those who get the benefits of any decision also bear an appropriate share of the burdens of that decision, while those who bear the burdens of a decision receive an offsetting benefit. That is what the requirement of equal treatment means. This kind of cost-benefit analysis, when understood to reflect the normative values that animate property law, is inherent in the way that moral people integrate other's interests with their own.

The concept of an appropriate assignment of burdens and benefits is not new to property law; it is prominent, for example, in analyzing servitudes. It is a central part of the economic foundation to law.[17] Yet the concept unifies property law in ways that have not yet been recognized, and, as used here, it supplements the economic approach with a better assessment of how relative costs and benefits ought to be determined. I present the idea of appropriately assigning burdens and benefits as a unified way of understanding individual responsibility for the harm that occurs to another. If an individual is responsible for the harm that another incurs, it is because the individual has failed to undertake a burden the individual should have undertaken or because the individual has received a benefit that the individual cannot morally keep without compensating the individual who conferred the benefit. Understanding how the law views the assignment of burdens and benefits as between individual ideal decision makers reveals a unified theory of individual responsibility under the doctrines that we now understand as negligence liability, strict liability, unjust enrichment, and no-liability regimes.

Moreover, the concept of appropriately assigning burdens and benefits provides a coherent definition of the idea of property. Because property involves a relationship between individuals over decisions about resources, an apt definition of private property is dominion over a resource that is constrained by the obligation to act as one would if the decisions about the resource appropriately assigned the burdens and benefits of resource use. In the vision presented here, rather than viewing property law to be addressing relationships between individuals over things, property law is about the relationship between individuals over an appropriate assignment of the burdens and benefits of decisions about a resource. Property is, in this way, a relationship between individuals about the relationship that each has with respect to a resource.

An appropriate division of the burdens and benefits of decisions will often depend on which individuals can reduce harm from their activity by making more reasonable decisions. But sometimes harm is unavoidable at reasonable cost, and the law must allocate the resulting social cost to one individual or another. In those circumstances, I advance the veil of ignorance to determine how to allocate the social cost. Behind the veil of ignorance, an ideal decision maker must make a decision without knowing the individual's status in the

---

[17] The focus on burdens and benefits differs from the cost-benefit analysis of economic analysis in two ways. First, the theory focuses on an individual's obligation in making decisions to appropriately consider the burdens and benefits of her choices. That means that the assessment of burdens and benefits is not an abstract mathematical calculation, but an individual determination that is influenced by the individual's knowledge and circumstances. Second, the values used to assign burdens and benefits do not turn on the willingness of an individual to pay to avoid a burden. The assignment depends on neutral values that reflect a fair assignment of burdens and benefits given the kind of values that a particular society has worked out to apply the concept of fairness.

world, and thus without knowing in what way the individual will be affected by the decision. From behind the veil of ignorance, decisions will have the kind of neutrality, and will be grounded on social values concerning the well-being of interacting individuals, that non-interested decision makers would take into account; those decisions are entitled to be called moral.

Although the full explication of the way the theory here is using the burdens and benefits concept will be developed throughout the book, a foreshadowing summary of how the burdens and benefits concept pervades property doctrine might help the reader understand the conclusions supported by the concept.

2.4.1 Trespass

A private property owner bears the costs, maintenance, and risk of property, or receives it in transfer from one who has borne those burdens.[18] Because the owner absorbs the property's burdens the owner generally has the exclusive right to benefit from her decisions. That accounts for the principle that generally an owner may exclude others from the property for any and no reason. Nonowners are generally not entitled to the benefits of the property because they bear none of its burdens. Because one person has no obligation to benefit another in the absence of a special relationship with the other, one is entitled to the fruits of the burdens that one bears. If others had a claim to use property without bearing the burdens of the property, there would be too little investment and too much private taking without compensation.

On the other hand, owners sometimes have obligations to be appropriately other-regarding concerning the well-being of potential users of property, which is why the law limits the right to exclude. Even then, the owner's only obligation is to appropriately assign the burdens and benefits of decisions about resources. A person knowingly buying property subject to a prior use buys property on which users have built up justified expectations – perhaps the prior users were authorized to be there. That expectancy exemplifies the burdens of investment the users have made in reliance on their unchallenged or privileged use. The new owner may not, therefore, exclude prior users without making sure that they get the benefits of their investment.[19] Presumably, when a person buys property subject to a prior use, the person adjusts the price he pays so that his burden of buying land subject to the prior use is offset by the benefits of a lower price.

---

[18] See Chapter 7.
[19] Race v. Castle Mountain Ranch, Inc., 631 P. 2d 680 (Mont. 1981).

An owner's duty to potential users often arises from an owner's choice about how to use her property. An owner using her property for a retail store benefits from her customers' patronage and therefore ought to bear the reasonable burdens of looking out for their well-being. The owner can exclude potential shoplifters (who would get the benefits of the merchandise without paying for it) but cannot exclude customers who benefit the owner by shopping there and who impose no dangers. An owner who hires (and therefore gets the benefit of) migrant workers cannot take that benefit without also accepting the burdens of letting social workers on the property to meet the needs of the migrant workers.

2.4.2 Nuisance

Under nuisance law, an owner who undertakes an activity that imposes a social cost on a neighbor benefits from doing so.[20] Because each owner has an obligation to take the well-being of neighbors into account, each owner ought to accept the reasonable burdens of reducing or internalizing the harm from its activity. For that reason, an owner's activity decisions must be reasonable, including decisions about where, how, when, and how frequently to do an activity, and an owner must compensate those injured by unavoidable harm from the activity when the harm is a type they ought to have taken into account when planning the activity. This obligates the owner to make sure that the activity bears burdens that reasonably match the benefits of the activity, and allows us to define the concept of reasonable decisions in this context.

2.4.3 Coordination between Concurrent Decision Makers

When two or more individuals own, or have the right to use, a resource, the value of the resource will be diminished if the concurrent decision makers do not effectively coordinate their decisions.[21] Effective coordination requires that each decision maker appropriately integrate the benefits from his or her decision with the burdens these decisions impose on the other owners or users. For common property, those with a right to use the resource must internalize the burdens that come from overuse, which generally occurs through private agreement or state regulation. If such coordination is impossible, transforming common property to private property helps to internalize the benefits and burdens of decisions. For property that is owned by more than one person, the law provides the mechanism for overseeing coordinated decisions and

---

[20] *See* Chapter 8.
[21] *See* Chapter 9.

making sure that burdens and benefits of individual decisions are appropriately distributed.

2.4.4 Coordination over Time between Sequential Owners

Covenants allow property to be burdened by promises to neighbors, but the law of servitudes is shaped by the requirement that those burdens be matched by benefits to the person making, or bound by, the promise.[22] The concepts that shape the assessment of servitudes – concepts of reasonableness, of changed circumstances, of notice, and of promises running with the land – all turn on whether the burdens and benefits of the promise remain appropriately assigned over time. Moreover, when resources are owned sequentially, which creates the need for the law to coordinate decisions about a single resource over time, the doctrine of waste embodies the duties that one owner owes to subsequent owners (for example, between tenants and landlords and between present and future estate holders) by virtue of their sequential relationship. This requires each owner/possessor who gets the present benefits of the property to also accept the burdens of saving appropriate benefits for future owners. Doctrines surrounding conditions put on the exercise of ownership by future owners require that the burdens of those conditions be justified by offsetting benefits of ownership.

2.4.4.1 Contract Law. Much of property law is the application of contract principles to agreements about resources. The law of landlord–tenant, governance of common interest communities, and promises between owners and users is based, I will maintain, primarily on contract principles. The fundamental contract principle is that the contract must appropriately assign the burdens and benefits of the promises that are exchanged, given the burdens that each individual has undertaken. The doctrines of consideration, mistake, fraud, duress, unconscionability, reasonable restraints, and implied terms work out what it means to appropriately assign burdens and benefits in these various relational contexts.[23]

2.5 ROLE OF PRIVATE AND PUBLIC LAW

The propositions supporting the theory here also illuminate the relationship between private and public law with respect to resource decisions. Private law

---

[22] *See* Chapter 10.
[23] These propositions are developed only implicitly in the theory here. I will develop these themes more fully in a book called *Contract Law and Social Morality*.

arises from one individual's claim that another individual has failed to give her well-being adequate respect – that is, from a claim that the defendant's behavior has failed to be appropriately other-regarding with respect to the plaintiff's well-being. This gives private law a unique function: to specify the factors, and their relative weight, that each individual ought to take into account when deciding how to act with respect to resources if that person is to appropriately integrate his or her interests with the interests of others by reasonably assigning the burdens and benefits of resource decisions. As I have said, owners may exclude individuals from their property for any and no reason when the owner need not take into account the well-being of others, but an owner's right to exclude is restricted when an owner is required to take into account the burdens of the owner's decisions on others. In this way, private law helps to solve coordination problems: when two or more people must coordinate their activity, private law determines the factors that each one ought to take into account in order to best coordinate their different interests by avoiding, or reasonably assigning, social cost.

What, then, is the role of public law, and how do we address the paradox that the state both constrains, and is constrained by, the concept of private property? How are we to understand the state's role when the state determines the scope of property rights at the same time that it is limited by the concept of property that it defines?

The theory advanced here gives property a core normative content that situates the role of the state by both justifying the need for the state to intervene in property relationships and limiting that intervention so that the state does not invade property's core normative content. The core normative content is that owners are promised an appropriate assignment of the burdens and benefits of decisions about resources when the state, representing the community, adjusts the burdens and benefits of ownership. Under the theories propounded here, the state exercises power under the Takings Clause to achieve collective purposes that could not be achieved through the market (because of the difficulty of coordinating private property use through consensual transactions) but may not exercise its takings power in the absence of such a market failure. Under the Takings Clause, the requirement that the state pay just compensation preserves the burdens and benefits of state decisions about property, mimicking the consensual transactions that the market is unable to provide. The state exercises a separate power by regulating property uses to adjust the burdens and benefits of ownership. Legislative regulation changes the factors that individual decisions makers must or must not take into account; the legislature exercises this power to allow the community (acting through its legislature) to make sure that owners account for a wider range of interests, over a broader time frame, than private law can ensure. However, the state is itself limited by the obligation to preserve a fair assignment of the burdens of regulation among owners by avoiding the assignment of undue burdens on some owners that ought to be borne by other owners.

2.6 CONCLUSION

This chapter has presented, in a generalized form, the propositions that animate this book's theory, in order to introduce the theory's vocabulary and provide a sense of how the separate principles relate to each other. In brief, the four propositions are:

1. that owners are constrained decision makers,
2. that the scope of decision making by owners with respect to the resources entrusted to them is governed by the community's norms of recognition,
3. that the primary coordinating norm is the obligation to be appropriately other-regarding, and
4. that other-regarding decisions will appropriately assign the burdens and benefits of decisions about resources.

The next four chapters describe and justify the four propositions in greater detail. The theory shifts focus from what individuals can do with resources to the way an ideal decision maker would make decisions about resources. This focus illuminates the way the law affects individual decisions so that the decisions show equal respect for the lives that individuals have chosen to live by requiring each individual to locate an appropriate assignment of the burdens and benefits of decisions about what to do with resources.

3   Owner as Decision Maker

The theory developed here suggests that the essence of ownership is the owner's right to make decisions about the resource entrusted to the owner, but that an owner's decisions are constrained because the owner must act as the owner would if the owner accounted appropriately for the social values implicated by her decision. In this chapter, I explore the idea of owner as decision maker and explain why it is important to a theory of social morality. In the next chapter, I explain the source and nature of the constraints on decisions under private law.

This chapter challenges the view that what is essential about private property is what owners can do with it. Property theory is built around the belief that owners have rights to do or refrain from doing certain things, and that ownership ought to be known by those rights, in particular by the rights to use and to exclude. Under this view, what is essential about property is what the law says about how owners behave. At best, such theories are theories of private property only, for they cannot account for common or government property. More to the point, such essentialist theories are only partially accurate, and cannot account for the many instances in which exclusion, use, and other behaviors are restricted; behavioral rights of ownership are not absolute, which makes behavioral characteristics poor candidates for any essentialist theory of property. Admittedly, shifting our analytic focus from what owners are allowed to do to focus instead on the scope of decisions that an ideal decision maker would make is subtle and slight. Nonetheless, the shift illumines important aspects of property theory.

The idea behind the concept of owner-as-decision-maker is familiar. When we talk about the rights of a private owner, we talk about the right to make a decision about the resource entrusted to the owner, but we recognize that the owner is constrained in the scope of decisions she may make. An owner has the right to choose among many lawful uses, but may not use the property in a way that significantly and unreasonably interferes with her neighbors. The owner has the right to exclude others, but may not exercise that right, for example, to prevent the state from undertaking a lawful search. Co-owners of land have the right to make decisions about the land, but their decisions are constrained by the equal decision-making rights of the other owners. Rights of nonowners are also defined by the decisions they may make and are limited by the factors they must take into account. Nonowners must respect a boundary, which implies a way of making decisions about where the boundaries are, but nonowners are allowed to tie up at a private dock to avoid the dangers of a sudden storm, which implies a different kind of decision.

As familiar as these ideas are, they deserve to be given a more central role in property theory. In the vision of property I present, the idea of owner as constrained decision maker is the central organizing concept of property law, the unit of analysis for how we understand rights and responsibilities over resources. Constrained decision making is what is essential about property; it is the raison d'être for property, and the invariant unit of analysis for evaluating property's social role. I elaborate on this point in Section 3.1. Constrained decision making is also, I claim, the best way of understanding the mechanism by which the law assigns rights and responsibilities about resources, for the concept of constrained decision making identifies the scope of permissible decisions about resources and therefore how individuals ought to act. It captures both the owner's right to have the community respect her decisions and the responsibilities that ownership imposes on owners to take into account factors appropriate to the decision they are making. It therefore provides a vision of the relationship between individuals in a well-ordered community and a vision of law's function in guiding individual decisions.

Property law puts the owner in the position of mediating between the owner's interests and the interests of others and functions to oversee an owner's mediating decisions to ensure that they are made on a socially appropriate basis. Property law also protects owner's rights by overseeing the decisions of nonowners with respect to the owner's property. This view of individual decisions as the mediating device the law uses to enhance social cohesion in the community is covered in Section 3.2. Finally, the notion of constrained decision making situates our understanding of the role of law in overseeing disputes about resources, and, in particular, our understanding of the relationship between private and public law. It suggests that the law's function, in both its private and public iterations, is to influence the kind of decisions that owners and nonowners make in order to align private and social interests. That idea is captured in Section 3.3, and it is employed in Part III of this book to locate the justification for, and limitations on, legislative regulation.

3.1 PROPERTY ESSENTIALISM

Our need to understand what is essential about a concept is grounded in our need to understand the appropriate method of thinking about the concept. Identifying what is essential grounds our understanding of the concept and provides the fulcrum around which we can develop insights about how the concept can be applied in concrete situations. To find what is essential, we look for a characteristic that is invariant, one that helps us integrate ideas around a central core – a characteristic that is indispensable to our understanding.

The essential characteristic of ownership, whether private or non-private property, is the right to make a decision about a resource. Any community faced with conflicting claims to resources must address two questions: (1) Which individual or group of individuals should make decisions about resources; and (2) By what process, and with what methodology, should those decisions be made? The identification of the decision maker determines the form that property takes. For private property, the decision maker is an individual or group of individuals who hold the right to transfer the property. For common property, the group of deciding individuals holds the right to use the property. The method the law requires for making decisions constrains the decisions. Naturally, different communities supply different answers to the question of how decisions about property are made (depending on their social structure and prevailing norms of cooperation), and within a community the answers differ for different resources and change over time as perceptions about social values change. However, no community can avoid the decision about who makes decisions and by what means the decisions are made. The assignment of decision-making responsibility is the social problem a community must address, and therefore the social problem that gives rise to all forms of ownership (even if a despotic dictator supplies the response).

Decision making is also a necessary condition of ownership. A person who has the right to make a decision about a resource has rights that nonowners do not have, and it is difficult to imagine calling an individual an owner if the individual does not have the right to make decisions about the resource. The claim that "I own my body" asserts the right to make decisions about one's body. The idea that I own a pencil but have no right to make decisions about the pencil (even to delegate decision making to someone else) seems impossible.

Constrained decision making is also the invariant characteristic of forms of property, which are distinguished by the nature of the decision making that accompanies them.[1] To take obvious examples, solely owned property

---

[1] The decision-making model affirms the temporal, spatial, and sharing dimensions of property noted by Laura Underkuffler (*see* Underkuffler (2003)).

designates the owner as decision maker and puts constraints on the owner/decision maker through private and public law. Jointly owned private property designates two or more decision makers and requires that they coordinate their individual decisions about various matters. Leases create a form of property in which decision making is divided and shared between landlord and tenant. Decision making may also be allocated over time so that various successive owners of property have decision-making authority at different times. A private owner's decisions distinguish one private owner from another and, I will argue, influence their responsibility to others. Owners of farms and owners of retail stores are both decision makers, but their different decisions distinguish their ownership, and, as we will see, their rights and obligations as well.[2] In these ways, constrained decision making is an invariant characteristic of ownership across different contexts in which private property is held.

Forms of non-private property are also distinguished by the character of the decision making they embody. Common property has common decision makers; the greater the number and diversity of "commoners," the greater the challenges of coordination through joint decision making.[3] It is decisions of the commoners that determine whether the commons will result in tragedy[4] or comedy.[5] For an open access commons, the number of commoners is unlimited. If the commoners are an identifiable and closed set – so that decision making is common on the inside but exclusive on the outside[6] – then the commons takes on some of the properties of joint ownership. If commoners have no right of exit, their decisions governing the commons take on one character. If the commoners have the right of exit, making the commons a liberal commons,[7] decision making is different yet. If a resource is held in common but the decision makers have no right to exclude, then the commons becomes open access property and decision making about the resource takes on still a different character.[8]

Property governance is also a matter of the form of decision making. Common interest communities identify areas of individual and collective decision making (realms of individual and common governance).[9] Condominiums and cooperatives are each distinctive in the way they distribute decision-making

[2] *See generally* Chapter 7, Exclusion.
[3] Aristotle (2000) ("Everybody is more inclined to neglect the duty which he expects another to fulfill").
[4] Hardin (1968).
[5] Rose (1994) at 105, Ostrom.
[6] Rose (1998) at 155.
[7] Dagan and Heller (2001).
[8] Eggertsson (2003).
[9] Heller (2005) and Dagan and Heller (2005).

authority, and entity forms such as partnerships and corporations are formed precisely because of the decision-making advantages that hierarchical decision making provides for determining resources use. Other resources are under the decision-making authority of the state, and are constrained by the procedures and political and legal requirements that the state must meet.

The concept of constrained decision making is also integrative across property theory; theories of private property, for example, can be understood in terms of how they highlight various features of decisions made by owners.[10] Theories of personhood stress the importance of the way people create identity by the decisions they make. Theories featuring autonomy stress the importance of decision making for the development and flourishing of the individual. Theories focusing on the incentive effect of property connect an owner's authority to make decisions to the kind of decisions they are likely to make. Kantian theories stress the freedom to make choices in a way that coexists with everyone's equal freedom to make choices. All theories of private property are built around a concept of individual decision making.

The idea that decision making is the essential characteristic of ownership is superior to any other essentialist theory, especially those theories that focus on what an owner may do with the property. Essentialists who focus on what an owner does – that is, on rights of owners to use or exclude – flounder on the problem inherent in any behavioral view of the law. Focusing on what an owner may do with a resource is problematic because the evaluation of what an owner may do is contextual. Owners of separate properties might engage in identical conduct with very different normative implications. Two owners of separate property may each deny a nonowner access to their land for a requested purpose; in one case, the denial may be lawful, in the other unlawful.[11] Such instances of exclusion are distinguished not by the behavior (the exclusion) but by the context and, in particular, the kind of factors an owner ought to take into account in that context when making the decision to exclude. If an owner is not required to account for a nonowner's interest in access when deciding whether to exclude, the exclusion is lawful. If the owner is obligated to account for the nonowner's interest in access and does not do so reasonably, the exclusion is unlawful. What makes the exclusion unlawful is not the owner's conduct (because exclusion is sometimes a right and sometimes not) but the nature and content of the decision an ideal owner

[10] Theories of property are evaluated in Alexander and Peñalver (2012).
[11] *Compare* Jacque v. Steenberg Homes Inc., 563 N.W.2d 154 (1997) (awarding punitive damages when seller of mobile home plowed a path through the owners' snow-covered property to deliver a mobile home to a neighbor) and State v. Shack, 277 A.2d 369, 374 (1971) (allowing defendants to enter plaintiff's property to aid migrant farmers).

would make in that context. When the exclusion is lawful it is because the ideal decision maker would have made the same decision about his behavior. When the exclusion is unlawful, it is because the conduct (the exclusion) would not have occurred had the owner acted as an ideal decision maker would in that context.

In other words, how an individual acts may not vary from one context to another, but the legality of how an individual acts depends on the circumstances because the circumstances tell us what factors the decision maker should have taken into account when making decisions.[12] By comparing actual conduct with the conduct of an ideal actor – one who took due regard of relevant factors – we can identify the legality of the conduct. The decision, not the way one acts, is what is essential about property.

3.2 DECISIONS AS A MEDIATING DEVICE

When individuals compete, they effectively disregard (or even intend) the negative impact of their decisions on the well-being of others. When individuals cooperate, they do so by taking into account the impact of their decisions on others, hoping that the other will do the same. Decisions of individuals mediate between cooperation and conflict, and thus between individuals and the resolution or generation of conflict. That is why individual decisions must be the unit of analysis for understanding human interaction. As we understand more about the belief systems that influence a person's decisions, we can improve our assessment of how to avoid conflict and encourage cooperation.

---

[12] This is not, of course, a property concept but a concept general to how we think about law. That is why there is no "negligence in the air." Palsgraf v. Long Island R. Co., 248 N.Y. 339, 341 (1928) ("proof of negligence in the air, so to speak, will not do") and why driving fast means one thing if done on a city street and another if done on a race track, See id., at 344 ("[O]ne who drives at reckless speed through a crowded city street is guilty of a negligent act ... [i]f the same act were to be committed on a speedway or a race course, it would lose its wrongful quality."). Assessment of most non-intentional behavioral decisions depends on the context. A driver is pulled over for going ninety miles an hour when the speed limit is seventy. Whether this is wrongful behavior depends on the circumstances. If the driver is taking a heart attack victim to the hospital but is not otherwise imposing undue risks on others, the driver may not be engaging in wrongful behavior. Therefore, we can understand different concepts of responsibility for objectively similar conduct only by evaluating the circumstances that led to the conduct. Circumstances matter because they inform our evaluation of how the actor ought to make decisions. Knowing that the actor was taking a heart attack victim to the hospital and was otherwise imposing only due risks on others indicates that the actor was taking into account the circumstances and factors that are appropriate in that situation. The actor's conduct was reasonable because the actor's method of making decisions was reasonable.

The decision-making concept is important because it sees each individual as the agent who, by the decisions she makes, mediates between her interests and the interests of others, producing either competition or cooperation. This helps us situate the law's role as a representative of the community. Under the vision presented here, the law functions by determining what factors a person must or must not take into account when making decisions about resource use. The law does this by determining when and how each individual must take into account the well-being of other individuals when making decisions and how those decisions ought to divide the burdens and benefits of decisions about resources.[13] When the law commands people to "be reasonable" it is saying that a person ought to make decisions based on the factors that a reasonable person would take into account in that situation. The law determines the set of factors that a person ought to consider, and how he ought to consider them, when making decisions. The law then evaluates conduct to see whether it is consistent with the conduct of a person who had taken into account the appropriate factors in the appropriate way, and the law rules accordingly.

Significantly, the law relies on individuals to make decisions in the appropriate way and recognizes the individual as the social intermediary by which the diverse interests of individuals are taken into account. The law seeks decisions that bring out the cooperative side of people and insists that individuals act in socially appropriate ways so that the law's work is minimized. It is the individual, not the law, that in the first instance integrates the individual's interests with those of others and finds an accommodation that creates the least conflict and the best fit in a community of diverse individuals.

To return to our exclusion example, the owner's right to exclude means that an owner may deny a nonowner access to the resource for any or no reason. When that is true, the law recognizes in the owner a scope of decision making that is absolute and unreviewable by courts. But when an owner is limited in her right to exclude, it is precisely because the owner is restricted in the kinds of decisions the owner may make; the owner is required to take into account factors that do not otherwise come into play. When a sloop ties up at a private dock to avoid the dangers of a sudden storm on a lake, the dock owner may not untie the sloop and set it out into the dangers of the storm.[14] That is because the scope of the owner's decision is constrained by the fact that the nonowner is already on the owner's property and by the circumstances of the emergency.

---

[13] The law's method for identifying the relevant factors is developed in greater detail in Chapters 5 and 6.
[14] Ploof v. Putnam, 71 A. 188 (Va. 1908). This principle is discussed in the context of the right to exclude in Chapter 7.

Decisions as a Mediating Device

The law asks the owner to be more cooperative, and evaluates decisions to see if they are sufficiently cooperative. Nonowners too are evaluated by the decisions they make. The law requires the owner of the sloop to compensate the owner of the dock for damages, which means that paying compensation is one of the factors the owner of the sloop must take into account when seeking refuge at the dock.[15] We can understand both the right to exclude and its limitations as implementations of the law's recognition of the factors a decision maker must or must not take into account when making decisions. The rights of ownership and nonownership are greater when the constraint on decisions is less; the rights are less the greater the constraint.

In this way, the focus on the owner-as-decision-maker simultaneously accounts for an owner's rights (those decisions the owner is permitted to make) and an owner's responsibilities (decisions the owner must avoid). An owner's rights and responsibilities are two sides of the same coin. Moreover, the decision-centric focus of the theory here simultaneously determines the rights and responsibilities of nonowners and owners who would be adversely affected by an owner's decisions.

The decision-centric approach has analytical value as well. By focusing on the basis for the owner's decisions, we can specify precisely the factors that are relevant and irrelevant to a decision in a particular context. Consider the right of a store owner to exclude from the store an African American customer thought to be a shoplifter.[16] From one perspective, the permissible scope of exclusion is formed from the clash of two principles: the freedom of business owners to exclude suspected shoplifters for legitimate self-protection and the principle prohibiting the owner from discriminating on the basis of race. Understanding the law at this level of generality is problematic, however, because the principles lead in two different directions. The store owner is likely to claim that he excluded a customer (who happened to be African American) not because of her race but because she was a suspected shoplifter; the customer is likely to claim the opposite. How is the law to know whether to apply the principle of self-protection or the principle of nondiscrimination?

This dilemma is resolved if we focus on the owner's decision and ask what factors the owner should take into account when deciding to exclude the African American. An appropriate accommodation of the freedom of a store owner to protect his investment and the freedom of the shopper to be protected against unjust discrimination requires a judgment about the level and kind of evidence the store owner ought to have had when making the decision

---

[15] Vincent v. Lake Erie Steamship Co., 124 N. W. 221 (Minn. 1910).
[16] *See* Singer (2011b).

to exclude. Assuming a centrist response to that issue,[17] it does not undercut the store owner's equal treatment responsibility to recognize that store owners have the right to take reasonable measures to protect against shoplifting, so that acting on the basis of objective evidence of a shopper's behavior that is associated with shoplifting ought not, by itself, be unlawful. As long as the objective evidence the store owner uses is racially neutral, uninfected by racial stereotypes, and applied evenhandedly, the store owner's decision can be upheld. Courts do not decide concrete cases on the basis of contesting principles but by defining the factors that an ideal decision maker may or may not take into account when deciding whether to exclude others.

In other words, with the decision-centric focus a court looks into the basis on which a shop owner ought to make decisions about how to treat customers, and this allows a court to get to a level of specificity that distinguishes an unreasonable decision (because it impermissibly took race into account) from a reasonable one (because it was a race-neutral attempt to prevent shoplifting). If we had perfect information about the factors a store owner took into account when deciding how to react to various customers, we could distinguish these two situations. Even without perfect information, the law can specify the kinds of considerations an ideal store owner (one who was trying appropriately to balance self-protection and nondiscrimination) would have taken into account when making the decision. The law can expect the store owner to have had objective, race-neutral criteria for identifying shoplifting and to apply those criteria evenhandedly. Store owners who make decisions following that protocol would be acting lawfully; store owners who did not would be acting unlawfully.

The focus on the decisions that underlie how people behave does not deny the normal association between law and behavior. When the law focuses on behavior, it is, without generally acknowledging it, actually looking behind the behavior to understand the decision-making process the actor must have used to determine the behavior. The decision-centric focus is, I believe, making explicit a mental operation in legal analysis that has often been taken for

[17] There may, of course, be other responses, depending on the background assumptions used to address the conflict. One polar position is that given the history of racial discrimination and the longevity of stereotypes, the store owner ought to be disabled from excluding African Americans without strong evidence of misbehavior by the customer, or ought to be subjected to high standards of proof of the risk of shoplifting. Under this resolution, the store owner's right of self-protection would be subservient to the customer's right not to be discriminated against. The opposite polar position is that shoplifting is a serious problem, a tax on all customers, and that the freedom of the store owner ought to override the possibility that exclusion would be racially based, absent a strong showing of racial bias. Either way, it is the basis of the store owner's decisions that are being evaluated.

granted. The law is asking this sort of question: If an individual in a particular context appropriately considered the factors she ought to have taken into account, how would she have behaved? If the actual conduct is different from the ideal behavior, the actor has acted wrongfully. If the actual conduct is consistent with the ideal conduct, the actor will have behaved correctly. This approach suggests that property ought to be known by the decisions owners and nonowners make rather than the behavior those decisions bring about.

This approach does not ask about a decision maker's motive; we are not inquiring whether the decision maker wanted to cause harm, or had an impure thought about others, and we do not care whether the decision maker was spiteful, angry, optimistic, or daydreaming. The reasons the decision maker behaved the way the decision maker did are irrelevant to the analysis. What matters is only the factors that an ideal decision maker would have used to make decisions about how to behave and whether the individual behaved as the ideal decision maker would have.[18]

3.3 DECISION MAKING AND LAW MAKING

The focus on decision making also allows us to define the relationship between private and public law in property matters, as I have already described. Private law assesses a defendant's decision making insofar as it affects a plaintiff who asserts that the defendant should have given his interests greater weight and respect. The law is then called on to determine whether the defendant behaved as she would if she made a decision that accounted appropriately for the factors that affect the plaintiff's well-being. Because all that concerns the court in resolving the dispute is the right of the plaintiff to be treated with equal respect and the obligation of the defendant to do so, the range of issues that can be raised in private law about the scope of an owner's decisions

---

[18] I adopt a distinction suggested by Jules Coleman between "reasons for action" in the sense of reasons for taking action (motive) and "reasons for action" in terms of reasons that people act on (that is, factors individuals use to make decisions). Coleman (2001) at 71–72. Often, if an individual's motives are impure, an individual will take into account inappropriate factors when making decisions. But so too might a person whose reasons for acting are pure, or even altruistic. And a person whose reasons for action are impure (motives) may make decisions that are beyond reproach in terms of the factors that a reasonable person would have taken into account. That is the sense in which courts say that an otherwise lawful act will not be rendered unlawful by a bad motive. *See* Bradford v. Pickles, (1895) A.C. 587 (H.L.) (lawfully drilling a well is not rendered unlawful by allegation that it was done for spite); Chapman v. Honig, (1963) W.L.R. 19 (C.A.) (U.K.) (vindictive eviction of tenant who testified against landlord); Allen v. Flood, (1898) A.C. 1 (H.L.); Holke v. Herman, 87 Mo. App. 125, 141 (1900) (collecting cases); and Letts v. Kessler, 54 Ohio St. 73 (1896) and Metzger v. Hochrein, 107 Wis. 267 (1900).

is necessarily limited. The plaintiff can claim that he should not have been denied access to the defendant's property, or that the defendant should not be emitting dangerous smoke from her factory, but the plaintiff may not claim that the defendant's decision to kill endangered species or fill in valuable wetlands was a wrong as to him.

Public law regulation further controls an owner's decisions about her property by specifying a broader range of interests that the owner must take into account – interests of the community that are not, by themselves, the source of an individual wrong. Like private law, legislative restrictions on land use operate by specifying the factors that decision makers may and must take into account when deciding how to use their property.[19]

3.4 CONCLUSION

This chapter has argued that the essence of ownership is the right to make decisions about resources. Once we focus on the owner as decision maker, we have identified both what is essential about property (whether property is held privately or non-privately) and also why property rights take different forms in different contexts (and therefore appear to be a bundle of sticks). The concept of owner-as-decision-maker also focuses on the individual owner as mediating between her interests and the interests of others, and allows the law to focus on the variable – the decision about a resource – that is most important in determining whether individual and social interests are aligned. Often, a society creates private property because it wants an individual to have the discretion to make decisions that are autonomous and personal; generally, social welfare is advanced by diffuse decisions coordinated by the market. But sometimes individual and social interests diverge unless the decision maker is required to take into account interests that would otherwise be ignored. The law functions to determine when and how other interests must be taken into account and, by doing so, seeks to align individual decisions with social interests.

---

[19] I elaborate on this distinction between private and public law in Chapter 13.

4 Ownership and Social Recognition

4.1 INTRODUCTION

In the last chapter, I argued that the essence of ownership is the right to make decisions about a resource, albeit decisions that are constrained by social obligations. In this chapter, I identify the source of the constraint on the decision an owner makes, advancing the concept of social recognition to position our understanding of the relationship between an individual and a community of individuals (whether acting as a social unit or as a political unit through the state).[1] Under this concept, property rights come from, and are limited by, the community (although not necessarily by the state). Rights conform to norms of recognition that the community has worked out over time. Rights are conditioned on constraints embedded in those norms that are designed to promote the interests of individuals vis-à-vis other individuals and vis-à-vis the community as a collective entity. Through norms and through law, the interaction of individuals shapes property rights and responsibilities in ways that reflect values important to the interacting individuals.[2] I explain the social recognition

---

[1] The concept of social recognition finds expression in communitarian theories of property. See, e.g., Radin (1993) at 168 ("...the very recognition of the existence of property rights is intertwined with our perceptions of their justice. There is no sharp demarcation between empirical and normative questions, and cultural commitments are reflected in the way we view either kind of question."). It is also prominent in moral theories (see Merrill and Smith (2007) (property rights must be accepted to be stable, and acceptance depends on the perception of their morality) and Waldron (1988) (moral theory tells us when claims must be accepted)). The theory is broadly reflective of Hume's theory that communities create their own justice norms by developing norms of mutual forbearance that acknowledge each other's claims to property, and in Adam Smith's notion that communities develop moral sentiments about the well-being of others that respond to the views of an impartial spectator (Smith 1759).

[2] Blackstone himself called for this inquiry. Although he posited an absolutist view of the right to exclude ("sole and despotic dominion") as one that "strikes the imagination and engages the affections," he called for a more studied view of "the original and foundation of this right," concluding that:

concept in this chapter. In the next two chapters, I complete the framework that allows us to see how the law assigns rights and responsibilities to owners and nonowners; I do so by identifying a way of thinking about the content of constraints under which decisions about resources are to be made.[3]

The social recognition concept addresses one of the most difficult questions in jurisprudence: Where do rights, and particularly property rights, come from? This chapter seeks to turn upside down the conventional view of property. Its basic claim is this: rights do not come from possession or labor or any other attribute of ownership. Rights come because, and to the extent that, the community, or a large proportion of the community, recognizes the justness of the claims of possession, labor, or other attributes of ownership. When it comes to property rights, the supply side is as important as the demand side.

This chapter addresses what Jim Krier[4] and others[5] have pointed out as the cooperation conundrum that plagues theories of the evolution of property. To be used effectively, commonly owned resources require coordination among individual users.[6] Private property addresses that coordination problem,[7] but the evolution of private property begs the issue of how a community that cannot coordinate the management of common property is able to coordinate successfully to develop a system of private property.[8] The conundrum is made greater as we think about evolution not in the context of abundance but in the context of scarcity, for scarcity increases both the need for, and the costs of, coordination. The cooperation conundrum too is addressed, I believe, if we focus not on the claims of dominion that people make but on the question of why those claims are accepted by others.

Evolutionary theories offer two general explanations for the development of private property: the intervention of the state to effectuate coordination (what Jim Krier likens to intelligent design theories) and the spontaneous emergence of coordinated solutions from individual decisions (what Krier likens to invisible hand theories). Under the latter theories, rights arise naturally as

...[W]hen law is to be considered not only as a matter of practice, but also as a rational science, it cannot be improper or useless to examine more deeply the rudiments and grounds of these positive constitutions of society. (Blackstone, Book 2, at 2)

[3] The theory purports to present a unifying framework to explain the emergence of a property regime in any social and cultural community. Nonetheless, in working out the application of the unifying framework I refer primarily to the experience of England and the United States.
[4] Krier (1992); Dukemenier and Krier (1988).
[5] Posner (1979) at 289, Rose (1990) at 50–51, and Michelman (1982) at 30.
[6] Hardin (1968); Demsetz (1967).
[7] Demsetz (1967).
[8] It also begs the issue of how a system of private property coordinates decisions of separate owners when resource ownership is so dispersed and fragmented that effective coordination through the market or through private agreements is impossible – the problem of the anticommons. *See* Heller (1998).

Introduction 75

interacting individuals seek to promote their self-interest.[9] For reasons that I will explain, these theories seem to rest on inadequate assumptions about the basis on which rights are recognized. Other theories are statist, and see property rights arising from a social and political compact, so that rights arise from, and are regulated by, the state. Such theories, however, present an inadequate specification of the relationship between the state and the individual and fail to account for the way that individuals react to claims to resources by other individuals or by the state itself. The social recognition theory integrates elements of each of these theories but supplies what those theories lack. As a theory of rights, it is a natural law theory, but one that focuses on how rights arise naturally from the way that individuals react to claims of right by others. The theory is Lockean, but not because it endorses Locke's labor theory. The theory is Lockean because it views Locke to present a theory of social recognition, and it views the labor theory to itself be socially recognized – an output of social recognition rather than an input into the natural law. As an evolutionary theory, the theory here encompasses insights from economics and game theory about how individuals learn to make better decisions, but it completes the economic theory of evolution by making explicit that claims to property are accepted on the basis of shared value formation.

[9] *See generally* Vermeule (2010). Early evolutionary theories posited the development of respect for property rights because those not possessing property would fail to challenge claims of ownership. J. M. Smith (1982). For example, Robert Sugden assumed that individuals in possession of property will fight to keep it, whereas individuals not in possession will defer to those in possession (*see* Sugden 2004). Like the possession models, the model I present assumes that rights come from claims that are either accepted or rejected; unlike a possession model, it does not depend on assumptions about human behavior in the face of claims based on possession, a point made recently by Carol Rose (2013). As the text argues, what is important in the evolution of property rights is not the fact of possession, but the fact that the claims of possession, including the breadth of possessory claims, are accepted by the community.

Herb Gintis suggests an evolutionary model built on behavioral traits to explain how individuals develop a normative disposition to respect property rights. The behavioral trait is the endowment effect, which suggests that individuals value a good they possess more highly than they value the same good when they do not possess it, which implies that individuals are more sensitive to losses than to gains (loss aversion). As a result, among individuals equally endowed with the ability to use force, possessors expend more energy defending their property than others are willing to expend to take it away, especially when other property is available for possession and the possessor is likely to be limited in her claims (because adding additional property would not yield additional benefits). Gintis (2009) at 201. The idea presented here is more general in two respects. It does not seek to identify any particular behavioral assumption that would lead individuals to develop a normative disposition to respect claims to rights made by others. It simply uses the decision not to contest an owner's claim as a proxy for shared beliefs that support the normative acceptance of a property claim, allowing the behavioral trait to be the dependent variable and the theory to be more generalizable. It also seeks to capture the idea that the acceptance of claims comes with, and is confined by, conditions that restrict the scope of the claim (and that therefore give rise to limitations on a claimant's rights).

Social recognition suggests that rights develop from the interaction of individuals and that rights take their strength from the values that communities develop to support the resolution of conflicts over disparate interests. It thus builds on Hume's notion that justice between interacting individuals depends on the values that individuals use to construct their sense of right action when they interact.[10] At the same time, because the social practices that people consider to be a just basis for interaction can themselves be justified by determining the values that individuals *ought* to take into account, the social practice can meet an independent standard of social morality. Social recognition suggests that property rights emerge from the interaction of individuals in a community in the face of conflicting claims, based on values that the community embraces as relevant to the resolution of conflicting claims, and that rights (and associated responsibilities) are then absorbed into the law as community values influence how lawmakers resolve disputes.

Under this view, rights are neither pre-political nor pre-community; rights evolve in response to social interaction, and they evolve from the way that individuals choose to interact with respect to claims over resources. Social recognition suggests that the appropriate evolutionary story of property must focus on the values that induce nonowners to accept claims of dominion over a resource.[11]

Norms of recognition are important for any cooperative interaction. In any social interaction, a variety of outcomes are efficient (wealth maximizing) in the sense that no person in the interaction can be made better off without making at least one person worse off (the Pareto criterion). Because there are multiple efficient equilibria, social interaction must determine which of the equilibria are acceptable to those who are interacting, and this requires those who are interacting to develop a norm to choose among the multiple equilibria. This norm is a norm of social recognition, and different norms explain why some equilibria are chosen over others. The equilibrium point that is chosen is the one that is recognized as fairly dividing the gains from social interaction. A simple diagram explains the idea. Say that A and B have the possibility of interacting in a way that benefits both. There is rarely a discrete wealth-maximizing point. Although all points of interaction that are

---

[10] Krier (2009); Binmore (2006).
[11] As I point out in Section 4.4.2, the famous Demsetz model of the development of private property from the commons assumes that claims of property rights are accepted by nonowners, but Demsetz did not model the basis on which nonowners give that acceptance; *see* Demsetz (1967). Paying attention to the supply side of property rights – that is, their acceptance – allows us to complete the evolutionary story begun by Demsetz. (Fitzpatrick 2006, and at 996) and (Komesar 2001).

Introduction

acceptable to both individuals increase their individual well-being (by definition), the division of the increased well-being is divided between them in different ways for different interactions; within the positive sum game there is a zero sum game in which one individual's gain is another individual's loss. In illustration I, A and B can interact to produce varying increases in well-being, producing a kind of social possibilities frontier that shows the Pareto efficient points the two can reach. Interaction that ends up at either point X or point Y is wealth maximizing in the sense that A and B are both better off from the interaction and neither's position can be further improved without making the other worse off, but the two points clearly have different implications for the well-being of each individual.

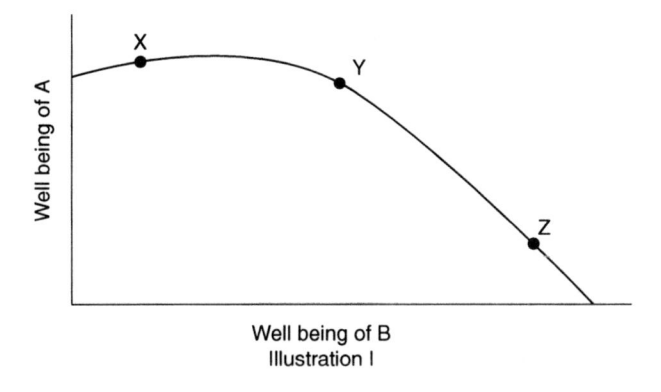

Well being of B
Illustration I

It is tempting to think that interaction will evolve toward point Y, which is wealth maximizing in both the Pareto sense and in terms of the total increase in well-being. But that assumes a social recognition norm that chooses that point over others and there is no a priori reason to think that individuals are always willing to share equally. Instead, the choice of the social recognition norm is one that arises from the interaction and represents the norm governing the division of gains of trade that the individuals bargain around. It is that social recognition norm that a property theory must identify.

As an evolutionary theory, social recognition depends on an important distinction, not always recognized, between theories of the origin of private property and theories of possession. A theory of the origin of private property specifies the way that private property, as opposed to some other form of property, arises from the state of nature (conceived of either as unowned or commonly owned property).[12] Resources can be held in various forms, and

---

[12] In this regard, the distinction frequently drawn, for example, by Richard Epstein (*see, e.g.*, Epstein 2009 at 4–6) between property that is unowned and property that is owned in common seems to be irrelevant; no story of the origin of private property depends on the distinction. It

a theory of the origin of private property must specify why the community recognizes individual claims to property rather than a collective form of ownership. This is a question prior to the issue of possession, which addresses the question of which individual has a just claim to private property. The claim "I possess and therefore I own" presupposes a community's recognition that the claimed resource can be privately owned; no claim to possession of waterways or air would give the claimant a right to exclude others. A theory of possession recognizes that if the resource is capable of being privately owned, we need a basis for awarding the property to one claimant rather than another (which we do based on some conception of possession), but possession does not itself justify nonowners' recognition that the resource should be subject to a private property claim.

Social recognition seeks to unify evolutionary theory across three important dichotomies: first, the dichotomy between invisible hand theories and cooperative interaction theories; second, the dichotomy between the universal and the contextual; and third, the dichotomy between statist theories and state-of-nature theories.

First, social recognition unifies our understanding of theories of cooperation, including, among others, cooperation through focal points, through behavioral traits, through repeated interactions, through kinship affiliations, or through individuals who make binding commitments.[13] Undoubtedly, many factors support cooperation: reasoned argument and disputation, information sharing, education, socialization, and religious traditions play important roles. Behind each of these theories, as well as behind game theory in general, is the notion that cooperation results when people share values and belief systems about the benefits and terms of cooperation – beliefs that not only coincide but that individuals understand to coincide (including the belief that cooperation can occur in the face of different value systems). Shared beliefs based on basic values are necessary because theories of cooperation depend on identifying what it is that allows one person to predict when another person will

---

is relevant only if a right of first possession is a theory of property. The view expressed here, to the contrary, is that possession is a theory of property only after a society has decided that a resource is subject to private ownership, in which event possession is a convenient and socially recognized way of awarding ownership rights to competing claimants. One in possession of flowing water does not own the water privately, and one whose property is above a common pool resource does not own the pool just because she is the first to extract a resource from it. Moreover, even when property may be owned privately, the concept of possession is hardly self-defining.

[13] See, e.g., Wiener (2011) (suggesting theories based on high benefits/low cost of cooperation, trust and reciprocity, issue linkage, and policy entrepreneurs).

Introduction

respond to a cooperative move with a reciprocal cooperative move.[14] Such shared beliefs, by decreasing the risks of making a cooperative move, increase the likelihood that an individual will make a cooperative move and that other individuals will respond with a cooperative move. If an individual does not have a basis for believing that others share the individual's beliefs about the value of cooperation and the values that lie behind the cooperation (including the value of accommodation), it is hard for individuals to make cooperative moves or to correctly interpret responses to cooperative moves.[15]

Shared beliefs reduce the distance between invisible hand theories and cooperative interaction theories. The former posit that individuals are led to cooperate simply by following their own self-regarding interest, letting their self-regarding interest determine when they cooperate and when to defect from cooperation.[16] Such theories suggest that as long as cooperation makes both parties better off, it will occur. However, the theories fail to account for the problem of opportunism as a barrier to cooperation. Cooperation requires that self-interest be advanced both ex ante and ex post; as a result, a viable theory of cooperation must contain a theory of how the cooperating individuals address the problem of opportunism. Theories of cooperative interaction, including the theory of social recognition, posit a mechanism to narrow the gap between ex ante and ex post results, and therefore help to explain the causal force that drives the invisible hand.[17]

Social recognition provides a theory of the evolution of institutions of cooperation that is both universal and contextual. The theory describes social interaction as a universal process that takes its values from the social context in which the process is carried out. It can therefore explain the evolution of

---

[14] An important distinction is between the *outputs of* cooperation and *inputs into* cooperation. Theories of cooperation must appreciate both when and why people cooperate and also when and why people fail to cooperate when cooperation would make them better off. Naturally, people cooperate to improve their mutual well-being. This is the output of cooperation, and it provides an incentive to cooperate. An example of such a theory is Ellickson (1991). However, positing that cooperation is welfare enhancing provides only half a theory because it does not put forth a theory to explain why welfare-enhancing cooperation is sometimes not achieved. Cooperation theory must therefore concentrate on the inputs into cooperation: that is, what it is that allows individuals to exercise their autonomy in favor of an outcome that also benefits another person. That is the focus of the theory developed here.

[15] The shared beliefs theory is therefore identifying the qualities that build trust, which ties it into the concept of social capital. *See generally* Fukuyama (1995). Trust plays a role in theories of property that emphasize social cohesion (*see* Dagan and Heller 2001 at 574 and Heller 2005 at 47).

[16] Individuals are, by hypothesis, self-interested, but self-interested behavior can be self-regarding or other-regarding. The distinction is explained in Section 5.1.

[17] *See* Section 4.2.

institutions of cooperation across societies. The theory does not assume a universal set of norms for enhancing or sharing well-being. Instead, it assumes a universal process that defines those norms, but it asserts that the norms that facilitate cooperation will differ from society to society depending on what kind of shared beliefs a society forms from the interaction of individuals, based on repeated social interaction. Those norms will differ over time as the social values that are embodied in shared beliefs change. Slavery involved shared beliefs among groups of individuals about the appropriateness of owning other persons, but those beliefs gave way (albeit slowly) to a set of beliefs that made such ownership impermissible.

Finally, social recognition bridges the distinction between statist theories of property and state-of-nature theories of property,[18] because social recognition explains the origin of private property whether it arises spontaneously from the interaction of individuals in a community without rights (the state of nature) or from authority of a governing power.[19] The theory therefore unites our understanding of the evolution of the feudal system in England, the evolution of state-owned property in the United States, and our understanding of the rise of private property among the American Indians. Just as a community may recognize or reject an individual's claim to property, the community may recognize that the claim is subject to institutional processes that the community has itself endorsed as an institutional means for mediating disputes between property owners and others. In other words, a community may cooperate by recognizing an institution that will make decisions that facilitate cooperation.[20] Under this conception, state institutions make decisions about

---

[18] Social recognition therefore avoids the polar position that all rights come from the state and the polar position that rights preexist the state. Under the conception here, the state functions to protect rights derived from the community, which functions as an independent source of rights. That is why rights can limit the state's authority to interfere with the rights, while enabling the state to regulate rights on behalf of the community as circumstances and community values dictate.

[19] It is not clear why Tom Merrill believes that "A theory that explains the evolution of property in a satisfactory fashion must be one that generates predictions that are unique to property and not one that would equally account for the development of other institutions, even if they perform overlapping functions" (Merrill 2002, at S334). Of course, state-of-nature theories are important in themselves (if that is what he means), but the co-evolution of property, representative government, and markets is too rich a story to ghettoize it.

[20] Individuals might, for example, agree to flip a coin to organize their cooperative endeavors; when they do, their shared belief in the benefits of that coordination method institutionalizes their cooperative decision making. Similarly, individuals might ask a friend to help coordinate their decisions, and the shared belief in that method of coordination creates an institutional basis for cooperation. In this way, institutions evolve from shared beliefs that institutions can make decisions that each individual will accept because of their shared commitment to the institutional method of coordinating decisions. The evolution of property systems need not be solely private or solely political. *See, e.g.*, Wyman (2005).

property relationships that are themselves recognized and accepted because individuals who recognize the pedigree of the state decision maker embrace a shared belief in the acceptability of the outcome of the decisions. Those institutions provide a social mechanism for shaping the rights and responsibilities that arise from social norms and socially developed expectations. Rather than viewing the state as being separate from the community or from individuals in the community, the social recognition concept understands the state as an institutionalized forum in which disputes about property resources are resolved. The social recognition concept does not separate the community, or individuals within the community, from their state. Institutions of governance (such as courts and legislatures) are themselves socially recognized, including institutions that are authorized to allocate rights and responsibilities over resources.

Because social recognition unifies our understanding of cooperative arrangements through private and state ordering, it encompasses property rights that are delegated from the sovereign to rights holders (the vertical aspects of social recognition) and rights that arise spontaneously from the state of nature (the horizontal aspects of social recognition). In its vertical forms, social recognition encompasses the concept of *delegation*, which is widely used in property theory when rights are distributed to individuals through a governance system. Feudal systems exerted social control through direct delegation from the sovereign to those who were given rights in land; the delegation determined the terms under which those rights and responsibilities were exercised.[21] Today, federal government decisions about the sale and use of the public land are clearly a basis for the community to recognize private property, just as the state exercise of its powers of eminent domain to take property reverses the process of social recognition. As to these vertical aspects of rights creation, social recognition suggests that recognition of the sovereign is recognition of the sovereign's right to decide who makes decisions about resources, as well as shared recognition that decisions made by the sovereign are worthy of respect because of their source. Recognition does not mean approval, of course, and it can be withdrawn, as the history of bloody (and not so bloody) struggles over forms of governance – and therefore over property rights created by the state – shows. But property rights created by the sovereign take their social recognition from the forces that recognize the legitimacy of the sovereign.

The social recognition concept also encompasses nonhierarchical ways by which rights are created. When private property evolves naturally from the state of nature, private rights exist because, and to the extent that, claims

[21] Simpson (1986).

to property are socially recognized. What turns property *claims* into property *rights* is the recognition by the community that the claims ought to be honored; it is that recognition that gives the claims moral force.[22] Although individuals and the community are continually negotiating the scope and content of such claims, the negotiation is always about which rights will be recognized and which will be contested.

The concept of social recognition rests on several ideas developed in this chapter. First, in Section 4.2, I argue that cooperation evolves from the development of shared systems of beliefs among individuals that allow them to predict, and rely on, how other individuals are likely to act in situations where cooperation is possible. In Section 4.3, I argue that the shared beliefs that enhance cooperation revolve around two distinct kinds of beliefs: shared beliefs about what makes individuals better off and shared beliefs about how the benefits of cooperation ought to be shared. I then discuss the forces that influence the content of shared beliefs about cooperation. I argue in Section 4.4 that the system of shared beliefs concerning claims to private property evolved because individuals formed shared beliefs as an alternative to threats of violence, making the formation of shared beliefs a way of moving toward a system of nonviolent resolution of conflicting claims to resources.[23] Under this conception, rejection and recognition of the claims made by the others are substitutes for each other, signifying either conflict or cooperation. Understanding how rejection or recognition, followed by conflict or cooperation, has created an iterative process for developing norms of acceptance allows us to understand why some claims to property are recognized today by most people without coercion. I claim that this evolutionary theory explains both property rights that arise from a state of nature and property rights that are created by a sovereign and change as conceptions of sovereign governance change. In Section 4.5, I then show how markets co-evolved with the institution of private property by showing that social norms supporting exchange have been subject to the same process of rejection or recognition followed by conflict or cooperation that led to the evolution of property. Property and markets coevolved because they both require norms of recognition governing the distribution of the burdens and benefits of human endeavor.

---

[22] James Penner has made this point by noting that in mature property systems, the only information an individual needs in order to respect another's property rights is the knowledge that the individual is not the owner. Penner (1997) at 75–76.

[23] *See, e.g.*, Schlatter (1973) (understanding property rights to be a social response of norm creation in order to avoid conflict over claims to property).

4.2 BELIEF SYSTEMS AND INSTITUTIONAL EVOLUTION

Because private property as an institution for coordinating decisions about resources has coevolved with institutions of state and the development of markets, it is worthwhile to understand property in terms of a general theory of institutional evolution. In this section, I present a framework for thinking about how institutions evolve from the interaction of individuals – a theory of evolutionary cooperation that depicts the development of institutions as resulting from the formation of individual belief systems, the development of shared belief systems among individuals, and finally the establishment of institutions that reflect and reinforce those belief systems.[24] Crucial to this framework is our ability to understand the kinds of values that individuals must hold if cooperative interaction is to lead to institutions. I intend this framework to be general enough to accommodate both social and temporal factors that influence the interaction between individuals in the face of conflict and cooperation. If the framework is successful, it ought to be commodious enough to identify the social and cultural factors that influence the development of institutions in different ways in various places. It ought also to be commodious enough to provide a basis for understanding, within any community, why norms and institutions change. Finally, it ought to account for the way that individuals form belief systems, the way those individual belief systems lead to conflict or cooperation, and the way that cooperative belief systems lead to the development of norms of cooperation and institutions that reflect the values underlying the cooperation.

An institution is an arrangement devised by humans that constrains and organizes human behavior,[25] a formalized way of expressing collective values that influence the way individuals make decisions. Institutions do not require an organization, although all organizations are institutions (because they are a forum for collective decisions). Money is an institution, as is language.

---

[24] The emphasis on shared belief systems is similar to that of Michael Taylor; see Taylor (1982) at 104–129, although the theory here, because it is one about institutions but not necessarily about community, does not depend on the kind of homogeneity that drives his theory. Nonhuman animals also exhibit territorial cooperative behavior, but obviously without the kind of belief systems that humans are capable of forming. See, e.g., Gintis (2009) at 205 and Mesterton-Gibbons, and Adams (2003). The fact that animals can cooperate without synchronized belief systems should not be taken to imply that humans can form respect for property rights without shared beliefs. Once humans developed even rudimentary grounds of reasoning, they were able to also develop the more complex systems that depend less on power, are able to survive even when resources become scarce, and are more sophisticated than a merely "mine-not-yours" system. See Krier (2009) at 156.

[25] North (1990) at 3.

Under this definition, property is an institution because it influences how people make decisions (by distinguishing between what is mine and what is not mine). Markets are institutions because they give individuals information (through prices), that people use to organize and implement their decisions. Mechanisms of governance are institutions, whether they are institutions of private or public governance.

The evolutionary story starts in a state of nature, with individuals capable of learning but with neither norms nor institutions to influence individual decisions. Individuals form belief systems that guide how they make decisions, belief systems about both physical phenomena and how other people will behave. They make decisions in light of those belief systems. The source of individual belief systems is underspecified in most evolutionary models, probably because we cannot directly test beliefs and so must rely on evidence of what people do to provide information about their beliefs. But we can acknowledge that belief systems reflect values that people develop; belief formation is, at bottom, a system of value formation. A person will believe that a sunset is beautiful because such a belief expresses something that the person finds to be valuable and that becomes a part of the person's identity. The value of the color of another's skin or other features also forms a similar kind of value-laden belief system. Individuals form belief systems about what they have to gain from cooperation and conflict and about the circumstances under which they are likely to see those gains.

When people interact, the nature and terms of their interaction depends on what each individual believes about the belief system of the other; an individual's decisions when interacting with other individuals, in other words, is based on beliefs about what other individuals believe.[26] Cooperation will not occur unless each individual who might cooperate believes that the belief system of the others overlaps with, or is compatible with, her own belief system.[27] Belief systems need not be the same for people to cooperate, but each belief system must be able to accommodate the belief systems of others. Individual belief systems can lead to either cooperation (if the individual believes that others will have a pro-cooperative belief system) or conflict (if an individual believes that others will have a noncooperative belief system). For each individual in

---

[26] Hume spoke of conventions that arise from "A general sense of common interest; which sense all the members of the society express to one another, and which induces them to regulate their conduct by certain rules," Hume (2000), Bk. 3, pt. 2, & 2 at 490. See also Sudgen (1998).

[27] Conventions develop from "mutual best response outcomes that are sustained by the fact that virtually all players believe that virtually all other players will best respond," (Bowles 2004, at 43).

Belief Systems and Institutional Evolution

each interaction there are two pairs of choices – each individual can either cooperate or not cooperate. Cooperation will result only if each chooses to be cooperative, and will be replicated only if the cooperation is deemed by each individual to have enhanced his or her well-being.[28]

Even if cooperation is not a likely outcome, evolutionary factors may move individuals to cooperate, at least in some settings. First, norms of cooperation can develop quite haphazardly from repeated experimentation and interaction, without either individual or shared purposiveness. If one individual makes a cooperative gesture, even unknowingly, the gesture is either reciprocated or not, which indicates either that the other party does not share the same cooperative beliefs or that the person initiating the interaction ought to adjust her belief system that led to the gesture. Although cooperation may not be a natural strategy, it can emerge if cooperative gestures are accepted and if the resulting cooperation reinforces the belief system of each individual in a way that facilitates cooperation. Second, belief systems formed to accept the possibility of cooperation are, in at least some circumstances, evolutionarily superior to belief systems that see everyone as an enemy. Survival depends on cooperation, and cooperation generally makes both parties better off, so it is not difficult to infer that those who survive move toward a belief in cooperative solutions, at least in instances where cooperation has worked in the past. Some evolutionists suggest that certain cooperative attitudes can become hardwired into genetic material because individuals with that material are genetically superior to people lacking that genetic makeup. The evolutionary path is rugged. Undoubtedly, throughout history many individuals believed that others would cooperate when they would not, and those individuals lived to regret it (if they lived at all). But the general advantage of cooperation and at least some evidence that humankind is making progress toward forming authentic communities out of the state of nature suggest that cooperative beliefs – that is, beliefs that others would cooperate – began to emerge. Over time, such belief systems became shared beliefs.

Shared belief systems reflect shared values and expectations. As the belief systems of individuals converge, cooperation is possible and the converging belief systems form norms – shared belief systems that guide behavior and reinforce beliefs (subject always to defection when the values that inform the beliefs change). It is but a small step from norms to institutions, for institutions

---

[28] It is important to note that cooperation can be in the direction of private property rights or of common property rights. Shared beliefs, for example, about the importance of access to the ocean may induce the community to resist claims to private property over navigable waters. On the evolution of common property as an alternative to private property, see generally Fitzpatrick (2006) and Field (1989).

too form around converging belief systems among individuals. Institutions and individual belief systems coevolve; institutions influence belief systems, and as the values that influence belief systems change, evolving shared beliefs influence institutions.[29] Because institutions and human behavior coevolve, individuals are able to understand their own interests in terms of the values that emanate from institutions, and those shared values become incorporated into the individuals' belief systems. Institutions provide a focal point to induce people to define their belief systems in ways that intersect with the belief systems of others.

The shared beliefs hypothesis is controversial. Many theories of cooperation seek to demonstrate that cooperation can result even if individuals think only about what the cooperation can yield them. The perfect market is an example. The elegance of Adam Smith's "invisible hand" is that, based on the assumptions of perfect competition, individuals can achieve productive cooperation even if each individual considers only her own self-regarding interest. No system of shared beliefs is necessary. Private arrangements based only on an individual's determination of her own interest (will I buy or sell at the market price) will yield a socially appropriate result. Many theories of cooperation purport to be able to model cooperation based only on self-regarding behavior rather than on a system of shared beliefs.[30]

I have already alluded to the reasons that invisible hand theories are incomplete. The model of perfect competition allows neither opportunism nor multiple equilibria. The assumptions of perfect information and instantaneous adjustment make opportunism impossible. Because the model of perfect competition already specifies the division of the gains of trade between producer and consumer (the gains above the reasonable cost of capital go to the consumer), the model has a single Pareto-efficient solution. Because the division of the surplus between producer and consumer is specified in the model, market participants have a single choice that does not depend on the choices of other participants.[31] When the possibility of opportunism and the existence of multiple equilibria are introduced into an invisible hand theory, cooperation

[29] James Krier helpfully points out the distinction between cooperative collective action (which I interpret to be institutionalized collective action) and natural convergence toward conventions of behavior (Krier 2009). I portray the distinction as showing different stages of evolution.
[30] Harsanyi and Selten (1988). The tradition goes back to the Scottish Enlightenment (Mandeville, 1705), continued in classical economics (Edgeworth, 1925), and continues in evolutionary biology (Dawkins, 1976 and Alexander, R. D. 1987). The hypothesis that markets can be organized on the basis of self-interested decisions has been confirmed through behavioral experiments by Vernon Smith. See (Smith (1982) and Smith and Williams (1992).
[31] In Section 4.5, I describe how that norm developed and became incorporated in the competitive model.

requires a mechanism for addressing opportunism and for selecting among multiple equilibria. Shared beliefs address the fear of opportunism and allow individuals to choose an equilibrium point.

If the shared belief hypothesis is true, it is relevant to ask the following question: Which shared beliefs are important inputs into cooperation? When cooperation depends on a unique outcome – when there is only one equilibrium outcome – cooperation is possible if both individuals share a belief that each will gain from the transaction that yields that outcome.[32] In that case, as in the case of the "invisible hand," cooperation does not require that one person care about the well-being of the other person in the transaction except to the extent that well-being is necessary to make the exchange occur. However, it is unlikely that many instances of social interaction are limited to one equilibrium point. In cases of multiple equilibria, there are two kinds of shared beliefs that must develop as a prerequisite to cooperation: shared beliefs about what makes each person better off and shared beliefs about the appropriate relative gain to each party from the cooperation.[33] Moreover, because markets, property, and private arrangements develop around multiple equilibria, both kinds of shared beliefs seem to be inherent in theories of cooperation as institutions coevolve. As I will explain now, the theory of cooperation developed here suggests that cooperation depends on norms of well-being maximization (making both parties better off or one party better off and the other party no worse off) and fairness (an acceptable division of the gains of cooperation).[34]

It is important to note that under the conception developed here norms of welfare maximization and norms of fairness are not defined outside of social

---

[32] It is not usual to refer to shared belief systems about whether each person gains from cooperation. Most theories assume that each person will independently determine whether he or she gains from cooperation. But shared beliefs about the gains from cooperation reduce search and transactions costs and allow negotiating parties easily to identify and exploit gains from trade.

[33] It is relevant that in the theory developed here it is not required that shared beliefs be about the benefit of cooperation to the community. Shared beliefs about the appropriate relative gains to the individuals are sufficient to bring about cooperation through private arrangements. In this respect, the theory here is congruent with state-of-nature theories: individual, private cooperative arrangements are all that are necessary to improve the well-being of the community when the community is considered to reflect the aggregate well-being of the individuals in the community. This does not, of course, take into account any need to provide for distributive justice, as I defined that term in Chapter 1, which explains why theories of distributive justice require an explicitly political aggregation method and cannot, under the belief systems that are now prominent, be achieved through private ordering.

[34] It is worth repeating that norms of efficiency and fairness are not identical across cultures or time. The norms that facilitate cooperation will differ from society to society depending on what kind of shared beliefs a society forms from the interaction of its individuals, and they will differ over time as the social values that are embodied in shared beliefs change.

interaction and imposed on interacting individuals. Instead they are formed through the social interaction and reflect the belief systems that the interaction forms. That is why norms can be context and society specific.

4.3 WHAT BELIEF SYSTEMS MATTER?

Here I support my claim that cooperative norms involve norms that enhance individual well-being and norms for acceptably sharing increases in well-being. Cooperative moves that enhance the well-being of each party but are not perceived by individuals to be made on acceptable relative terms will be rejected. Cooperative moves that acceptably enhance the well-being of two individuals but do not create new well-being (such as purely altruistic moves that shift well-being from one person to another) do not lead to (or need) cooperation; cooperative moves must be more than zero sum games. If this is correct, then if institutions are to evolve outside of environments of coerced cooperation they must reflect a mixture of norms that individuals perceive to be increasing their well-being and that also comport with an acceptable sharing of increases in well-being among people.

At first glance, the assertion that cooperation depends on a norm for sharing well-being seems quixotic. It implies that someone who stands to gain from cooperation would refuse to cooperate just because his share of the gains is disproportionately low. But the claim is not that individuals generally refuse to cooperate when the gains from cooperation are disproportionate. The claim is that cooperation depends on an acceptable sharing norm and that *sometimes* disproportionate gains make cooperation impossible. This assertion is supported by theory and empirics. The theory of bilateral monopoly suggests that many transactions do not occur because the surplus is large and each party knows that the other party has few options. One would expect that in cases of large surpluses bargaining would be easy, but just the opposite is true. Because more is at stake, the gains from trade are more difficult to divide.

As for empirics, evidence from game theory and behavioral economics supports the idea that cooperation turns on both a welfare-increasing norm and a welfare-sharing norm. The ultimatum game, for example, shows that even in one-shot games where the participants are anonymous, the participants are willing to reject monetary rewards that they consider to constitute an unacceptable division of the rewards of cooperation.[35]

---

[35] Guth and Tietz (1990) and Guth, Schmittberger, and Schwarze (1982). Under conditions of anonymity, two players are shown a sum of money (say $20.00) and Player One is asked to offer an amount of money to Player Two. Player One can make only one offer and Player Two can either accept or reject the offer. Because Player Two is better off with anything, one would

What Belief Systems Matter?

Let me model my claim that cooperation depends on two norms by presenting the fable of exchange.

Many years ago, two cavemen meet on a path. One had spent the day stoning rabbits and had four rabbits on a line. The other had spent the day trapping birds and had five birds on a line. There was no scarcity of rabbits or fowl in the area, and the technology of catching rabbits and birds was known to each one, so either of them with only a little time and effort could have independently hunted for the game the other had.

Perhaps each had the game he preferred, but it is plausible to think that (ex post) they each might find the game the other had to be attractive (perhaps fueled by a sense of envy). They each could forcibly take the other person's game, but in this story they are of equal strength and weight and neither one had an advantage in weaponry. Although cavemen, they were rational decision makers, and they figured out that under these circumstances force was a less attractive way of getting the game they wanted than to hunt for it independently. For this reason, neither challenged the right of the other to possess the game he did; they recognized the property claims of the other and each was therefore secure in his property right.

It might not have occurred to them at first, but over time they might have thought about the possibility of exchanging the game they had for the game they wanted. Under what circumstances would an exchange take place once they had stumbled on to the possibility of exchange? Thinking about this, each might intuit that if the cost of bargaining was greater than the cost of hunting for the game he wanted, he would avoid any bargaining. (Perhaps one of the cavemen was named Coase.) So it might not occur to them to even think about the possibility of exchange if the prospect of haggling was more expensive than the alternative way of satisfying their desires.

On the other hand, they might enter a bargaining process if they had reason to believe that the bargaining would be less expensive than independently hunting for the game they wanted. Perhaps it was dusk and the cost of hunting was going up because of the anticipated darkness. Taking into account the strength of their desire for the type of game each did not have, how would each person think about the cost of bargaining? First, each would think about the rates of exchange that would likely be the basis of the bargaining – that is, on the range of rates of exchange between rabbits and birds that each would consider

think that Player Two would accept any offer. However, in a wide variety of settings, Player Ones offer very substantial amounts and Player Twos generally reject very low offers. The results are not what one would expect if each player was motivated solely by what is best for him or her individually. Gintis (2009) at 57–58. On the similar phenomenon in the contract law, *see* Fehr, Hart, and Zehnder (2011).

to be acceptable. Each would assess the potential rates of exchange to identify those that would make him individually better off, looking at the net gains from what he got and what he would give up for each rate of exchange. Each would determine, for example, whether an exchange of two rabbits for each bird would make each better off individually, given their preferences for rabbits and birds and alternative ways of obtaining rabbits and birds. That would eliminate some potential rates of exchange – those that would leave one of them no better off. Each would then evaluate the rates of exchange that the other caveman might consider; that is, each would try to predict the rates of exchange that the other caveman would think made him better off. They would look for a shared belief about the rates of exchange that would be mutually beneficial. Unless each caveman had a basis for predicting overlapping, mutually beneficial rates of exchange there would be no incentive to bargain because each would know of the high cost of bargaining under those circumstances.

Therefore, the possibility of bargaining under the circumstances of the fable would depend on a particular set of shared beliefs: the ability of each to successfully predict the rates of exchange that would satisfy the other, comparing that to the rate of exchange that would satisfy the decision maker, and predicting that there might be matches in the rates of exchange each would accept. This prediction would be facilitated if they had some reason to believe that their rates of substitution for rabbits and fowl responded to similar factors. Without that prediction, it would be hard to see why they would invest in the bargaining process. Put another way, bargaining would be facilitated by any source of information that would allow them independently to predict that the range of acceptable rates of exchange between rabbit and fowl would overlap. As sources of information became regularized, they might even be able to predict what rates of exchange would be normal in that situation and, if they both made the same prediction, a norm governing possible rates of exchange might easily develop to facilitate the exchange.

Assuming they each could predict the mutually acceptable rate of exchange (one that would make each better off), and that they each predicted that there would be sufficient overlap to justify bargaining, they would then have to consider another factor: the cost of bargaining over which rate of exchange to pick. They would face a circumstance of multiple equilibria and would need a basis to choose among them. They would each ask themselves this question: From among the rates of exchange that are acceptable to both of them, how difficult will it be to decide which rate of exchange to choose?[36] Exchange, as

[36] Theoretically, there could be a single, unique rate of exchange that would satisfy their need to be made better off by the transaction. Although that removes the need to choose among multiple equilibria, it also increases transaction costs by requiring the parties to find the unique rate of exchange.

explained in Section 4.1, is generally a game with multiple equilibria, and a prerequisite to exchange is that the parties have a basis for choosing among equilibria.

Choosing from among multiple equilibria would depend on a shared (or normal) way of thinking about how the benefits of the bargain ought to be divided between them. Even if they could identify a range of rates of exchange that make them each better off, each rate of exchange would have different wealth-distributing effects, benefiting one person more than the other. If they bargain knowing that they share the same sense of how the gains from trade ought to be divided, then each could predict that it would not be too costly to agree on the rate of exchange they should choose and bargaining could proceed. But if there were no ground for developing an independent but common understanding governing the division of the gains from trade, they would predict that the bargaining would break down and, with that prediction, bargaining would never start.

The moral of the fable is this: successful trades maximize well-being, but before individuals enter the bargaining process, each individual must make predictions about two things: the relative ease of finding rates of exchange that make them both better off (the well-being–producing prediction) and the relative ease of choosing from among the possible rates of exchange (the well-being–sharing prediction). Unless individuals form shared beliefs about both aspects of exchange, exchange will not take place. This is intuitive: two or more individuals, and by extension a community of individuals, cannot make a bigger pie without, ex ante, having an acceptable basis for determining how the pie will be divided. In a community without norms for dividing the wealth from bargaining, either no one will engage in the cooperation necessary to make the pie bigger or the resources used to cooperatively make a bigger pie will be consumed in fighting over how to divide the pie after it is made.

Therefore, the possibility of cooperative bargaining to increase well-being will depend on whether the bargainers think that they share beliefs about two matters: the rates of exchange that will make them both better off and the rates of exchange that they would each consider to represent appropriate and acceptable divisions of the gains of trade. Turning this around, we have identified the two sources of impediments to bargaining over exchange that constitute transactions costs (in addition, of course, to the actual expenditure of time and effort to undertake the bargaining, part of which is spent discussing the shared beliefs about rates of exchange and the division of the gains of trade). If the law wants to function to maximize well-being, the law must work to support two types of shared beliefs (norms) that guide the conduct of the bargainers: norms governing the shared and cooperative *production* of well-being and norms governing the shared and cooperative *division* of well-being. A cooperative strategy depends on both.

Thus far, I have argued that social cooperation requires shared beliefs about the basis on which cooperation will take place. I have also argued that cooperation requires two kinds of shared beliefs: shared beliefs about how to make the pie bigger and about how to divide the additional pie. I now illustrate and apply this framework to explain the development of two institutions, property and markets, showing how norms to create well-being and norms to divide well-being are embedded in our understanding of these institutions.

4.4 THE EVOLUTION OF PROPERTY

Property institutions develop either spontaneously from the state of nature (horizontally) or through a governance structure, which occurs when an individual or group with authority over resources allocates rights and responsibilities to the resources (vertically). Both evolutionary paths can be explained using a simple model. I first present the model and then show how it influences our understanding of the evolution of property in both its horizontal and vertical applications.

4.4.1 *The Violence/Norm Development Trade-Off*

The evolutionary story is of a community of people deciding between cooperation and conflict.[37] Private property starts its evolutionary path when one person makes a claim of dominion over a resource.[38] Others in the community have two options: they may accept the claim or reject it, signaling either cooperation or conflict. Each option has implications.

If the claim is accepted, the right is secure (as long as acceptance continues) and the accepted claim functions as a property right by virtue of its acceptance; the acceptance of the claim gives people a reason for recognizing and respecting it. If we put the threat of violence aside, the claim would be accepted because it comports with some belief about the "rightness"' or "legitimacy" of the claim, given its nature, scope, and content in light of the norms that the community has developed to assess such claims. Acceptance will, in other words, reflect a shared belief system about claims to control a resource.

---

[37] The model here is suggested by North, Weingast, and Wallis (2009). *See also*, Hirschleifer (1982). Significantly, the framework demonstrates the rise of both property rights and the state from the state of nature.

[38] Carol Rose has observed that the function of possession in property theory is to communicate that a claim is being made. *See* Rose (1994) at 13–18.

The Evolution of Property

The terms of acceptance make up the conditions under which the claim may legitimately be exercised, and, because the acceptance comes from the community, it necessarily embodies a norm of cooperation that the community embraces. This system of claim and acceptance functions much like the rule of law, for when it occurs, both the rights holder and the community have a basis for making decisions about the scope of the claim and its existence, and both justify the community in enforcing the norm against nonconformers (even if the nonconformer may be working to change the dominant norm of acceptance).

This is a Lockean story.[39] One person picks an apple from a tree and claims it as hers. There is enough and as good for others. The others too want to make claims to an apple under similar circumstances. They accept the original claim and, because of its acceptance, the claim becomes a right.[40] This occurs because the claim was based on a happy confluence of beliefs that legitimize the claim (it is the product of her labor) and suggest that the claim is made on acceptable terms: each person may claim property as long as there is enough and as good for everyone else. Both the belief about what makes claims legitimate and about the terms of the claim constitute the social recognition of the claim, for acceptance of the claim is based on a belief that all who pick an apple from the tree ought to be wealthier by that act when the act deprives no one of what he or she needs for life.

The world is not Lockean, of course. The claim may not be to an apple; the person who picks an apple may, by virtue of that act, claim the entire apple orchard or all the apples in the world; the claim may not leave as good and as enough for others.[41] The claim may be too broad to be accepted under the prevailing belief systems. Or, even if there are plenty of apple orchards, the claimant and community may misunderstand the conditions on which the

---

[39] Standard interpretations of Locke focus on the labor theory of property. The theory here suggests that it is not adding labor to resources that gives rise to rights but the non-claimants' acceptance of the claim that adding labor to resources gives rise to rights. Locke's labor theory is successful to the extent that individuals accept the claim that certain kinds of value added give rise to rights.

[40] As Carol Rose has written, "the would-be 'possessor' has to send a message that others in the culture understand and that find persuasive as reasons for the claim asserted." Rose (1994) at 25.

[41] The example is not farfetched. Portugal claimed the exclusive right to sail to India via the route around Africa because Vasco Da Gama was the first to sail (and therefore "possess") that route. This led to one of the classic works on property rights (Grotius 1916). A frequent criticism of John Locke's theory of property is that Locke could not specify the scope of the claim that could be made when an individual added his labor to what was in nature. By positing that acceptance of the claim is based on a norm recognizing the existence and scope of the claim, the theory of social recognition addresses that criticism.

claim was accepted; they may be operating under different norms of acceptance. Perhaps the claim to an apple orchard was accepted on the implicit condition that people without means continue to be able to pick and eat apples from the orchard (a norm of acceptable sharing). That norm defines the contours of the property by defining the conditions under which the owner's claim is accepted. If the owner does not honor that condition, the community may reject the claim and seek to revise the terms under which the claim was accepted.[42]

If the community does not accept the claim, or its conditions, under prevailing norms of recognition, individuals in the community will reject it, in which case conflict is the only option until norms of recognition change.[43] If individuals in the community hold different norms of acceptability, they may pick sides, with some supporting and others resisting the claim. If the claimant (supported by her coalition) presses her unaccepted claim, the only option is violence, by which I mean the threat to impose harm, physical or otherwise, on others. Then the claimant and the community resort to self-help to settle the claim; whether the claim is eventually accepted or rejected depends on the relative ability of each side to inflict harm on the other side. If the violence comes from the claimant, the violence is associated with the decision to make, and thus to try to enforce, the claim, and the claimant is seeking to create a norm that moves in the direction of recognizing the claim. If the violence comes from the community, it is associated with the decision to reject the claim, and seeks to create a norm of recognition that would accept the claim only on narrower grounds.

In this way, violence and norms of recognition are substitutes.[44] The claim can be settled by violence or by the development of a norm of recognition – the development of a shared understanding of the terms under which the claim ought to be respected. Norms of recognition are a way of avoiding the harm from violence, whereas the lack of norms of recognition leads to the harm from violence.

Both violence and norms of recognition are relative and relational, of course. A norm of recognition expresses a relationship between claimant and

---

[42] Norm formation is contextual, of course, and may not lead to regimes of private property. Where the property is mobile, and exclusive appropriation is therefore difficult, norms may develop in favor of common property (see Heller 2006) at 45 (as to oysters); Demsetz (1967) (concerning Indians in the Southwest).

[43] As Hobbes pointed out long ago, two people who want the same thing that cannot be shared "endeavor to destroy or subdue one another." Hobbes (1968), ch. 13 at 184.

[44] Anderson (2002) (emphasizing that fighting over property rights was a negative-sum game, so that entrepreneurs devised local rules outside of formal government rules).

community, a relationship that recognizes both the basis for, and the limitations of, the claim. Norms of violence are relational because mutual threats of violence revolve around the relative ability of each side to impose harm on the other. The mix of recognition norms and violence norms that will shape the property relationship depend on the relative strength of the two options that the claimant and the community face, as they each implicitly trade off the possibility of accepting a recognition norm and the possibility of using violence. If the claimant has a relatively strong ability to impose harm through violence, the claimant will be able to support the claim by threatening the harm. Some norms will be accepted to avoid violence. As the ability to impose harm changes in response to the changing technology of violence and the ability of the community to organize, the claimant will want to substitute a recognition norm for the violence that has protected his claim. Violence becomes relatively more costly and less effective as the negotiation of recognition norms become less costly and (relatively) more effective. Recognition norms soon become voluntary and socialized rather than coerced and political.

An important factor influencing the rate of substitution between violence and norms of recognition is the ability of the property claimant to make concessions if the community accepts the claim. The claimant can adjust the terms of the claim to make sure that the community will be better off if it accepts the claim, thus making the community more inclined to do so.[45] The claimant can do that by reducing the size of the claim, by giving the community access to the resource on terms acceptable to the community, or by agreeing to absorb the cost of internalizing externalities that arise from the use of his property. The claimant, in looking for ways to enhance the acceptability of the claim (in order to reduce the cost of protecting the claim through violence) will seek to mold the claim in a way that demonstrates how acceptance of the claim will fit a norm of the acceptable division of the gains of cooperation. The norms affecting the terms of the claim and the acceptance of the claim develop together, and together they form a basis for the community to accept the property owner's claim. Once the norms of well-being enhancement and well-being distribution are worked out, the claim becomes a right that is worthy of respect (as long as the norms are stable). It is then not difficult for the community to enforce the norm against people who fail to comply with it.

States emerge naturally in this evolutionary story because, as many have pointed out, states lower the cost of enforcing prevailing community norms

---

[45] This feature of property evolution is highlighted in Banner (2002), which, however, assumes a political basis for making the distribution. The suggestion here is that negotiating the distribution of the surplus can also occur in pre-political communities.

and provide an opportunity for the orderly change of norms in response to changed circumstances and changing social values. Because norm development is a substitute for violence, it makes sense to institutionalize norm development through governance in order to limit self-help and violence as means of changing shared belief systems. The state monopolizes violence and marginalizes self-help by providing a mechanism for social recognition of claims over resources. The state functions as a forum for social recognition insofar as it depends on the acceptability of the governance mechanism to substitute for individual recognition of rights and responsibilities. Importantly, however, the state functions to assert and influence community norms of recognition as to both rights and responsibilities of individuals over resources. The state is not designed to protect private property as an end but to protect the rights of owners that reflect the terms of recognition on which private property is founded.[46]

This model allows us to organize our understanding of the evolution of property when it arises spontaneously from a state of nature and also when it arises from hierarchical governance.

4.4.2 Evolution from the Commons: The Demsetz Theory

Property rights often emerge from the state of nature, without a formal governance structure. The violence/norm development model explains how that occurs, but it does so in a way that is different from conventional understanding. Take, for example, the theory advanced by Harold Demsetz from his reading of how property rights developed among Labradorean Indians in the eighteenth century.[47] His theory is generally understood to show that private property emerges because of the efficiency of private over common property. Although his model is incomplete, the violence/norm-development idea completes his model in a way that Demsetz anticipated. The Demsetz model was built around the concept of welfare enhancement; the social recognition

---

[46] Although mature property systems within a state channel social recognition through legal institutions, the social recognition concept is very much at work. Custom and prior use are forms of social recognition that limit the claims of property owners, putting some decisions of private property into the commons. See, e.g., State ex rel. Thornton v. Hay, 254 or 584 (1969) (dry sand portions of beaches are open to public based on customary usage). Social recognition also justifies reducing access to otherwise common property. See, e.g., Tyler v. Wilkinson, 4 Mason 397, 401 (D.R.I. 1827) (giving owner of mill "use of so much of the water of the river, as has been accustomed to flow through [a canal] to and from their mills") and Ghen v. Rich, 8 F.150 (Dist. Mass. 1881) (endorsement of reasonable custom that has been "recognized and acquiesced in for many years").

[47] Demsetz (1967).

model around the concept of acceptability. Both are necessary elements of the model.

The Demsetz model suggests that as the relative values of resources change, the benefits of, and demand for, private property will increase in response to those changes. As the value of beaver pelts increased (as beaver hats became popular in Europe), the Labradorean Indians developed a system of private property out of once common property. Demsetz described the benefits of creating private property in terms of the internalization of externalities, making three broad types of arguments: (1) that private property supplies superior incentives for the development of resources relative to a system in which resources are open to others; (2) that private property eliminates or at least reduces the overuse associated with common access regimes; and (3) that by reducing the number of individuals who must agree on any effort to internalize externalities, private property makes it easier to agree on controlling spillovers between private owners, such as those from flooding or pollution.[48]

Understood in this way, the Demsetz model explains why people make claims to own private property (because the benefits of private property are greater than the costs) and why those claims may be accepted, on efficiency grounds, by the community (because, by internalizing externalities, private property preserves the resource, provides incentives to develop the resource, and lowers the cost of coordinating resource use with other owners). At the same time, the model is not, as thus described, complete. Two criticisms are prominent in the literature. The first is that Demsetz does not provide a causative story because he cannot explain how the transformation of a resource from common to private property occurs.[49] We must ask: What factors drive the cooperation that leads to private property if there is no state to force cooperation?[50] The emergence of cooperation over claims of property from a state of nature is the very story that the evolution theory is trying to explain. Moreover, the causative story is difficult to discern because Demsetz did not explain why the costs of exclusion would go down as the value of the resource goes up. One would think that as a resource gets more valuable the cost of excluding people from the resource would go up, because people would be less likely to accept the claimant's claim, and that should decrease the value of private property.[51] Finally, Demsetz did not explain why the owner would want to internalize the externalities of resource use; doing so adds to the cost

---

[48] Merrill (2002); Krier (2009); Banner (2002).
[49] Krier (2009).
[50] Rose (1994) at 39 ("cooperation, then, is a preference ordering that the classical property theorists weren't counting on in theory, but that they can't do without.").
[51] Field (1989).

of owning private property while benefiting only nonowners. Detail must be added to the Demsetz model to complete the evolutionary story.

Demsetz's theory actually alluded to those details, but he hid them in his assumptions. Demsetz assumed, without exploring its content or implications, a social recognition norm that made the claims of private property acceptable to the community. His vision of private property assumed that an "owner of property rights possesses the consent of fellowmen to allow him to act in particular ways."[52] This is, of course, true in a mature property system, but would be true in a system emerging from the state of nature only if the claim is acceptable to the community, and that occurs, as my model suggests, only if the claim comports with community norms that determine whether the claims are appropriate under the circumstances. Later he repeats the notion that "private ownership implies that the community recognizes the right of the owner to exclude others from exercising the owner's private rights,"[53] signaling his understanding that ownership and community recognition go together.

To complete the Demsetz theory, we must identify the community's shared beliefs that made the claims to property acceptable to the community. The negotiation of the recognition norm need not be formal; we can imagine that it follows the evolutionary path of offer and acceptance, trial and error, mutation and response. We also know that many claims failed to be acceptable to those excluded, so that violence was a necessary part of norm formulation. But slowly the claims were made and accepted, and the threat of violence was replaced by a norm of recognition. That completes the causative story that Demsetz omitted. Claims were accepted because each claim involved a defined and discrete area of a relatively small territory, with plenty of other areas left for others. Moreover, the claims were subject to a norm that individuals who needed to hunt beaver for food could do so as long as they left the pelts for the owner of the land. Acceptance provided the missing causal story. Because reciprocal claims were recognized, the cost of enforcing them did not go up as the value of the pelts went up. And owners assumed the burden of internalizing externalities because that was one of the implicit conditions put on the rights so that the community would recognize the rights.[54]

[52] Demsetz (1967) at 347.
[53] Id. at 354.
[54] The evolution of property rights is not unidirectional. As the cost of exclusion by an individual owner goes up and the transactions cost of governance of the commons goes down, common property may be more efficient than private property (Field 1989). Social recognition reduces the cost of exclusion for both private property and restricted-access common property and is therefore a priori neutral as to these two forms of property. One might conjecture, however, that there is a relationship between social recognition and the quality of the governance of the commons on the ground that outsiders give more deference to the rights of common owners when the commons is well-governed. Social recognition is, after all, grounded on a sense of

The Evolution of Property

Some careful studies of the evolution of property rights make the norms of recognition explicit, including both norms that increase well-being and norms for the division of increased well-being.[55] More important, even studies of property evolution that do not mention a recognition norm reveal evidence from which the recognition norm can be determined; a close reading of those studies makes the formation of recognition norms apparent.[56] The causal direction revealed by these studies is clear: private property is not honored because it is private property; it is private property because it is honored by the community.[57]

> propriety. And if a restricted access commons allows some entry, social recognition is likely to go up, increasing support for restricted access common property. In a sense, the finder's fee that whalers give to finders of beached whales is both an incentive to report the "find" and a way of building support for the custom of "capture" in the whaling industry. See Ghen v. Rich, 8 F. 159 (D. Mass 1881) (enforcing custom governing killed whales and reasonable salvage fee for the finder).

[55] See Ellickson (1989) and Schorr (2005).

[56] Most empirical studies of the rise of property rights from common property concentrate on the development of rights, rather than on the limitations on those rights. Accordingly, they often leave unanswered the question of the implicit recognition norms that induce individuals to respect the claims that have been made. A close reading of those studies, however, shows that the claims were in fact limited, and this implies that the claims were accepted by others because they fell within acceptable norms for such claims. This could not have occurred had a recognition norm not developed that allows the claim of right to be accepted. See, e.g., Libecap (1978) (once the Comstock lode was discovered, and property rights became more valuable, the Gold Hill District developed written rules regarding the establishment and maintenance of private holdings); Ellickson (1991) (reporting on division of responsibility between cattle owners and grassland owners, forming an implicit agreement that cattle need not be fenced in, that grassland owners would accept the damage to their property from trespassing cattle, but that cattle owners would pay for personal injury and damage to livestock); Acheson (1998) (reporting on norms governing lobster fishermen on Maine coast); Dow (1985) (reporting on informal norms for dividing whales when more than one individual contributed to its death and for dividing whales that were found); Anderson (2002) at 499 (in environment of abundance, "when a cattleman rode up some likely valley or across some well-grassed divide and found cattle thereon, he looked elsewhere for range"); later, cattlemen resorted to associations to develop rules protecting their property and excluding outsiders; Kettles (2004) (possession rights for street vendors last only a day, until a person has claimed the same spot by custom; frequent disputes over custom usage are worked out informally).

[57] In this respect, we might read Locke as a summary of the general class of recognition norms that seemed to be relevant in seventeenth-century England. The outline of recognition norms suggested by Locke's theory of property consists of the following:
  a. A claim that has required some effort by the claimant (labor condition).
  b. A claim no larger than the claimant can effectively exploit (the "no waste" condition).
  c. A claim that left enough so that no other potential claimant (based on a prediction of the number of claimants and the size of the resource pool) would be inconvenienced (the "as much and as good" condition).
  d. Conditions on the claim that would accommodate special needs and situations (the "special access" condition).
  e. Conditions on the claim that would require the owner to internalize unreasonable externalities.

4.4.3 The Co-Emergence of Sovereignty and Property

The violence/norm development model also explains the evolution of property rights that arise from sovereign decisions rather than spontaneously from the state of nature. The close connection between sovereignty and property rights will surprise no one. Because violence and norm development are substitutes, and because state sovereignty depends on either institutionalized coercion or social recognition, the recognition of the sovereign and recognition of social norms about resource allocation go hand-in-hand. States, whether democracies or autocracies, depend for their power on either violence or recognition, just as individual claims to private property do. Norms that accept sovereign power also accept sovereign decisions about resources. And violence that would destabilize the state stems from the community's unwillingness to accept existing norms of social ordering, including social ordering through both governance and rights in property. States and property regimes co-evolve because sovereignty and resource control respond to the same question: Who ought to decide about resource use and on what terms should the decision be made? Governance is social control because states use decisions about resources as the means of social control. A socialist state will endorse one kind of property regime and a democratic state a different type. In hierarchical systems, the form of property is hardwired into the form of the state, and the evolution of property reflects the forces that influence the form of state.

In other words, state institutions evolve for the same reason that property institutions evolve. Norms that justify the acceptance of state regimes change as communities modify the values that support those norms and as technology and coalitions of violence change.[58] In some tribal communities, tribal chiefs make decisions about resources, so that the property system used by the tribe reflects individual decisions to recognize the decision of the chief. Such systems look hierarchical, but only because deference to a tribal leader is supported by the community's system of beliefs that allows the community to accept the leader's decision. The norms and belief systems that support community acceptance of the leader's decisions are forged over the years by threats of violence; they change as values that support the norms change and as power relationships change.

Nontribal governance systems are often erected on violence. William the Conqueror subjugated the ruling tribes of England and set up the feudal property system as a form of explicit social control. Because the property regime is

---

[58] As Carol Rose has argued, property is the mainstay of propriety – that is, the socially recognized distribution of power within a society (Rose 1994) at 58–64 (describing various concepts of the proper social order throughout history).

The Evolution of Property

a system of governance, the mix of violence and norm development that supported the property system also supported the system of governance, and the property and governance systems co-evolved in response to the shifting ability of the lords to credibly threaten to change the status quo through violence and the desire of the king for more revenue from productive uses of land. Norm development both supports and erodes the system built on threats of violence. On the one hand, norm development legitimizes the exercise of authority, creating norms of recognition that support the sovereign's authority. On the other hand, evolving power relationships create the possibility of renegotiating the existing system of property rights (and governance structures) and norms change to reflect the new possibilities. The Magna Carta symbolized both a shift in relative power between the king and the lords and the creation of new norms to justify the shift in property rights and governance that responded to that power.

The evolutionary path is hard to predict and will take different turns in different communities, depending on the trade-off between violence and norm development.[59] The important point is that this kind of social recognition links property regimes and governance regimes because governance is reflected in decisions about resources. Mature property systems in the West reflect the historical flattening of both governance and property regimes as governance and ownership shift from crown to the people, and as the current rights of private ownership increase to reflect new understandings about the relationships between individuals and the state.

The violence/norm-development model also provides a foundation for understanding how state institutions respond to changes in norms of recognition. The acceptability of slavery – and therefore the acceptability of property in other individuals – reflected a norm of acceptance that highly influenced state recognition of that form of property. As social norms began to change and the norm of recognition of property-in-persons began to erode, the norms of recognition began to be absorbed into state policy and states began to change the formal legal recognition that justified slavery. In many countries, the law changed peacefully to reflect the norm of recognition; states changed policy to

---

[59] Naturally, government intervention to shape property regimes gives rise to suspicions of interest group politics that will change the evolutionary path and replace social recognition with interest group recognition (Levmore 2002 and Banner 2002). This is a change in the form but not the substance of social recognition. The violence that precedes changes in the form of government, say the overthrow of monarchs, is an expression of the lack of social recognition that reflects the interests of the members of the community. As part of the evolutionary story, democracy channels social recognition into interest group politics and allows the community, through elections, to keep interest group politics within manageable bounds as an alternative to violence.

reflect evolving social norms and to preserve the norms of recognition that supported their own legitimacy. Yet, in the United States, where the federal structure divided authority vertically, the appropriate norm of recognition about property in humans was decided by violence, and even then the development of a norm of recognition for full personhood is taking years to evolve.

4.5 THE EVOLUTION OF THE MARKET

It is no accident that private property and markets co-evolved, for neither exists productively without the other. It is accepted that well-defined property rights facilitate transactions and therefore make markets possible. Equally, dividing resources into private bundles and assigning dominion over them to individuals would be hopelessly unproductive if the bundles could not be traded to improve their value as relative beliefs about value change over time.[60] Because markets and private property are codependent, their coevolution was no accident. Both markets and private property evolved through the evolutionary mechanism already described, in response to related changes in social organization and values. In this section, I demonstrate that relationship by showing that markets, much like private property, evolved because of shared norms of recognition about the sorts of transactions that ought to be validated. And, contrary to contemporary understanding of markets, I maintain that, much like property, markets reflect two kinds of norms: shared beliefs about ways of increasing individual well-being and shared beliefs about the appropriate distribution of the well-being that has been created.

The market, when operating well, is a powerful force for wealth creation. It is also, I maintain, imbued with norms of recognition that govern the terms under which wealth is divided. The intuition is straightforward. Markets, by allocating resources to higher uses, increase material well-being. But markets also determine the division of rewards between sellers and buyers, and this distribution of well-being requires norms about how the gains from market transactions – the surplus – ought to be divided. Today, we take it for granted that the market functions to maximize consumer surplus by distributing to producers only the cost of production (including a competitive return to capital). But this is, I claim, a socially constructed notion of the appropriate division of wealth between consumers and producers. Historically, a community's understanding of how the market functions in allocating resources has depended on

---

[60] This is the central insight of the tragedy of the anticommons, which exists to the extent that the market does not allow fragmented property rights to be reassembled into bundles that allow more effective decision making. Heller (1998).

The Evolution of the Market

how the community has viewed the appropriate division of rewards between seller and buyer; even today, norms of recognition about that division influence how a community establishes its market institutions.

I hope to show that we ought to organize our understanding of market efficiency to recognize two kinds of norms: norms about allocative efficiency (wealth generation) and norms about how the gains of allocative efficiency ought to be divided between producers and consumers. In the view presented here, the "efficiency" justification for holding producers to a competitive return is in fact a normative judgment about what return is appropriate. It is a judgment about the division of rewards between consumer and producer, not a judgment about what an efficient output would be under a particular market's cost structure. We call the division of the surplus between producer and consumer an efficiency judgment only because that division is in the hands of economists, who wield the efficiency hammer. In fact, the division of returns between producer and consumer – where the norm of acceptable division of wealth is intertwined with the concept of allocative efficiency – is where society has waged battle over the fair distribution of the benefits of the market as a method of allocating decision making about resources. A community that finds a more appropriate division of returns will change the division.

To be clear, I am not challenging the competitive model or the efficiency justification for markets. My claim is that the concept of a socially recognized division of well-being generated by the market is wrapped into our definition of efficiency, but ought to be identified separately. We ought, in other words, to separate the value of allocative efficiency and the value of awarding the market surplus to consumers. Allocative efficiency occurs when deadweight loss is minimized, which happens when consumer surplus is maximized within a given cost structure. At that point, assuming no externalities, all consumers who are willing to compensate society for the cost of producing the goods are able to purchase them, and no person who is unwilling (or unable) to compensate society for the cost of the goods can acquire them. With allocative efficiency, society can get no more out of its resources because any expansion of output would result in greater costs than benefits. The pie is as large as possible.

But, as I argue here, the market can be set up in many ways to achieve this efficient outcome; there are multiple equilibria that satisfy the demands of allocative efficiency. The market can be allocatively efficient whether producers make a reasonable return or a higher return. A community therefore needs a method for choosing how the market surplus ought to be divided. It must define what costs count as a cost of production, and there are many ways of doing that. As an illustration, if we define cost to include a competitive return plus 10 percent, the conception of the allocatively efficient output would not change, but the division between consumers and producers would. As a matter of allocative efficiency, we would still want output to increase up to the point where marginal demand equals marginal supply, we would still want to eliminate deadweight loss (given our cost curves), and we would still want those consumers who are willing to compensate society for the cost of producing the product to be able to get the product. Yet the division of the resulting surplus would depend on whether the relevant cost of production includes the extra return of 10 percent. Either market would be allocatively efficient but the division of the gains from the market would respond to different ideas about the appropriate division of the surplus between consumers and producers.

Some economists will resist this conclusion because the extra 10 percent given to producers is thought to be unnecessary to induce productive investment and therefore to be waste; we would call this unproductive rent seeking. There is, however, no allocative reason to make that choice in one way rather than another; the judgment about which costs of production consumers ought to pay is unlike the one about the judgment over how the market, once it is set up, allocates resources. To be sure, output will be less with the higher cost structure, but that is not a matter of allocative efficiency. That is a matter of how society wants to divide between consumers and producers the wealth generated by the market.

Let me provide several illustrations to show the value of separating issues of allocative efficiency from the norms for the division of wealth. Labor laws (or any other law that increases the cost of production) cannot be evaluated on the basis of allocative efficiency. Labor laws express the notion that producers (and, through them, workers) should be given a greater share of the surplus generated by the market. One can argue against labor laws on the ground that consumers deserve that share of the surplus, but that is an argument about the division of rewards between producer and consumer, not an argument about allocative efficiency.

Consider also that for the perfectly discriminating monopolist there is no inefficiency, even when its costs are calculated to include no more than a reasonable return on its investment. Because the perfectly discriminating monopolist can charge each customer exactly what the customer is willing to pay, it will, like the seller under perfect competition, expand output until marginal cost equals marginal revenue. There will be no deadweight loss and no allocative inefficiency from underproduction. But there will also be no consumer surplus, for the entire benefits of the market will inure to the seller, not to buyers. Whether this is an appropriate division of the gains from trade is a question about the division of rewards from the market, not about efficiency.

The issue is whether it is socially acceptable for the perfectly discriminating monopolist to reduce the consumer surplus to zero.

As another example, consider the problem of appropriating the returns from innovation. Under conditions of perfect competition, producers are rewarded for their investment of capital but not for their investment in innovations that can easily be copied. That is because under conditions of perfect competition information about innovation is translated immediately to competitors, who can easily utilize the innovation. As a result, the incentive to innovate is lost. In these terms, the market depends on imperfect competition – that is, rewards to innovation that can be captured because the producer has, or is given by law, the lead time to capture the returns necessary to insure the investment. The issue then is: How much imperfect competition is appropriate?

The lead times that are necessary to induce investment are generally spoken of in terms of efficiency, not in terms of the division of wealth between producer and consumer. Under the efficiency view, imperfections or interventions in the market are necessary to induce investment, and it is expected that the benefits of the investment will offset the higher costs of inducing the investment. Yet the justification can also be expressed in terms of the return that the producer deserves, not in terms of what allocation of wealth is best, with resource allocation following the determination of a deserved return. Under the concept of social recognition, a higher-than-normal return in the short run is deserved because of the investment in innovation and, accordingly, resources can be moved from consumers to producers to reflect that sense of appropriate producer reward. This was not lost on common law judges. The law sometimes intervenes in markets to give producers the advantage of lead time, as it did in the hot news case; when it does, it calls the competitive tactics that would reduce lead time "unfair competition."[61]

Markets, as we understand them, developed over centuries from a constant contest between producers and consumers over the division of market surplus, with the pendulum swinging between greater percentages for producers and greater percentages for consumers. The conflict has been about the appropriateness of different divisions of profits, given perceptions about the role of producers and consumers. The medieval notion of a "just price," and the vacillation in our understanding of markets between increasing market barriers (thus increasing the return to producers) and reduced market barriers (reducing the returns to producers) are all part of the evolution of what it means to divide the gains from an efficient market.

---

[61] *See* Int'l News Serv. v. Associated Press, 248 U.S. 215 (1918).

A landmark decision in this struggle was the 1410 *Schoolmaster Case*, a pivotal one in the development of our modern conception of rights and property in competitive markets. Two schoolmasters of the only school in an English town sued a person who opened a second school, claiming that by diverting their future customers the second schoolmaster had taken their property. The claim was rejected, establishing the principle, now foundational, that no producer has a property right in his prospective profits, and that reducing producer surplus by fair competition is not a wrong against a competitor. In current terms, we would understand that competition allows pecuniary externalities and favors consumer surplus over producer surplus. That was not, however, the grounds on which the competitor prevailed. Although competition had reduced prices from 40 pence to 12 pence, the benefit to consumers was not mentioned in the opinion. Instead the opinion focused on whether it was appropriate for the second schoolmaster to take expected profits away from the original schoolmasters. The result depended primarily on a sense of the appropriate gains, and the appropriate sense of who "owned" those gains, in the competitive struggle. The harm inflicted through fair competition was not actionable.

It should not surprise us that norms governing the appropriate division of well-being are embedded in our understanding of markets, just as they are embedded in our understanding of the norms that support the concept of private property. Markets not only allocate property, they create claims to property by creating wealth, and they recognize and honor claims to that wealth. Markets therefore function around norms that, as in the property context, either accept or reject claims to the wealth that the market creates. Human decisions, reaction to relative prices, and norms governing the division of returns between consumers and producers influence whether the claims are rejected or accepted. Two final examples illustrate the point. It is thought that when the price of a product goes up, the amount demanded will go down as consumers find other supplies to be relatively more attractive. This can be explained, as economists do, by the simple notion that higher relative prices make a product less attractive, which induces self-interested consumers to substitute new, relatively more attractive products. But there is a different behavioral explanation for this phenomenon – one based on a norm of recognition. Consumers might move away from a product whose price has gone up out of a feeling that the price is no longer acceptable as an appropriate expression of the division of gains between consumers and producers. This happens frequently when gasoline prices rise, and this is a behavioral trait based on a vision of the appropriate relationship between price and the recognized appropriate return to producers.[62]

---

[62] *See also* Kahneman, 2011 at 306 (existing price is reference point so that deviations may be seen as unfair).

Conclusion

Finally, it is worth noting that norms of recognition are embedded in assumptions of the model of perfect competition – namely, the assumption that consumers are indifferent to all information about the product except price and perceived quality – which assumes a norm that people will be only self-regarding. But consumer behavior sometimes follows a different norm. Consumers sometimes want to benefit producers from their home state, or producers from poorer countries who are guaranteed a particular return. Sometimes consumers, acting out a negative norm, seek to direct their spending away from people of a certain racial or religious group. In other words, consumer behavior in the face of the possibility of transacting sometimes reflects a norm that reflects a consumer's understanding of the acceptable terms on which producers and consumers ought to share the benefits of exchange.

The norms of recognition that govern consumer behavior in the market capture a major theme of the theory developed in this book. Human decisions are built on a mix of self-regarding and other-regarding values. We sometimes choose a product with the lowest price, and sometimes a product that benefits a group we would like to benefit (even at a higher price). This mix of self-regarding and other-regarding attitudes is highly influenced by norm development, as well as by the law (which is itself based on norm development).[63] Institutions reflect the mix of self-regarding and other-regarding values that people develop in a community and therefore reflect the beliefs about efficiency and the appropriate division of returns that enable people to cooperate to design institutions. Institutions arise out of that cooperation, reflect the mix of self-regarding and other-regarding values, and then engage in the process of changing the mix of self-regarding and other-regarding values as the institution evolves toward a stable unity of the two values.

4.6 CONCLUSION

Property theory and other theories of evolutionary cooperation might consider the importance of the formation of shared beliefs and the recognition of the claims and interests of others that flow from those shared beliefs. Social recognition of those claims and interests through shared beliefs are what makes cooperation possible. They are what make institutions that foster cooperation possible. And they are what make automatic compliance with the law possible.

---

[63] Antidiscrimination laws require transactions to be based on factors other than race or other impermissible characteristics. They therefore force transactions to be based on self-regarding aspects of quality and prices, and not on negative other-regarding characteristics. Country-of-origin labeling laws support transactions in which consumers make market decisions because they think that the country of origin matters.

It is the social recognition that comes from shared beliefs that gives property rights theirs scope and moral force.

This chapter has argued that shared beliefs that make cooperation possible come in two types – shared beliefs about how to make each cooperating individual better off and shared beliefs about the relative benefits of cooperating. Except in the most abstract circumstances, the two conditions must be satisfied simultaneously for cooperation to take place.

5 Other-Regarding Decision Making

Thus far, I have developed two propositions: that ownership arises because the community recognizes an owner's right to make decisions about the resources entrusted to the owner, and that social recognition imposes implicit conditions on how an owner exercises that right.[1] An owner's decisions that are within the authorized scope of decision making constitute the rightful exercise of decision-making authority; decisions outside that authorized scope constitute the wrongful exercise of decision-making rights because they do not sufficiently respect the well-being of others. Nonowners must respect the owner's rightful decisions and may challenge the owner's wrongful decisions. This chapter and the next identify methodologies for determining the scope of decision making the community has authorized the owner to exercise and for determining whether a particular decision is inside or outside the authorized scope of decision making. Together, this chapter and the next develop a theory of appropriate decision making about resources that describes the method each individual ought to employ if the individual desires to make moral decisions.

In this chapter, I develop the concept of other-regarding decisions as the methodology the community expects an individual to use to determine how to behave. Here we must distinguish between an individual's general obligation to think about the well-being of others and a decision maker's specific responsibility to take another's well-being into account when determining how to behave. We can assume that each individual has the general obligation to consider whether her activities implicate the well-being of others. But often that obligation is fulfilled when an individual concludes that her decisions do not require her to consider the well-being of another. In those circumstances, the individual need not make specific other-regarding decisions because the

---

[1] An owner may be an owner of private property or an authorized user of common or shared property.

individual has fulfilled her general obligation by concluding that her decisions need not incorporate the well-being of others. The more specific obligation to make other-regarding decisions comes about only if an individual has a duty to take the other's well-being into account as she determines the means she will use to reach her goals.

Under this specific other-regarding obligation, each individual, when under a duty to another, must act as he would if he had appropriately incorporated the well-being of others into his decisions, using values that the community has developed to reflect the appropriate assignment of rights and responsibilities among free and equal individuals. Other-regarding decisions serve as the community's mediating device to facilitate cooperation and resolve potential conflicts. When all individuals in a community acts as they would if they had appropriately accounted for the well-being of others, the collective assignment of rights and responsibilities means that no different decision could make one individual better off without making other individuals worse off, and that the assignment of rights and responsibilities to individuals is acceptable to each individual because it reflects neutral values of appropriate social interaction. In this chapter, I explore the origin and scope of the duty to make other-regarding decisions. When the community entrusts a resource to an individual it is asking owners and nonowners to act as the ideal decision maker would.

In the next chapter, I focus on the content of ideal, other-regarding decisions. There I argue that ideal, other-regarding decisions must appropriately assign the burdens and benefits of decisions about resources, and I provide a way of thinking about whether a particular assignment of burdens and benefits can be considered to be neutral enough to be recognized as moral by the community. This chapter is about the methodology of moral decision making; it situates our understanding of the existence and general scope of the obligations we owe one another. The next chapter is about the content of moral decisions; it identifies the values that the ideal decision maker will use when she determines the scope of her obligations.[2]

The concept of other-regarding decision making is not new in legal theory.[3] The requirement to be reasonable, as interpreted in the Hand formula, is the

---

[2] The general approach described in these two chapters is relevant to all domains of private law and is therefore not necessarily grounded on values that animate the property system. I express the theory using the open-ended terms of appropriateness and reasonableness. The methodology for discerning the content of those terms, the veil of ignorance, is advanced in the next chapter. The values of the property system are further explored as the theory is applied in Part II of this book.

[3] Hanoch Dagan and Michael Heller have discussed this idea in the context of conflicts of interest between people who must jointly make decisions about property. Dagan and Heller (2005) at 39. I expand the concept they use into a general theory of how individuals ought to incorporate the well-being of others into their decisions.

requirement to invest in another's well-being when the benefits of doing so offset the costs. I raise the concept of other-regarding decisions to the centerpiece of a theory of property in order to pull together some central strands of legal theory. The law's command to act as if one had made a decision appropriately accounting for the well-being of others is fully consistent with the idea that people act from rational self-interest, for in a wide variety of settings it is rational to be other-regarding. That point is developed in Section 5.1. That section also argues that other-regarding decisions are what make cooperation possible, and develops the idea that the concept of other-regarding decision making can be understood to be a fundamental building block for theories of cooperation. Section 5.1 also distinguishes between other-regarding decisions and altruistic decisions, which preserves the important distinction between the kind of decisions that private law requires and decisions required by morality but not by law.

Section 5.2 addresses the question of when an individual has the duty to take into account the well-being of others and the scope of the other-regarding obligation when it applies. Even in the face of a general obligation to others, the ideal decision maker must decide *when* the well-being of others is relevant to the decision he is making. That is the issue of duty; it asks this question: Under what circumstances must an actor take into account the well-being of others? The other dimension of other-regarding decisions is *how* a decision maker makes decisions when the decision maker has the obligation to take into account the well-being of others. That is the issue of the scope of the duty (and the scope of the decision); it asks this question: What factors must an ideal decision maker take into account, and with what weight, when the decision maker is obligated to account for the well-being of others? The issue of when a decision maker must account for the well-being of others is important because an individual who has no duty to others need not take the other's well-being into account when making decisions; the uninvolved observer is not required, under private law, to save a drowning person. But when an individual is charged with looking out for the well-being of others – that is, when the individual must be specifically other-regarding – the individual must appropriately incorporate the well-being of others into the individual's decisions. When an individual gets behind the steering wheel of a car, and *because* she gets behind the steering wheel of a car, she accepts the obligation appropriately to consider the well-being of others.

The other-regarding concept unifies and integrates economic and philosophical approaches to law. This idea is developed in Section 5.3. Behind every decision – and therefore behind human behavior – is a way of thinking about one's behavior. Every action is preceded by a way of making a decision about one's action – a methodology of making decisions. Although, as discussed in Chapter 3, the law cannot assess directly the methodology of decision making an individual uses, the law can assess the way an ideal decision maker would behave in a particular situation if the ideal decision maker used a morally appropriate methodology of decision making. The law can determine how an individual *ought* to act by replicating the methodology that the individual ought to have used when deciding how to act, and by determining whether the individual's behavior is consistent with the behavior of the ideal decision maker. If the law needs to determine, for example, whether an individual is driving her automobile too fast, it does that by replicating the methodology the driver should have used when deciding how fast to drive. The law cannot know whether driving at seventy miles an hour is reasonable under the circumstances without first determining what methodology the ideal driver would have used to decide how fast to drive. The law is not judging the individual's methodology, only her behavior. Yet the law assesses the behavior by determining how the individual would have behaved had she used the ideal other-regarding methodology.

As a matter of moral decision making, the law is saying the following: act always as you would if you had used the appropriate, ideal methodology of decision making. This is an imperative that is constant no matter what the context and no matter what the consequences for the person making the decision. At the same time, the ideal, other-regarding decision maker is also using a methodology of consequences because ideal decision making specifies which consequences an individual ought to take into account when making decisions and how the decision maker is to assign weight to the consequences. The law has absorbed this view of moral decision making into private law because the law determines when an ideal decision maker is allowed to ignore the well-being of others and when and how an ideal decision maker must take the well-being of others into account. Other-regarding behavior results from the ideal integration of the well-being of the decision maker with the well-being of those affected by the decision. As I mentioned, when every person engages in appropriate other-regarding behavior, no other arrangement of rights and responsibilities would be socially beneficial, and rights and responsibilities have been distributed on grounds that respect the equality of individuals. When one or more individuals avoid other-regarding behavior, conflict results and aggrieved individuals can ask courts to determine which decisions ought to be changed, and to induce those changes with appropriate remedies.

5.1 THE RATIONAL PERSON AND OTHER-REGARDING DECISIONS

It is important to understand the relationship among rational decisions, self-regarding decisions, and other-regarding decisions, which I do using the conventions of behavioral game theory.[4] Individuals make rational choices in the sense that they make decisions designed to allow them to achieve their goals. Rational decision makers define their own ends and are subject only to the modest requirement that their decisions, to be rational, must be consistent over time, given the individual's circumstances when he or she makes the decision. Rational preference-satisfying decisions are self-interested decisions, but they need not be selfish or exclusively self-regarding decisions; decisions can be shaped by preferences for equality or fairness as the decision maker understands those terms. Although we can assume that human decision making is self-interested in this preference-satisfying sense, rational self-interested decisions can be either self-regarding or other-regarding. Self-regarding decisions are decisions in which the decision accounts only for the probable reward of the decision to the decision maker; a self-regarding decision maker cares about other individuals' decisions only insofar as those decisions influence the actor's reward. Transactions in a perfectly competitive market are generally self-regarding because decision makers normally care about the well-being of others only to the extent that the other can make the decision maker better off. A buyer looks at the market price and decides whether to buy, without considering the benefits of the purchase to the seller; a seller looks at the market price and decides whether to sell, caring about the well-being of the buyer only to the extent that the buyer can pay the seller's price.

Alternatively, self-interested decisions can be other-regarding. These are decisions in which the decision maker is willing to invest resources or absorb costs to improve another individual's well-being. Even in the marketplace some decisions are other-regarding. Some citizens of Michigan, for example, are other-regarding because they decide to buy automobiles made by Detroit companies rather than less expensive or better quality automobiles (as they would define those terms) made by foreign companies; they sacrifice their self-regarding interests (quality or price) on behalf of the well-being of others. Under this typology, all decisions are self-interested, but some are self-regarding and some have a mixture of self-regarding and other-regarding motivations. Self-regarding decisions depend only on the well-being of the decision

---

[4] The definitions here draw directly on Gintis (2009) at 6.

maker; other-regarding decisions also take into account the well-being of one or more other individuals.

The other-regarding decision concept hovered over the last chapter. That chapter established that individuals cooperate when they are each made better off and when they share beliefs about how the gains from cooperation ought to be divided. An individual's decision that cooperation makes him better off can be based on only self-regarding factors, for the decision maker considers only the effect of the decision on his own well-being (taking the well-being of the other person as exogenous to the decision). However, to act on shared beliefs about an appropriate division of the gains from cooperation requires an other-regarding decision because it requires at least one cooperating individual to accept a sacrifice in her own well-being in order to facilitate another individual's well-being. To return to the example in the last chapter, individuals considering an exchange identify a range of rates of exchange that make them both better off, which requires the individuals to have overlapping self-regarding decisions. They also need to determine which rate of exchange to choose, and as each individual makes that decision, one individual's gain will be another individual's loss. One or both of the individuals must therefore accept a lower relative benefit from the exchange so that the other individual can receive a higher relative benefit. There is, as we said in Chapter 4, a hidden zero sum game embedded in the positive sum game of cooperation. When one individual accepts a lower gain so that the other individual can accept a higher gain, the individual is making an other-regarding decision. Other-regarding behavior serves as the cooperation gene – the attitude on which cooperation is built in markets, social arrangements, and political activity.[5] It is therefore not surprising that the concept of other-regarding behavior is emerging in the social science literature as a key component for understanding cooperative behavior.[6]

In some disciplines, scholars use the term *altruistic* as a synonym for other-regarding. That is understandable because altruistic and other-regarding decisions share the characteristic that the decision maker sacrifices her own well-being to improve the well-being of others. However, for the purpose of legal analysis, at least, it is relevant to distinguish between altruistic and other-regarding decisions, a distinction that turns on the nature of the self-interest that motivates the decision. An altruistic decision is one in which the only benefit to the decision maker is to satisfy the decision maker's desire to make

---

[5] Rose (1994) at 27 ("for property regimes to function, some of us have to have other-regarding preference orderings").
[6] *See* Ostrom (2002), Jones (2004), and Baron (1993).

someone else better off. A gift to hunger relief is self-interested and altruistic because it makes the decision maker better off only by making the decision maker feel good about making someone else better off. This is altruistic self-interest because it does not achieve any of the decision maker's ends except the goal of helping others. An other-regarding decision incorporates the well-being of others with the well-being of the decision maker so that the decision maker can achieve her own preferences. The decision maker considers the well-being of others in order to improve the decision maker's well-being (other than just the well-being of doing something for another person). Slowing the car down when streets are crowded makes the decision maker better off by integrating the decision maker's self-regarding impulses (the impulse to accomplish one's goals quickly) with the decision maker's other-regarding impulses (to do so without imposing undue risks on others). The motivation for such a decision is to honor the reciprocal, transactional nature of the cooperative relationship with others so that the decision maker can achieve her own goals while honoring other's goals.

The distinction between other-regarding and altruistic decision-making is important for two reasons. First, the distinction preserves the concept of other-regarding decisions as one useful in thinking about cooperation. Altruistic decisions are not transactional and do not implement any goal of the decision maker except that of making someone else better off. They implement distributive justice because they do not suppose that any recipient has a claim to altruistic behavior from any other individual. Other-regarding decisions express the reciprocity inherent in cooperation. An individual is other-regarding because being so enhances the successful coordination of disparate activities. Second, the distinction between other-regarding behavior and altruistic behavior also reflects an important distinction between decisions an individual makes to benefit another out of moral compunction (altruism) and the decisions a person makes to benefit another out of legal compunction (other-regarding decisions). As we see in the next section, private law does not require altruistic decisions, and public law requires altruistic decisions in the name of the community rather than in the name of corrective justice between interacting individuals. That distinction is important for the concept of legal duty, as I explain in the next section.

5.2 OTHER-REGARDING DECISIONS AND LEGAL DUTY

The obligation to make other-regarding decisions is not implicated in every decision an individual makes because not every decision implicates the equality principle. The obligation to be other-regarding does not, for example, require that an individual deciding whether to use her property for a cornfield or a cigar store take into account anyone else's well-being. To be sure, that decision affects other individuals, but nothing about that decision is relational in a relevant sense. Because the concept of other-regarding decisions requires a way of determining *when* an individual has the obligation to consider the well-being of others, the theory must distinguish between duty and no-duty, which is a pivotal concept in the common law. In this section, I present a theory of the no-duty and duty principles that allows private law to identify when one has the obligation to take into account the well-being of others. Under this conception, duty and no-duty are dichotomous; for each decision an individual makes, the individual is either obligated or not obligated to take into account the well-being of others. At common law, the no-duty principle is the prevailing principle, and the concept of duty serves to trigger obligations to take into account the well-being of others (and thus to trigger legal intervention). When obligations are defined by legislation, obligations need not reflect the no-duty principle and, in fact, contain a broad range of obligations that would not be recognized by the common law.

5.2.1 The No-Duty Principle

Under the no-duty principle, an actor's obligation to another in common law arises only from a relationship that the individual has with the other: a relationship that reflects a choice the actor has made. The law imposes no freestanding obligation to benefit fellow citizens. An actor is under no general obligation, without some basis for finding a relevant relationship, to expend energy in helping another because, under the common law, the other has no valid claim to be helped by the actor. There is, in other words, no duty to rescue another, even when rescue is relatively effortless, and no person who is in need can claim that this or that stranger has failed in her obligations by failing to rescue him. Although controversial,[7] this is an accepted principle of the common law, despite the recent expansion of the obligations of one individual to another when the appropriate relationship exists.[8]

---

[7] *See* Landes and Posner (1978) at 106–08 (looking at the duty to rescue from an economic perspective); Levy (2010) (arguing that all states should enact a "bad-Samaritan" law); Lipkin (1993) (addressing the objections to a general legal duty to rescue); Waldron (2000) (arguing that the law is capable of securing help for those in need or danger by a state-enforced good Samaritan law instead of simply a moral duty to help); Weinrib (1980) (arguing for a reconsideration of the common law position against a duty to rescue); Yeager (1993) (arguing that the common notion that affirmative duties are intolerable is less prevalent than most observers suggest).

[8] The expansion of obligations has come in tort through product liability, whereas in property it has come through landlord– tenant law. In fact, the expansion of responsibility in both

The no-duty principle raises three kinds of issues. First, and most important, it seems to be at odds with our moral intuitions that individuals sometimes ought to be responsible for the well-being of others, even in the absence of a prior relationship. Second, it suggests (unconventionally) that duties are not imposed by courts, but are recognized by courts from the decisions that an individual has already made. Finally, the no-duty principle seems to be belied by the doctrine of necessity, which, by requiring an owner to allow those in physical danger to use her property, seems to be property law's equivalent of a requirement of easy rescue. Each of these issues begs us to clarify the relationship between the common law and individual obligations, as well as the distinction between private and public law.

My defense of the no-duty principle is a defense of the principle at common law. I do not attempt to refute the moral intuition that one ought to help another when help is badly needed and relatively easy to provide. A recent expression of the moral argument supporting an obligation of easy rescue comes from Ronald Dworkin. Given the need for each individual to live in the balance between two intersecting values – due regard for the way one has chosen to live one's own life and equal regard (although not equal weight) for the lives of others – an individual will sometimes be in a situation in which the endorsement of both principles requires an individual to sacrifice his own projects and preferences for the projects and preferences of others. As Dworkin says:

> We must show full respect for the equal objective importance of every person's life, but also full respect for our own responsibility to make something valuable of our own life. We must interpret the first demand as making room for the second, and the other way around...[t]here is a limit to how far I can consistently ignore something that I claim has objective value. I cannot be indifferent to its fate.[9]

If this is true, then sometimes an individual must make something valuable out of her own life by recognizing the equal importance of another person's life.

It is not necessary to refute this argument to support my claim that the common law ought not impose a general non-relational duty to benefit another, not even a duty of easy rescue. Sound reasons support the divergence between an actor's general moral obligations and an actor's moral obligations at common law. Consider two points. The first is that the common law is but a

---

domains reflects judicial reassessment of the relationship between suppliers and their customers given access to information and specialization of functions.

[9] Dworkin (2011) at 272–74.

subset of the law, so that the failure to incorporate the moral obligation of easy rescue within the common law does not create a necessary divergence between the law and moral requirements. The moral duty of easy rescue can be, and is, incorporated in law in many ways. The second point is that there are good reasons courts do not incorporate the obligation of easy rescue into the common law.

The common law addresses claims by an injured individual against another individual that the other is responsible for, and ought to correct, the harms the injured person suffered. It deals only with the division of responsibility between individuals when bad things happen to one of them. Public law deals with harms more broadly, and the law finds many ways of incorporating an individual's moral obligation for the well-being of others into the law without incorporating the obligation of easy rescue into the common law. Law can, and does, offer rewards or indemnities to rescuers.[10] Legislation sometimes imposes a duty of easy rescue that is enforceable by victims. Criminal law can express the sense of the community that the failure to easily rescue another ought to be punished. And social norms can exert a strong law-like force of reputational rewards and sanctions to support rescue. Moral intuitions are incorporated in law in many ways, but the common law and the redress it provides may not be the appropriate vessel for the moral duty of easy rescue.

The crucial distinction is between what an actor ought to do (the moral issue) and what another individual can claim from the actor if the actor fails to do what the actor ought to do. The common law enforces corrective justice, which treats only the bilateral relationship between two individuals; it does so by dividing responsibilities between them. In the context we are discussing, it always asks: What responsibility does individual A owe to individual B, and vice versa? It does not ask about the moral action of one person only, but about the moral character of the interaction of two or more persons, taking into account, and giving equal weight to, the personhood of each individual in the context of their interaction. The common law is about a claim that one person may make against another based on the division of responsibility to avoid harm between the two of them. The moral obligation of beneficence and easy rescue is about what an individual ought to expect of himself. The common law is about what an individual can claim (using the coercive power of the

---

[10] *See generally* Ripstein (2000). *See, e.g.,* Haynes v. Harwood, [1935] 1 K.B. 147 (C.A.) (no assumption of risk in rescue); Perpich v. Leetonia Mining Co., 118 Minn. 508, 512, 137 N.W. 12, 14 (1912) (rescuer may recover from imperiled person for injuries sustained in a rescue attempt, unless rescuer acted with extreme recklessness); Echert v. Long Island R.R., 43 N.Y. 502 (1971) (same); Wagner v. Int'l Ry. Co., 232 N.Y. 176 (1921) (a reasonable rescuer may recover against the negligent person who caused the need to rescue).

Other-Regarding Decisions and Legal Duty

state) from another. These are separable concepts and good reasons suggest that every *"ought to"* that moral reasoning imposes on an individual should not be translated into an enforceable claim by another individual for redress.

There are, of course, practical problems in enforcing a common law duty to rescue: knowing where the duty to benefit another ends;[11] how the would-be rescuer ought to address the many questions about the need for, and costs of, rescue; and the problem of determining who among several possible rescuers ought to execute the rescue. Even putting these aside, the common law fails to incorporate a doctrine of beneficence and easy rescue because the values that would compel a person to make the rescue are foreign to the values that govern the claims that one person may make against another.

Arthur Ripstein has provided the most persuasive philosophical defense of the proposition that corrective justice precludes one person from making a claim to be benefited by another person when the would-be rescuer is not associated in a relevant way with the risk the claimant faces.[12] He draws the important distinction between the common law, which deals with the division of responsibility between individuals, and public law, which deals with the division of responsibility between the individual and the state.[13] This distinction orients the further distinction between claims an individual has against other individuals and claims an individual has against the community (in the person of the state). Claims against the state are claims of distributive justice, whereas claims against individuals are claims of corrective justice. In both realms, choice must be grounded in the responsibility one takes for one's own life in the context of equal respect for others. Naturally, that means that when an individual is attached in an appropriate way to the risk of loss another faces, the individual must, when making choices, give appropriate significance to the harm another might incur. This is because it is the individual's own choice that leads the individual to be attached to the risk of harm another might face,

---

[11] Even the most persuasive expression of the doctrine of easy rescue requires the rescuer to draw difficult lines between her interests and the interests of the victim, mediated by the immediacy of the victim's plight (what Dworkin calls the "confrontation factor").

[12] Ripstein (2006) at 1411.

[13] In actuality, Ripstein draws a distinction between private law and public law, but I believe he is thinking of the distinction between the common law and public law. Private law addresses the relationship between individuals by assigning rights and responsibilities to their relationship. All common law is private law because common law courts have no other authority, but the legislature may adjust the rights and responsibilities as between individuals and therefore may make private law. Good Samaritan laws impose duties as to individuals in need and thereby adjust the rights and responsibilities as between individuals (a private law function). The strong no-duty pull of the common law is reflected in how infrequently legislatures pass Good Samaritan statues with civil remedies, but such legislation is possible.

and the other is entitled to be free from the avoidable consequences of that choice.

By the same reasoning, the would-be rescuer ought to be free of the choices of the one who would otherwise absorb a loss. As Ripstein says:

> Independence from another person's choice is important not because it is thought of as the best way of promoting successful choice, but rather because it implies the more general idea of reconciling the purposiveness of separate persons – each of whom has a special responsibility for his or her own life – through a set of reciprocal restraints. ....[Y]our independence from the choices of others is to be understood as your entitlement to be the one who decides what purposes you will pursue with the means that are at your disposal.[14]

Based on the independence of each individual to choose her own goals and means of reaching those goals, each individual must be independent of the choices made by others, which is what gives the decisions of each individual their independence.

> The idea that each person has responsibility for his or her own life limits the means individuals are able to use for their purposes. In particular, my special responsibility for my life is only consistent with your special responsibility for yours if each of us is required to keep from using the other, in pursuit of our purposes.[15]

Claims against another individual must therefore flow from choices that the other has made. Unless a claim against another flows from such a choice, an individual's life is his own responsibility, or the responsibility of the community, and not the responsibility of an individual who stands outside of relationships that have already been formed. This account is Kantian because "Kant approaches private law through its relationship to freedom, understood as independence from the choices of others."[16]

The moral *ought* looks at the situation from the standpoint of the would-be rescuer only, and does not take into account the moral status of the victim's claim. Once we account for the moral status of the victim's claim, we find it hard to see why the victim can impose on a stranger an obligation to help avoid a loss. Even if the victim's position is determined only by that person's bad

---

[14] Ripstein (2006) at 1403.
[15] Ripstein (2006) at 1405.
[16] Ripstein (2006) citing Kant (1797) at 30.

luck, by what right does the luckless victim assert a claim that a stranger should bear the consequences of that bad luck? Hypothetical problems involving children in danger are meant to sway our moral judgment about the relationship between adult rescuer and child, but they ignore the moral relationship between the would-be rescuer and the person who put the child in danger.

This parsimonious view of the duty to rescue is consistent with autonomy theories of property. Private law sees each person as an autonomous actor, fully endowed with the freedom to make decisions that do not positively interfere with the projects and preference of others. Each person is an individual of purposive agency, and for each person to fulfill her individuality she must be able to develop her talents in directions she finds to be important, toward goals she values, and by means that enhance her journey. That implies that each actor has the freedom to make decisions without taking into account the well-being of others unless the actor has surrendered or used her autonomy in a way that fairly implies an obligation to another.

Personal autonomy demands that the decision to benefit or rescue another be made freely and not under the compulsion of the victim, for that is the only way by which personal autonomy can be fully realized. As a reciprocal value, autonomy strengthens the individuality of the would-be rescuer by protecting the rescuer from claims that would change the rescuer's projects and preferences, while protecting the person to be rescued, for no person may make claims against him. Importantly, the reciprocal autonomy protected by the common law strengthens the bond between would-be rescuer and victim. When the victim is rescued voluntarily, as moral decision making (but not the common law) requires, the victim knows that the rescue is an act of grace, not an act compelled by the community. The very voluntariness of the rescue builds a bond between rescuer and victim that would not be there if the law put a price on the failure to rescue. Acting voluntarily out of concern for another's well-being builds the bonds of community that might not be there if the act were done to avoid legal liability to the victim.[17]

In my earlier book, I show how this conception of an actor's freedom from claims of easy rescue by others is integral to our understanding of obligations

---

[17] Indeed, under some plausible assumptions, imposing liability for failure to rescue may reduce the public recognition accorded to other-regarding acts, which could actually reduce the incentive to rescue others. Landes and Posner (1978) at 122. Some philosophers agree that, in Jeremy Waldron's words, Good Samaritan laws will "subvert altruism by replacing other-regarding motives with a self-regarding fear of legal penalties." Waldron (2000) at 1064, citing Hunt (1959) at 18–20 (1959) and Moore (1997) at 747–48 (1997). The relationship between explicit economic incentives and an actor's social preferences to help others is subject to a growing literature (Bowles and Polania-Reyes 2012).

in tort law, one not weakened by the great expanse in tort obligations.[18] The same concepts shape property law. As I will argue in more detail in Chapter 7, the no-duty concept underlies the right to exclude. An actor who asks to take a mobile home across another's fallow field is asking the owner to confer a benefit that the owner has not fairly agreed to confer. The actor is asking the owner to be other-regarding in a way that the owner has not accepted by the choices the owner has made. If the law were to impose the obligation to confer this benefit – that is, if the law were to require that the owner surrender the right to exclude – the law would be requiring the owner to look out for the well-being of others even when that obligation cannot fairly be implied by any choice the owner has previously made. Such an imposed obligation would easily undercut social interchange as individuals made claims against each other without the other's express or implied consent.[19]

5.2.2 Duty

Under the duty principle I advance, an individual's obligations come from a decision the individual has made. Duties are self-imposed, and recognized by law, not created by law; they arise when an individual makes a decision from which it can reasonably be inferred that the individual, if acting morally, would understand that the decision implies the obligation to take into account the well-being of others when making future decisions. Often, the decision that triggers the obligation to account for the well-being of others is made in the context of a relationship, for relationships are evidence that the person, by virtue of having entered into a relationship, has assented to incorporating someone else's well-being into her own well-being. But in the concept that I advance, duty does not depend on relationships; it flows from the kind of decisions an individual makes about the activities she will undertake. Duty arises from decisions about activities because the choice of an activity implies the decision to accept the obligation to think about the well-being of others.

Under this conception, the law's role is to recognize those decisions from which it can be inferred that a reasonable person would have made the decision only if the person had also accepted the obligation to think about the well-being of others. The idea that duty arises from an individual's activity decisions

---

[18] Gerhart (2010) at 114–118.
[19] This account is, I believe, consistent with "the traditional everyday morality of property" that is "recognized by all members of society." Merrill and Smith (2007) at 67 and 91–92. Everyday morality encourages individuals to confer benefits on strangers but we would not expect the beneficiary to have an enforceable claim against the would-be rescuer for failing to do so.

preserves the individual's autonomy and therefore protects the no-duty principle. On the other hand, duty arises from activity decisions because some decisions are made with the knowledge that the decision implicates the well-being of others and therefore requires the individual to make the decision only if he is willing to assume the burden of other-regarding behavior. For example, if one starts a rescue, that decision implicates the well-being of the person to be rescued; the obligation to complete the rescue reasonably flows from that decision. More broadly, tort law recognizes that duty is automatic when an individual engages in an activity that creates a risk for another. That is because the decision to engage in an activity that risks the well-being of others implies that the decision maker is ready to take that well-being into account (reasonably). A person who gets in her car to drive (thereby creating a risk) knows that if she does not drive carefully she imposes risks on others, and ought to decide to drive accepting the responsibility to invest in the resources necessary to avoid unreasonable harm.

In the property context, an owner's obligation to take into account the well-being of others flows from two kinds of decisions the owner might make. First, the obligation sometimes flows from the owner's decision to purchase the property. By virtue of their purchase, owners assume duties to neighbors and, for example, to those who have customarily used land before the purchase. The doctrine of necessity imposes an obligation on owners that flows from an owner's decision to buy property (although, as we will see in Chapter 7, it is a far more limited obligation than is generally imagined). Second, owners accept obligations to others when owners decide to use their property in certain ways. Activity decisions often imply that those undertaking the activity ought to look out for the well-being of others. The decision to operate a common carrier, or a retail store; the decision to employ migrant workers; the decision to give employees access to the Internet, and many more, create the duty to attend to the well-being of others. This vision of property law's duties is developed in Chapters 7 (exclusion) and 8 (nuisance).

5.3 OTHER-REGARDING DECISIONS AND DEONTIC OBLIGATIONS

The law asks individuals to make decisions as an ideal decision maker would make them. This is the requirement of the reasonable person. The law does not want an individual to act unreasonably under any circumstances, given the circumstances. That means that the law requires that individuals behave as if their behavior was governed by an appropriately moral methodology of making decisions. That obligation – the obligation to act as if the individual decision maker were using an ideal, moral methodology – is not contingent on the consequences of the decision for the decision maker or anyone else. The method of making decisions is a categorical obligation – one that does not vary with circumstances or consequences. It is not hypothetical because neither circumstance nor consequence changes the obligation to act as one would if one had used the appropriate decision-making methodology. Even if one is deciding whether to lie to Nazis to protect Jews in hiding, one is not excused from the obligation to act as an ideal decision maker would if she were using a moral methodology of decision making.

Stated in this way, the obligation of the reasonable person to use an appropriate method of making decisions serves as an interpretation of Kant's Categorical Imperative. In its first iteration,[20] Kant's Categorical Imperative provides that an individual must always "act only on that maxim whereby thou canst at the same time will that it should become a universal law." Each word of the Imperative expresses an important part of Kant's philosophy, but two aspects of the Imperative claim our attention here: the command to search for a maxim to guide action and the command to search for a maxim that can be called universal.

The first part of the Categorical Imperative directs individuals to act only in accordance with a maxim. One should therefore avoid acting unless one can employ a principle of the required kind when deciding the means for achieving one's ends. This expresses an individual's obligation to reason – a particular method of making decisions – or to act as if one had reasoned. This part of the Imperative separates the process of reasoning, or thinking about, one's action from the act itself, by saying that acting must be based on, or operate as if it were based on, a maxim determined through reason.[21] Because one must act as if one had reasoned before acting, Kant is saying that one must act as if one had adopted a methodology of deciding how to achieve one's ends that leads to a maxim of the appropriate kind.[22] The requirement is methodological, not

---

[20] In the course of his metaphysics Kant repeats the Categorical Imperative in three other ways in order to emphasize a different imperative when acting. Each variation supports the interpretation of the Categorical Imperative developed here (Gerhart 2010).

[21] Deigh (2010) at 146 (the principle one chooses to achieve one's end is a first-order principle; the Categorical Imperative is a second-order principle that regulates the first-order principles. The Categorical Imperative "given that it represents a requirement of practical reason, is itself, then, an imperative that dictates with unconditional necessity....Faithful application of the Categorical Imperative in one's deliberations, that is, not only shows what the moral law requires but also reinforces the judgments of ordinary men and women about right and wrong.").

[22] We can distinguish between two statements: (1) that an individual must use a certain methodology before acting. and (2) that an individual must act only as she would act if she had used such a methodology. Kant reads as if he is saying the former, and is therefore imposing

substantive. It is about the way individuals decide what means to employ to achieve their goals, when they would act morally, and not about the action or behavior brought about by the method of reasoning in various contexts. In this respect, Kant's emphasis on reasoning toward a maxim is entirely about *how* individuals make choices, not about the choices individuals make.

The second requirement of the Categorical Imperative is that the maxim be one that the deciding individual could will to be universal in the sense that it could be made into law for all human beings.[23] The principle of universality does not mean, as is sometimes supposed, that the maxim must be true in all times and places. Rather, the principle of universality means that the maxim must meet two tests: coherence with the conception of the principle as a universal law and coherence with the act of will required to make it universal law. If those two tests are met, then the principle is universal because anyone would reach the same principle in the same circumstances. "To Kant's way of thinking, as long as you are able to form the idea of everyone acting on the principle of your action when they find themselves in situations similar to yours and as long as you can will consistently with your decision to act on this principle in situations like yours, then your acting on the principle is lawful."[24]

This interpretation of the concept of universality avoids the misinterpretation that has distanced Kant's thinking from other ways of understanding personal decision making, including the methods of game theorists and economists. Some have understood the word "universal" to be "true in every time and place." This broader interpretation of the word "universal" ought to be avoided. First, it would wrest the meaning of the Categorical Imperative from the examples Kant used to explain it. Kant's examples did not purport to ask the decision maker to look for a broad and general rule of behavior that was independent of the context of the decision. Kant illustrated the Categorical Imperative with a number of examples, each of which occurred in a particular, not a general, context. Kant demonstrated, for example, why it is wrong for an individual to lie in order to obtain a loan; Kant's justification turns on a particular set of contextual assumptions. The maxim derived in that example yielded a maxim for that situation (one that met the standards of the

---

an obligation to reason before acting. Under this view, even if an individual acts in a moral way, the individual acts immorally if the individual has not acted for the right reasons. For the purposes of determining an individual's *legal* obligations, that moral obligation is too stringent because the law is unable to determine by what method an individual decided to act in one way rather than another. It is therefore natural for the law to require an actor to act as if the actor had made the decision using the appropriate methodology, using the actions of the ideal decision maker as the standard for evaluating an individual's conduct.

[23] Deigh (2010) at 145
[24] Deigh (2010) at 145.

Categorical Imperative), but Kant did not purport to claim that the maxim about lying would also be true in other contexts.

Second, as has often been pointed out, the broader reading of the word "universal" leads to troubling results. Although most individuals accept and implement the general principle that one ought not tell a lie, most individuals simultaneously believe that if an individual can save lives by telling a lie (perhaps by misdirecting Nazis searching for Jews hidden in the attic), the appropriate maxim is that the individual *should* lie. The awkward conclusion that one must be truthful when asked a question by Nazis seeking to incarcerate Jews is required if the word "universal" is read to mean "always true in every context."

Further, Kant insisted on internal coherence in the choice of a maxim, and a broad reading of the word "universal" would violate the requirements of consistency. For Kant, internal coherence serves as a logical constraint on the search for the appropriate maxim. If a maxim about behavior were required to be true in all times and circumstances, it is difficult to see how any maxim would maintain its internal coherence, for coherence implies that the principle would not contradict itself. But the maxim "do not lie" – a universal maxim in the broad non-contextual sense – contradicts itself if one has promised to hide Jews from the Nazis. Either the promise is a lie or the decision maker must lie when Nazis ask whether there are Jews hiding in the attic. This internal inconsistency between these "universal" maxims disqualifies either maxim as one that meets the coherence requirement of the Categorical Imperative.

Finally, if the goal of the Categorical Imperative were to derive a set of maxims of behavior that individuals should follow regardless of context, Kant's appeal to reason and the will would be subverted. If the universal maxim was "be truthful in all declarations," an individual would need reason only insofar as an individual found reason necessary to compare the individual's behavior with the universal behavior required by the maxim. An individual would have to reason about what a "truthful declaration" was, but not about whether a particular declaration violated a maxim that ought to be applied in that situation. This would reduce the exercise of the will to an exercise of deductive reasoning (what is a truthful statement, and does my statement fit that definition?), rather than an exercise of the will in the way Kant intended – as the implementation of thoughtful human choice. The interpretation that allows the maxim to respond to the decision's context makes the requirement of using a methodology of reasoning meaningful. It requires a method of reasoning that would produce a maxim that one would will to be applied every time that decision was made in that context, whether it was made by the decision maker or by someone else. That maxim would be adopted by all individuals who undertook the kind of moral reasoning compelled by the reasoned search for such a maxim. The universality of the maxim relates not to the maxim as a broad rule but to the maxim as a response to the decision the actor faces.[25]

The correct interpretation of the word "universal" – the one that emphasizes universality within a particular context – makes Kant's moral philosophy congenial with theories of individual decision making used in game theory and economics. Under the law's approach, Kant is suggesting that an individual should choose a course of action for achieving her goals – that is, choose a maxim – that is universal in all times and places for the type of decision that the decision maker is making. Hence, the word "universal" refers to a maxim that is always a valid response to the question the decision maker is addressing, whatever the consequences for the decision maker. This implementation of the Categorical Imperative retains the *imperative* but also takes into account the different contexts in which individuals must make decisions.[26] The Imperative is about the methodology of thinking and about the required maxim that results from using that methodology, but the maxim applies only in situations that are similar to the situation that gave rise to the need to reason. It is not the maxim that is imperative; it is the way of reasoning about the maxim that is imperative. And what is imperative about the way of reasoning is that an individual must reason toward a maxim that the individual would

---

[25] The only evidence that Kant intended a definition of the word "universal" that would mean "true regardless of the context" is the letter published under Kant's name in a Berlin newspaper. See Kant Edition (1889), Appendix I. There, Kant responded to an article by an unnamed "French philosopher" who argued, much as the interpretation here suggests, that one ought not be morally compelled to tell the truth to murderers who are looking to kill a friend. Kant's response was: "To be truthful (honest) in all declarations is a sacred unconditional command of reason, and not to be limited by any expediency." This seems to support the interpretation that says the Categorical Imperative is to derive a maxim that is universal regardless of the context. Yet Kant's apparent statements about truthful declarations can be understood in two ways that are consistent with the context-centered interpretation of the word "universal" that I endorse. First, Kant may be striving in the letter for a distinction between declarations that are untruthful and the obligation to disclose facts in response to a question. Kant may be correct that if one speaks one must tell the truth, but that maxim allows one to refuse to answer questions. Second, we might distinguish between actions for which the appropriate maxim must be non-contextually universal (such as truthful declarations) and actions for which the appropriate maxim can be contextual (such as whether to invest in abatement technology to remedy conflicting land uses).

[26] This interpretation does not imply that all maxims must be particularized or that maxims may not have a generality that reduces the cost of discovering and applying the appropriate maxim. It only implies that maxims need not be so general as to lead to results that could not themselves be considered to be moral, or that lead to contradictions between generalized maxims. On the optimal generality of any rule, there is a trade-off between the rule's normative "fit" for the decision maker and the information costs of ascertaining which of several particularized rules applies in a particular situation. *See generally* Merrill and Smith (2007) at 1853; Merrill and Smith (2000) and Smith (2003).

choose as the ruling maxim even if the individual were not the person facing the consequences of the decision. It is universal in the sense that all individuals would develop the maxim if they thought about a maxim in that situation, even if they were not in the position of the decision maker. Under this reading, individuals must act as if they had adopted a methodology of reasoning that leads to a maxim that they could use in that situation, one that they would use in every identical situation, and one that they would want to have used even if they were not in the position of the decision maker.

Under this interpretation, individuals are required to act as they would if they used the method of decision making that an ideal decision maker would use. This methodology has two fundamental requirements. First, the maxim must be neutral enough so that it is one the decision maker would pursue whatever the decision maker's position, regardless of the consequences for the decision maker. Second, it is one that would garner consent from other individuals in the community who used the proper method of making decisions. That methodology requires, I claim, decisions that are appropriately other-regarding. The content of those decisions is the subject of the next chapter.

5.4 CONCLUSION

In this chapter, I have argued that the obligation to be other-regarding implicates the question of when an individual has the obligation to incorporate the well-being of others in one's decisions, and the question of how, when an individual has an obligation to make other-regarding decisions, the individual must appropriately integrate the individual's self-regarding and other-regarding interests. In the next chapter, I develop the methodology by which an individual can determine what the appropriate integration ought to be. This chapter elucidated the no-duty principle that animates the common law, so that we can later understand the ways in which the no-duty principle animates property law. The chapter also introduces the concept of other-regarding decisions and relates that concept to an interpretation of Kant's Categorical Imperative. The theory relies on the distinction between the requirement to act as if one had used a moral methodology of making decisions (the categorical obligation) and the action itself. It therefore focuses on how an ideal decision maker would actually make decisions. The categorical requirement that one act as one would act if one were an ideal decision maker allows legal theory to focus on the factors that a person ought to take into account when making decisions and thus to separate the categorical from the consequential by separating consequences that must be taken into account from those that may not be taken into account.

6 Assigning Burdens and Benefits

6.1 INTRODUCTION

Thus far, I have developed the idea that owners are decision makers, and that in property law decisions by owners and nonowners must be other-regarding in the sense that, when their obligations require it, individuals must appropriately attend to the well-being of others. I therefore developed a concept of duty – when a decision maker must attend to the well-being of another – and introduced the idea that through property law courts are defining that duty and its scope when individuals make decisions about resources. In this chapter, I provide an account of how a person who is expected to be other-regarding makes decisions that can be called moral. Here, I define what we mean when we say that individuals must be *appropriately* other-regarding, and I present a methodology of thinking about how the ideal decision maker ought to think about her self-interest in terms of a blend of self-regarding and other-regarding attitudes – the methodology of thinking from behind the veil of ignorance.

Here we look at the normative content of property law – the values that individuals must account for when they make decisions about resources, and the method by which they must account for those values. As explained in Chapter 1, property is given its normative content – its ability to express social values – by the decisions that owners and nonowners make if they would act in the way an ideal decision maker would, and by the values that individuals are required to take into account when making decisions if their conduct is to be called moral. The law serves to recognize and enforce those values by specifying the requirements of the ideal moral decision maker.[1]

---

[1] This chapter concentrates on the rights and responsibilities of individuals when making decisions about private property. The basic idea – that decision making about property must account appropriately for the assignment of the burdens and benefits of the decision – applies equally to regimes of common property and to legislative regulation of property. The implications

The central message of this chapter is that when deciding whether and how to be other-regarding, an individual must appropriately assign the burdens and benefits of decisions about resources. The basic intuition is captured by the notion that an individual should not reap where he has not sown. From the standpoint of rights, an individual who bears the burdens of, say, investing in an apple orchard, ought to reap the benefits of that investment.[2] From the standpoint of responsibilities, an owner who seeks the benefit of retail customers ought to bear the burden of reasonably looking out for their well-being. At the same time, the aphorism that one may not reap where one did not sow is not invariably true. Individuals benefit from the investment of others all the time.[3] The notion that property law adjusts the burdens and benefits of ownership and nonownership is contained in economic models built on cost-benefit analysis, and it finds expression in court opinions and property theory,[4] especially in property doctrine relating to servitudes. The concept is put to broader use here because I offer the burdens and benefits concept as the central normative core of property law, expanding on the economic approach by developing a methodology for determining the values that must be used when assigning burdens and benefits.

So central is the burdens and benefits principle that it can be understood to define property. We can say that property is the normative right of owners and nonowners to an appropriate assignment of burdens and benefits when individuals make decisions about resources. It is a measure of what owners receive when they acquire a right (no one else may reap where the owner has sown), the measure of limitations on what they acquire (no right to impose unreasonable burdens on those who benefit the owner), an authorization for state regulation (to make sure that owners take into account a range of burdens and benefits important to the community), and a limitation on state regulation (because the state may not inappropriately assign the burdens of

---

for common property regimes are worked out in Chapter 9, the implications for legislative regulation in Chapter 13.

[2] The idea of investing in an apple orchard and being allowed to reap the value of the apple orchard is, of course, a version of Locke's labor theory of value. As articulated in Chapter 4, however, I am using the labor theory not to justify the existence of the right, but to define its scope. The right and its scope come from social recognition of the claims made in the name of the labor theory, not from the labor theory itself. The labor theory is not the source of the right but the source of the recognition of the right by non-claimants. It holds no independent significance until, and to the extent that, it is recognized by a community.

[3] Consumers in a competitive market reap consumer surplus in excess of their expenditures; one farmer's investment in bees may benefit a neighbor who depends on the bees to pollinate her plants. Investment frequently yields positive spillovers.

[4] See, e.g., Heller (2005) at 43 (discussing allocation of burdens and benefits in governing the commons).

Introduction

regulation).[5] Ownership is dominion over a resource (the subject matter of the right) that gives the owner the right to an appropriate assignment of the burdens and benefits of ownership (the scope of the right).

Even beyond property law, however, the concept that ideal decision makers will appropriately assign the burdens and benefits of decisions about property unifies our understanding of private law. The theory defended here is one about the responsibility of one individual for the well-being of another individual – that is, social morality – and the theory applies whether the relationship between the individuals arises out of what are conventionally called torts, contracts, property, or unjust enrichment. An individual's obligation to appropriately assign the burdens and benefits of decisions about resources is a unified theory that specifies the circumstances under which one individual is responsible for the harm that befalls another individual.

Under the theory propounded here, private law asserts that the core responsibility of all individuals is to make an appropriate assignment of the burdens and benefits of their decisions, and that the assignment of burdens and benefits of decisions must follow the requirements of equal freedom. This, in turn, requires the actor to weigh the interests of others equally with the actor's own interests, using values that are neutral as between victim and injurer. The requirements of equal freedom follow the familiar distinction between intentional and non-intentional harm. If the actor knows only of the risk of harm, the actor acts without the intention to harm, and the requirements of equal freedom divide the harm between the injurer and the victim (the injurer is responsible for harm that could have reasonably been avoided, and the victim is responsible for the residual harm). In this sense, actor and victim share responsibility for the harm. On the other hand, if the actor acts with knowledge, to a substantial degree of certainty, that harm will result, the requirement of equal treatment allocates the harm either to the actor or to the victim, but the harm is not shared between them. This is a case of unilateral responsibility for harm. The requirements of equal freedom manifest themselves in the two ways that an individual is responsible for the harm that befalls another individual: when an actor fails to give the other the care that the other is due

---

[5] The essence of the theory of private property developed here is that owners are protected from the undue imposition of burdens by other individuals. The theory developed in Part III is that owners are also protected against the undue imposition of burdens by the state. Under this view, the constitutional protection of property against either a taking (the Takings Clause) or a deprivation (the Due Process Clause) is not protection of the resource itself, but protection of the assignment of burdens and benefits to which the owner is entitled. The conception of undue burdens is different in the legislative realm than in the common law realm the difference rests on an understanding of the relationship between common law and legislative regulation of property.

(a regime of shared responsibility) and when the actor, even though acting reasonably, has the duty to repair harm that cannot be avoided with the exercise of due care (a regime of unilateral responsibility).

Unlike conventional theories of responsibility, however, the theory here suggests that the failure to repair is, in fact, the failure to make a reasonable decision about whether to repair, and, for that reason, the theory here integrates under the fault principle the failure to exercise due care and the failure to reasonably repair. Actors make two kinds of decisions: What kind of care to take and whether to repair the harm that cannot be eliminated by the exercise of due care. Those decisions are either faulty or not, and responsibility follows from a faulty decision and not otherwise. Under this approach, there is no room for strict liability, which I view to be a legal artifact that artificially divides rather than unifies our understanding of human responsibility. In the view presented here, cases conventionally thought of as strict liability are those in which either (1) the actor failed to take due care in deciding where, when, how, and how often to undertake his or her activities; or (2) the actor has unreasonably failed to repair harm that should have been repaired. Strict liability gets absorbed into either the duty to take due care or the duty to repair when a reasonable person would do so.

I therefore start, in Section 6.2, by showing that many "strict liability" cases are, in fact, cases in which an actor has made unreasonable activity decisions and that other "strict liability" cases are in fact those in which the actor unreasonably refused to repair damage the actor caused.[6] Briefly, the consolidation of responsibility under the fault principle is based on two intuitions: (1) first, if I reasonably borrow my neighbor's hose to put out a fire in my house, I do so with the expectation that I will return the hose intact or pay to restore the hose to its condition when I borrowed it; and (2) second, if a friend mistakenly leaves her wallet at my house, I will, if I want to act reasonably, return the wallet to avoid unjust enrichment. I explain why it is important to view these cases as ones of fault rather than strict liability, and I show that each is a matter of appropriately assigning the burdens and benefits of decisions.

In Section 6.3 I continue to focus on the duty of due care and the duty to repair by explaining how the equality principle determines the way an actor ought to think about the burdens and benefits of his decisions. The obligation to avoid undue harm is imposed when the actor does not intend the harm (in the sense of not knowing, with a substantial degree of certainty, that it will occur) and reflects a regime of shared responsibility: the actor is responsible for harm that can reasonably be avoided and the victim is responsible for

---

[6] The thought is not new. See Smith (2004) at 382.

The Fault Principle

harm that cannot reasonably be avoided. I show how the equality principle justifies that level of responsibility and not more. The obligation to repair harm is imposed when an actor knows, with a substantial degree of certainty, that harm will occur and when a reasonable person would repair the harm. The principle of equality also justifies that form of responsibility because it is invoked when the injurer ought to incorporate that harm into the injurer's decisions because the failure to do so would show a lack of respect for the victim's equal dignity.

The two general classes of responsibility – responsibility for avoiding harm and responsibility for repairing harm – both require a method of comparing well-being across persons. I address this issue in Section 6.4. The obligation to avoid harm by taking due care requires each individual to determine when her self-regarding interests must give way to her other-regarding interests. The obligation to repair harm requires the reasonable person to determine when the failure to repair harm that cannot reasonably be avoided would be unjust; this requires the individual to understand how the requirements of equal freedom dictate that another should be free of the consequences of the individual's activity choices. I argue that the requirements of equal treatment are best determined by how individuals would reason about equality from behind the veil of ignorance, and I show how the thought experiment of the veil of ignorance allows us to reason about the morality of decisions in interpersonal relationships.

Taken together, these three sections demonstrate the unity of private law[7] by developing a theory of responsibility that shows why and when an injurer should have done more to protect her victim's well-being.

6.2 THE FAULT PRINCIPLE

The concept that decision makers must appropriately assign the burdens and benefits of decisions about property unifies our understanding of private law behind the fault principle, and leads to two forms of responsibility for the well-being of others: the duty to take due care and the duty to repair when repair is the reasonable decision.[8] In this section, I explain why the four major

---

[7] I have not yet worked out in detail the application of this framework for contract law. The broad outlines are straightforward. When entering into a bargain, each party has a duty to take into account the well-being of the counterparty. Therefore, its responsibility in interpreting the contract and compensating the counterparty for undeserved losses flows from its obligation to insure that the burdens and benefits of its decisions are appropriately assigned. That explains, among other things, doctrines of restitution, promissory estoppel, and the good faith requirement of contract interpretation,

[8] I proposed a theory of duty in Chapter 5. This chapter subsumes that theory in responsibility for taking due care, which is triggered only if the injurer has a duty to the victim.

categories of responsibility – no responsibility, negligence responsibility, strict liability responsibility, and unjust enrichment responsibility – in fact collapse into either the duty of due care or the duty of reasonable repair.

I first argue that the fault principle accords with how individuals think about their responsibility to others and is therefore superior to strict liability as the doctrinal home for either the duty of due care or the duty to repair. I then argue that strict liability collapses into either the duty to take due care or the duty of reasonable repair, each of which is a fault-based concept.

The idea of strict liability creates doctrinal disarray and drives a wedge between the way individuals and the legal system think about responsibility. Under the conventional legal view, courts choose which standard to apply – negligence, strict liability, or unjust enrichment – and the choice determines the outcome of the case. Doctrine is therefore overlapping and in tension. Negligence responsibility is thought to compete with strict liability as a governing standard; negligence is thought to be for normally dangerous activities, and strict liability is thought to be for abnormally dangerous activities. We understand the relevant classification by asking: In this particular context, should we apply fault liability or no-fault liability? Strict liability is for liability without fault, which sometimes, as in *Vincent v. Lake Erie Steamship Co.*,[9] swallows up unjust enrichment. Sometimes strict liability is for liability without harm (but with fault), as in trespass cases, but that kind of strict liability appears to overlap with unjust enrichment, which is also about liability without harm (assuming that the failure to repair is not harm). This classification system divides rather than unifies our understanding of responsibility. Under any of its iterations, the classification system assumes that the classification defines its own rules of application, quite apart from how individuals think about their own responsibility.

Not only does this classification system reflect doctrinal disarray, but the approach separates the way the law looks at responsibility from the way that individuals understand their own responsibility, making the standards external to the way people interpret and evaluate their behavior. An important distinction is between the law as an institution that tells people how to behave and the law as an institution that tells people how to think about how they ought to behave. All agree that the law functions to mediate between the *is* and the *ought* – that the law plays a vital role in establishing norms of appropriate behavior. But the law should also model how individuals ought to think about how to behave, and in that respect the concept of strict liability drives

---

[9] 109 Minn. 456 (Minn. 1910). See the various points of view developed in the electronic symposium about the *Vincent* case at http://www.bepress.com/ils/iss7.

The Fault Principle

a wedge between the law and society. Under the conventional classification system, the analyst is asking "to what verbal standard should the law hold the defendant?" It is not asking "to what standard of conduct ought the defendant hold himself?" The legal standard, being external to the individual, is divorced from the way an individual thinks about her own responsibility for the well-being of others. An individual does not say: "Should I hold myself to a no-fault standard?" The individual says: "Am I responsible for the harm to the injured person, either because I acted wrongfully or because in fairness I ought to repair their harm?" Similarly, if an individual says to himself "this activity is abnormally dangerous," the individual does not think to himself: "therefore I will be responsible for all the harm my activity causes." The individual thinks: "therefore, I should be really careful."[10] A standard that is external to the individual whose sense of responsibility the law is attempting to influence necessarily creates a disjunction between how the law thinks about responsibility and how individuals think about responsibility. This, in turn, creates a disjunction between law and the social behavior the law is trying to affect.

This wedge between how people think about how to behave and how the law tells individuals how to think about how they behave is unfortunate. To effectively control human behavior, and to ensure respect for itself, the law ought to adopt ways of thinking about how to behave that match how individuals themselves think about their behavior. The classification system the law now uses does not do that. Individuals adopt a unified way of understanding the responsibility that flows from their decisions. As I have argued, if an individual borrows a neighbor's hose to put out a fire in her home, she understands that she does so with the implicit obligation to return it without damage or to repair the damage. She does not say: "I am holding myself to a standard of no-fault liability." She says: "I know that I am responsible for the hose I borrowed even though I was perfectly reasonable in borrowing it."

Under the approach advocated here, the relevant classification for determining responsibility depends on the decisions the individual makes because that reflects how individuals think about their responsibility to others. Different

---

[10] This example illustrates why strict liability for abnormally dangerous activities is not a meaningful legal category. The more dangerous the activity, the more careful a reasonable person will be. The negligence standard adjusts automatically to the dangerousness of the activity, making the special category for abnormally dangerous activity redundant if that standard is thought to designate activity that is "really dangerous." Having strict liability for abnormally dangerous activities puts the law at odds with how people normally make decisions, creating a disjunction between the commands of the law and the way people think of their responsibilities. The interpretation I provide in this section for the concept of abnormally activities closes that disjunction by focusing on dangerousness along a different dimension of decisions about an activity.

kinds of decisions implicate different assignments of burdens and benefits and therefore different levels of responsibility. Individuals do not depend on some external definition about what they are doing (i.e., whether the activity is abnormally dangerous) or about a legal standard of responsibility (fault or no-fault). Conceptually, responsibility as an internal standard of behavior depends on an individual answering the following question: "Given the decision I am making, and its context, what factors ought I take into account if I want to act as an ideal decision maker would act?" That, I maintain, boils down to asking: "What is the appropriate way for me to think about the assignment of the burdens and benefits of my decision?"

Understanding the law in terms of the fault principle comports with the way individuals think about their own responsibility for the harms that befall another and therefore aligns the law's approaches to responsibility with the way individuals approach questions of their own responsibility. Moreover, it unifies our understanding of responsibility by making fault the exclusive ground for responsibility, where fault is sometimes in how one undertakes one's activities and is sometimes in failing to repair harm that would otherwise lie with the victim. This approach sees wrongful behavior and wrongfully refusing to repair harm to be forms of decision making that ought to be subject to legal intervention.[11]

The strategy is to recognize the different contexts in which one person must attend to the well-being of others and to use those contexts to understand why liability seems sometimes to be based on faulty conduct and at other times is to be based on faulty decisions to avoid repairing harm.[12] In this regard, the concept of strict liability embodies the concepts of due care and of the unreasonable failure to repair, both of which are fault-based concepts. As applied to property, it is helpful to focus on various activity decisions that an individual makes, which include both what use they make of their property (the traditional focus of property law) and the care with which they exercise that use.

When an individual has an obligation to others, no-fault liability disappears if we recognize the relationship between behaviors and repair and affirm their content in the fault concept. In some instances, an individual is responsible

---

[11] I use the word *activity* to encompass an individual's decisions about how to use her property. Property theory generally revolves around an owner's right to use the property. I borrow the idea of analyzing *activities* (rather than *uses*) from tort theory in order to allow us to disaggregate use decisions into various activity dimensions and to show the unity between torts and property.

[12] The two basic forms of responsibility were developed in Keating (2012), which is closely followed here. The treatment here differs by proposing, for reasons given in the text, that we view the failure to repair harm to be a form of unreasonable behavior rather than as strict liability.

The Fault Principle

for the harm to another because the individual has behaved wrongfully, in which case responsibility comes from faulty behavior. Negligence liability is the most prominent example. We can call this responsibility for primary conduct – that is, responsibility from behaving in a way that can be described as faulty. In other instances, however, an individual is responsible for the harm to another not because the harm was wrongfully inflicted but because even the harm from rightful conduct may be a wrong if the harm is not repaired. The most famous example, the *Vincent* case, held that a ship that damages a dock while reasonably, and with privilege, staying at the dock to avoid the dangers of a storm must nonetheless compensate the owner of the dock for damages to the dock. The steamship's primary conduct was reasonable, and yet the steamship company was required to compensate those who were hurt by its activity.

Similarly, in unjust enrichment the obligation to repair flows not from faulty behavior but from the faulty refusal to repair. Under that doctrine, an individual who is benefited by another's activity is required to compensate the individual conferring the benefit if it would be unjust not to compensate the individual. A builder who erects a home on another's property with the good faith and reasonable belief that it is the builder's property is generally entitled to be compensated for the benefit the building provides to the property's owner. Unjust enrichment cases are liability without fault in the limited sense that the injurer's primary conduct is not faulty. They are, nonetheless, cases about the kind of decisions a reasonable person ought to make, for they rest on the principle that sometimes an individual ought to accept the obligation to repair a victim's harm even though the individual has not acted unreasonably. Obviously, the individual who must pay for receiving an unsolicited benefit has done nothing wrong, but the loss imposed by failing to compensate for the benefit constitutes a wrong.

Although distinct, responsibility to take due care and responsibility for reasonable repair are linked through the fault principle. One form of responsibility is conduct-based harm (harm that results from faulty conduct); the second is harm-based harm (harm from rightful conduct that becomes a wrong when an individual fails to repair the harm). This can also be understood as the difference between responsibility for primary conduct (how one behaves before causing the harm) and responsibility for secondary conduct (how one behaves after the harm is incurred). Responsibility for wrongful conduct in the primary sense arises from misbehavior. Responsibility for wrongful conduct in the secondary sense arises from reasonable behavior that nonetheless requires compensation if harm results. Conduct-based responsibility is unconditional responsibility; if one engages in wrongful conduct, one is obligated to repair the harm. Wrongfully failing to repair the harm from rightful conduct is conditional liability – an individual may engage in the conduct as long as the individual makes reparations. Conduct-based harms are about unreasonable conduct; the failure to repair is about unreasonable harm (harm that unreasonably exists because it should have been repaired). Each is fault-based responsibility because both faulty behavior and faulty refusal to repair are based on decisions that an ideal reasonable decision maker would not have made.

Under this typology, strict liability is sometimes faulty primary behavior and sometimes faulty failure to repair. An individual undertaking activities must take reasonable care in how she carries out her activities. In the property context, that means an owner must invest in reasonable precautions to prevent harm (of a certain type) to his neighbors.[13] That is one branch of the law of nuisance, and it requires the property owner to invest in abatement technology in the same way that the law of negligence requires a driver to invest in reasonable precautions against harm.

Under the reasonable care requirement, individuals must also make reasonable decisions about where, when, how, and how often to undertake activities. These are called activity-level decisions in the torts literature, and they relate not to how carefully one does an activity but to other decisions an individual makes about her activities. Here the strict liability moniker is used to describe circumstances in which the decision maker has been reasonably careful in how she undertook the activity but could have reduced harm with more reasonable decisions about where, when, how, and how often to do her activities.[14] The decision about the activity is faulty in the sense that an individual, had she been reasonably other-regarding, would have made different decisions about where, when, how, and how often to do her activities. This category of responsibility crosses traditional tort and nuisance boundaries and shows us their essential unity. Under traditional tort cases, keeping a lion in the backyard is an unreasonable decision about location (an "abnormally dangerous activity"), whereas, under nuisance law, keeping a lion in the backyard is a nuisance. A driver could drive more carefully (due care), a factory could install scrubbers (due care), a gasoline truck could take a more reasonable route (location decision), a pig farm could locate farther from a retirement community (location decision), and a jazz trumpeter could practice with a mute (method of undertaking the activity) or only when neighbors are not at

[13] The qualification that harm must be *of a certain type* is necessary because, under nuisance law, an owner is not responsible for insignificant harms or for harms to a hypersensitive individual. The justification for these outcomes is discussed in Chapter 8.
[14] *See* Gerhart (2008). Many nuisance cases involve this kind of wrongful activity. The application of this principle to activity decisions is discussed at greater length in Chapter 8.

The Fault Principle

home (when to do an activity). Indeed, because both care in doing an activity and care in where, when, how, and how often to do an activity turn on whether the injurer's conduct is faulty in the primary sense, they can be fruitfully combined as forms of due care decisions.

If faulty activity-level decisions assume part of strict liability's work, what about the parts of strict liability that flow from failure to repair a harm caused or a benefit that it would be unjust to retain? In what way is this form of responsibility fault based?

The idea of strict liability for failure to repair a harm comes from *Vincent v. Lake Erie Steamship Co.*[15] This kind of responsibility responds to the moral intuition that if I borrow my neighbor's hose to put out a fire in my house, I will borrow it on the understanding that I will return it without damage. Common morality of the kind normally practiced by neighbors suggests that using another's property may be the reasonable thing to do, but that doing so is reasonable only if the property is returned in the condition in which it was borrowed. That is what *Vincent* and nuisance law require.

This common moral intuition is, in fact, an implementation of the reasonable person standard. Reasonable individuals invest in reasonable precautions when they undertake activities. In a normal negligence case, a case addressing how one conducts himself, individuals are asked to take due care by building the cost and inconvenience of due care into their activities. A case such as *Vincent* is no different. The steamship was entitled to stay at the dock by the doctrine of necessity; its activity was lawful. The harm to the owner of the dock *was* the precaution that was necessary to avoid damage to the ship; if that cost had not been borne, the ship and its crew would have been endangered. What the *Vincent* court did was what all negligence cases do. It made sure that individuals, in order to act reasonably, pay for the precautions of their activities; because damage to the dock was the precaution that reduced its risk, the steamship company was required to pay for it, and it could not thrust that cost on others (in this case, the owner of the dock). The steamship company could undertake the primary conduct (staying at the dock) only on the condition that it compensate the property owner who provided the precaution that justified staying at the dock in the first place.

Vincent can be recast as a nuisance case. The steamship's decision to stay at the dock was a nuisance because one property owner (the steamship company) inflicted harm on another property owner (the dock company) in order to protect the steamship company's property values. The activity of staying at the dock was reasonable (in the sense that the steamship was entitled to stay

[15] 109 Minn. 456 (Minn. 1910).

at the dock and the activity was done with reasonable care) but the steamship company could obtain the value of that activity only by imposing the cost of achieving that value on another property owner. The central moral core of the nuisance doctrine is clear: reasonable people do not enhance the value of their property by imposing significant[16] costs on others without agreeing to compensate the others for their harm.[17] More generically, in nuisance law courts are saying that investments in activities on property, although reasonable, may only be made if the owner who reaps the value of the investment also pays the cost of securing that value. Reasonable property owners and reasonable investors know this.[18]

A parallel nuisance case is *Boomer v. Atlantic Cement.*[19] There a cement factory did as much as it reasonably could to prevent harmful emissions[20] and was, for that reason, entitled to continue emitting the particles, but it was nonetheless required to pay for the harm it caused. Its obligation to repair the harm came not because its primary conduct was faulty, but because it was unreasonable to fail to repair the harm. In these kinds of cases, a reasonable person would undertake the activity only on the self-imposed condition that if the activity causes harm the individual would repair the harm. The obligation arises from the activity but not from the due care decisions an individual makes. It arises from the obligation, given the nature of the activity, to undertake the activity on the condition that any harm from the activity will be repaired.

The duty of reasonable repair also encompasses the concept of unjust enrichment, which is invoked when an individual is benefited under circumstance where it would be unjust not to compensate the person providing the benefit. The concept makes generous appearances in property law, including

---

[16] The idea that nuisance is actionable only for significant costs is necessary to account for those nuisance cases that refuse to shift responsibility to the injurer.

[17] Such nuisance cases are frequently understood as a private taking for which compensation is required, the private counterpart to the state's power of eminent domain. Eminent domain gives the state the power to take property for public use if it pays just compensation. It would be unusual indeed if a private party could, without paying compensation, engage in conduct that would take another's property while the state could not.

[18] This is evident, for example, in environmental impact fees.

[19] 26 N.Y. 2d 219 (N.Y. 1970).

[20] 26 N.Y. 2d at 222 ("In large measure adequate technical procedures are yet to be developed and some that appear possible may be economically impracticable"). Although the court did not discuss whether the cement plant could have been put in a more reasonable location, it is probably true that moving the cement plant to locations with fewer neighbors would greatly increase the cost of cement because of transportation costs. The location of this cement plant was probably reasonable given the relevant tradeoffs. *See generally* Dobris (1989–1990).

in cases where the plaintiff in good faith and reasonably builds on the defendant's property. In such cases, the defendant owns the building by virtue of owning the land on which the building was built, but the defendant is required to compensate the plaintiff for the improvement to the land in order to avoid unjust enrichment. In this form of responsibility, the defendant has committed no wrong; the obligation to compensate the plaintiff arises because it would be unjust for the defendant to fail to compensate the plaintiff for the benefits the defendant received.[21] The fault lies not in being enriched but in the failure to repay the plaintiff for the enrichment. Whereas a nuisance case involves a faulty failure to repair harm, an unjust enrichment case involves a faulty failure to repay a benefit that it would be unjust to keep. The notion that it is unreasonable to accept certain kinds of benefits without paying for them is the flip side of the notion that it is unreasonable to impose certain kinds of burdens on another without paying for them.

More broadly, what makes unjust enrichment unjust is the sense that burdens and benefits are not shared justly. The fair apportionment of benefits and burdens is what unites trespass law, for example, with unjust enrichment law. In trespass law, the benefits and burdens are allied on the side of the owner. The owner absorbs all the burdens of ownership and is able to reap all the benefits. One cannot lawfully pick an apple from an owner's apple tree without permission, which is, for normative reasons that will become clear later, the benefit of ownership. But if a nonowner mistakenly and in good faith builds a structure on an owner's land, the nonowner has absorbed the burden of building that structure, and it would violate the fair sharing of burdens and benefits to allow the owner to absorb all the benefits of that investment. Courts have long acknowledged that one who trespasses on another's property, cuts down and carries off trees, and makes them into barrel hoops may keep the benefits of her efforts if she compensates the owner for the trees she took. Similarly, courts are increasingly establishing doctrine that allows the mistaken improver or one with a mistaken encroachment to recover something for her burden.[22]

---

[21] By contrast, wrongful enrichment is taking something from the plaintiff through faulty conduct; as in a negligence case, it involves a wrong independent of the enrichment. See Birks (2001).

[22] The duty that gives rise to the obligation to repair a benefit that it would be unjust to keep comes from the relationship between the parties. In property law it arises from the duty that neighbor owes neighbor. In contract law it arises from the duty that contracting parties owe each other.

In summary, we can think of responsibility for the harms that befall another as flowing from four dimensions of an individual's decisions about her activity:

Fault in Activity Decisions[23]
Unreasonable decisions about how careful to be
Unreasonable decisions about where, when, how, and how often to do an activity

Fault in Failure to Repair[24]
The harm from primary activity
The benefits accepted and unjustly retained

Before moving on to show how the equality principle provides a justified methodology for the assignment of burdens and benefits in the two forms of responsibility, let me summarize the main points of this section. Responsibility flows from an individual's choices about what to do with his or her life. Some, but not all, of those choices implicate responsibility for the well-being of others, and the scope of responsibility depends on the choices the individual has made. Responsibility therefore flows from an individual's activity decisions and is tied to how much care an ideal decision maker would put into his activities and whether an ideal decision maker would undertake his activities only on the understanding that repairing harm is a central part of that activity. Under the typology developed thus far, when an individual chooses an activity, the individual must consider how careful to be when she undertakes her activities, whether to undertake her activities with the implied promise to compensate others for the harm her activities cause, and whether to undertake her activities with an implied promise to compensate another for the benefit the other has conferred on her. Each of these decisions requires the decision maker to appropriately assign the burdens and benefits of the decision. Each form of responsibility demands that individuals make reasonable decisions,

---

[23] These two categories of fault-based decisions about primary activity are aspects of due care. They describe the two dimensions of care that all individuals must take when they are under an obligation to exercise due care on behalf of another.

[24] Although the two categories of responsibility in the failure-to-repair category are different, they share the characteristic that they require the individual to determine whether she should repair the harm. For that reason, they are responsive to identical methodologies, albeit from different directions. In the category for "failure to repair harm from primary activity," the individual is asking whether his activities should bear the cost of harm. In the category denominated "failure to repair benefits conferred and unjustly retained" the individual is asking whether an individual is responsible for returning benefits conferred.

The Requirements of Equal Freedom

and each is therefore an implementation of the reasonable person standard. People ought to expect to be held to that standard, and the law can demand neither more nor less from an individual.

Of course, none of the categories of responsibility is self-defining or automatically applied. Each requires a methodology of application: a definition of due care, an identification of which activities can be undertaken only on the condition that harm from the activity be repaired, and an identification of which benefits cannot justly be kept. In order to develop such a methodology, we must understand each form of responsibility as an expression of the requirement of equal freedom.

6.3 THE REQUIREMENTS OF EQUAL FREEDOM

A just society is one that shows respect for the equal freedom of each individual, and the law is just if it reflects the requirements of equal freedom. Several propositions flow from this principle. First, each individual may chose his goals and means of reaching those goals, subject only to the equal freedom of every other individual to do the same. Such freedom is essential because it forms the basis of individual autonomy and responsibility. From the perspective of autonomy, it preserves choice, and therefore the opportunity to grow as an individual; that is why the theory here depends on the choices an individual has made. On the other hand, it imposes responsibility, for it casts on the individual responsibility for the choices she makes, including the burdens that normally come with those choices. The principle of equal freedom also requires that the individual respect the equal freedom of every other individual and that she exercise her freedom in a way that appropriately accounts for the equal freedom of others. The assignment of burdens and benefits must be done in accordance with the requirements of equal freedom.

In this section, I show how the two categories of responsibility – the responsibility of due care and the responsibility to reasonable repair – respond to the demands of equal freedom.

Entitlements are statements of the responsibility of injurer and victim to each other and to themselves.[25] An entitlement awarded to a victim says that

---

[25] The convention of referring to the injurer and the victim does not denote responsibility; it simply denotes the person who feels she has a claim against another and the person against whom the claim is brought. A victim is a claimant, not a person with a just claim, and an injurer is a person against whom a claim has been made, not necessarily a person who is responsible for the harm. Injurer and victim are in a relationship by virtue of the fact that one may have caused harm to another (including the failure to repair harm). Causation and harm create a relationship that, if proven, is sufficient to justify the court in determining whether it wants to intervene to shift the loss.

the injurer should have acted differently toward the victim (either behaving differently or repairing harm that could not be avoided). An entitlement awarded the injurer says that there is nothing the injurer needs to do in terms of his responsibility for the victim's burdens. The award of an entitlement is a bilateral statement, saying something significant about an injurer's and a victim's responsibility to each other and also to themselves. It reflects the fact that, under a regime of equal respect for the freedom of every individual, each individual is responsible for both her own life, and, when the circumstances call for it, for the equal freedom of other individuals. Importantly, the question of which party should be awarded the entitlement is separate from the question of what remedy protects the entitlement or even whether the entitlement must be purchased.

The two general categories of responsibility – responsibility for behavior and responsibility for repair – correspond to two different ways in which burdens and benefits of decisions are allocated. Decisions about how careful to be are governed by a regime of shared burdens. The injurer is required to exercise due care but is not responsible for harms that could not be eliminated with due care. Decisions about whether to repair another's harms are governed by a regime of unilateral responsibility; the duty to repair is either there or not. A regime of non-liability applies in all other instances – that is, when the activity is done with sufficient investment in due care, when the activity does not require the actor to be other-regarding, and when the activity results in benefits that it would be just to keep. In other words, responsibility is either shared (because one individual extinguishes her responsibility to the other by taking due care, leaving the other to avoid the harm by his own due care decisions) or responsibility is unilateral (because it requires one individual or the other to be responsible for the harm that cannot be avoided with due care).

What accounts for the different forms of responsibility and how do the different forms of responsibility reflect the equality principle?

6.3.1 Shared Responsibility, Avoidable Harm

The regime of shared responsibility is associated with situations in which individuals act without knowledge of the harm and the harm might be avoided if either injurer or victim, or both, took greater care to protect the well-being of themselves and potential victims. It is therefore associated not only with due care decisions, where comparative negligence makes the regime of shared burdens explicit, but also with decisions about where, when, how, and how often to undertake an activity (the range of activity decisions that are now associated with strict liability). It is associated with the privilege of a nonowner

The Requirements of Equal Freedom

to go on the owner's property, when both the owner (victim) and nonowner (injurer) have the ability to avoid the harm if they think more carefully about the equal freedom of the other. A farmer who houses migrant workers on his land has a duty to those workers by virtue of the benefit they provide him. A migrant worker is therefore entitled to reasonable access by social workers, and owner and nonowner share responsibility for reasonably eliminating the harm that one or the other would suffer if the counterparty did not invest in due care.[26] A regime of shared responsibility also applies to those nuisance cases in which a different decision by one or both of the neighbors could avoid the harm. If the harm can be avoided at reasonable cost by moving or otherwise modifying one of the activities, the party who can avoid the harm should do so (leaving separate the issue of who should pay for the activity change).

The regime of shared responsibility is justified by the equality principle. If an individual has a duty to look out for the well-being of another and can avoid harming that well-being at reasonable sacrifice of her own interests, the individual ought to do so. But responsibility ends at the point where due care is taken, and losses beyond that point fall on the victim. The victim may be the least cost avoider and the no-responsibility principle inherent in shared responsibility puts pressure on the victim to protect himself. Each individual, in choosing an activity, must be prepared to invest reasonably in efforts to minimize the social harm the activity imposes. If an individual does otherwise, the individual is using the other as a means to her ends, not as an end in itself. In accident law, the victim may have caused the harm through contributory negligence. In nuisance law, the victim may be able to avoid the harm by investing in reasonable abatement technology.

Even when the harm cannot be avoided by reasonable care, the regime of shared burdens that allows losses to lie where they fall is justified by the need to maximize individual freedom consistent with the equal freedom of other individuals. A basic tenant of responsibility is that people ought not be responsible for harm they cannot control. Because the common law invokes the system of shared responsibility when an actor does not know of the harm that will result, that harm, once due care has been taken, lies effectively beyond the actor's control. Such harm, when it occurs, must, like the harm from lightning, lie where it falls. In this way, no individual's activity is privileged over any other individual's activity by virtue of the nature of the activity, and each individual is free to pick activities without fear that the choice of activity, by itself,

---

[26] Courts have made this interrelationship explicit. Social service providers must respect the privacy and other property interests of the farmer; the farmer must grant effective access. Each is a way of sharing responsibility for harm that can be avoided.

imposes an unequal burden on the individual. The injurer who takes due care is not held responsible for the harm that another suffers, because nothing within the reasonable control of the injurer would avoid the loss.

The justification for applying the principle of equal freedom to relieve an injurer of responsibility is that each party wants to make choices about, and engage in, activities free of the burdens that other persons might impose by *their* choice of activities. When the injurer does not know that harm will result, the law imposes burdens on both the injurer's and victim's activities (the burden of due care) and allows the unintended burdens that cannot be avoided with due care to lie where they fall. The assignment of unavoidable burdens is a kind of default position, the best we can do to deal with forces that are beyond human control. The allocation of unavoidable burdens is not itself justified except out of respect for the equal freedom of the injurer not to be required to unduly circumscribe her activities. As a result, the assignment of the unavoidable burdens is by luck – a morally neutral assignment reflecting the unavoidability of the burden and the fact that, because it is beyond the scope of human control, it must lie where it falls.

Equal freedoms imply the equal freedom to impose harms and the equal freedom to absorb burdens. This occurs when the benefits of the injurer's activity do not depend on imposing burdens on others. A driver benefits from the activity of driving without imposing burdens on others because there is no necessary harm to the other. The benefits of driving do not depend on the imposition of burdens once the driver takes reasonable care, and the law therefore allows the driver to be free from burdens that could not be avoided.

Put another way, the division of burdens and benefits in this way is justified because decisions about due care implicate the freedom of two individuals, each of whom wants to undertake his or her chosen activities without the restraint imposed by the other individual's freedom of activity. If the law were to impose all the burdens of unintended harm from the two activities on one of the individuals, it would be imposing a burden that the individual undertaking the activity could avoid only by abandoning the activity. The benefits of the activity would be lost.[27] The failure to repair the harm is not unreasonable because the harm was not knowingly inflicted, and we do not want the person undertaking the activity to do so under the condition of having to protect against even unavoidable risks. That would impose too great a burden on the injurer's activity.

[27] This is an application of the concept of reciprocity. Each activity undertakes the reciprocal burden of due care, and each accepts the reciprocal burden of harm that cannot be controlled by human decisions – that is, the harm that comes from bad luck. No individual is allowed to ask another individual to bear that individual's bad luck because no person has a claim against another to relieve the harm he or she suffers as a result of bad luck.

6.3.2 Unilateral Responsibility: Unavoidable Harm

A system of shared responsibility functions to eliminate only harm that can be avoided by due care – that is, to eliminate harm that can be avoided by the reasonable surrender of freedom by either injurer or victim. It leaves open the question of how a court ought to define entitlements with regard to the harm that cannot be avoided with a reasonable surrender of freedom. In cases where harm is reasonably incurred, courts must confront the question of whether the loss should lie where it falls or be shifted to the injurer. These are regimes of unilateral responsibility: when a loss cannot reasonably be avoided, the court must confront the question of which party should bear the loss. There are two situations. In the negligence regime, courts allow the loss to lie where it falls once injurer and victim have taken due care; that is the essence of negligence – losses that cannot be avoided are borne by the victim. On the other hand, where an actor knowingly imposes a loss, courts identify losses that must be repaired (cases conventionally thought of as strict liability or unjust enrichment), courts will shift the loss to the injurer (the person who injures another by not repairing an unreasonable loss).

The justification for this category of unilateral responsibility is its inevitability. Losses happen, and if they cannot be avoided through reasonable care they must fall on, or be assigned to, either the injurer or the victim. If one neighbor needs to practice his trumpet because he is a jazz musician and his neighbor needs quiet because she is a math genius working on a theorem, the court must decide which neighbor is entitled to a remedy against the conflicting use of the other.[28] If the interference can be abated without awarding an entitlement (perhaps by installing soundproofing), the court must determine which neighbor is required to pay for abating the interference, which is the same as awarding an entitlement to the other party.

The difficult justificatory question is how the court determines whether losses should be shifted – that is, whether the burden of a loss of well-being should be on the injurer or the victim. Because the injurer knows of the harm, the injurer knows of the possibility of repairing the harm, and the injurer therefore cannot avoid the choice of whether to repair the harm. Unlike the instance of shared burdens, where the injurer does not know of the harm and therefore is not required to make a choice about the harm (only a choice about the level of care she takes), when the actor knows of the harm, the actor

---

[28] If the interference can be abated without awarding an entitlement (perhaps by installing soundproofing), the court must determine which neighbor is required to pay for abating the interference, which is the same as awarding an entitlement to the other party.

must make a decision about whether to exercise that choice in the victim's favor in order to uphold the requirements of the equality principle.

This form of responsibility corresponds to the demands of equal freedom because the choice of an activity that knowingly causes harm subjects another to an unfreedom that the other ought to bear only if the harm is socially sanctioned by a norm that allows the loss to lie where it falls. Because the harm is knowingly imposed, it would disrespect another individual's equal freedom to be subject to the choices the actor has made when the harm is not the kind that the society, for institutional or normative reasons, recognizes as a legitimate product of the activity.

Nuisance law illustrates this principle. One who knowingly creates a nuisance is responsible for the harm caused unless the harm is understood in that society to be the kind of harm that is a legitimate product of the activity. The principle applies the notion that it is wrongful to knowingly use another's property to increase the value of one's own property because doing so privileges an injurer's use of property over a victim's use of property. Privileging one's property in that way shows disrespect for the equal freedom of the other unless it is done under circumstances sanctioned by a community norm. Nuisances that are consistent with the norms of the community – those that are insubstantial or not unreasonably imposed – lie where they fall because if they did not the victim would be violating the equal freedom of the injurer by imposing a burden on the injurer that the norm determines ought to be his. The rule against hypersensitivity is similarly justified. An individual's hypersensitivity is bad luck, but it is not bad luck that a neighbor ought to be required to anticipate or absorb.

The privilege to compete follows the same geometry of unilateral burdens. Injury inflicted through fair competition is privileged by a community norm that sanctions the injury as a legitimate byproduct of the competitive activity. Injury inflicted through unfair competition – that which the norms of the community suggest are not an important byproduct of the activity – must be repaired by the injurer.

Similarly, the requirements of equal freedom compel an individual to disgorge himself of unearned benefits out of respect for the person conferring those benefits. The obligation is incurred when the benefits are ones that the benefiting individual would normally have acquired only by taking on burdens, and when the person conferring them would ordinarily not have taken the burdens in question if the individual were not able to also reap the benefits of the burdens. If individual A benefits individual B under such circumstances, and individual B were not required to compensate A in those circumstances, B would not be respecting A's equal freedom because B would end up with an unearned benefits and A would end up with an undeserved burden (one without offsetting benefit). A would not have exercised her freedom to burden herself in that way, and B would not have expected to exercise his freedom to benefit in that way without also taking on burdens. Two individuals starting in a position of equal freedom would end up in a position of unequal freedom because one would be made better off at the expense of the other, without any offsetting increase in the other's freedom. If B is to show respect for the equal freedom of A, individual B must, to act morally, compensate individual A for the unearned benefit. This is the reasonable thing for B to do because the requirements of the reasonable person are to show respect for the equal freedom of the other.

In sum, we can understand the unity of the fault principle in the following way: individuals must avoid activities that impose unreasonable harm on others. This applies to all activities, including driving and making cement. Individuals must therefore take due care in how they undertake their activities, investing in reasonable measures to reduce harm. And, individuals must also make reasonable decisions about whether to repair the harms another incurs, using a methodology of thinking about repair that takes into account the requirements of equal freedom. Victims win when the injurer has failed to take due care, when the injurer has knowingly taken something from the victim that the victim is not required to share, when the decision to undertake the activity implies a decision to repair harm from the activity, and when the injurer unreasonably refuses to repay unearned benefits. Injurers win when they are under no duty to the victim, when they take due care, and when they are entitled to undertake their activities without agreeing to repair harm from those activities.

6.4 THE METHODOLOGY OF MORAL DECISIONS: THE VEIL OF IGNORANCE

We have seen that courts must determine whether the activities of the injurer or the victim should bear the harms of human activity that are effectively unavoidable, and it does so under circumstances in which each activity is entitled to equal respect. What methodology ought courts use to make such an interpersonal comparison, and can the law develop a methodology that mirrors the way we want individuals to think about the well-being of other individuals? Because the assignment of entitlements inevitably involves a thought experiment, the central issue is which thought experiment is most appealing.

Methodologies that facilitate the kind of comparisons the law must make are one of two types. Some methodologies seek to award entitlements on the basis of the value of the activity to the individuals (and thus to society). I reject such methodologies for the reasons given in Subsection 6.4.1. Other methodologies seek a principle for awarding entitlements that responds to a neutral evaluation of the basis on which the well-being of one person can be sacrificed for the well-being of another. I explain and support those methodologies in Subsection 6.4.2.

6.4.1 Comparative Individual Valuations

Distributing unavoidable costs might be done to maximize the value of the two activities. That is a plausible goal because it implies that society could not be made better off with any other assignment of costs. That, indeed, is how Coase articulated the solution to the problem of social costs. He suggested that courts should attempt to "maximize the value of production"[29] or engage in "weighing up the gains that would accrue from eliminating these harmful effects against the gains that accrue from allowing them to continue."[30] Comparing the personal or social value of two activities is not, however, a self-defining objective and, in any event, misses the more important point that entitlements to be free from harm ought to be based on a social valuation of the activities.

One might ask whether the trumpet player's interest in practice is more valuable to him than the need of the mathematician for quiet. This might lead one to ask what options each has and by how much awarding the entitlement to each person would improve the quality of his or her life, a kind of qualitative valuation. This, of course, runs into the problem of comparing interpersonal welfare and raises questions of whether we should adjust our assessment of the value of the interests by taking into account the social position of the two neighbors. Should it matter that the jazz trumpeter is a wealthy son of a rich family or a starving artist? Should it matter that one of the neighbors is disabled and cannot easily leave her condominium? All sorts of circumstances could influence the value of each person's interest in an entitlement, so that each case would have to be decided anew, without any sure way of determining which factors would influence the decision one way or the other.

Some read Coase to suggest that courts should determine what solution the parties would have bargained for if there were no transaction costs, which amounts to a test of which party is willing to pay the most for the entitlement, a thought experiment that puts entitlements up for auction based on some

---

[29] Coase (1960) at 15.
[30] Coase (1960) at 26.

hypothetical system of imputed value.[31] This monetizing approach asks each neighbor how much he or she would be willing to pay to have the entitlement, which would use willingness to pay as a proxy for the value of the interest each has in being awarded the entitlement. Under this approach, we could avoid making decisions based on idiosyncratic circumstances by asking how much most people in the same situation would be willing to pay for an entitlement of that type. This is the market-mimicking device that economists advance. That runs into another problem, however, for wealth is not distributed equally, and using willingness to pay as a measure of the value to each of the neighbors would undoubtedly be skewed by the preexisting distribution of wealth. Ronald Dworkin has suggested that we solve that problem of skewed preferences by imagining that wealth is evenly distributed, so that willingness to pay would reflect only distribution-adjusted preferences for the entitlement and not the preexisting distribution of wealth. That approach might be integrated with Amartya Sen's notion that we must adjust for the capabilities of each of the neighbors by also imagining that the neighbors have both equal wealth and equal capabilities.

All of these bargaining solution exhibit a degree of circularity.[32] How much one is willing to pay for an entitlement depends on whether one owns or does not own the entitlement. Individuals generally pay more to keep something they own than they do to acquire something they do not own. Because we are trying to determine which individual "owns" the entitlement, it is circular to construct a hypothetical bargaining situation in which individuals would bargain for the entitlement without knowing who owns the entitlement.

The well-known difficulties of determining how much each neighbor values an entitlement to be free from the harm miss a more fundamental objection: each of the methods for determining the value that individuals put on the entitlement assumes that the distribution of the entitlement ought to be based on individual valuations rather than on the rate of exchange that society expects for the valuations. In my view, each of these methods misunderstands the role of the individual in determining entitlements and is based on confusion about the way an individual's valuation of her interests develops into entitlements. An individual's valuation of an interest represents a claim that tells us what that individual wants; whether the claim will be recognized is quite another matter. Bargaining for entitlements also misses the central basis on which exchanges of well-being take place. The valuation methods ask how neighbors would organize an exchange over the entitlements, but valuing one's interest

[31] Posner (2003) at 52.
[32] Kennedy (1981) and Kelman (1979).

is only one part of the exchange process; even as a market-mimicking device, comparing individual valuations of a potential entitlement is an incomplete approach. I argue that entitlements are created not by the valuations put on things by individuals in isolation, but by the way those valuations are socially understood in terms of the tradeoffs between various individual evaluations. Because there is no market in entitlements, we need to construct a method of determining the tradeoffs between various claims to entitlements.[33] The valuations that transform claims into entitlements must preexist, and stand outside of, individual valuations rather than follow from them.

The crucial distinction is this: the law creates entitlements so that individuals can organize their relationships around the expectations embodied in the entitlements, including (when exchanges are not blocked) exchanging entitlements when the exchange yields higher value to both individuals. But entitlements are not created by the value that people put on them. Entitlements are created by the relationships that people form, and they reflect the values that people embody in their decisions as they form relationships. Entitlements are an ideal type, reflecting norms of ideal behavior as people interact.

In Chapter 4, I showed that the creation of the institution of private property depended on members of the community accepting claims to resources when those claims are consistent with terms that the community considers acceptable. Other entitlements, including legal entitlements, form in the same way that property rights emerged. Entitlements mature from claims to entitlements when people have a reason for accepting the claim and respecting it, based on their beliefs about whether the values that lie behind the entitlement are acceptable to them as members of the community. Those values are not the values that individuals put on entitlements in support of their own interests, but the values that individuals put on social interaction generally, ones that are formed and reformed over the years and that embody values people use in their successful cooperation.

In other words, the reason the law ought not award entitlements on the basis of how two individuals value the entitlement is that we are then asking

[33] I argue, in other words, that entitlements are not subject to an auction, even if we equalize the resources available to people who engage in the bidding. Auctions occur when people accept the rules of the auction, which specify that the object of the exchange be auctioned off to the highest bidder. But an auction is only one exchange mechanism, one in which people are willing to exchange on the terms specified in the auction. Other types of exchanges occur under different rules of exchange. Exchange in competitive markets occurs under rules that specify that only price takers may engage in exchange. Exchanges that occur under conditions of bilateral monopoly follow a still different set of norms of exchange. When society is dealing with something as fundamental as the right to be free of a cost imposed by another individual, an auction model seems sterile.

The Methodology of Moral Decisions: The Veil of Ignorance

them only their self-regarding interest, not their other-regarding interests, and are not inquiring into the social rate of exchange between the interests of the two people. Entitlements ought to reflect the social rate of exchange between the interests represented by two activities, for the social rate of exchange is the only legitimate way of comparing the social welfare of the two activities.

Here I repeat the claim I advanced in Chapter 4. Markets work not only by asking each individual to determine how much the exchange is worth to her; markets also ask each party to determine what terms of exchange would be acceptable to them if an exchange could take place. Each individual facing a possible exchange evaluates what is "in it for them" at various rates of exchange. That is the process akin to determining the value of an entitlement, and that process determines how much each person would give up in order to get the benefits of exchange. But that determination is not the only one the parties make. The individual evaluation of the benefits of exchange – that is, how much the exchange is worth to each individual – must be coupled with a determination of which rates of exchange of well-being are acceptable to each individual. That second determination asks the basis of the comparative valuation and requires cooperation to find a rate of exchange that is acceptable to both individuals. The range of acceptable rates of exchange determines the basis on which the bargain is formed and therefore establishes the outcome of the bargain, which in turn determines the entitlement of each party to the exchange. In this way, entitlements in exchange are not developed and awarded to the one who values the exchange the most but are awarded on the basis of which rate of exchange between the independent valuations is acceptable to both of the parties. If a market-mimicking device is to be used to award entitlements it must take into account not only how much each party values the entitlement but also the rate of exchange that each party find to be acceptable in the exchange.

In summary, both quantitative and qualitative methodologies for addressing competing claims problematically assume that individual valuations are determinative for the creation of entitlements, whereas, in fact, it is the valuations of the rate of exchange between the individual valuations, and their acceptability to each of the parties, that determines the creation of entitlements. The parties are determining not only the benefits of the entitlement for each of them individually, but also the division of burdens and benefits that each would accept in order to get those benefits. The parties must arrive at a division of burdens and benefits that they each understand as acceptable. As a result, we must ask: What is it that makes the rate of exchange of individual valuations acceptable to each of the parties? More concretely, we must ask: Given the way that people normally think about how to trade the need for quiet and the need for loud activities, what rate of exchange are they likely to use to determine the entitlements to noise and loud activities? That is, we need a theory that allows us to evaluate the various kinds of tradeoffs that people make. For that we must look to the methods people normally use to make comparisons of well-being.

6.4.2 Neutral Valuations

Philosophers seeking consilience between deontic and consequential theories have proposed several methodologies that might be used to determine when an individual is entitled to have his unavoidable harms absorbed by another individual. For Adam Smith, the impartial spectator would evaluate the sentiments of individuals. For Thomas Scanlon, courts might award entitlements by looking for a principle that no individual could reasonably reject.[34] For Derek Parfit, courts would look for a "principle that is optimific,[35] uniquely universally willable, and not reasonably rejectable."[36] Each of these methodologies seek a neutral valuation of comparative well-being that allows the analyst to determine which consequences matter and how we ought to think about a principle that takes seriously the equal freedom of each individual.

Despite the erudition of these theories, the veil of ignorance seems to be a superior methodology for thinking about how courts ought to award entitlements. I defend the veil of ignorance here not in comparison to the inherent merits of the other theories, but because the veil of ignorance comports with the way individuals think about their responsibilities in their everyday affairs.

The veil of ignorance is a thought experiment that allows an individual to reason about the appropriate way to make a decision (and the appropriate decision to make) when the individual must integrate her self-regarding and her other-regarding obligations. It asks this basic question: If the individual did not know her status in the world and therefore did not know how she would be affected by the decision she is making, what factors would she take into account, and how would she take them into account in making the decision? The objective is to ask the individual to put aside her self-regarding impulses by taking away her ability to reason from the consequences that reflect her status in society and to reason instead toward a decision that she would make if she did not know her status. Behind the veil of ignorance, the decision maker would acknowledge that the decision would have different consequences for

---

[34] Scanlon (1998) at 189–90.
[35] For Parfit the term "optimific" pulls in the optimizing quality of utilitarian theory.
[36] Parfit (2011).

different individuals, depending on their actual status in society, but would not know the impact on her. By keeping the decision maker ignorant about how the rule would affect her, the veil of ignorance provides a method of neutral decision making – in the sense of requiring the decision maker to reason toward a decision that would be made regardless of personal consequences – one that implements the requirements of moral decisions under the equality principle. The veil of ignorance is a variation of the principle that has almost universal acceptance across societies and religions: do unto others as you would have them do unto you if you were in their position.[37] It is commended by both its universality and its particularism.[38]

The veil of ignorance neither denies decisions have consequences, nor does it require non-consequentialist reasoning.[39] It does, however, require the decision maker to make a reasoned decision about which consequences matter and how consequences matter, and it rules out the possibility that the decision maker will give undue weight to the consequences that reflect the status of the decision maker. The veil of ignorance recognizes that decisions must be made on the basis of assertions about how the empirical world works and that some consequences of decisions matter. It simply rules out reliance on consequences that would be given undue weight when the decision maker knows what is at stake for her in the decision.

Reasoning from behind the veil of ignorance does not provide answers. It provides a way of thinking about the values that one ought to take into account when making decisions. It allows discussion and debate to focus on how one ought to think about moral decisions and to highlight various points of view that must be considered (or may not be considered) when determining what action is moral. Two issues are prominent behind the veil of ignorance. First, analysis can focus on what factors are impermissible when reasoning from behind the veil of ignorance; second, analysis can focus on how an ideal decision maker would assign the burdens and benefits of her decision as between the various individuals affected by the decision.

---

[37] Binmore (2006).
[38] The methodology of the veil of ignorance illustrates how a universal obligation can coexist with local variations in ethical behavior. The near-universal prevalence of the Golden Rule shows that the methodology of personal decision making can be universal even though its application can result in different moral decisions made under that requirement in different cultures and religions. The implementation of the universal requirements of a moral decision will vary with the values that are taken into account in making the decision and will therefore result in a wide variety of social systems, each of which is considered, by its participants, to be moral.
[39] The obligation to act as if one had used a methodology of moral decision making behind the veil of ignorance *is* obligatory and non-consequential; the actual decision process takes some, but not all, consequences into account.

As for the first issue – the determination of which factors are impermissible from behind the veil of ignorance – the word "status" denotes those factors about an individual that are relevant to the decision but are likely to be given undue weight by the individual making the decision. Status relates to the socioeconomic position of the decision maker and identifies factors that would allow the decision maker to either gain or lose from the decision. It identifies the self-interested impulses of the decision maker that must be held in check in making decisions. A farmer who employs migrant workers and must decide whether to deny social workers access to the property must reason toward a decision without knowing his status as either a farmer or a migrant worker. The interests of the farmer as farmer would be relevant to the decision, of course, because the burden on the farmer is relevant to the decision. But behind the veil of ignorance the farmer would have to reason toward a decision that he would be comfortable with if he did not know his status in the world. If he had to live as a migrant worker with the maxim he came up with, would he accept the treatment under that maxim as just? The decision maker would take into account general knowledge about the relative position of farmers and migrant workers, but not whether he would profit from the decision by being a migrant worker or farmer.

The second order decision determines what decision a person would make if the person would make a decision based only on permissible factors. This determination depends on the values the person would take into account when determining the relative weight to be given to the interests of the individuals who would be affected by the rule. Would an ideal decision maker believe that imposing on the farmer's ownership interests would do more harm than burdening the migrant worker's ability to receive social services? As economists have reminded us, this is a form of cost-benefit analysis in the sense that we are assigning entitlements based on a comparison of two possible states of the world. Unlike much economic analysis, however, the terms of the comparison would not be influenced by ability to pay or by the preexisting social status of the individuals. That is ruled out by the veil of ignorance because the social status of the decision maker is ruled out. Instead, decision making must be based on abstract thinking about the values society expects an ideal decision maker to use to compare two states of the world. Because the farmer and the migrant workers are entitled to equal respect, they are also entitled to have their interests determined on the basis of values that are neutrally determined, not determined by their status.

That means that in thinking about each individual's loss of autonomy or capability or personhood from the award of the entitlement, the decision maker would have to think about how society expects those indicia of well-being to be accounted for when the well-being of each cannot be accommodated. The law is asking: What is our social construction of the values that support decisions about resource use? Importantly, the decision maker behind the veil of ignorance does not need to know what the law says on the subject. The purpose of the examination behind the veil of ignorance is to determine which party has an entitlement to be free of harm; that, of course, is the question of what the law is. What the decision maker behind the veil of ignorance needs to know is the values that underlie the law – the values of autonomy, capability enhancement, and personhood – and how the community in which the entitlement is being questioned would view those values in the context in which the decision must be made.[40]

The determination made in this way is value-laden because the decision maker must resort to values that are commonly used in the community for making decisions of that kind.

6.5 CONCLUSION

In this chapter, I have argued that moral, other-regarding individuals make decisions that assign the burdens and benefits of their decisions in an appropriate way. When an individual has a duty to others, the individual's duty consists of the duty of due care and a duty to reasonably repair another's harm that could not have been avoided. The duty of due care is the duty to be reasonably other-regarding, which requires the individual to take burdens that benefit another. The duty of repair depends on whether the victim is entitled to compensation for the injury that the victim would otherwise have to bear alone. The law determines such entitlements by asking the individual to make decisions from behind the veil of ignorance, reasoning about how the individual would want to be treated if the individual did not know which party was the injurer and which the victim. This requires an assessment of how the community is likely to view the relative value of the freedom from harm that must be allocated.

---

[40] Behind the veil of ignorance decision makers will have to decide a range of other issues about how to account for the consequences of decisions. Many of these will be context specific. The decision maker may have to determine whether to adopt an attitude of risk aversion, for example. This is likely to be context specific, which will require the decision maker to determine whether the average decision maker in that context would be risk averse or risk neutral.

PART II

APPLICATIONS

Part I developed a theory of private law that explains and justifies the law's role in coordinating decisions about resources by individuals. This part applies that theory to the property areas of greatest significance in private law: exclusion, nuisance, concurrent decision making, and decision making over time.

Chapter 7 argues that the right to exclude is best understood and justified as an expression of the no-duty principle of private law, whereas limits on the right to exclude are explained and justified by the duty principle. Chapter 8 suggests that neighbors have an obligation to other neighbors to reasonably reduce the social harm of their activities, and it explains how the law allocates reasonably unavoidable harms to reflect equal respect for the activities of each individual. Chapter 9 suggests that when owners have joint decision-making authority over a resource (because of their equal right to own or their equal right to use the resource), the law provides a framework for decision making that maximizes the possibility of cooperative outcomes. Chapter 10 argues that when ownership is divided over time, the law functions to protect the market so that it can represent the interests of future owners and to regulate the relationship between successive owners so that no owner imposes burdens on future owners that are not offset by countervailing benefits.

7 Exclusion

The right to exclude is the most characteristic and central right of ownership. But it is not unlimited.[1] The right to exclude gives way when a nonowner is privileged to use, or has an irrevocable license or easement to use, the owner's property. This leads to the following disjunction. The right to exclude is justifiable on economic and philosophical grounds, and we understand why nonowners are privileged to use an owner's property under various circumstances. But if we are to understand the right to exclude and its limitations as rights that flow from a unified theory of social values, we need what property theory has not yet provided – a normative basis for locating the boundary between exclusion and access, one that justifies how and why, in particular cases, the law favors exclusion over access or access over exclusion. What social value explains and justifies the right to exclude and simultaneously explains and justifies why the right to exclude is sometimes limited?

The right to exclude at private law has a distinctive analytical structure that reflects the exclusion/access dichotomy. Following Tom Merrill and Henry Smith, we can understand exclusion cases as coming in two categories. The core exclusion concept is that an owner may exclude for any and no reason. When a case is put in this category, the owner need not give good reasons, or even any reason, for excluding. Indeed, nonowners are to infer the owner's right to exclude – the command to "keep out" – from the fact of ownership. A boundary marker is its own "keep out" sign. As a result, an owner's decision to exclude an individual who has neither a privilege nor permission to enter the property is not subject to judicial scrutiny, and the state may not

---

[1] Scholars who claim that exclusion is the essence of property do not deny that the right is limited. Their point is that if an individual has no basis for excluding someone, the person can hardly be thought of as an owner. Even the owner of a retail store may exclude shoplifters.

unjustly interfere with it.[2] If someone wants access to the property, she must seek the owner's permission and pay the price the owner exacts. The state stands behind that right. If an individual accesses the property with no permission or privilege, a court will generally impose a remedy designed to deter such conduct, such as an injunction or punitive damages, even if the owner suffers no compensable harm from the incursion. The unlawful incursion is harm enough.

When courts limit the right to exclude, they put the exclusion case in a different category. When a nonowner is privileged to enter the property, courts evaluate the owner's reasons for exclusion in light of the nonowner's interest in access to the property. In this category of cases, the reasons for exclusion become relevant and the right to exclude *is* subject to judicial oversight. Courts then undertake a kind of a balancing test to determine the border between exclusion and access. When the balance is in favor of access, they allow access without any payment for the privilege.[3] And even when access is not itself privileged and the nonowner is a trespasser, courts sometimes enforce the right to exclude not with a deterrent remedy, but simply by requiring the defendant to compensate the owner for the harm that the incursion caused.[4] Then, the amount of harm from the incursion measures the scope of the owner's rights.

This dichotomy between cases in which courts do or do not examine the interests of the nonowner determines the analytical method used in the case. Because exclusion cases fall into one of two categories, with different implications in each category for the relationship between the state and owner, and the owner and nonowners, it is important to be able to identify and justify how and why courts put a case in one category rather than another – that is, the boundary between exclusion and access.[5] We ask the following question: "What values is the court following when the court makes the categorization decision?" In this

[2] As we will see in Chapter 12, when a state interferes with the right to exclude, even by regulation, it is a taking that is just only if the state pays compensation.
[3] Moreover, when access is privileged the burden of communicating the desire to exclude may fall on the owner. Under some circumstances, a nonowner is privileged to gain access to the owner's property *unless* the owner makes the intention to exclude clear, in which event the privilege to enter the property is the default rule.
[4] As I show in Section 7.3, if the nonowner's incursion into the property resulted from a good faith and reasonable mistake, courts generally award only compensatory damages.
[5] Existing theory addresses this question in generalizations that beg the question of why courts balance the interests in some cases but not others. One possibility is that courts balance the interests of owners and nonowners in every case and put cases in the exclusion category whenever the balance tips in favor of the owners, but not otherwise. Although the possibility is real, recognizing the possibility does not help define the border between exclusion and access. We still need to know what sorting mechanism courts use to undertake the balance. Information cost theory does not define the boundary between exclusion and access because, as developed thus far, it does not tell us why courts seek to conserve information costs in some cases but not others.

chapter, I present a theory of exclusion that allows us to distinguish these two kinds of exclusion cases on the basis of the values that impel courts to treat cases one way rather than another.[6] In the class of cases where balancing is necessary, I identify why and how the balancing occurs. And I relate the remedy courts impose in exclusion cases to the nature of the underlying wrong.

7.1 EXCLUSION AS NO-DUTY

The right to exclude is justified because it implements the no-duty concept that animates private law. The right to exclude is limited when an owner has a duty to take into account the well-being of others. Our theory of obligations marks the border between exclusion and access.

The no-duty concept, as developed in Chapter 5, embodies the principle that an individual who has made no choice to take responsibility for another's well-being is under no duty to benefit another. The right to exclude is the right to say "no" to the individual who wants the unearned benefit of using the owner's property. An individual cannot go onto an owner's property for the same reasons that an individual cannot go into an owner's wallet. Because the owner has no duty to benefit others until the owner has made a choice that implies that the owner has accepted responsibility for another's well-being, the owner has the right to exclude for any and no reason until the owner makes a decision from which the law can infer that the owner has accepted a limitation on the right to exclude. When courts address limitations on the right to exclude, the no-duty concept gives the owner full authority to ignore the well-being of nonowners.[7]

---

[6] Statements that a trespass is an entry without consent or privilege distinguish between the concept of consent and the concept of privilege as a ground for providing nonowners with access. The consent of the owner may be implied in fact from the owner's actions or implied in law from norms of access that bind the owner unless the owner has informed nonowners that he does not follow the norms. Privileged access is thought to be the creation of the law, as in the doctrine of necessity or the many exceptions to the right to exclude in particular circumstances. I am arguing that the distance between these concepts is narrower than conventionally understood. As the text makes clear, courts find that access is privileged because of decisions the owner has made, such as the decision to use her property as a retail store. If that is true, then privileges are themselves based on a kind of consent that is inferred from the decisions the owner has made. Consent implied in law can come either from norms that bind the owner as owner or from decisions from which it might fairly be implied that the owner, by that decision, has consented to the nonowner's access. In effect, the law is saying: "Here are the decisions you have made and here are the consequences of those decisions."
The theory thus builds on the concept of consent that is well-understood.

[7] The concept of duty takes on a different contour when an owner is dealing with the rights of other owners. As I argue in Chapter 8, neighbors have the obligation to consider the well-being

More concretely, an individual who asks to take a mobile home across an owner's fallow field is asking the owner to confer a benefit that the owner has not fairly agreed to confer.[8] The owner's decision to use his property for a farm in no way implies that the owner has agreed to consider the well-being of others when deciding issues of access to the farm. The mobile home seller is asking the owner to be other-regarding in a way that is not part of the obligations the owner has accepted by its use of the property. If the law were to impose the obligation to confer this benefit – that is, if the law were to require the owner to surrender the right to exclude – the law would be requiring the owner to look out for the well-being of others even when that obligation cannot fairly be implied by any choice the owner had previously made. Such an imposed obligation would undercut social interchange because people would make enforceable claims against each other without the other's express or implied consent.[9]

Because the owner has no duty to think about the well-being of others, there is no warrant for balancing the owner's interest against the nonowner's interest; the owner can exclude for any and no reason. This explains, therefore, why the right to exclude does not depend on the owner showing a compensable harm. The right to exclude does not depend on the injury that would otherwise incur when a nonowner invades the decision-making autonomy of the owner and seeks to appropriate, without warrant, the owner's resources to other uses. The injury from unprivileged access is in upsetting the assignment

---

of neighbors, which gives nuisance law its unique structure and distinguishes nuisance from exclusion.

[8] Jacque v. Steenberg Homes, Inc., 563 N.W.2d. 154 (Wis. 997). Although owners often give permission for others to use property in cases such as this, the owner here had a good reason for denying permission. A relevant fact from the case is *when* the nonowner, the mobile home seller, asked for permission to cross the owner's land. The owner's denial of permission may have had as much to do with the timing of the defendant's request as it did with the substance of the request. The defendant knew he needed to secure the owner's permission (for defendant had no claim of privilege). Yet the defendant did not seek permission before he set the price for delivery of the home (even though the cost of delivery would depend on whether defendant could go across the property). The owner was entitled to be asked for permission at the time the nonowner needed to decide how much to charge for delivery. Instead, the defendant either assumed he would get permission, a sign of disrespect for the owner, or charged the buyer a high price for delivery and then lowered his cost of delivery by seeking a shortcut. We might conjecture that the homeowner intuitively understood that the defendant had put him in an unfair position by seeking permission to use the land only after the terms of the contract has been negotiated. One can also conjecture that the homeowner would have felt differently about the use of his land if the permission had been sought before the deal closed.

[9] This account is, I believe, consistent with "the traditional everyday morality of property" that is "recognized by all members of society." Smith and Merrill (2007) at 91–92. My sense is that everyday morality respects the moral obligation to confer benefits on strangers but would not expect the person benefited to have an enforceable claim to the benefit.

of burdens and benefits that are protected by the no-duty concept. An owner bears the burdens of ownership: purchase, upkeep, and risk. Unless the owner has in some way agreed to share the benefits of that investment with others, the owner is entitled to the benefits.[10] The biblical and legal admonition to reap only where one has sown expresses the ethical and functional imperative that one who carries the burdens of ownership ought to also reap the benefits of ownership.[11]

The doctrine of necessity might appear to impose a duty to benefit those who are in physical danger and, in that way, to implement the moral duty to rescue others. When the owner of a sloop ties up to an owner's dock to avoid a dangerous and unavoidable storm, the dock owner is disallowed, under the doctrine of necessity, from casting the sloop into the dangerous waters.[12] This looks as if the dock owner must allow his dock to be commandeered by another in order to avoid greater harm. Is this not the duty to allow someone to benefit from an owner's property? It is, but it is important to put the doctrine of necessity in the proper context.

In the next section, I will make two kinds of arguments about the doctrine of necessity in order to establish that it does not give courts a general warrant to balance the interests of owner and nonowner whenever a court thinks the interests of the nonowner are important. First, I will argue that most cases decided under the rubric of necessity are better explained as applications of the narrower duty concepts I develop here. Second, I will argue that even when properly applied, the doctrine of necessity is actually far narrower than the simple reading generally given it. It applies only when a nonowner is already on the property, and it requires that the nonowner exhaust all other reasonable means of self-protection. Importantly, it does not disable the owner from making her property unavailable for rescue.[13] Thus narrowed,

[10] Henry Smith has made a similar point in the context of information theory:
Ownership concentrates on the owner the benefits of information developed about – and placed bets on – the value of the asset ... [S]uch owners make bets in situations of uncertainty and are rewarded or punished depending on how those bets turn out later when the uncertainty is resolved. The owner develops information about the attributes and potential uses of the asset he owns, but he may not be able to communicate his prediction about future values to others at reasonable cost. Smith (2004) at 1729.

[11] This account is also consistent with the accounts of property that emphasize the value of an owner's autonomy. Dagan (2011) at 96. It goes beyond other accounts, however, by also emphasizing that it is an actor's exercise of autonomy that gives the actor the duty to take into account the well-being of other individuals.

[12] Ploof v. Putnam, 71 A. 188 (Vt. 1908).

[13] The owner has no a priori obligation to build a dock that provides a refuge for people in a storm, and nothing in the doctrine of necessity disables the owner from making the dock inaccessible to nonowners. Property owners routinely erect fences and other barriers that disable people from using the owners' property in an emergency.

the doctrine of necessity stands for the proposition that once a nonowner, because of an emergency, is on the owner's property, the owner is limited in the choices the owner may make with respect to that use of the owner's property. For reasons I will elaborate below, this is consistent with the concept of duty that animates private law.

7.2 LIMITATIONS ON EXCLUSION AND AN OWNER'S DUTY

The right to exclude privileges the decision-making autonomy of the owner over the well-being of the nonowner, but the right to exclude is not, as we have said, absolute. Just as the right to exclude is supported by the values underlying the no-duty principle, the right is limited by the duty principle. Owners assume obligations for the well-being of others by the decisions they make; when an owner's decisions take on an obligation, an owner may not exclude nonowners unless the exclusion is reasonably necessary to protect a legitimate interest, after taking into account the legitimate interests of nonowners. This section elaborates the concept of duty that animates private law and shows how and when the concept of duty limits the scope of an owner's right to exclude.[14]

We often talk about duty arising from a "special relationship" between the parties. The source of that special relationship is, in the theory developed here, the owner's decisions that trigger the obligation to be other-regarding.

An actor takes on many obligations by granting permission, of course, and the right to exclude is limited by the scope of the permission the owner has given.[15] Licenses grant permissive access, and many affirmative easements

---

[14] Some limitations on the right to exclude relate not to an owner's duty to other individuals, but to an owner's duty to the state. Owners must allow reasonable access so that public officials can perform their public functions. *Restatement (Second) of Torts* § 202–210 (1965). Section titles convey the range of state privileges: (abatement of public nuisance by public official); (entry to arrest for criminal offense); (entry to recapture or to prevent crime and in related situations); (forcible entry of dwelling to arrest, recapture, prevent crime, and related situations); (entry to assist in making arrest or other apprehension); (entry to execute civil process against occupant of land); (entry to execute civil process against non-occupant of land); (entry pursuant to order of court); and (entry pursuant to legislative duty or authority).

[15] Rawls & Assocs. v. Hurst, 550 S.E.2d 219 (N.C. Ct. App. 2001) (finding vendor's implied consent to occupy premises precluded trespass claim); Maint. Equip. Co. Inc. v. Godley Builders, 420 S.E.2d 199, 202 (N.C. Ct. App. 1992) (requiring construction company to get permission from tenant, who occupied land owned by railroad, before grading and bulldozing adjacent property); Shell Oil Co. v. Murrah, 493 So. 2d 1274, 1275 (Miss. 1986) (holding company liable for trespass when company only obtained permission to conduct seismic exploration of plaintiff's property yet proceeded to run a seismic line across plaintiff's property without additional permission); *See also, Restatement (Second) of Torts* § 167–170 (1965) (effect of consent of possessor); (conditional or restricted consent); (consent restricted as to area); (consent conditioned

are created by express or implied grant. Because permission is an exercise of autonomy, it does not violate the values underlying the no-duty principle. But the obligation to be other-regarding is not limited to permissive relationships. An actor surrenders the decision-making autonomy protected by the no-duty principle when the actor makes decisions (in the exercise of decision-making autonomy) from which the duty to take into account the well-being of others can fairly be implied. Just as the no-duty principle protects an actor's decision-making autonomy, the duty concept reflects the consequences that attach when an actor has exercised her autonomy in a way that implicates the well-being of others. Although the concept of the duty to be other-regarding is not prominent in property theory, it ought to be, for property law, like contract law and tort law, is about how an individual ought to understand herself in relation to other individuals.

Duties are imposed because they are the natural consequence of choices people make. This principle is well-developed in tort law. A person getting behind the wheel of a car surrenders decision-making autonomy by the very decision to subject others to the risks inherent in the actor's driving; the actor must therefore make reasonable decisions while driving. Similarly, a supplier of goods or services, has, by virtue of going into business, surrendered decision-making autonomy and accepts the obligation to think reasonably about the well-being of those the supplier serves. The duty extends even to risks that the actor did not create. A landlord has the obligation to tenants to reasonably protect them from muggers, and a store owner must take reasonable steps to protect a customer who suffers a seizure while in the store. These obligations are fairly implied from the decision to be a landlord or a store owner.

These examples from tort law have their counterparts in property law. When, for example, an owner uses his property to erect a steel mill, the obligation to think about the well-being of others is fairly implied from the owner's knowledge that the steel mill will cause pollution that adversely affects the well-being of others. The law of nuisance is built on an obligation of each owner to other owners, one that flows from the choices each owner makes about how to use her property. Similarly, limitations on the right to exclude flow from decisions the owner makes and from the owner's relationship to people on the owner's property. As this chapter shows, an owner's duty to take into account the

---

or restricted as to time). Permissive privileges for nonowners to use an owner's property are, of course, implied by law, as in the case of irrevocable licenses and many easements. McCaig v. Talldega Pub. Co., Inc., 544 So. 2d 875 (Ala. 1989) (finding co-op agent did not trespass and had right of access for limited purpose of inspecting and servicing co-op equipment); Moore v. Schultz, 91 A.2d 514 (N.J. Ct. App. Div. 1952) (finding that defendant had a right of *profit a prendre* in gross to extract sand and gravel from plaintiff's land).

well-being of nonowners when making exclusion decisions is fairly implied from three circumstances: (1) an owner's decision to buy property subject to preexisting burdens, (2) an owner's decisions about how to use property, and (3) an owner's relationship to individuals who are on their property. These circumstances determine the scope of the right to exclude and justify the instances in which an owner must grant reasonable access to nonowners.

7.2.1 Obligations Implied by Use

As we have seen, owners' decisions about how to use property generally impose on them no obligations to take into account the well-being of others when deciding whether to allow a nonowner access; an owner's decision to use land as a homestead or farm does not impose the obligation to think about the well-being of those who want to use the property to transport a mobile home across the property to a neighbor.[16] That is because nothing in the decision to use the property in that way implies the obligation to take into account the well-being of someone who wants to use the property as a transportation corridor. The owner absorbs all the burdens of ownership and is under no obligation to share the benefits of ownership with another.

In other contexts, however, owners, in the exercise of their autonomy, make decisions concerning the use of the property that fairly imply that the owner has accepted the duty to think about the well-being of others. As a prominent example, a decision to open a retail business implies a series of obligations to take into account the well-being of customers, including obligations to reasonably protect the customers' safety and to allow access unless there is a good reason for denying it. The reasoning is straightforward. The store owner gets the benefits of attracting customers, and the benefits of their business; from this benefit it can fairly be implied that the owner ought to accept the reasonable burdens of that benefit.[17] For that reason, the law recognizes obligations of a retail business owner that it does not recognize for the owner of a home,[18] and the law works out the content of those obligations by considering how the

---

[16] Jacque v. Steenberg Homes Inc., 563 N.W.2d 154 (Wis. 1997).
[17] By contrast, the owner of the farmhouse in the mobile home case did not get any benefit from the seller of the mobile homes and therefore, by deciding to use the property as a farm, did not agree to accept any burdens with respect to the seller of the mobile homes.
[18] An owner's decisions about how to use the property determine the kind of expectations that people have about when and how they will be given access to the property, which allows us to distinguish between the right to exclude from a home and the right to exclude from a business. That is why "the social context in which the property operates and the types of uses prevalent there affect the assignment of legal rights and obligations." Singer (2000) at 43.

Limitations on Exclusion and an Owner's Duty

owner ought properly to balance her interests with the interests of others. The decision to open a retail store serves as a decision to take into account the well-being of others, and courts work out the scope of that right by looking at how the community has constructed norms of access that reflect the appropriate assignment of burdens and benefits.

The scope of a retailer's right to exclude depends on how a court assigns the burdens and benefits of exclusion, given the need to accommodate the interests of both owner and nonowner. Although the cases are few and, for the most part, old, Joseph Singer has made the point that the owner of a retail business retains exclusion rights that are different from other retail sellers, such as common carriers.[19] Care must be taken in interpreting these decisions, however. A court may confirm a retail owner's right to exclude, without articulating a basis for that conclusion. The right to exclude could be affirmed if it is based on appropriate reasons, even if the court does not articulate the reasons. Or, a court could justify exclusion rights for a class of cases if the court feels that the benefits of a bright-line rule outweigh the benefits of a case-by-case approach. This could be justified on the basis of conserving information costs. Under this approach, the court would be saying that the value of a more fine-tuned resolution of the issue would not be worth the additional expenses of the inquiry to differentiate between cases where the owner had a reasonable basis for exclusion and cases where the owner did not. It seems clear, for example, that a store owner who excludes suspected shoplifters on the basis of non-discriminatory and objective criteria might well retain the right to exclude, so that litigation would focus on the quality of the decision-making process used by the owner, rather than the effect of the decision.

In any event, any notion that retail sellers have a greater right to exclude than common carriers is a vestige of both formalism and racism that cannot be long-lived because it cannot withstand analysis of whether assigning burdens to nonowners on the basis of race or other matters of status is permissible.[20] It is a regrettable comment on the common law that it could not address exclusion on the basis of race, but the public accommodations laws have helped create a social norm in which courts ought to feel fully empowered to forbid the right to exclude on the basis of factors unrelated to the legitimate purposes of the owner's business. Overall, it is hard to escape the conclusion of the New Jersey Supreme Court that "when property owners open their premises to the

---

[19] Singer (1996).
[20] This analysis also suggests, of course, that exclusion based on impermissible personal factors, such as race, can be, and ought to have been restricted by the common law. *See* Singer (1996) at 9 (both public perception and fundamental legal principles today suggest that businesses open to the public have a duty to serve the public without unjust discrimination).

general public in the pursuit of their own property interests, they have no right to exclude people unreasonably."[21]

This approach explains the unsurprising result in *Pruneyard Shopping Center v. Robin*.[22] There a shopping center attempted to exclude students who set up a card table in the shopping center's central courtyard to seek support in opposition to a proposed United Nations resolution. The state, citing First Amendment grounds, refused to allow the exclusion. The Supreme Court found that this limitation on the right to exclude, although authorizing a physical invasion of the shopping center's property, was nonetheless not a taking. Without specifying the precise scope of the shopping center's right to exclude, and acknowledging the shopping center's right to adopt reasonable time, place, and manner restrictions, the limitation on the right to exclude, although grounded in constitutional values, also recognized that the right to exclude depends on an owner's decision about how to use its property. Because the shopping center was designed to be a semipublic place, it was not hard to see why their right to exclude would be limited by countervailing interests in access.

Similar reasoning about the use decisions owners make justifies the outcomes in the migrant worker cases.[23] In these cases, an owner's duty to allow social service workers reasonable access to meet with migrant workers housed on the farm can be implied from the owner's decision to house the migrant workers on the farm. The obligation does not attach to the owner as owner

---

[21] Uston v. Resorts Int'l Hotel, Inc., 445 A. 2d 370 (N.J. 1982).

[22] 447 U.S. 74 (1980).

[23] State v. Shack, 277 A.2d 369 (N.J. 1971); Asociacion de Trabajadores Agricolas de Puerto Rico v. Green Giant Co., 518 F.2d 130, 138 (3d Cir. 1975) (requiring union members to prove that no other reasonable way existed to access migrant workers than entering on the defendant's private property); Petersen v. Tailsman Sugar Corp., 478 F.2d 73 (5th Cir. 1973) (requiring company to grant labor union officials and religious workers access to Jamaican migrant worker camps); United Farm Workers Union, AFL-CIO v. Mel Finerman Co., 364 F. Supp. 326 (D. Colo. 1973) (holding that operator of camp had to allow union to enter migrant camp subject to reasonable constraints); Velez v. Amenta, 370 F. Supp. 1250 (D. Conn. 1974) (holding that tobacco growers' association, which ran a migrant workers camp, could not deprive the migrant workers of their civil rights, regardless that the camp was private property); Franschina v. Morgan, 346 F. Supp. 833 (S.D. Ind. 1972) (holding that migrant workers were tenants, and were therefore entitled to receive guests); Folgueras v. Hassle, 331 F. Supp. 615 (W.D. Mich., 1971) (finding in favor of state workers' access); Lee v. A. Duda & Sons, Inc., 310 So. 2d 391 (Fla. Dist. Ct. App. 1975) (holding that a corporation that provided legal assistance to migratory workers had right of access to migrant worker camps subject to restrictions to give notice and visit at reasonable hours); Baer v. Sorbello, 425 A.2d 1089 (N.J. Super. Ct. App. Div. 1981) ("One is not answerable to a charge of criminal trespass where his purpose is to ascertain working conditions and make available state or charitable services on behalf of migrant farmworkers."); People v. Rewald, 65 Misc. 2d 453 (N.Y. Co. Ct. 1971) (finding that because privately owned migrant workers camp was partially open to the public, the landowner could not arbitrarily deny a reporter access).

but to the owner as one who, by hiring and housing migrant workers, undertook an obligation reasonably to consider their well-being. The owner gets the benefits of the migrant worker's labor and therefore ought to bear the burdens that appropriately attach to those benefits. That obligation does not violate the owner's autonomy or the values underlying the right to exclude because it does not impose a burden that the owner does not impliedly accept by his decision to hire the migrant workers. Developing reasonable obligation-based limitations on the owner's right to exclude is an appropriate assignment of responsibilities because an owner who is not willing to accept such reasonable burdens is not respecting the equal freedom of the migrant workers. The scope of the obligation requires the owner to provide the minimal access that gets the migrant workers assistance without interfering with the owner's privacy or operations.[24]

Many limitations on the right to exclude flow from an owner's choices about how she uses her property. Limitations on the right to exclude that appear under the doctrine of irrevocable licenses and easements created by implication, necessity, or estoppel each arise from decisions an owner has made about the use of her property. A license to use the owner's property generally implies that the license will be revoked only under reasonable circumstances.[25] When

[24] The controversial aspect of the migrant worker cases was not the duty to consider the well-being of the migrant workers, but the question of whether their well-being might have been accommodated by allowing them to meet with the social workers outside the premises. Had that been a reasonable alternative, the owner would not have been unreasonable in prohibiting access. But this issue was resolved by most courts against the owner. According to the court in *State v. Shack*, "[migrant workers] are unaware of their rights and opportunities and of the services available to them [outside of camp: thus] they can be reached only by positive efforts tailored to that end ... [o]ne of the major problems ... is [migrant workers'] lack of adequate direct information with regard to the availability of public services...." *Shack*, 277 A.2d at 372–73. The only court upholding the right to exclude in a migrant workers case did so on the ground that the migrant workers could meet with the social worker off the premises. Associacion de Trabajadores Agricolas de Puerto Rico v. Green Giant Co., 518 F.2d 120 (3d Cir. 1975) (requiring persons seeking access to migrant workers' labor camp to produce proof that no other reasonable options existed for reaching the desired audience).

[25] Standard property doctrine is that licenses are revocable. Chicago & N.W. Transp. Co. v. City of Winthrop, 257 N.W.2d 302, 304 (Minn. 1977) (holding that a license is generally revocable and not an encumbrance on the land). That view is justified because simple permissions to use property are generally not given under circumstances that would make revocation unreasonable. However, in a broad range of circumstance, the right to revoke the license – and thus to exclude – is limited because of the circumstances under which permission was given. Messer v. City of Birmingham, 10 So. 2d 760 (Ala. 1942) (a licensee, on revocation of license, is entitled to reasonable notice and opportunity to remove the improvements erected on licensor's premises); Rhodes v. Otis, 33 Ala. 578 (1859) (a license coupled with an interest or an executed license are exceptions to revocability); Shearer v. Hodnette, 674 So. 2d 548, 551 (Ala. Civ. App. 1995) (license may become irrevocable when the licensee has expended money or labor in reasonable reliance on the continued existence of the privilege); Mize v. McGarity, 667

an owner allows another to use the property under circumstances that justify invocation of the doctrine of estoppel, the right to exclude for that purpose is limited. Finally, the separation of one parcel of land from another under circumstances where use of one of the parcels is necessary implies a limitation on the right to exclude.

Courts sometimes decide cases under the doctrine of necessity that are better explained on an obligation-based theory that recognizes the natural consequences of choices the owner has made about how to use her property. A railroad has a duty to its passengers, and a railroad's decision to close the railway station and send its waiting passengers into an impending storm is an unreasonable exercise of that obligation. Even when a court frames its decision in terms of the doctrine of necessity, the court in reality is working out the railroad's obligations to treat passengers reasonably given the railroad's preexisting duty to consider their well-being. Similarly, if an owner creates an "attractive nuisance," the owner has accepted the duty to think about the well-being of a child who might enter the property, even though courts sometimes refer to the doctrine of necessity to explain their reasoning.[26] And if an owner knows of a trespasser and the hazard the trespasser faces, the owner has a duty to the trespasser because the decision to create or fail to abate a risk (a decision about use) imposes the obligation to think about the well-being of those who are known to be on the property.[27] And the owners of a guard dog must think reasonably about the well-being of those who might come onto the property (whether they come on the property with implied permission or from necessity).[28] Here, too, the appropriate basis for the decision is not the doctrine of necessity but the decision an owner has made about the use of her property.

S.E.2d 695 (Ga. Ct. App. 2008) (finding that because licensees contributed to the cost of constructing and maintaining a joint driveway they gained an irrevocable license); Lee v. Regents of Univ. of Minn., 672 N.W.2d 366 (Minn. Ct. App. 2003) (holding that if a licensee has property on the premises in question, she is entitled to reasonable notice of revocation of license). I state the irrevocability rule in terms of the reasonableness of the revocation because I think that it is a mistake to state a rule as if it had no exceptions, when, in fact, exceptions arise in a variety of circumstances. The focus of analysis ought to be on the circumstances under which the license may be revoked rather than on the fact that in many instances it is reasonable to revoke the license.

[26] See Lambert v. W. Pac. R. Co., 26 P.2d 824, 825 (Cal. Ct. App. 1933) (holding that defendant owed a duty to children trespassers when defendant left attractive nuisance on property).

[27] See Restatement (Second) of Torts § 336 (1965) (activities dangerous to known trespassers); Restatement (Second) of Torts § 337 (1965) (artificial conditions highly dangerous to known trespassers).

[28] See Rossi v. Del Duca, 181 N.E.2d 591 (Mass. 1962) (finding a minor privileged to enter the defendant's property by necessity; the defendant was liable to the minor for defendant's dog attacking the minor while she was permissibly on his property).

7.2.2 Obligations Implied by Purchase: Historical Usage

An owner's obligation to consider the well-being of nonowners, and therefore to think reasonably about the circumstances under which a nonowner might be excluded, may also arise from the decision to purchase property. Property comes with preexisting or customary uses, and those uses bind the owner when the owner is making decisions about the property. When it can fairly be said that the owner must have known about prior or customary uses, the decision to buy the property is a decision to accept the limitations that custom imposes on the right to exclude.[29] Prior and customary uses serve as a kind of non-legislated zoning, forming a set of unstated expectations that owners take on when they purchase the property. It does not impermissibly infringe the owner's autonomy to say that the decision to buy the property knowing of the preexisting uses is a decision by the owner to reasonably respect those uses. Indeed, a person who has respect for his own decisions will accept responsibility for burdens that come with the property.[30]

The most straightforward illustration of this principle is *Race v. Castle Mountain Ranch, Inc.*[31] Plaintiffs had built and used summer cottages around a lake with the permission of the owner, who benefited from the plaintiff's use in a variety of ways. Defendant bought the land, knowing of this use, and tried to get the seller to exercise his right to terminate the license, but the seller refused. The court held that even though the plaintiffs' use was governed by a contract with an at-will termination clause, the defendant could not exclude plaintiffs until the plaintiffs had stayed there long enough to reap the value of their investment in the summer homes; the court imposed a constructive trust on the defendant for the purpose. The defendant had limited the scope of his right to exclude by buying the property under circumstance that required the defendant to respect the plaintiffs' ability to get the benefits of their investment.

Similarly, when a person acquires an ownership interest in beachfront property that historically has been used by the public, and the property is not to be used in some different way, the owner takes the land subject to the implied

---

[29] Du Mez v. Dykstra, 241 N.W. 182, 183 (Mich. 1932) ("[R]ecognition of the general custom of owners of wild lands to permit the public to pass over them without hindrance.")

[30] The idea that the purchase of property comes with preexisting burdens is central, of course, to the law of servitudes, which imposes obligations on purchasers who have notice of reasonable burdens that run with the land. It also suggests that when community values require it, purchasers must also respect the habitat and preexisting wildlife on the property. Here, we examine only the burdens that purchasers take with the property in the context of preexisting uses by humans that serve to limit the right to exclude.

[31] 631 P. 2d 680 (Mont. 1981).

duty to consider reasonably the well-being of the nonowners.[32] When the community custom is to hunt on the undeveloped portions of property, the owner accepts the property subject to the obligation to look out for the hunter's well-being, which includes letting people continue customary use that does not disrupt the owner's use.[33] By virtue of custom, the owner is understood to buy the property subject to the norms that are recognized by the community and, through the purchase, to have ratified those norms and impliedly agreed to take into account, reasonably, the well-being of nonowners when making decisions about the property. The autonomy of the owner is not compromised because the owner could always buy property that comes without the implied restrictions, and can adjust to the burdens by paying less for the property.

Many cases decided under the rubric of "necessity" are enforcing customary usages that can be fairly thought of as an obligation that one accepts when purchasing property. In these cases, the duty to allow others access to the property comes not from a general balancing of interests but because owners have accepted the customary rights of nonowners to come onto the property. Some cases are a part of the law of easements, where the decision to allow another to use the land for specific purposes is implied as an obligation of ownership. Other cases suggest a custom that allows travelers on the highway to drive over private property next to the highway in order to get around an obstruction in the highway.[34] Such cases are not really cases of necessity but reflect the obligations that owners assume from prior custom and historical usages. These cases seem to reflect the law of neighbors rather than the doctrine of necessity. One group of cases creates exceptions to the trespass rule for activities that start on the defendant's land but, because they are beyond the defendant's

---

[32] *See* Matthews v. Bay Head Improvement Ass'n, 471 A.2d 355, 363–64 (N.J. 1984) (holding that the public has a right of access to privately owned dry-sand beaches); State *ex. rel.* Thornton v. Hay, 462 P.2d 671, 679 (Ore. 1969) (enjoining defendants from constructing a fence to block dry-sand portions of their beachfront property from the public); Moody v. White, 593 S.W.2d 372, 374 (Tex. Civ. App. 1979), *disapproved of by* Severance v. Patterson, 2010 WL 4371438 (Tex. Nov. 5, 2010) (affirming a mandatory injunction against defendants to remove motel and lounge that infringed the public's right to an open beach).
[33] Freyfogle (2007) at 29. *See also*, McConico v. Singleton, 1818 WL 787 (S.C. May 1818) (holding that hunters have a right to hunt on unenclosed lands).
[34] *See* Dwyer v. Staunton, 4 D.L.R. 393 (1947) (driving across field when snow blocked the public highway is privileged); Taylor v. Whitehead, 2 Dougl. 745, 99 E.R. 475 (1781) (where common highway is out of repair, by the flooding of a river or any other cause, passengers have a right to go on the adjacent ground). Morey v. Fitzgerald, 56 Vt. 487 (1884), *superseded by statute as recognized in* Town of Calais. v. Cnty. Road Com'rs, 795 A.2d 1267 (Vt. 2002) (finding that when a public highway is out of repair and impassable, a traveler may lawfully go over the adjoining land, and that interference with private property is justified by necessity).

control, spill over into the plaintiff's land – as from straying sheep, dogs, and cattle.

7.2.3 Necessity and Private Takings

The foregoing analysis suggests that an owner has no general duty to consider the well-being of nonowners when making exclusion decisions, but that an owner's obligations to think about the well-being of nonowners arises from decisions an owner makes concerning the property. Once the obligation to think about the well-being of others arises, the owner must make reasonable decisions about whether to exclude another from the property; the owner must reasonably consider the well-being of others in light of the owner's own self-regarding interest. Under this theory, the obligation to think about the well-being of others arises, or is implied, from decisions of the owner rather than from a balance of interests of the owner and nonowners. There is no balancing of interests until the court determines that the owner has accepted the well-being of nonowners as part of the owner's projects and preferences. Duty does not arise from the fact that the use is very important to the nonowner, which precludes any general claim that the nonowner's use of the resource is more important than the owner's use.

The doctrine of necessity seems to be at odds with this approach, for this doctrine seems to create an owner's duty by balancing the interests of the owner and nonowner rather than from the owner's autonomous choices. In its most general form, one might say that a person is privileged to use the property of an owner whenever that use is necessary to avoid greater harm or inconvenience to the nonowner. In a more restricted form, one might say that the owner's right to exclude is limited when the nonowner's physical safety is in danger. Either formulation suggests that an owner's duty not to exclude arises from a balance of interests rather than because of an owner's decision from which the duty can fairly be implied. In the classic case, the owner of a dock is not permitted to force a sloop away from the dock and into an impending and dangerous storm; the privilege to stay at the dock as a nontrespasser is implied from the dangerous circumstances, rather than because of any decision the dock owner has made.[35] That looks like the imposition of a duty to allow another to have access to the dock rather than a duty that is accepted by the dock owner because of some decision the dock owner has made.

---

[35] Ploof v. Putnam, 71 A. 188 (Vt. 1908).

The doctrine of necessity's threat to the right to exclude is accentuated by its remedial aspect. When a nonowner is privileged by the doctrine of necessity to use the owner's property, the nonowner is required to compensate the owner for any harm. This is the famous *Vincent* case;[36] the owner of a ship was privileged to stay at the plaintiff's dock when a storm arose (because that was the reasonable thing to do), but the owner of the ship was nonetheless required to compensate the dock owner for damages his decision imposed. If an owner's duty to let another use her property is determined by balancing the owner's rights against the nonowner's rights, and if the nonowner's only responsibility is to compensate the owner for harm, then the right to exclude has been transformed into a duty to let others use the property whenever the nonowner is willing to compensate the owner. Certainly, the mobile home seller who wanted to deliver his mobile home across the owner's property would be happy to compensate the owner for any harm his use caused.

In other words, the notion that an owner's duty to allow access to the property comes from comparing the interests of owners and nonowners threatens to undermine the right to exclude for any or no reason. It does little good to try to confine the doctrine of necessity to instances in which the nonowner would otherwise be in peril of physical danger (although courts and commentators have tried to confine it on that basis). Not only is the doctrine of necessity not used in that way, but even that limited application would undermine the no-duty justification for the right to exclude for any or no reason.

How, then, are we to understand the doctrine of necessity in a world in which we want to give content to the right to exclude that is not predicated on a balancing test?

As I argued in the prior two subsections, most cases that allow access under the rubric of "necessity" are in fact ones in which the owner has a duty to consider the well-being of the nonowner because of the owner's prior decisions. These are not really cases of necessity because the obligation to account for the well-being of nonowners comes not from the need of the nonowners but from the preexisting relationship between owners and nonowners. Most of the "necessity" cases involve a relationship from which the obligation to think about the well-being of nonowners can be implied. That leaves only a small number of "necessity" cases, such as *Ploof v. Putnam*, that appear not to involve a preexisting obligation.

Cases of "necessity" in this narrow sense ought *not* be understood as standing for a general obligation to let another use one's property whenever the nonowner's benefits outweigh the damage to the owner. Instead, the doctrine

---

[36] Vincent v. Lake Erie Transp. Co., 124 N.W. 221 (Minn. 1910).

of necessity should be understood as a limitation on the self-help remedies available to the property owner when a nonowner is already on the property, and therefore as rulings limiting the owner's remedies for protecting the right to exclude. Under this view, the right to exclude is limited because once a person is on another's property and faces risks or hazards, the relationship between the owner and nonowner has changed. To understand the narrow scope of the doctrine of necessity, recall that it does not apply to individuals not already on the owner's property. An owner is not required to build a dock in order to benefit sloops on the lake that might otherwise face dangers. Nor is the owner of property on a lake prohibited from building a barrier around her beach that would make it impossible to seek shelter on the property. The doctrine of necessity in the pure duty-to-benefit sense applies only after the nonowner has sought shelter on another's property. It is no accident that *Ploof v. Putnam* was a case by the owner of the sloop against the owner of the dock for wrongfully casting the boat away from the dock; the case was about the remedies an owner can use against a nonowner once the nonowner is on the property.

The justification for imposing the obligation to consider the well-being of a nonowner in such cases is that a nonowner who is on the owner's land has a different relationship with the owner than one who is not on the land. The analogy here is to the owner's duties to trespassers to protect them from physical injury on the property. Despite the older doctrine that an owner owes a trespasser only the most minimum level of care, it is now clear that once a trespasser is on the land, the owner who knows or reasonably should know of the trespasser's presence cannot ignore that fact when deciding how to act in relation to the risks the trespasser faces. In the context of the discussion here, to passively stand by and allow the trespasser to be injured is not a form of self-help punishment for trespassing that an owner is allowed to employ. This philosophy of other-regarding behavior animates the obligation of owners in the spring gun cases.;[37] an owner is not allowed to deter trespassers with self-help remedies that involve undue force. The law curbs self-help remedies because even when the entry is unprivileged, the fact that the trespasser came on the property establishes a relationship that the owner must recognize – one that limits the owner's remedies.

An owner owes an obligation of other-regarding behavior to those on her land because the owner must determine whether the nonowner's presence is privileged. Ownership of the land implies that the owner will take into account the reason that an individual has come on the land when deciding

---

[37] Katko v. Briney, 183 N.W.2d 657 (Iowa 1971).

how to act toward the potential trespasser. Under the doctrine of attractive nuisance, when the owner is implicated in attracting the potential trespasser to the property the relationship is clear. But it is equally true when the owner is not implicated in attracting the nonowner to the property. When a road is blocked and a traveler moves onto the adjacent land to get around the blockage, the obligations of owners may privilege that use,[38] and therefore limit the right of the owner to resort to self-help. The reason the trespasser is on the land creates a special bond with the owner, one that creates the obligation to act only after taking into account the well-being of the potential trespasser. This, in turn, often limits the right of the owner to seek self-help when exercising the right to exclude.

Although information costs generally weigh in favor of the right to exclude,[39] if a person is on the owner's land, the information costs swing in the other direction. A nonowner's presence on the land requires the owner to determine whether the presence is privileged. The nonowner could be on the land for any number of reasons, some benign and privileged and some trespassory. The protection of those persons requires a relatively bright-line rule protecting their interests until the owner has determined the status of their use of the property and whether non-harmful means are available to remove those who are not privileged to be there.

Undoubtedly, this is a "thin" invasion of the right to exclude, available only when a nonowner's need for access to property is compelling or made in the good faith belief that her presence is privileged. Nor is the right to exclude limited once the owner determines that the nonowner's incursion is unprivileged. The only point is that the doctrine of necessity does not require that the right to exclude be subject to a balancing test unless the nonowner is on the property and on it for a compelling reason.

Under this interpretation, the doctrine of necessity creates no general duty to take into account the well-being of potential nonowners of the land; nor does it impose a broad exception to the notion that, in the absence of a special relationship, one has no duty to benefit others. The difference between accepting reasonable responsibility for those who come on one's land and accepting responsibility for those who are not on one's land but would like to be is the difference between owing a duty to the special class of entrants on land and owing a general duty to benefit others. Admittedly, in cases of duty to trespassers and the doctrine of necessity, the duty seems to be thrust upon

---

[38] *See* Dwyer v. Staunton, 4 D.L.R. 393 (1947) (allowing defendant to drive across plaintiff's field when snowstorm blocked a public road).
[39] Merrill and Smith (2000).

the owner, because it requires the owner reasonably to take into account the well-being of others even though the owner has made no prior decision that would itself imply this obligation. But this obligation is justified by the fact of ownership. The benefits of owners are matched by the burden of thinking differently toward those who are on the land (whether lawfully or unlawfully) because once they are attached to the land their well-being is, in many ways, in the hands of the owner. Because the law allows entry for some purposes, it also limits the self-help remedies available when people come on the land.

7.3 REMEDIES IN EXCLUSION CASES

The remedy invoked to protect the right to exclude also reflects the concept of duty underlying property law.[40] Property rule protection (an injunction or punitive damages) requires the nonowner to pay a price set by the owner (that is, to buy the right to avoid the injunction by paying an owner's premium or punitive damages). Sometimes, the right to exclude is protected only by a liability rule – a judicially determined price for the invasion of the right (generally, compensatory damages). If a nonowner's entry is continuing or can be apprehended ahead of time, the right to exclude is usually protected by an injunction.[41] Ex ante, unless access is privileged, the nonowner must

---

[40] On remedies, see Parchomovsky and Stein (2009) (identifying differences between ex ante and ex post protection of ownership and developing remedial proposals that address those differences).

[41] See Friess v. Quest Cherokee, L.L.C., 209 P.3d 722, 726 (Kan. Ct. App. 2009) (granting injunction against defendant because legal remedies were inadequate); Ellis v. Wren, 1 S.W. 440, 442 (Ky. 1886) (granting an injunction for removal of stones from plaintiff's property); Pile v. Pedrick, 31 A. 646 (Penn. 1895) (granting injunction against defendant and requiring removal of foundation wall that extended onto neighbor's property by 1 3/8 inches); Baker v. Howard Cnty. Hunt Club, 188 A.223, 231 (Md. 1936) *distinguished by* Montgomery v. Remsburg, 810 A.2d 14 (Md. Ct. Spec. App. 2001) (granting injunction against fox hunters to prevent hunters and their hounds from crossing onto plaintiff's property); O'Brien v. Murphy, 75 N.E. 700, 702 (Mass. 1905) (allowing an injunction for "inconvenience and annoyance from repeated trespasses, though relatively harmless ... even if a recovery of nominal damages at law would afford full compensation."); Amaral v. Cuppels, 831 N.E.2d 915, 920 (Mass. App. Ct. 2005) (granting a injunction to prevent defendant country club from allowing golf balls to fly onto the plaintiff's property); Sharpiro Bros., Inc. v. Jones-Festus Properties., L.L.C., 205 S.W.3d 270, 279 (Mo. Ct. App.2006) *distinguished by* Postnieks v. Chick-fil-A, Inc., 647 S.E.2d 281 (Ga. Ct. App. 2007) (granting permanent injunction against a business traversing their heavy vehicles over the plaintiff's property and damaging a parking lot); Parkinson v. Winniman, 344 P.2d 677 (Nev. 1959) (awarding injunction against defendant who threatened to continue trespassing); Strawberry Valley Cattle Co. v. Chipman, 45 P. 348, 352 (Utah 1896) (granting an injunction for repeated and continued trespasses by defendant's sheep on the plaintiff's land); Cornelius v. Corry, 2006 N.C. App. LEXIS 2135, at *9 (N.C. Ct. App. Oct. 17, 2006) (granting injunction for removal of a home that encroached on the plaintiff's property by 22 feet); O'Connor

buy the right of access from the owner. If the entry has already occurred, the court must choose between compensatory damages[42] (because there is nothing to enjoin) and some form of punitive damages (which functions like an injunction).[43] It is the remedy for past incursions that interests us. If the entry was unlawful and the court awards only compensatory damages, the defendant is privileged to use the property as long as the defendant compensates the owner for the harm done. This is a far different kind of right to exclude than a right that is protected by an injunction or punitive or continuing damages. How does a court decide to use one remedy rather than another?

The choice of remedies, like the right to exclude, turns on a conception of duty – this time on the nonowner's duty to the owner. Nonowners have a duty to respect both the owner's right to exclude and the boundaries of the owner's property, a duty that reflects the norm of recognition that supports private property rights. A court's choice of remedy will reflect the respect the nonowner has shown for that obligation. When the trespass is non-privileged and intentional[44] courts invariably impose at least compensatory damages.

---

v. Smith, 2010 U.S. Dist. LEXIS 114752, at *2 (S.D. Tex. Oct. 28, 2010) (granting injunction to prevent defendant from trespassing and searching for an alleged buried treasure on plaintiff's property); Crook v. Sheehan Enter., Inc., 740 S.W.2d 333, 337 (Mo. Ct. App. 1987) (granting punitive damages when defendant entered property without plaintiff's permission).

[42] Even for continuing trespasses, if the trespass resulted from a reasonable and good faith encroachment, courts will often award only compensatory damages. McKean v. Alliance Land Co., 253 P. 134 (Cal. 1927), *distinguished by* Carey v. Bowie, 19 P.2d 1032 (Cal. Ct. App. 1933) (denying an injunction to remove a de minimis encroachment when $10 in compensatory damages compensated plaintiff); Golden Press, Inc v. Rylands, 235 P.2d 592, 595 (Co. 1951), *declined to extend by* Hunter v. Mansell, 240 P.3d 469 (Colo. Ct. App. 2010) (denying injunction and granting compensatory damages for a slight encroachment on plaintiff's property); Teasley v. Buford, 876 So. 2d 1070, 1083 (Miss. Ct. App. 2004), *declined to extend by* Patterson v. Holleman, 917 So. 2d 125 (Miss. Ct. App. 2005) (granting compensatory damages for a trespass claim); Hollister v. Ruddy, 48 A. 520 (N.J. Sup. Ct. 1901) (reversing award of punitive damages but granting compensatory damages against defendant for trespass and cutting down tree); Eischen v. Hering, 622 N.W.2d 771 (Wis. App. 2000) (allowing compensatory damages for defendant's trespass and removal of fence and trees).

[43] Shell Oil Co., v. Murrah, 493 So. 2d 1274 (Miss. 1986) (awarding punitive damages against defendant who ran a seismic line across plaintiff's premises); Fareway Hgts. Inc. v. Hillock, 300 A.D.2d 1023 (N.Y. App. Div. 2002) (awarding punitive damages against developers who intentionally excavated a ditch without a landowner's consent); Maint. Equip. Co. Inc. v. Godley Builders, 420 S.E.2d 199, 203 (N.C. Ct. App. 1992) (awarding punitive damages for a trespass action against a builder who graded and dumped dirt on plaintiff's property); Jacque v. Steenberg Homes Inc., 563 N.W.2d 154, 165 (Wis. 1997) (awarding $100,000 in punitive damages for intentional trespass by mobile home company); Doyle v. Arthur, 222 Wis. 2d. 624 (Ct. App. 1998) (awarding punitive damages for intentional trespass by neighbor).

[44] This is a weak requirement of intention, requiring only the intention to do the act. *See Restatement (Second) Torts* § 158 (1965) ("One is subject to liability to another for trespass, irrespective of whether he thereby causes harm to any legally protected interest of the other, if he intentionally (a) enters land in the possession of the other, or causes a thing or a third

But whether they move beyond a liability rule to a property rule depends on whether the nonowner has been appropriately other-regarding. As a general rule, when courts feel that a nonowner is acting without reasonable regard for the rights of the property owner, they impose a form of deterrent remedy that requires the nonowner to purchase the right from the owner; when the nonowner has acted reasonably and the incursion is the result of a mistake, courts impose only compensatory damages. In this way, courts act on the notion that nonowners too must be reasonably other-regarding, but reasonable nonowners need only compensate the owner for the harm imposed.

A nonowner's duty to avoid trespassing involves the duty to seek permission for non-privileged entry, as well as the duty to make reasonable decisions about boundary lines and the validity of privileged and permissive entry. For potential nonowners, property rights present formidable information issues.[45] A nonowner must decide whether access is privileged by custom or implied consent, or whether permission is needed to cross the boundary. Other information requirements surround the location of the boundary; the nonowner must ask where the boundary is, and determine how much effort to take to verify the boundary. Still other information requirements surround the putative permission the nonowner has received. The nonowner must ask whether the putative permissions are authentic and authoritative. In addressing these issues, an actor must determine whether it is reasonable to rely on the information she has, or whether she must get more information before going ahead. A court's choice of remedy largely turns on that decision. The failure to get information that a reasonable person would obtain, or acting in the face of information that would reasonably induce forbearance, makes the entry in bad faith, and justifies a court in granting property rule protection.[46] On the other hand, acting honestly on the basis of information a reasonable person would rely on under the circumstances makes the entry in good faith (albeit mistaken).[47] If entry is in bad faith, courts award punitive damages; if it is in good faith, they award compensatory damages.

> person to do so, or (b) remains on the land, or (c) fails to remove from the land a thing which he is under a duty to remove.").

[45] See Merrill and Smith (2000) at *8 ("When property rights are created, third parties must expend time and resources to determine the attributes of these rights, both to avoid violating them and to acquire them from present holders. The existence of unusual property rights increases the cost of processing information about all property rights.")

[46] See Seismic Petroleum Serv., Inc. v. Ryan, 450 So. 2d 437, 440 (Miss. 1984) (allowing jury to award punitive damages when the defendants trespassed after two of the defendant's employees had already been arrested and charged with trespass on the same land); Hood v. Adams, 334 S.W.2d 206, 208–09 (Tex. Civ. App. 1960) (awarding punitive damages when defendant had actual knowledge of his trespass).

[47] See Horn v. Corkland Corp., 518 So. 2d 418, 420 (Fla. Dist. Ct. App. 1988) (holding that punitive damages are not appropriate for mistaken trespass); Chesser by Hadley v. Hathaway, 439 S.E.2d

This also explains why courts sometimes award punitive damages for entry over the objection of the owner, as in *Jacque v. Steenberg Homes Inc.*[48] while in other cases of deliberate trespass over the objection of the owner, punitive damages are not imposed.[49] How then do courts determine whether the entry was in good faith? The cases come is several formats. In one format, the trespasser believes the boundary was in one location when it was, in fact, in another location.[50] In a second format, the trespasser claims that he had permission to enter the property, either because someone connected with

---

459, 464 (W.V. 1993) (refusing punitive damages when defendants were unaware that they were not the owners of the trespassed land at the time of the trespass); Eischen v. Hering, 622 N.W.2d 771 (Wis. App. 2000) (refusing punitive damages when plaintiff mistakenly believed that tree line, not stone fence, was the property line); Crowe v. Bellsouth Telecomm., Inc., 2009 WL 3241847, at *5 (M.D. Ala. Oct. 2, 2009) (refusing punitive damages when trespass was committed by mistake and construction employees believed no permission was needed to enter plaintiff's property).

[48] Jacque v. Steenberg Homes, Inc., 563 N.W.2d 154 (Wis. 1997).

[49] Friess v. Quest Cherokee, L.L.C., 209 P.3d 722 (Kan. App., 2009) (gas company proceeded to install natural gas pipelines on landowner's property with knowledge of encroachment and thus plaintiffs were entitled to injunction, but court declined to award punitive damages); Chesser by Hadley v. Hathaway, 439 S.E.2d 459, 464 (W.V. 1993) (refusing to award punitive damages despite defendants being warned by plaintiff about timbering on the property as defendants believed they had permission despite warnings); Eischen v. Hering, 622 N.W.2d 771 (Wis. App.2000) (not awarding punitive damages when defendant removed stone fence on plaintiff and defendant's property line, despite warnings that the fence was on the boundary line and not solely on the defendant's property, as removing the fence despite these warnings was not outrageous enough to warrant punitive damages); Dwyer v. Staunton, 4 D.L.R. 393 (1947) (refusing to award punitive damages despite defendants driving across the plaintiff's field to get around a blocked public road and despite the fact that plaintiffs had been warned they did not have permission to do so).

[50] *See* Vick v. Tisdale, 324 So. 2d 279 (Ala. Civ. App. 1975) (holding that defendant was not liable for punitive damages when defendant mistakenly entered plaintiff's land using an out-of-date map); Wood v. Neuman, 979 A.2d 64 (D.C. 2009) (holding that in a neighborly feud the plaintiff was entitled to $5000 in compensatory damages despite the fact that the trespassing defendant mistakenly believed the condominium association granted the defendant permission to enter the plaintiff's yard); Goshgarian v. George, 161 Cal. App. 3d 1214 (1984) (allowing punitive damages when defendant siphoned water from his swimming pool onto an adjoining lot that he believed he could rightfully access); Horn v. Corkland Corp., 518 So. 2d 419 (Fla. App. 2 Dist. 1988) (holding plaintiff was not entitled to $25,000 in punitive damages when defendant got written permission from a person he thought was property owner and was unaware that waterway crossed plaintiff's property); Lanier v. Burnette, 538 S.E.2d 476 (Ga. Ct. App. 2000) (awarding compensatory damages but not punitive damages when defendant erected fence on the plaintiff's property without consent but there was no evidence of willfulness and intention); Weaver v. Stafford, 8 P.3d 1234 (Idaho 2000) (holding that punitive damages were appropriate when defendant removed fence between defendant's and plaintiff's property, filled in irrigation ditch running in plaintiff's property, and erected new fence that encroached on plaintiff's land); Pehrson v. Saderup, 498 P.2d 648 (Utah 1972) (denying treble damages when defendant mistakenly thought lilacs were growing on his property but instead were growing on plaintiff's property); RESTATEMENT (SECOND) TORTS § 164 (Intrusions under Mistake).

Remedies in Exclusion Cases

the property had given him permission or because he had permission to do one thing on the property and assumed that also gave him permission to do something else.[51] In a third set of cases, the entry is ancillary to the nonowner protecting a different right, either to take control of property that was pledged in a debt or to get rid of what the trespasser considered to be a nuisance.[52] In each case, the good faith of the nonowner depends on whether the nonowner acted reasonably considering the information she had before her. If the nonowner enters the property without a reasonable basis for believing that he has permission or that he is on his side of the boundary line, the jury can impose punitive or exemplary damages.[53] However, where the entry is the result of a good faith belief in the defendant's permission to enter or in the location of the boundary, the owner is not entitled to have the jury consider punitive damages.[54] Thus, where the defendant hires people to log his property, lies about the boundary line, and expresses disregard for where the boundary line

---

[51] *See* Beetschen v. Shell Pipe Line Corp., 253 S.W.2d 785 (Mo. 1952) (regardless that employees of the defendants mistakenly believed they had a right to fence a 10-foot strip of land, the court awarded punitive damages because the defendant's easement over the strip of land did not include the right to fence, and that fact was evident from the proceedings in a condemnation suit); Maint. Equip. Co. v. Godley Builders, 420 S.E.2d 199, 205 (N.C. Ct. App. 1992) (holding that permission from a third party does not excuse trespass and awarding both punitive and compensatory damages); Dahlstrom Corp. v. Martin, 582 S.W.2d 159, 164 (Tex. Civ. App. 1979) (refusing to grant punitive damages when company did not know, even though the company should have known, the company was not leasing the land from the landowners because the comp any mistakenly believed the lease had already been executed).

[52] Yearian v. Columbia Nat. Bank of Columbia, 408 N.E.2d 63 (Ill. Ct. App. 1980) (reversing award for punitive damages, but allowing compensatory damages for physical damage to car, when bank agent mistakenly repossessed the plaintiff's car, instead of similar-looking car, when bank agents did not act willfully or wantonly despite the fact they did not check the license plate; *see* JCB, Inc. v. Union Planters Bank, NA, 539 F.3d 862, 874 (8th Cir. 2008) (awarding punitive damages against bank trespassing on debtor's property to repossess property). Of course, when repossession is not in good faith, courts award punitive damages. Kibbe v. Rohde, 427 A.2d 1163 (Penn. 1981) (awarding punitive damages against defendants for intentional trespass when defendant mistakenly believed they had security interest enforceable against the plaintiff's farm equipment).

[53] *See* Weaver v. Stafford, 8 P.3d 1234 (Idaho 2000) *overruled on other grounds by* Weitz v. Green, 230 P.3d 743 (Idaho 2010) (holding defendant liable for trespass and punitive damages for disregarding boundary lines and erecting a fence encroaching several feet onto the neighbor's property); Wilen v. Falkenstein, 191 S.W.3d 791, 802–03 (Tex. App. 2006) (awarding punitive damages when defendant knowingly directed tree trimmers to trim neighbor's tree).

[54] *See* Russell v. Irby, 13 Ala. 131, 136 (1848) (holding that the trespasser was liable only for compensatory damages when trespasser accidently cut timber on another's land); Isle Royale Mineral Co. v. Hertin, 37 Mich. 332, 335–36 (1877) (holding good-faith trespasser liable for only compensatory damages). *Cf.*, Cubit v. O'Dett, 16 N.W. 679, 680 (Mich. 1883) ("Absence of bad faith can never excuse a trespass, though the existence of bad faith may sometimes aggravate it.").

is, the defendant is subject to punitive damages.[55] On the other hand, good-faith (albeit mistaken) belief about the location of the boundary line, where the defendant has no reason to doubt her own belief, results in only compensatory damages. Even when the defendant is taking down a stone wall (which might normally be thought to be a boundary line), as long as the defendant reasonably believes that the boundary is beyond the wall (where a line of trees was) the defendant is responsible only for compensatory damages.[56]

The duty to investigate requires that the nonowner have an honest belief in the lawfulness of the entry and that the nonowner have no basis for thinking that more information to clarify the situation would be worth the additional effort in terms of the accuracy of the decision to enter.

7.4 CONCLUSION

This chapter has examined an owner's right to exclude and its limitations in order to explore the values that impel courts to justify the right to exclude when the owner is not harmed, the boundary between exclusion and inclusion, and the remedies for a breach of the rights thus determined.

Focusing on the content of the decision to exclude allows us to understand the right to exclude in terms of a theory of the duty of one person to take into account the well-being of others. Under this reading, the right to exclude reflects the general common law orientation that an actor has no duty to benefit others unless the actor has made a decision that implicates another's well-being. Because ownership itself, without more, does not implicate that obligation, an owner has no duty to benefit others and may therefore exclude others for any and no reason. But in a significant subset of cases, an owner will make a decision that fairly implies that the owner has undertaken to look out for the well-being of others, and, in those cases, the right to exclude is limited by the owner's obligation to meld the owner's well-being with the well-being of others.

---

[55] *See* Stearns & Culver Lumber Co. v. Cawthon, 56 So. 555, 557–58 (Fla. 1911) (holding that when a trespasser makes no effort to ascertain boundary line the trespasser cannot claim unintentional or mistaken trespass); Wimberly v. Barr, 597 S.E.2d 853, 858 (S.C. Ct. App. 2004) (holding defendant liable for punitive damages when defendant trespassed after being told of the property line on at least three occasions); Doyle v. Arthur, 222 Wis. 2d 624 (Ct. App. 1998) (holding defendant liable for disregarding property lines and knowingly instructing loggers to plow a logging road and destroy trees on the plaintiff's property).

[56] Eischen v. Hering, 622 N.W.2d 771 (Wis. App. 2000).

8 Nuisance: Spatial Coordination

Sometimes property owners make decisions about the use of their property that interfere with each other. One owner, a jazz trumpeter, wants to use his condominium to practice his trumpet; his neighbor, a mathematical genius, wants to use her adjoining condominium to quietly contemplate the mysteries of mathematical theorems. The decisions made by each owner are incompatible because the sound from the jazz trumpeter affects the mathematician, while the mathematician's request for quiet adversely affects the jazz trumpeter. There are social costs to be allocated.

Although the neighbors can (and often do) address the interference and allocate the costs through private agreement, the neighbors need law to help overcome barriers to bargaining. Importantly, there are multiple ways of addressing the interference, but each antidote requires the neighbors (and the law) to allocate costs. The interference would be avoided if one neighbor moved (a location decision), but any move is costly and the neighbors (and the law) must determine who should pay the cost. If soundproofing will abate the problem, the neighbors (and the law) need to determine who should pay for the soundproofing. If allocating separate times for trumpet practice and mathematical theorizing is a workable solution (another activity change), the neighbors (and the law) need a framework for making that allocation. If the harm to one neighbor can be addressed only through compensation, the neighbors (and the law) need to know who should compensate whom for how much. In short, the neighbors (and the law) must decide how to coordinate the conflicting decisions by requiring one owner to change her decisions (by moving, abating, or compensating) in light of the decisions of the other owner. This is the realm of private nuisance law.[1]

---

[1] Activities that are illegal under legislation are per se nuisances and do not create the kind of interpersonal coordination problem discussed here. They embody a determination that by virtue of their illegality, the activities ought not be carried out anywhere.

Nuisance cases present the community, and neighbors within the community, with a complex coordination problem: because the decisions of one owner may impose social costs by conflicting with the decisions of other owners, and vice versa, the community must figure out how best to coordinate those decisions to either avoid the social cost or to assign an entitlement to one party or the other. In terms of the equality principle, the law addresses this question: What set of rights and responsibilities will affirm the equal freedom of each owner to use her property as she likes, subject only to the equal freedom of other owners to use their property as they like.[2] The law cannot avoid a decision, for continuing the status quo without intervention is a decision that adversely affects the person harmed by the interference. Solving this coordination problem appropriately has perpetually perplexed the law.

In this chapter, I present a framework for thinking about the tradeoffs among the multiple possible solutions to the problem of social cost by focusing, as our theory suggests, on the decisions of each of the neighbors, a framework that focuses on understanding the factors that each individual ought to take into account when making decisions in the face of possible conflicting decisions of his or her neighbors. In Section 8.1, I discuss the conceptual issues raised by these reciprocal interferences, and explain why Coase's theories are best understood as identifying the social choices that must be made when individuals make decisions that are interdependent (where the effects of one individual's decision depends on the content of another individual's decision). I then address a conundrum haunting property law: the boundary between nuisance and trespass, showing in Section 8.2 how the concept of duty helps to chart the boundary between exclusion and unreasonable interference. I then suggest an appropriate framework for thinking about the just resolution of nuisance cases, focusing on two kinds of issues. First, as I discuss in Section 8.3, the neighbors (and the law) must determine whether social costs can be avoided by changing the activity of one (or both) of the neighbors. Second, the neighbors (and the law) must determine, for those social costs that cannot reasonably be avoided, whether they should be allocated to the activity of one neighbor or the other. I discuss this determination in Section 8.4.

8.1 THE CONCEPTUAL FRAMEWORK

One cannot get far in discussing nuisance without touching base with the work of Ronald Coase, for his abiding contribution was to identify and unravel the conceptual issues raised by the interdependent decisions of individuals.

---

[2] Simpson (2009).

The Conceptual Framework

Understanding the problem of social costs as one of interdependent decisions allows us to create an approach for addressing it.

8.1.1 *The Conceptual Problems*

The conceptual issues flow from Ronald Coase's famous demonstration that nuisance problems are problems of reciprocal cost.[3] In nuisance cases, each owner, while making decisions about the scope and nature of activity on his or her property, imposes a cost on the other – a cost that is external to the decision maker because it is absorbed by someone else. In our example, the trumpeter's practicing imposes a cost on the mathematician, and the mathematician's need for quiet imposes a cost on the trumpeter. The costs are reciprocal because the cost would not occur if the other owner were not there or had otherwise changed his or her behavior. The sound of a jazz trumpeter practicing would cause no harm if the mathematician were not next door, and the mathematician's demand for quiet would be unnecessary if there were a quiet-preferring individual next door.

Coase's demonstration that nuisance problems result from reciprocal costs posed two conceptual issues, one about causation and the other about the distribution of the costs generated by the interference. In the environment of reciprocal costs, how are we to understand the concept of causation? The jazz trumpeter is inflicting a cost on the mathematician neighbor in the sense of creating a stimulus that brings about the harm, whereas the mathematician neighbor is not creating a reciprocal harm-causing stimulus. Yet, as Coase demonstrated, each neighbor is a "but for" cause of the harm; if each neighbor were not there, there would be no harm. Nuisance law therefore works with two different causal ideas: one based on a "but for" test and the other based on the notion of initiating a stimulus that has a harmful effect. We need to determine whether one person's responsibility for the harms that another incurs ought to be based on one of these causal concepts or on some other basis.[4]

---

[3] Coase (1960).
[4] Courts act as though causing an effect – one-way causation – were the relevant causal concept, apparently disregarding Coase's notion of reciprocal causation (*see* Smith (2004) at 998) and Simpson (2009) at 22). Yet, causing harm is not a nuisance and responsibility does not following from causation. *See, e.g.*, Fontainebleau Hotel Corp. v. Forty-five Twenty-Five. Inc., 114 So. 2d 357 (Fla. 1959). A case has been made that nuisance is a strict liability tort, in which event causing harm in the one-way non-Coasian sense would be an operative concept. *See* Keating (2012). My view that nuisance is a fault-based tort is explained in Chapter 6 and in Gerhart (2010), and elaborated here.

Similarly, because nuisance cases present problems of reciprocal costs, they raise difficult conceptual issues about which party should be responsible for which costs. Because each neighbor is imposing a cost on the other, the relevant issue is to determine on what basis society ought to allocate the cost of the interference to one neighbor or the other. Should the interference be considered a cost of the activity of the mathematician or of the jazz musician? A choice to allow the jazz trumpeter to practice is the choice to distribute the cost to the mathematician's activity. But if the jazz musician is required to change his activity or to compensate the mathematician, the choice is to distribute the cost into the activity of being a jazz musician. How are we to know whether the cost should be distributed in one direction or the other?

The conceptual issues of nuisance require us to pay special attention to methodological issues. It is not possible to think about nuisance cases by applying a test or principle. Addressing nuisance problems requires one to consider the comparative advantage of avoiding the cost by moving or modifying one or both of the activities, which can be done in a variety of ways. It also requires one to determine who should pay for changing the way the activity is carried out and whether compensation should be required for activities that cannot reasonably be avoided. That is why legal doctrine can do no better than to point us in the direction we need to go, suggesting that a nuisance is a significant and unreasonable interference with the right of another to enjoy her property.[5] Given the variety of circumstances in which nuisance arises and the variety of factors that are relevant to the law's mediating function, nuisance law is no place for principles, rules, or doctrine. No sooner does a court utter "*sic utero*" or say that "coming to the nuisance is a wrong," then the next court turns around and contradicts the principle. What is needed is not doctrine but a systematic way of thinking about such interferences, one that allows us to make judgments about the relevance and weight of various factors the neighbors ought to take into account when they make activity decisions about their property. I present such a framework in this chapter.

8.1.2 *The Framework of Interdependent Decisions*

In order to fully exploit Ronald Coase's insights about reciprocal costs and causation, we need to understand the problem of social cost as a problem of individuals making interdependent decisions and to center our analysis on the appropriate content of each of the decisions.

---

[5] *Restatement (Second) of Torts* § 822 (1977).

The Conceptual Framework

Let us start with the concept of economic externalities. Although the term "externality" is contested, even within economics, the orthodox narrow view of externality is a cost that ought to be borne by the decision maker because, in the absence of transaction costs, others would pay more to avoid the cost than the decision maker would pay for the freedom to impose the cost.[6] The reason this kind of inefficient externality is of interest is that it distorts appropriate decision making, creating a gap between individual and social welfare. A steel mill emitting smoke is making use of a social resource, clean air, without having to include the cost of that resource in its prices. That creates a disparity between the higher social costs of the company's steel and the lower cost that is included in the price of the steel. The consequence is that steel's price does not reflect the full social cost of the steel and therefore does not send an accurate signal to consumers about the resources they consume when they buy steel. Buyers overconsume steel, buying more than they would if they had to compensate society for the full social cost of the steel. By internalizing the externality – that is, by including the true cost of using the air in the price of steel – the market is able to match private and social costs (all other things being equal) and decisions about resource use are made in a socially constructive way.

This is well-known, but it reminds us that the failure to internalize an externality is of significance because of the way it distorts decisions that ought to have taken that externality into account. For the market to effectively coordinate decisions about resources, the signals it gives through prices must contain all the information a buyer needs to make a socially appropriate decision; without that, the invisible hand cannot match individual and social benefits. When prices contain inadequate information, decisions are distorted and the market cannot effectively coordinate decisions about resource use.

---

[6] If, in the absence of transaction costs, those harmed by the activity would organize and pay the neighbor to change his or her activity, the external harm is an economic externality because it increases social wealth to internalize it. Demsetz (1967). This occurs, for example, if the cost of the harm is greater than the cost of avoiding the harm, which is why negligence law requires that individuals take reasonable precautions. If an actor is offered a sum of money to avoid the cost and does not accept it, the cost is not an external cost because the decision maker has taken the cost into account in the decisions the actor makes; the refusal to accept the payment signifies that the decision maker finds the right to impose the harm more valuable than those who incur the harm. Dukeminier et al. (2010) at 47. This formulation, however, assumes that the entitlement was correctly assigned in the first place. If it was not, then because the value of giving up an entitlement will often be greater than the value of the entitlement to someone who must purchase it, the externality may not be internalized in the right direction. That formulation also assumes that the money offered to the entitlement holder accurately reflects the decreased value of all individuals who incur the cost, which assumes that coordination of interests by non-entitlement holders is frictionless.

More generally, the problem of reciprocal cost is not just the fact that someone must bear the cost. Some costs cannot be avoided at reasonable expense; some costs – like some accidents – are unavoidable without imposing more expense on society than is saved. The problem of reciprocal costs is not the harm itself but the related problems that are caused because of the way imposing some costs on the community distorts socially appropriate decision making. The harm is a problem because it reflects a cost that one person should have taken into account, but did not, when making decisions about his or her activities.

This suggests that we can understand the essential point of Coase's analysis to be about the nature of decision making that brought about the interference (compared with the decision making of an ideal decision maker) rather than about the interference itself. Coase's insight is that the decisions of two owners in nuisance cases are interdependent in the sense that the effect of each decision depends on the decision made by the neighbor. The decision of the jazz musician to practice where and when he does causes harm because it is interdependent with the decision of the mathematician to work on her theorems at the same time and place. Harm occurs because the two decisions interact in a way that makes costs inevitable. The social cost of one actor's decision depends on, and is determined by, another person's decision, and vice versa.[7]

This characterization of Coasian insights helps us freshly address the conceptual problems of nuisance. Because the problem of nuisance is the problem of interdependent decisions, neither owner's decision is obviously correct or obviously wrong. As an interdependent decision, the decision's impact is determined by how the decision interacts with the decisions of neighbors. The decision to operate a pig farm is not unreasonable in itself; in the right time and place the decision to open a pig farm would produce little social cost. The decision to operate a pig farm is cost-producing only in the context of decisions made by neighbors. If neighbors decide to open a retirement community next to the pig farm, the decision to operate the pig farm could impose a significant social cost because of the way that decision interacts with the decision to open the retirement community next door. Because there are reciprocal interdependent decisions, the reverse is also true. The decision to open a retirement community imposes social costs because of the way it interacts with the decision to operate a pig farm.

---

[7] The question the law is asking is whether a decision maker who was taking the appropriate factors into account would have behaved the way the neighbor did. Nuisance law is saying that if all activities are governed by the decisions of an ideal decision maker, some social costs will be avoided and non-avoidable social costs will be borne by the activity that ought to bear them.

The Conceptual Framework

Because the decisions of neighbors are often interdependent, any owner's activity or use decisions can be evaluated only in the context of that owner's understanding of the decisions made by others; the individual decisions take their meaning from the decisions of others because their effect depends on decisions of others. And, because decisions by neighbors occur in situations where each has a chance to evaluate and predict the decisions of neighbors, each neighbor/decision maker, when acting as an ideal decision maker, has a basis for taking into account what one knows or can reasonably find out about one's neighbors' decisions. When a steel factory is looking for a location for a new plant, it knows whether people are likely to move into its neighborhood, and has a chance to take that information into account when deciding where to build the plant. And homeowners moving into a neighborhood have an opportunity to find out whether they are, or are likely to be, sharing their neighborhood with a cement plant. As a result, when we evaluate the decision of the cement company or homeowner, we must do so on the basis of how an ideal decision maker might have, or should have, taken into account the likely decisions of the other decision makers.

Because the problem of coordinating interdependent decisions underlies the problem of social cost, we can approach the problem of social cost by focusing on the conflicting decisions of the individuals in light of what they ought to have considered about the likely decisions of others. We can determine which activity should bear which cost by asking this question: Which neighbor, acting as an ideal decision maker, ought to have taken the possibility of interfering decisions into account as she made decisions about the use of her land, and how ought that information have influenced her decisions? Nuisance cases force the law to assign responsibility for the factors the neighbors take into account in decision-making, given the factors that we expect each individual to take into account when making decisions in light of the decisions that his or her neighbors can be expected to make. This, of course, is the question of how other-regarding each neighbor should have been.

Focusing on the decision making of each owner and the quality of that person's decision also allows us to approach freshly the causation issue. The focus on decision making suggests that rather than concentrating on which actor caused the harm we ought to concentrate on which actor made an unreasonable decision that caused the harm (including the possibility that an individual made an unreasonable decision not to compensate the other for harm caused). The fact that a person made a decision that caused harm is not the problem or the source of responsibility (even if the decision has, in some sense, brought about the harm); it is that the decision of one (or both) of the parties was unreasonable given the factors that each party should have taken into account, including the effects of the decision under reasonable assumptions about the likely decisions of the neighbor. The source of responsibility is not the decision but the unreasonable decision, and once we identify the relationship between the unreasonable decisions and the harm we know which party has "caused" the harm in a way that is relevant for imposing legal responsibility. But we are then not speaking of causing harm in the general sense of cause and effect; we are referring to causing harm in the sense of being responsible because of the unreasonable decision that brought about the harm. The causative question is not independent of the issue of who ought to be responsible for the harm and what it is that makes that person responsible.[8]

Given these conceptual shifts, we can create an appropriate framework for approaching nuisance cases. Under the view presented here, the law's function in nuisance cases is to assess the decisions made by each neighbor in light of what each neighbor should have understood about the decisions (past, present, and future) of other neighbors (assuming that the other neighbors will make reasonable decisions). That assessment will include an appraisal of the factors that should have influenced each decision given the existing and likely future decisions of the neighbor. It addresses this question: In view of the contextual facts that a reasonable person in the position of the decision maker would know, what kinds of considerations ought the decision maker have taken into account to reach a reasonable decision about its activities, given the reasonable decisions its neighbors are likely to make? Each actor is required to make reasonable decisions given what it knows about the background facts and the likely decisions of others. Reasonable decisions are those that are made with appropriate regard for the well-being of others (that is, the social costs that would otherwise occur), given the projects and preferences of the others as the actor reasonably understands them. Under this approach, the law functions to evaluate the decisions of each owner in light of how each owner should have thought about the well-being of other owners.[9]

---

[8] This is, of course, the role of causation in negligence liability. Causation is a constituent part of assigning responsibility because if the harm would have occurred anyway, an actor is not responsible for the harm. An actor is not responsible just because the actor is the "but for" cause of the harm, which is the intuition that Coase reminded us of when he criticized courts for assigning responsibility on the basis of which party caused the harm. Causation is relevant to responsibility only if what made the decision unreasonable caused the harm. And causation is a source of responsibility only if the actor is also responsible for the circumstances that linked the actor to the harm. See Gerhart (2010) at 108 and 133. In tort law, making a decision that caused harm is a source of responsibility only if the decision was unreasonable, and then only if the decision is connected to the harm in a specified way.

[9] Under this vision of nuisance, courts ought not compare the utility of neighbors' activities. Comparing utilities suggests that society must give up the utility of one of the activities in order to get the utility of the other activity, as if we were ranking decisions that people have made

The Conceptual Framework

This process of making decisions in light of the anticipated decisions of others assures that each individual makes decisions that match the burdens and benefits of decisions about resource use, given the likely decisions of others. If one individual ought to move to a more reasonable location, that reflects the burdens that a reasonable person would absorb in those circumstances. If one person would compensate the other for unavoidable harm, the compensation represents the amount necessary to restore the appropriate assignment of burdens and benefits of the activity decisions of the other individual.

Because an individual's harm can be addressed either by reducing it or compensating for it, we can recognize two kinds of nuisance cases, with two different ways of thinking about how to address social costs. In one kind of nuisance case, the social cost could be avoided if one (or both) neighbors modified how they undertook their activity. We can call this an activity-change solution. One neighbor (or both neighbors) can adjust their activity, either by discontinuing it, by investing in technology that abates the harm (such as soundproofing), or by changing the location or timing of the activity. This is an internalization function because the neighbor absorbing the additional costs of his or her activities (by discontinuing, abating or moving the activity) is avoiding the external harm by absorbing the cost of avoiding the harm.[10]

This type of internalization is the internalization of the negligence regime. To avoid acting unreasonably, an actor must invest in reasonable precautions, which is similar to absorbing the cost of harm that, by making reasonable changes in activities, could have been avoided. If a factory could reduce the harm by installing scrubbers, and the cost of installation is less than the harm avoided by the installation, the factory ought to do that. If a pig farm has the choice between two locations that serve its purposes equally well but one location imposes more damage than another, the owner will have to choose the lower-cost–imposing location, even at a higher price (if the higher price is offset by decreased damage to neighbors). The owner has an obligation to be other-regarding and that obligation requires the owner to absorb burdens that save a neighbor from equivalent or greater harm.

In the nuisance context, this solution can be achieved by enjoining the activity that causes the harm. An injunction in these circumstances will induce the defendant to absorb the costs of making activity changes unless those costs are

---

about their lives. It suggests, for example, that we decide whom we value most, jazz trumpeters or mathematicians. That choice is impossible to make and is not the kind of decision that courts ought to be making. The law instead is asking which actor ought to bear the cost of either changing his or her activity or absorbing the cost of the interference, given the way society generally looks at the responsibility of one person for the well-being of another.

[10] This is the concept of internalization advanced by Demsetz (1967).

greater than the value of the activity, in which event the defendant will avoid the harm by shutting down the activity (so that the injunction is equivalent to the determination that the activity itself is an unreasonable one). Alternatively, a court could achieve the same result by requiring the defendant to compensate the plaintiff, but only when the court is sure that the cost of avoiding the harm by changing the activity is less than the harm that must be compensated. If the cost of avoiding the harm is greater than the damage from the harm, the remedy will have no impact on the defendant's activity and will simply be a transfer payment to the neighbor. That transfer payment would not reduce the interference and must therefore be justified on some other ground, which is the function of the second kind of nuisance case.

In a second kind of nuisance case, social cost cannot be avoided: either no change in an activity of the neighbors will reasonably reduce social cost or the court needs to decide which neighbor ought to bear the cost of changing an activity to avoid the harm. When dealing with the social cost that cannot be avoided, the court faces a second (and different) kind of cost-allocation issue. In this type of case, the law cannot function to avoid the social cost (either because no change in activity decisions would be reasonable or because someone must incur the cost of reasonable activity changes). Rather, the law is allocating responsibility for the social cost that cannot be avoided – allocating the cost of the harm to one party or the other (or to both) by awarding an entitlement to avoid the harm.

In this kind of nuisance case, compensation is the only reasonable remedy. By our hypothesis, the objective is not to change anyone's primary behavior (as occurs when an activity is enjoined) but to allocate an unavoidable social cost. Moreover, in this kind of case, the law is not determining whether the activity decision of either neighbor is unreasonable or inefficient; by the terms of our analysis, no reasonable decision could have avoided the harm. The law is deciding who should absorb the cost of the unavoidable harm – that is, in which direction the harm should be allocated. We might conceptualize the issue as follows: In the context of a particular case, which party should, when making decisions about its activity, build the cost of unavoidable harm into the cost structure of its activity, so that the harm is one of the factors it takes into account when making decisions? That is the individual who is required to be other-regarding by absorbing the cost of repairing the harm as part of its activities.

These two types of nuisance cases reflect the difference between negligence and strict liability. In a negligence regime, the only cost that is internalized is the harm that could have been avoided had the actor taken reasonable precautions. The other harm is internalized into the activity of the victim, for there is

The Conceptual Framework

no recovery for harm that could not be prevented by the injurer's reasonable precautions. Strict liability, by contrast, distributes all the harm and therefore corresponds to the second kind of nuisance case. The unavoidable social cost is distributed to one neighbor or the other.[11] Either the victim bears the loss because the victim is not negligent (a case of strict no-liability) or the injurer bears the loss even if not negligent (a case of strict liability).

To illustrate the framework suggested by our theory and the relationship between the two types of nuisance cases, consider a cement factory that emits smoke harmful to neighboring homeowners. As Coase demonstrated, this is a problem of reciprocal costs, requiring us to ask whether the social cost of the smoke should be allocated to the activity of the cement factory or into the activity of the homeowners. Our analysis has broken this into two questions, one related to each neighbor's decisions about its activity and one related to each neighbor's obligation to pay the costs that cannot reasonably be avoided.

As to activity decisions, we should ask whether the cement factory or the homeowners are in the best position to take into account the harm when making decisions about their activity. The cement factory must consider where it should locate and what abatement technology it might use, because these activity decisions might be the least-cost solution to the problem. The homeowners ought to consider their location decisions (did they "come to the nuisance") and whether they can avoid the harm at least cost by some form of self-protection. If the cement factory was there first, it could be that the homeowners are fully compensated for the harm because they pay lower prices for their property (in which event the plaintiffs ought to be the homeowners who sold their property at the lower price, not the homeowners who bought the property). The law should, in other words, identify the least cost avoider.

Assuming that harm cannot be avoided with reasonable activity decisions, or that the court has to decide who should pay for the cost of those reasonable decisions, the law must determine in which direction the costs should be distributed; should it be a part of the cost of the activity of making cement or the cost of owning a home? In the case of the cement factory, the decision to require the factory to compensate the homeowners is tantamount to saying the activity of making cement ought to be undertaken only if the owner of the factory undertakes the activity with the understanding that if harm occurs, the owner will compensate those injured. I have already given the economic

---

[11] Theoretically, the unavoidable harm could be split between both activities if no better allocation method were available. In fact, however, courts allocate the harm in one direction. Either the victim bears the loss because of the victim's negligence (a case of strict no-liability) or the injurer bears the loss even if not negligent (a case of strict liability).

rationale for that internalization decision – namely, that in the absence of internalization, consumers might buy too much cement instead of other material because the cost of cement does not reflect the full cost of its production.[12] The result can also be understood in terms of either unjust enrichment or as an application of the doctrine of *Vincent v. Lake Erie Steamship Co.* When the cement company decides to use a resource that it shares with another (clean air) and to which all have an equal claim, it must do so with the understanding that it will compensate the other for the damage caused by its resource use.[13]

Thus far, I have presented a conceptual framework of the considerations that are relevant in nuisance cases. This analysis allows us to chart the domain of nuisance law, which I do in the next subsection, and then to delve more deeply into each of the two ways of addressing the social costs presented in nuisance cases.

8.2 DUTY AND THE DOMAIN OF NUISANCE

The concept of duty helps us chart the domain of private nuisance law. Neighbors have obligations to neighbors by virtue of having purchased land in a neighborhood; the obligation to be other-regarding with respect to a neighbor comes from the decision to become a neighbor knowing that some uses of land could impose harms on others. A neighbor is one who might be affected by an owner's activity decisions. The duty of neighbors is reciprocal, a reflection of the problem of reciprocal costs that their interdependent decisions can bring about; each owner owes to every neighbor the obligation to think reasonably about her use of the property.[14]

This conception of obligation begs the question of what we mean by "neighbor." The ownership and spatial aspects are clear: (1) neighbors must be owners, for the obligation in private nuisance derives from ownership and runs to other owners; and (2) neighbors must be near enough so that their decisions might interfere with each other. But the spatial aspect of neighborliness also has temporal implications, for neighborhoods change and the identification of

---

[12] Even if the price is not too low, the cement company may be making too much profit, earning a supra-competitive return because its shareholders do not have to pay the true cost of production.

[13] In this sense, nuisance law supplies an antidote to the tragedy of the commons, requiring individuals who withdraw resources from the commons to pay for those resources.

[14] Public nuisance, which is not discussed at length in this book, concerns the relationship between owners and nonowners. Because nonowners are using public (common) property, public nuisance protects users of common property from decisions of owners of private property. The concept of the duty of an owner to others is the same in public as in private nuisance, although in the case of public nuisance the duty is owed to the users of common property.

neighbors therefore change as well. Circumstances change, and with changed circumstances come changing obligations. This presents nuisance law with a particular temporal dimension – the obligations to neighbors shift as the neighborhood changes – and a particular ex post problem. Decisions that are reasonable ex ante may become unreasonable over time, and nuisance law must deal with changing obligations in response to changing circumstances.

Because of its broad scope, the concept of duty plays little role in assigning the burdens and benefits of resource decisions in nuisance cases, but it can help us chart the border between trespass and nuisance, a border that has proven tenaciously difficult for courts to define. The problem is easy to see and difficult to address. If a person walks over another's boundary, the person is, unless privileged, a trespasser. But if the person sends smoke across the boundary the person is, if responsible at all, responsible for a nuisance. What accounts for that difference?

The traditional judicial distinctions are unappealing. The law has tried to distinguish between trespass and nuisance on the basis of the owner's interest that is being protected under the two doctrines. Trespass is thought to protect an owner's interest in exclusive possession, whereas nuisance protects an owner's interest in use and enjoyment. But it is impossible to cleave these two interests. One's use and enjoyment is protected by keeping people off the property, just as exclusive possession can be threatened if one is dispossessed by invading particles. The appellations *exclusive possession* and *use and enjoyment* appear to be labels attached to explain conclusions reached on other grounds, not justifications for putting a case in one category rather than another. The attempt to distinguish between trespass and nuisance on the basis of the means of invasion is also unworkable. Dust and smoke are thought to be "indirect" invasions even though they constitute a physical incursion, whereas stepping over a boundary is thought to be a direct invasion, even when it imposes no actual harm. The terms *direct* and *indirect* also seem to be characterizations attached to distinctions drawn on some other basis. The notion that tangible incursions are trespasses whereas intangible incursions are nuisances is also artificial – depending, as it does, on a definition of those terms that is not consistent across cases. Sometimes things that seem tangible are classified as intangible and vice versa. Whether the interference arises from the use of the plaintiff's land or the defendant's land is closer to a workable distinction, but by itself is of little help because by definition there must be an effect on plaintiff's rights for either trespass or nuisance.

What distinguishes trespass from nuisance, and therefore accounts for their treatment in different analytical categories, is the concept of duty. It will be recalled that in trespass cases the interests of owner and nonowner are not balanced against each other until a court finds that the owner has a duty to consider the well-being of the nonowner. In nuisance cases, the interests of the neighbors are always balanced against each other. The distinction between balancing in all cases (nuisance) and balancing only when the owner has a duty to the potential user (trespass) derives from the different function that duty plays in determining the right to exclude and the right to use. Because neighbors always have duties to each other, cases involving conflicting land use require no prior determination of whether one person has an obligation to another; courts can assume there is a duty and proceed to define the scope of each neighbor's duty. By contrast, in trespass cases there is no need to "balance" competing interests if the owner has no obligations to one who wants access to the property. In those kinds of cases, courts use a different analytical apparatus because they need to make a prior determination about duty and, in the absence of a duty to the nonowner, the incursions are trespasses.

This analysis suggests that what distinguishes trespass from nuisance is not the interest of the owner who claims an invasion or the means by which the invasion occurs, but the obligation of the owner to take into account the interests of the one causing the invasion. If the invasion is caused by a neighbor's use of her land, the court knows that it needs to balance two sets of interests because the plaintiff and defendant share reciprocal duties. Balancing is inevitable when neighbors injure each other by their land use decisions because each neighbor has an obligation to make reasonable land use decisions in light of the decisions of his or her neighbors. On the other hand, if the incursion is not from a neighbor's land use, there is no reason to believe that the owner has a duty to the person causing the incursion, and courts must make a preliminary determination of whether the owner owes the person making the incursion any obligation.[15] The potential user's decision is not grounded on her ownership rights but on her personal right to have the owner take her well-being into account (as we have seen, in trespass cases there is no warrant to undertake a balance of interests until the court finds that the owner has, for one of the reason outlined in Chapter 7, an obligation to take into account the well-being of the potential user. When the potential user is a neighbor, her rights arise from her use of the property and the case cannot be addressed without balancing interests.

The distinction between obligations growing out of a defendant's use of his property and obligations growing out of an individual's right of access to another's property has not always honored by courts, but that is because the

---

[15] If a neighbor walks across a boundary with neither permission nor privilege, doing so, of course, is a trespass. It is not a nuisance because it does not arise from the neighbor's use of the land.

law followed a formal, not a functional approach. Moreover, the law seems to be moving in the analytical direction recommended here. Consider the encroachment cases. When a neighbor builds an addition to her home that crosses a neighbor's boundary, courts historically treated this as a trespass; it was, after all, a physical incursion. Classifying encroachment cases as a trespass led to severe results; because encroachments are not privileged, the normal trespass remedy was to enjoin the trespass (a continuing one), which required that the encroaching structure be torn down, no matter how minor the encroachment or how major the loss imposed by the remedy. Under the analysis suggested here, those cases ought to be treated, and increasingly are treated, as nuisance cases because they arise from a neighbor's use of her land and are thus covered by a reciprocal duty to avoid unreasonable interferences with a neighbor.

Under the nuisance approach, courts can and still do enjoin encroachments, for encroachments often occur in circumstances where the builder did not do enough due diligence before the structure was built. And even for innocent encroachments – those done in good faith and with reasonable consideration of boundary lines – courts require compensation for the incursion. But the fact of encroachment – the unprivileged trespass – is no longer the sole basis for imposing liability; the liability is imposed because of one neighbor's unreasonable interference with the rights of another neighbor. Courts are properly treating encroachment cases as nuisance cases rather than trespass cases. That frees courts to avoid remedies that would be socially harmful by requiring a builder to destroy structures built by reasonable mistake, and to use damage remedies to compensate the owner whose property has been invaded.

8.3 AVOIDING SOCIAL COSTS THROUGH REASONABLE DECISIONS

The theory developed here understands law to influence behavior by influencing the way individuals make decisions in an interconnected world. As a result, we can understand nuisance law by understanding the kind of decisions that the law expects an ideal decision maker to make, focusing on the factors an ideal decision maker ought to take into account when making decisions. In the class of cases discussed in this section, the harm can be avoided if one or more neighbors make more reasonable decisions about where and how to undertake their activities, and the law requires an individual's behavior to conform to that of the ideal decision maker.

In this class of cases, nuisance law asks each owner to consider the reasonableness of her activity decisions in light of the reasonably predicted activity decisions of her neighbors. The law, in other words, must determine which owner's decisions ought to accommodate the projects and preferences of the neighbor. This is a matter of establishing how each owner/decision maker ought to think about the other owner/decision maker's well-being and then determining which decision maker ought to accommodate to the decisions of the neighbor. Cases in this class are like negligence cases: the harm could be avoided by either the victim or the injurer, and the law asks which individual can avoid the harm at least cost. One or both individuals must invest in reasonable precautions by modifying the activity to avoid harm to the other. As in negligence cases, the least cost avoider can be one party or the other, or the harm can be avoided at least cost by some combination of changed decisions of both parties.

Because this type of case is built on negligence principles, the idea that the law requires decision makers to make a fair division of burdens and benefits is conceptually easy to understand. Each party must invest in its activity up to the point where an additional increment of investment will be offset by a benefit to a neighbor, taking into account the kind of values that the social norms of the neighborhood require for that kind of decision. When each neighbor does that, the burdens and benefits of decisions about resources are appropriately allocated.

What property law adds to the general negligence framework is a methodology of accounting for changed circumstance – something that is often unneeded in accident law, where little time elapses between the decision that leads to the harm and the harm itself. In property law, activity decisions made at one time may give rise to interferences at a later time because of intervening circumstance. That challenges the negligence concept because the original activity decision may be reasonable when made but may become unreasonable because of changing circumstances. Here, the analogy is to product liability, because manufacturers are under a continuing responsibility to understand changes in technology that might make their products safer – a changed circumstance for which a reasonable manufacturer would account. Similarly, even if the decision to engage in an activity is reasonable when made, changing technology and changing neighborhoods may require the decision maker to reconsider the reasonable activity decision.

The remedy in this type of case follows from the assessment of responsibility of each party. As in negligence cases, responsibility can be shared by the parties or assigned to one individual or the other. If responsibility falls solely on one individual rather than the other, that party bears the costs of changing his or her activity. The court can enjoin the unreasonable activity, confident that the effect of the injunction will be to induce the individual to invest the resources necessary to change the activity. Alternatively, a court may award compensatory damages to the same effect (if the court determines that the cost of changing the activity decision is less than the cost of the harm). If only one neighbor made an unreasonable decision, that owner ought, for that reason, to absorb the cost of changing the decision; the owner can reverse the decision she made and implement the decision she should have made. If owner A locates his pig farm near an existing housing development, the determination that the pig farmer chose an unreasonable location leads to the conclusion that the pig farm ought either to move or to invest in abatement technology (if available). In these cases, the demonstration that an owner made an unreasonable decision demonstrates the appropriate accommodation to address the interference. The law asks that owners compensate the victims for the harms that occurred in order to tell the decision makers that they should have taken that cost into account when making their decisions.

If costs can be avoided by both neighbors, the nuisance case looks much like one involving negligence and contributory negligence, and the court must use some notion of comparative responsibility to determine what changes each neighbor is required to make to avoid the harm. And the court may require one party to change its activity and that the other party help pay for that change. Owner A may choose an unreasonable location (in light of B's existing use), but once A has invested in the location it may be cheaper from a social perspective to require B rather than A to move. In that case, the responsibility for the interference may be assigned to one party but the burden of reducing the interference may be assigned to a different party. The party responsible for the interference then pays the party responsible for reducing the interference to do so.

Two general dimensions of activity decisions are involved: where an activity is done and how an activity is done.

8.3.1 Where an Activity Takes Place

Individuals make decisions about where to engage in their activities, and sometimes the activity becomes a nuisance only because of where it is carried out. As the Supreme Court colorfully put it: "A nuisance may be merely a right thing in the wrong place, like a pig in the parlor instead of the barnyard."[16]

Each decision maker is responsible to make a decision about the reasonable location for her activity, given what the decision maker reasonably understands about existing and future land use patterns. The reasonable location

[16] Village of Euclid v. Ambler Realty Co., 272 U.S. 365, 388 (1926).

depends on the burdens and benefits of each of the decision maker's options, and requires the decision maker to minimize harm to others by choosing a location where the sacrifice of benefits just offsets the burdens that would otherwise be borne by the neighbor. A reasonable decision maker will accept the burdens of a less desirable location when those burdens are offset by reduced harm to a neighbor. In other words, the relevant factors a decision maker ought to take into account include the decision maker's location options, the costs and benefits of those locations for the well-being of the decision maker, and the costs imposed on neighbors at the various locations. That obligation is borne by each neighbor. The task of each decision maker is to integrate what it understands about the interests of its neighbors at the various locations with its own projects and preferences in a way that fairly treats the interests of the neighbors.

Many nuisance cases test location decisions. The doctrine of "coming to the nuisance" suggests that those who make land use decisions ought to take into account the well-being of those already there; the first-in-time notion privileges first inhabitants because it gives second comers information they ought to take into account when making decisions. Under that doctrine, one who moves toward a nuisance cannot complain about the nuisance; straightforwardly, a person choosing a location is assumed to know surrounding land use patterns, and is expected to take those patterns into account when determining the value of his or her property. When land uses that would create a conflict are reasonably knowable, a decision maker is expected to reflect the conflict in determining the price of the property, and may therefore not complain about it. But the coming-to-the-nuisance doctrine requires only that the decision maker make reasonable investigation of the surrounding area before making a location decision. Where the individual moving toward the nuisance could not reasonably discover the nuisance, or where the person was given false information, the decision maker has not, by the decision about location, accepted the burdens of the location.

The notion of coming to the nuisance is not, however, an invariable rule.[17] Circumstances change, and sometimes even first comers bear the risks of their location decisions. Consider *Foster v. Preston Mills Co.*,[18] for example. There, the blasting to create access to a logging operation caused mink on a nearby

---

[17] In *Sturges v. Bridgemen*, for example, one of the analogies the court used is to a blacksmith's forge that had once been on a barren moor, where a residence had recently been built. According to the Bridgemen court, it would be "in an equally degree unjust, and, from a public point of view, inexpedient that the use and value of the adjoining land should, for all times and under all circumstances, be restricted or diminished by reason of the continuance of acts incapable of physical interruption..." [1879] 11 Ch.D. 852 at 865.

[18] 268 P.2d 645 (Wash. 1954).

mink farm to eat their young, thereby decreasing the stock of the mink farm. The court ruled in favor of the defendant blasters, despite the following facts: the blasters came to the nuisance,[19] the mink farm had apparently chosen a reasonable location,[20] and the blasters "caused" the harm in the sense of setting off a stimulus that brought about the harm. Finding that "it is the exceedingly nervous disposition of the mink, rather than the normal risks inherent in blasting operations, which therefore must, as a matter of sound policy, bear the responsibility for the loss here sustained," and that the noise "was no more than a usual incident of the ordinary life of the community," that court denied the plaintiff any recovery.[21] The basis of the decision is clear. One of the risks of operating a mink farm is the risk that the mother mink will become excitable from surrounding noise. That is a risk that ought to be borne by those operating mink farms, not by the surrounding community and the mink farm operators should not be able to impose costs on neighbors to take extraordinary measures to protect the mink from themselves.[22]

Similarly, a home owner may not be able to complain about noise from a nearby drag racing track if the drag racing operation is in a reasonable location. Where a neighborhood deteriorated after a home owner moves in, and now includes a major interstate highway, an airport, and numerous railroads and commercial establishments, the neighborhood may be the most reasonable location for drag racing; despite the incremental costs imposed by drag racing, the owner is not able to claim that it is a nuisance. The law cannot protect a property owner against lower property values caused by changing neighborhoods.

On the other hand, nuisance cases involving location decisions do not always require the party that ends up in an unreasonable location to absorb the cost of its unreasonable location. In *Spur Industries, Inc v. Dell E. Webb*

---

[19] The defendants had been logging in the area for fifty years; however, from all we know in the record, this was the first time they had blasted in the area.

[20] The mink farm was near a major interstate highway and two railroads, but the mink had become inured to the noise from those sources.

[21] *Id.* at 359. The trial court had apparently found neither a public nor a private nuisance, and the opinion dealt primarily with the scope of liability for an abnormally dangerous activity such as blasting. The reasoning of the court under strict liability seems equally relevant to the nuisance claim.

[22] By contrast, where a mink rancher had bought land next to the village dump to operate a mink ranch, the mink rancher was able to hold the city responsible for damage to the mink farm from smoke caused by burning at the dump during breeding season. Although the ground of the jury determination is not clear, it may be influenced by the prior sale of the land by the village to the mink ranch, for the effect of the decision is to impose a kind of implied contractual obligation not to operate the dump during mink breeding season in a way that would injure the sensitive mink.

Development Co.,[23] for example, the operator of a feedlot and the operator of a neighboring retirement community simultaneously moved their operations closer to each other, so that eventually the interference at the boundary between them was significant. Because the interference was caused by contemporaneous decisions that seemed, by both neighbors, to discount the impact of their decisions on other neighbor, it was not unjust to require, as the court did, that they share the cost of moving the feedlot. Although social costs would be minimized by moving the feedlot (because the feedlot was in the way of an expanding Phoenix, Arizona), the retirement community developer was responsible for paying for that result, because the developer's decisions to move closer to the feedlot had unreasonably brought it about.

8.3.2 Decisions about How an Activity Is Done

When land use decisions conflict, the impact can sometimes be avoided if one (or both) of the parties change how they do the activity. A jazz trumpeter who wants to practice can install soundproofing; a factory can install scrubbers. Or, owners can change how often or when they do an activity. Neighbors are required to think about whether they ought to invest in abatement measures in order to avoid social costs. Accordingly, each owner is expected to invest in reasonable abatement measures whenever the cost of doing so is offset by the reduced harm to the neighbor.

Sometimes, both owners have abatement options. In that case, the relevant model reflects the division of responsibility between two actors who can both invest in precautions to reduce the risk of harm. In tort cases, when harm can be avoided by either the injurer or the victim, courts look to a rule of responsibility that asks the least cost avoider to invest in precautions, or courts divide responsibility for investing in abatement measures between two owners, depending on their relative ratio of costs and benefits. Similarly, in nuisance cases, courts must look to the least cost avoider to determine which combination of measures reduces harm with the least social burden.

This analysis explains the otherwise surprising result in *Sturges v. Bridgman*,[24] one of the cases providing an important illustration in Ronald Coase's article of social cost. There, a doctor's office adjoined a bakery, and the doctor constructed his examination room so that it was contiguous with the back wall of the bakery. Although the doctor "came to the nuisance" and, in one sense, "caused" the interference (which did not occur before the expansion), the

[23] 108 Ariz. 178 (1972).
[24] [1879] 11 Ch. D. 852.

court enjoined the bakery from continuing to use its equipment in a way that interfered with the doctor's practice and patients. Brain Simpson's detailed review of the case suggests the justification for this result. Apparently, the baker's equipment could be moved away from the wall or otherwise modified with little expense,[25] whereas the doctor needed the additional room in order to avoid examining patients in his dining room. The injunction may simply have represented the belief that the baker was the least cost avoider.

That analysis does not completely address the nuisance issue, of course, for we must still ask who should pay to move the equipment to avoid the harm – the baker or the doctor? When rights and remedies were thought to be conjoined, the failure to ask this question may be understandable. Under a modern approach, which sometimes determines that the party that is the least cost avoider is not the party who is responsible for the decision that led to the conflict, the court can order that one neighbor abate the interference and that the other neighbor pay for the abatement. The identification of the least cost avoider is separated from the identification of who should pay for the abatement because abatement addresses the reduction of social cost, and payment responds to the question of responsibility for the social cost. Responsibility depends on which neighbor's decisions were faulty given what both should reasonably have known about the decisions of the other neighbor. With this understanding, it might well be that a modern court, recognizing the responsibility of the doctor for "coming to the nuisance," would require the doctor to pay the baker to move the machines that "caused" the harm. Even if the baker is the least cost avoider, it is not clear why the doctor, who got the benefit of the construction, ought to be able to impose the costs of removing the harm on the baker.

8.4 THE DISTRIBUTION OF UNAVOIDABLE COSTS

When neighbors cannot avoid social costs by making reasonable activity decisions, or when courts must determine which party should bear the cost of reasonable investments to avoid the harms, courts must determine which neighbor should bear the costs. In making that determination, they are essentially deciding which costs ought to be a part of an actor's activity and which ought not. When a mathematician needs quiet and a jazz trumpeter needs to practice, we need to know who should pay for the soundproofing, or, if

---

[25] The judge gave the baker the time "to make the necessary alterations to his premises; and no doubt he would find some skillful mechanic in London who would tell him how to work these machines without making any noise at all." *Id.* at 859. *See* Simpson (2009) at 38, 41.

soundproofing will not address the problem, which party should absorb the loss. Should the mathematician be allowed to claim compensation, or should she be made to put up with the loss? This is the process of awarding an entitlement to avoid the loss to one party rather than the other.

This is among the most difficult issues the law faces. In terms of the terminology they use, courts sort cases into two types: insignificant harm (for which the loss lies where it falls) and significant harms (for which the loss is shifted).

8.4.1 Insignificant Harms

Courts recognize a category of social costs they call "insignificant." In these cases, no relief is given and the cost lies where it falls. Generalizations about this class of cases are difficult because the meaning of "significant" is unclear. A social cost could be insignificant because it is not the kind of cost for which we want other people to be responsible. One might, for example, say that the loss of profits by a monopolist schoolteacher when another schoolmaster came to town is an insignificant cost, which would be a ruling on the merits and a statement that we want the loss to lie where it falls because inflicting losses through fair competition is privileged. Other cases may use the term "insignificant" to signify social costs that are insignificant in relation to the administrative costs of adjudicating them in court. It would be rational for the judicial system to refuse to expend scarce resources on cases of little social cost. And the rule denying recovery to a peculiarly sensitive plaintiff denies that plaintiff undue control over his neighbors.

It is nonetheless noteworthy that the law uses the word "significant" as a filter to determine whether the cost should be distributed to the plaintiff or the defendant. In other contexts of interfering decisions (for example, in the general law of torts) no such filter is used. The "significance" of the harm and the sensitivities of the plaintiff are simply factors that courts take into account when they determine whether the actor made a reasonable decision. What is different about the law of neighbors?

Because the duty of neighbors is a reciprocal duty, there must be special room in the law of nuisance for cases in which the plaintiff ought, out of a spirit of neighborliness, to absorb the social cost of being a neighbor. It is clear, for example, that if an individual has a particular sensitivity to odors or aesthetic propriety, the individual ought not be empowered to impose the social cost of that sensitivity on another by claiming that the other has caused a nuisance. More broadly, neighborly duties include the duty of accepting certain idiosyncrasies of other neighbors. Norms of neighborliness include norms of

The Distribution of Unavoidable Costs

open discussion about difference and open acceptance of differences. The duty of acceptance and accommodation is a way by which the law forces neighborliness and invites neighbors to expand their view of each other's tastes and aesthetic palate. Indeed, the law needs to withhold its power when what appears as a nuisance is in fact derived from a prejudice that the community ought to fight. We can view the smells coming from neighboring kitchens to be nuisances or we can accept the difference, and the law does not want to get in the business of determining, for example, whether the Asian couple that is cooking down the hall is a nuisance to Caucasian sensitivities.

The concept of insignificant harm signals that some harms ought to be accommodated rather than suppressed.

8.4.2 Significant Harms

When harm cannot be avoided, the law must award an entitlement to avoid the harm to one neighbor or the other. In Section 6.4.1, I argued that the comparative valuation of the activities is not a meaningful methodology for distributing costs. I have also argued that sometimes the law wants the individual to pay the social costs because the law wants that person's decision to reflect those costs. Here I argue that thinking about the division of costs from behind the veil of ignorance is a workable methodology for determining how the costs ought to be distributed.

8.4.2.1 The Role of Norms. The *Vincent* case reflects a simple social norm: when using another's property to protect one's own, one ought to agree to compensate the other if the other's property becomes damaged. This norm governs the division of burdens and benefits when property entitlements have already been assigned. But norms also influence how the law assigns entitlements. Norms reflect standards of behavior that most people use to make decisions about their activities. They tell us how people form expectations about their activities and therefore how people value various decisions that they must make about their activities. People interact based on norms of behavior that are constantly being renegotiated in social settings, and those norms reflect valuations that people put on claims to entitlements in different settings. It is the valuations that lie behind the norms of behavior that give rise to entitlements, for when those valuations signal that claims to entitlement will be accepted under the prevailing norms, the claim to an entitlement matures into a right. Human behavior reveals those valuations by revealing the way people normally act. In awarding entitlements, then, what is important is not the valuation put on them by the individuals but the valuation that courts put on the claims based on the court's best assessment of how the values that people normally use in social interactions ought to be understood in the context of the interaction before the court.

For example, a norm of quiet establishes a baseline from which the law can determine how the belief systems of interacting individuals will influence decisions about when and where to engage in noisy activities. Such norms therefore help the law recognize in which direction entitlements ought to be allocated. The law might logically say that the norm of quiet after certain hours implies that those engaging in loud activities will build the cost of avoiding interference with that norm into the cost of their activities. Jazz trumpeters would expect to pay for soundproofing or to arrange practice space in other locations during the hours of normal quiet.

As helpful as norms are in the law, they beg issues of interpretation. Norms are contextual and must be interpreted to determine in what context the norm would be followed. Norms must also be interpreted to determine what they imply about the rate of exchange between the interests of separate individuals. Finally, norms need to be interpreted to determine whether they reflect a fair division of the burdens and benefits of interactive behavior. I suggest that the veil of ignorance is helpful in putting the norms into a larger framework for determining the fair terms of human interaction.

8.4.2.2 The Veil of Ignorance. To restate the argument thus far, asking how valuable each person thinks the entitlement is to her activity does not allow a court to determine what the entitlement ought to be. In addition to the individual valuations, the court must evaluate the terms under which each individual would find the rate of exchange between the interests to be acceptable, the terms under which they will both agree on an acceptable division of burdens and benefits. That second determination requires reference to norms that people use when they interact with other people. If quiet is the predominant norm, then determining the entitlement requires the court to assess under what circumstances individuals usually accept a breach of that norm. But norms too need to be interpreted, both to know what they are and to determine whether they are just norms.

The veil of ignorance provides a thought exercise that allows courts to understand values that underlie human interactive behavior in a way that is not limited to the hypothetical valuation of rival claimants. Under this methodology, our hypothetical jazz trumpeter and mathematician would be asked to resolve the interference they face on terms that they would consider to be acceptable but without knowing whether they were the jazz trumpeter or the mathematician. They would have to reason to a resolution that they would accept if they were in the position of one of the parties, without knowing which position they were in. In order to make that determination, they would have to take into account social norms and practices as they understand them and determine how those norms would influence the division of the burdens and benefits as between the neighbors. We can consider how that reasoning might go in both our hypothetical case and actual cases.[26]

In the *Fontainebleau* case,[27] a hotel built an additional tower on its property, north of its existing building; the shadow cast by that tower impaired the value of the cabana area of the neighboring Eden Roc hotel. The Fontainebleau tower was probably in a reasonable location. Locating the tower on the south side of the existing building would produce no added benefit for the Fontainebleau Hotel, and there was no reason to think that the Fontainebleau hotel chose the northern location in order to cast a shadow on the Eden Roc (even though there were allegations that the Fontainebleau was aware of, and understood its benefit from, the interference). No activity decision could be questioned that would allow one of the parties to avoid the interference. The question, rather, was whether the Fontainebleau was required to bear that cost – and make it a part of the Fontainebleau's decision making when it decided where and whether to build the tower. If the Fontainebleau resort ought to have taken that cost into account, then a court would be justified in requiring the Fontainebleau to compensate its neighbor for the harm, which would then have become another cost of building the tower. But if the decreased value of a neighbor's property is not one of the factors that the Fontainebleau was required to take into account, then the neighboring hotel would be entitled to neither an injunction against the building nor compensation for its loss.

---

[26] The discussion in the text also implies that the division of burdens and benefits and the distribution of costs need not be answered the same way in all communities or in a universal way over time. Because the cost distribution question turns on social values that are used in awarding entitlements to people with different interests, a community's values determine whether the cost of air pollution ought to be internalized into the price of steel or into the price of living near a steel mill. The internalization question cannot be avoided, but how we answer it depends on the values we use to understand how a community decides which party should bear the cost. In advanced Western and wealthy countries, we take it for granted that the cost of air pollution ought to be internalized into the production process. That is a value judgment that given our wealth and the accumulated damage to the quality of air from emissions, we lose comparatively little if we make buyers of steel bear the cost of the pollution. Not so in a developing country such as China. There internalizing the cost of air pollution into the production process rather than into the general population cost could stifle the country's growth. It may be wrong to base growth on the lungs of those susceptible to the air pollution, but it is not incoherent to fail to internalize the cost of air pollution into the price of steel.

[27] Fontainebleau Hotel Corp. v. Forty-Five Twenty-Five, 114 So. 2d 357 (Fla. Ct. App. 1959).

Behind the veil of ignorance, we might reason as follows: in urban settings, people are not normally expected to take into account the impact that their building has on the light their neighbors receive. Land costs are expensive, especially for beachfront property, making building vertically a better option than building horizontally. Internalizing the cost of casting a shadow by requiring compensation for the harm the shadow causes would compensate the neighbor for something the neighbor had no right to expect. After all, the neighbor had a means of avoiding the cost. The neighbor could buy additional land in order to provide a buffer for the areas of its property that needed light, or it could have located its cabana in a way that did not make it susceptible to harm from its neighbor. Moreover, if the Eden Roc had wanted to build an additional tower on its property, it probably would have put the tower on the north side of its building, casting a shadow on *its* northern neighbor. It would have reasoned, just as the Fontainebleau did, that it would lose less by building on the north side of the building because it would obstruct the view of the north-facing windows, which were already less desirable because they lacked the southern sun, and in order to preserve its own cabana area. It is doubtful whether the Eden Roc would have thought of compensating its neighbor for the harm from the shadow it cast. Finally, the administrative cost of such a requirement would be great because it would be difficult to quantifying the damage, which would vary by season and weather.

The veil of ignorance also allows us to think about how the law might award entitlements to the mathematician and the jazz trumpeter. In general, the social value of quiet seems to predominate over the social value of loud activities. This is partly a function of the prominence of activities that require quiet over activities that require noise. It is also a function of the fact that a person undertaking no activity is likely to choose a quiet environment over a noisy one. The norm for those who must engage in noisy activity is to concentrate that activity in areas where there is noisy activity, so that we can expect a natural selection of areas where noise is accepted. This, in turn, suggests that quiet is the norm.[28] The musician and the mathematician would each choose this way of thinking about the problem because of its neutrality; it does not require one to determine whether jazz playing is more important than working out mathematical formulas. They would each approach the situation from a posi-

---

[28] Landlords often play a coordinating role for activities representing conflicting interests among neighbors by enforcing restrictions that determine ex ante the rules of behavior for the building. As part of this coordinating function, landlords might well find it profitable to set up rules that favor loudness over softness, in the hope of attracting tenants whose projects and preferences incline them toward noisy activities.

tion of neutral appreciation of the activity that each has chosen because each would not know whether he or she engaged in one activity or the other.

8.5 CONCLUSION

Neighbors must make two kinds of decisions that are relevant to the law when they determine how to use their land. First, they must decide how they can make reasonable decisions about their activities by taking into account the effect of their decisions on others when they choose where and how to do an activity. Second, they must decide whether to build into the cost of their activity the costs that would otherwise be borne by others. The former determination asks owners to think about the well-being of others in a reasonable way; the latter asks them to think about whether their decisions about their activity ought to include the social costs of the activity. The law functions to induce individuals to make those decisions in accordance with social values that construct the meaning of neighborliness.

9 Concurrent Decision Makers

When more than one person owns, or has the right to use, property, decision making is shared and property law must determine how decisions ought to be made in a way that allows productive collective decisions while protecting the interests of individual decision makers. The law functions to set up a framework that determines how each individual ought to account for the well-being of other individuals with rights in the property, seeking to identify the factors that an ideal decision maker would take into account in the context in which the decision is made. The theory of responsibility developed here allows us to model the decisions of interacting co-owners and co-users.[1]

It is important to distinguish between co-owners and co-users. Co-owners – those with an undivided interest in the whole of the property – exercise concurrent decision making over a resource that could be held individually. Accordingly, they must share decisions about use, exclusion, and transfer of the property, acting as if they had a single voice but accounting for their individual interests. By contrast, co-users, that is those with rights to common property, have claims to a resource that can never be held individually; they can make decisions only about their use of the property (including the exclusion of individuals who are not authorized to use the common property),[2] but cannot transfer the property or exclude each other.[3] A third kind of concurrent decision making occurs when owners of land above a common pool

---

[1] I do not address decision making through hierarchical governance regimes, such as common interest communities, partnerships, and corporations, where the governance regime determines how decisions are made and where constraints on decision making come from bylaws and judicial review for reasonableness.

[2] It is common now to distinguish between open access common property (where access is available to members of the public) and exclusive access common property (where access is limited to identified individuals or classes of individuals).

[3] Under this definition, a lake or a meadow is a commons even though the fish in the lake or grass in the meadow can be privately owned and consumed.

resource seek to exploit the resource. In this situation, each surface owner has an interest, but not an undivided interest, in the pool (an interest reflected in the percentage of land above the pool that each owns), but one surface owner's decisions about use affect other surface owners. Their interests are a hybrid between co-owners and co-users. I will call those resources *shared resources*.

Each of these contexts require concurrent decision making because each gives more than one person decision-making responsibility over the resource. The tragedy of the commons is therefore a potential barrier to efficient resource use in each of the contexts.[4] Each context allows voluntary exit from the concurrent decision making: co-owners by partition (or, for joint tenancies, severance and partition), co-users by relinquishing their claim to the commons, and shared resource owners by selling their surface or subsurface rights.

An important distinction among the different forms of concurrent decision making concerns the consequences of exit. For co-owners, exit results in the owner retaining ownership of the same quality as before partition; only the scope of the ownership and dominion is reduced. An owner of a one-quarter undivided interest in land ends up, after exit, owning a full interest in one quarter of the land (or its equivalent). For co-users and owners of shared resources, exit means that the decision maker gives up or transfers a claim to the resource. An owner of land over a common pool resource will sell the land. An owner of lakefront property will sell the property. The owner of a farm that depends on common grazing land will sell the farm or convert it to a different use. In other words, the different types of decision makers cash out in different ways. For co-owners, the owners who exit "cash out" the value of their interest. For co-users or owners of a shared resource, the decision maker who exits will "cash out" the right to use the resource and the potential benefit of cooperative solutions.

In any concurrent decision making, society faces the need for productive cooperation among the concurrent decision makers, which requires concurrent decision makers to make productive cooperative decisions in the face of divergent preferences and interests. This, of course, requires, as in the case of nuisance law, that each decision maker take into account, in a reasonable way, the impact of her decisions on the well-being of others in the group, given the actual and likely decisions of the others. When each concurrent decision

[4] If a summer home is owned by twenty-four individuals, the summer home is susceptible to the same kind of overuse and competition for use that affects a common meadow or fishery. If several (or more) individuals own property over a common pool, overuse and competition for use have the same potentially negative effects.

maker does this, the decision makers will maximize their joint interest, given their individual interests.[5]

9.1 CO-OWNERS

The law functions to facilitate productive use of co-owned property by making exit from co-ownership easy and by encouraging independent decision making when independent decisions are consistent with the rights of other co-owners. Each co-owner has both exit and voice, which facilitates cooperation to the extent that cooperation is possible, and preserves the rights of each co-owner when cooperation is not possible.[6] Co-ownership imposes the option of cooperating or accepting the consequences of exit.

9.1.1 *Ease of Exit*

Ease of exit is the greatest facilitator of cooperation. With few exceptions, any owner has the unconditional right to sue for partition.[7] Ease of exit facilitates cooperation by giving all co-owners the option to get the value from their ownership (as they define it) when cooperation is impossible. Co-owners face the following choice: cooperate or partition. As a result, ease of exit facilitates cooperation by asking all co-owners to weigh the benefits of their co-ownership

---

[5] Property law does not assume that society has an external standard that determines which uses of resources are productive and which are not; it has no external standard for evaluating the wisdom of joint decisions. It seeks only to ensure that the joint interests of the owners or users will be maximized in a way that is satisfactory to the individual co-owners and users.
[6] *See generally*, Hirschman (1970).
[7] Courts will disallow partition where the partition would disproportionally disfavor one of the parties. In these cases, courts are not viewing the value of exit in enhancing cooperation; they are viewing exit by one of the parties as the disproportionate imposition of burdens on one of the parties. Thus, when a bank became a co-owner of property, it was not allowed to sue for partition because the other owner needed to live in the house, and partition would have effectively evicted the family, depriving them of the benefits of ownership. As harsh as this result was for the bank (which wanted to get its money out of the house), the decision to deny the partition and thus block exit did not affect cooperation between the co-owners. The bank could build its cost of forced co-ownership into the cost of its lending operation, and its losses from forced cooperation were outweighed by the benefits to the family that needed to stay in the home. Newman v. Chase, 70 N.J.254 (1976). *See also*, Condrey v. Condrey, 92 So. 2d 423 (Fla. 1957) (parents who conveyed property to son and daughter-in-law as joint tenants in order to support a cooperative living arrangement could not have intended the son to seek severance and partition, which would have the effect of forcing the parents to move) and Hassell v. Workman, 260 P. 2d 1081 (Okla. 1953) (partition would deny one cotenant substantial profits and impose a big tax liability, whereas the petitioning cotenant could sell his cotenancy for a substantial profit).

against the costs of their co-ownership, which insures that each owner who values the co-ownership has an incentive to compromise his differences with other owners in order to keep the co-ownership alive. In this sense, easy exit gives each co-owner both exit and voice and supports cooperative solutions to shared concerns.

Although ease of exit is important for inducing cooperation, courts allow co-owners to reduce the exit option by agreeing not to seek partition for a reasonable time given the circumstances.[8] This is not a paradox. Courts know that cooperation is context-specific and that co-owners know whether the law's default position for individual decisions and easy exit will enhance or retard cooperation. Co-owners are therefore allowed to modify the ease of exit by agreeing ex ante not to resort to partition for the period of time necessary to make their cooperation enduring or to resort to partition only under certain circumstances. Courts generally uphold such agreements where they function to increase cooperation and refuse to uphold the agreements where they last unreasonably long or are not tied to the goal of facilitating cooperation.[9] Even restrictions on partition that are imposed by the grantor on grantees are generally permitted when they are reasonable, but the reason for prohibiting partition must be limited in time and be related to the grantor's reasonable purpose.[10]

9.1.2 Overseeing Individual Decisions

The law also facilitates cooperation among co-owners by intervening to determine whether the individual decisions of co-owners appropriately account for the well-being of the other owners. The law does not require agreement on every decision about the property. Instead, it allows individual owners to make decisions that affect the other owners, subject always to the requirement that

---

[8] *Restatement (Second) of Property* § 4.5 (reporter's note 2c).

[9] *Compare* Nagel v. Kitchen, 44 N.E.2d 853 (Ill. 1942) (enforcing implied agreement not to partition where co-owners developed a plan to manage the property and that plan would be destroyed by partition); Twin Lakes Reservoir & Canal Co. v. Bond, 401 P.2d 586 (Colo. 1965), cert. denied 382 U.S. 902 (Colo. 1965) (similar) *with* Harrison v. Domerque, 78 Cal. Rptr. 797 (1969) and Rosenberg v. Rosenberg, 108 N.E.2d 766 (766 (Ill. 1952). The case of *Raisch v. Schuster*, 47 Ohio App. 2d 98 (1975) is not to the contrary. There, the court construed an agreement that required a majority vote for all decisions about the property, including transfer and sale, to imply an agreement not to seek a unilateral partition. Because the agreement had no time limit, the court struck down the implied agreement not to seek partition. In that case, it was not even clear that the parties had intended to agree not to partition. A reasonable agreement not to seek partition is not a restraint on alienation because any co-owner can transfer her interest subject to the restriction.

[10] *Restatement (Second) of Property* §4.5.

the decision maker shares the burdens and benefits of those decisions with other co-owners. By allowing individual decisions that are subject to the rights of co-owners, the law allows one owner to shift the burden of decision making to the other owners, requiring the other owners to either challenge or accept the decision. This pattern of individual decision making subject to law-supplied default rules enhances cooperation by allowing co-owners to negotiate around the decisions made by individual co-owners. Productive uses of the land (at least in the eyes of one co-owner) are facilitated without reducing the value of the property to other co-owners because other owners have the right to object.[11]

Thus, if the property is rented by one co-owner, the law entitles co-owners to their share of the proceeds.[12] If one co-owner lives on the property, the others cannot object unless they are also in a position to, and want to, use the same property. Co-owners are expected to share in the reasonable and necessary expenses for the maintenance of the property, including taxes, debt service, insurance, and normal upkeep. A co-owner who has paid these expenses may sue the other co-owners for contribution. On the other hand, co-owners may not unilaterally impose discretionary expenses on other co-owners. A co-owner who invests in improving the property may not seek contribution from co-owners or sue them for unjust enrichment, although she may be awarded the value of the improvements in an action for partition, and, if the costs generated income, the co-owner investing in those costs may deduct them when accounting to the other co-owners for the income. Similarly, a co-owner may not unilaterally impose costs on other co-owners, as by cutting timber that the others would like to preserve.[13]

A difficult issue arises if one co-owner possesses property that could otherwise generate income, because such use deprives the non-possessing co-owners of income, and this gives the possessing owner disproportionate benefits from the property. The law approaches this issue by allowing individual co-owners to benefit from possession without paying a co-owner unless the co-owner objects; the nonpossessing owner is not entitled to receive a portion of the possessing owner's benefit unless the nonpossessing owner has been "ousted." In the absence of an ouster, the opportunity costs of the possessing owner are

---

[11] This is a mini-version of social recognition because it allows rights to form when individuals with the right to object fail to do so.
[12] This paragraph is drawn from Massey (2011).
[13] Threatt v. Rushing, 361 So. 2d 329 (Miss. 1978). *See also*, Chosar Corp. v. Owens, 370 S.E.2d 305 (Va. 1988) (giving cotenants veto power over coal leasing rights) and McCord v. Oakland Quicksilver Mining Co., 64 Cal. 134 (1883) (allowing mining without approval of all co-owners.)

not a measure of the nonpossessing owner's loss.[14] Because of the disproportionate benefits given the possessing owner (subject to objection) this result appears to be inequitable; by making the nonpossessing owner's interests subject to the decisions of the possessing owner, the nonpossessing owners are deprived of the income-producing benefits of ownership but retain their share of the burdens.

The result is understandable as a way of enhancing cooperation. First, it requires the nonpossessing owner to make a good faith claim for possession, so that the possessing owner has an ability to evaluate the conflict in interests that result from simultaneous claims for possession. The requirement of a good faith claim respects the decision-making right of the possessing owner while protecting the rights of nonpossessing owners. Second, the requirement of an ouster reflects a social norm that gives meaning to the concept of property. Although possessing property can be understood in economic terms by its opportunity costs, and although individuals decide whether to buy or rent property based on opportunity costs, individuals do not normally think of possession in terms of opportunity costs. An individual living in a home is not doing so to conserve expenses; the person is living there as an expression of her attachment to the property or the activities the property provides. Because individuals do not think in terms of opportunity costs when they decide whether and how to possess their property, it would disserve their decisions if they had to take opportunity costs into account to satisfy the nonpossessing owner who does not wish to possess the property. Hence, one co-owner's right to possession is limited only by the actual interest of other co-owners in possession.

9.1.3 Severance of Joint Tenancies

One of the difficult issues of joint tenancy[15] law is why a joint tenant is allowed to sever the co-ownership without giving notice to another joint

---

[14] Thus, even when property is used to rent lots for a trailer park, a co-owner who puts his own home trailer on one of the lots is not required to pay the non-ousted owner for the market value of the lot. Martin v. Martin, 878 S.W. 2d 30 (Ky. Ct. App. 1944). In the absence of an ouster, that is simply not a basis on which an owner who wants to use the lot should be required to compensate a co-owner; that is not one of the factors they should be required to take into account. Not all jurisdictions agree with this result. See, e.g., West v. Weyer, 46 Ohio St. 66, 72 (1888) and Cohen v. Cohen, 157 Ohio St. 503 (1952).

[15] Tenancies by the entirety – a form of tenancy for married couples with the right of survivorship that is severed only by death, divorce, or the agreement of both co-owners – are no longer prominent. Consistent with the importance of exit, it is worth noting that such tenancies were developed when ease of exit from marriage was discouraged and fell into disuse when ease of exit from marriage was favored.

tenant.[16] An owner who conveys her interest to a third party automatically severs the joint tenancy and turns it into a tenancy in common, even if the other co-owners do not know about the severance. This is unusual because a co-owner who transfers her interest is depriving the other co-owners of a valuable right – the right of survivorship. It is odd enough to give one joint tenant the power to deprive another of a valuable right; it is even more surprising that a joint tenant can do that without informing the other person of the change in the legal relationship. A co-owner who loses the right of survivorship but does not know of the loss cannot rearrange her affairs to account for the change.

Yet the law functions in this way to facilitate cooperation. The no-notice rule allows easy exit while avoiding the recriminations that might occur if notice were required. This is especially important in the context of a marriage because a spouse may not want to end her marriage, and relative marital harmony, even if she gives up the right of survivorship. As long as the severing owner accepts the burdens of the severance by giving up her right of survivorship, she has accepted the burdens of the benefits she gets from severance. The unfairness to the co-owner is mitigated by his notice of the circumstances that reflect the deteriorating relationship.

The law's central function with respect to the severance of joint tenancies is to make sure that one joint tenant cannot get the benefits of severance without accepting the burdens of the severance – that is, the loss of the right of survivorship. When a joint tenant appears to want to sever the joint tenancy if she is the first to die, but also to retain the right of survivorship if she is not, courts are not likely to find a severance against the unknowing and un-consenting joint tenant.[17]

9.2 CO-USERS AND SHARED OWNERSHIP OF COMMON POOL RESOURCES

9.2.1 *Co-Users*

Private law plays a relatively small role in coordinating decisions about usage among authorized users of common property. Tort law provides the "rules

---

[16] The major case is *Riddle v. Harmon*, 162 Cal. Rptr. 530 (Ct. App. 1980), where a wife deeded her interest in a joint tenancy to herself as a tenant in common, without notice to her joint tenant husband, and then left her interest in the land (now as tenant in common) to someone else. This was held to successfully deprive the husband of his rights of survivorship when the wife died. This result has been rejected by legislation in some states. *See*, *e.g.*, Calif. Civil Code § 683.2c.

[17] *See*, *e.g.*, Harms v. Sprague, 473 N.E.2d 930 (Ill. 1984) (mortgage does not sever joint tenancy where mortgagor would not have claimed severance had he survived).

of the road" that coordinate uses of the highway and similar common property, but it generally regulates only risks of physical harm. Traditionally, tort law played a relatively minor role in coordinating use decisions that had only an economic effect; the economic impact doctrine precluded tort law from coordinating rights to use among co-users. Only recently have courts relaxed the economic impact rule to protect the users of common property against economic harm from risky conduct that reduces the resources available to the common owners. Common law coordination of decisions about surface water usage has been more successful, but otherwise neither tort law nor property law, in their private law iterations, have successfully coordinated user rights in a way that would avoid the tragedy of the commons. In light of the impotency of common law with respect to the coordination problems arising from use decisions, the rise of environmental law as a legislative topic is not surprising.

A significant development in property theory in the last three decades has been the advance in our understanding of the ability of co-users, through private arrangements, to address the tragedy of the commons. Based on intensive fieldwork and a network of investigators, Elinor Ostrom has shown that the assumptions behind the idea that common use ends in tragedy (in particular, the assumptions of self-regarding decision making and high transaction costs) do not always hold true.[18] In certain situations, co-users of common property can put aside their self-regarding instincts and overcome transaction costs to set up successful governance regimes for the commons – wholly outside of traditional political regulation.

These case studies of successful self-governance by co-users confirm the theories developed in this book. They are, for example, a confirmation of the evolutionary theory developed in Chapter 4, a demonstration of the idea that other-regarding decisions enable cooperative solutions, and an explication of the circumstances under which other-regarding norms are likely to develop.

As in the evolutionary theory developed in Chapter 4, co-users of property are faced with the option of cooperation or conflict. Conflict comes in the form of a race to exploit the resource, with familiar consequences; cooperation comes in the form of establishing a governance regime that will limit conflict by accounting in appropriate ways for the individual interests of users and the collective interests of users as a group. The choice between conflict or cooperation, like the choice between accepting or contesting a claim to property rights, requires the individuals with common use rights to assess their beliefs about whether the collection of common owners has formed the

---

[18] See, e.g., Ostrom (2010) (Nobel Prize acceptance speech); Ostrom (2000); Ostrom (1990); Ostrom and Dietz (2002). See also, Singleton and Taylor (1992).

kind of common belief systems that would make cooperation possible. In the absence of individual beliefs in the possibility of a common belief system, individuals are likely to be wary of cooperation (for fear of opportunism by others). Once individual users become convinced of the possibility that a large collection of individual users hold common beliefs (including beliefs about the social sanctions for defectors), they will begin to act cooperatively, hoping that others will not take advantage of the limitations they have placed on their self-regarding interests.

The implementation of common belief systems requires that individuals adopt other-regarding decision making, refraining from self-regarding decisions (overexploitation) when their self-interest suggests that a sacrifice of their short-run self-regarding interests will, in cooperation with others, achieve their long-run interests. In this context, individuals are other-regarding when they curtail their use of the commons in order to coordinate with other users to preserve the stock of resources and ensure the long-run health of the commons. They act like a reasonable driver (a common user of roads) who sacrifices her interest in getting to her destination quickly in order to reduce the risk of harm to others, preserving the commons for herself and others.

Studies of successful governance of the commons are therefore important because of the insight they provide about the circumstances under which individuals with a collective interest form common belief systems that turn conflict into productive cooperation. Cultural homogeneity builds trust and facilitates the formation of common belief systems (including belief systems about the degree of monitoring that will be necessary). The ability to discuss common objectives allows collective interest to become a part of each participant's belief system. The homogeneity of individual interests allows each individual to predict the belief system of other individuals. The formation of cooperative ventures in allied areas produces common beliefs and trust that individuals can use to replace conflict with cooperation. When common belief systems allow common users to coordinate their uses they create a system of rights that are worthy of moral respect because of their source in the community's recognition of rights and responsibilities of individuals.

Cooperation among co-users is, however, different from cooperation among co-owners. In that connection, the theory developed here casts light on the debate about whether governance of the commons ought to encourage or discourage exit.

In the last section we saw that for co-owners the ease of exit is an important way to encourage cooperation. The work of Elinor Ostrom and her colleagues, however, suggests that for common property, ease of exit will make cooperation more difficult.[19] That view had led to the belief in some quarters that successful governance of the commons requires an "illiberal commons" (one that discourages exit), a view that is countered by those who favor governance through a "liberal commons," one in which ease of exit is preserved.[20] The debate between advocates of a liberal and illiberal commons is a false one, however; the distinction between liberal and illiberal commons is a distinction between two different forms of property holdings, not a debate about the role of exit among common users of property. Clarifying that distinction sheds light on the varieties of common property.

When individuals have only the right to use a resource, private agreements governing use of the commons are likely to be difficult to arrange; the benefits of cooperation are likely to be greatly outweighed by the benefits of unilateral exploitation. That is because individuals with only a right to use a resource cannot credibly threaten to exit the property in order to induce cooperation, for exit gives them no benefits, while exploitation gives them benefits (albeit only in the short run). Indeed, because of their inability to get any value out of a common resource if they exit, the best strategy for co-users is to exploit the resource as quickly as possible. That is why successful governance of common property is often linked to restrictions on exit. Once restrictions on exit are in place, co-users begin to understand that their best long-term interest is in cooperating. Because they are locked into this resource as a source of wealth, they might as well preserve the long-run source of their wealth.

But this "no exit" strategy is not required when an individual with a right to use the common property also has an interest in an underlying asset whose value is influenced by the right to use the property. If access to a common meadow is available only to landowners near the meadow, or if access to fish is available only to owners of property on the lake, the value of the underlying asset goes up if the owners can coordinate their use decisions in way that enhances the long-term value of the asset to which their use is tied. Any person seeking to sell the underlying asset would want the selling price to reflect the long-term value of the use rights that go with that asset and is therefore more likely to cooperate than one who holds only the right to use the meadow or fish. Put differently, any buyer of the underlying asset is likely to pay more for the asset knowing that the owners of the right to use the resources that make that asset more valuable have already coordinated the long-run value of their use rights.

---

[19] See Ostrom (1990), McKean (1992), and Simon (1991).
[20] Dagan and Heller (2005).

Under those circumstances, cooperation does not require restrictions on exit.[21] The value of the right to use the commons becomes embedded in the privately owned asset and the sale of the asset would reflect the value of the common right. Those with use rights could exit by selling the private asset, which facilitates cooperation by allowing those who have invested in cooperative solutions to receive the value of those cooperative solutions when they sell the underlying asset. As in the case of co-owners, the threat of exit then becomes a way by which cooperation is facilitated.

In other words, the requirements of an "illiberal commons," where exit is sticky, apply to common property in which use rights are not attached to an underlying asset. Restrictions on exit then facilitate cooperation. The possibility of a liberal commons exists when the value of use rights is tied to the value of a separate asset. Then, ease of exit facilitates cooperation. The different kinds of common property demand different strategies toward exit.

9.2.2 *Sharing Owners of Common Pool Resources*

Owners of land that lies above deposits of oil, gas, and water that migrate underground without regard to surface boundaries, or that can be extracted only by underground drilling across surface boundaries,[22] share a resource in a unique way, for one person's extraction of the resource, and the means that person's uses for the extraction, will affect another surface owner's ability to exploit the resources of the pool. Yet the law has examined rights to such subsurface pooled resources through inadequate paradigms, applying either a private property or a co-ownership paradigm, and wavering between the two. Under the private property paradigm, each owner has a claim to the resource lying underneath his property. Under the co-owner paradigm, each surface owner has an interest in the entire pool (although not an undivided interest). Neither paradigm is adequate to the task of regulating decision making with respect to common pool resources. Regulation of rights to such resources ought to be addressed under a paradigm of shared ownership, one

---

[21] Tellingly, advocates of the liberal commons refer to arrangements in which the common property is tied to the value of an underlying asset, such as common interest communities, condominium associations, marital property, and partnerships. *See* Dagan and Heller (2001). They are therefore referring to a different kind of common right than is Elinor Ostrom.

[22] Traditional extraction of oil, gas, and water involved drilling within surface property lines; slant drilling (i.e., drilling beneath property lines on the surface), was forbidden as a trespass unless the surface owner's permission was obtained. The development of the technology of hydraulic fracturing (the cracking of shale to release deposits of oil and gas) now enables and requires horizontal drilling, which usually requires that the drilling cross property lines.

that recognizes that decisions by any surface owner are interdependent with decisions of other owners, and the law ought to approach the regulation of such resources through sharing norms, rather than through coordinated unilateral decisions.

Coordination problems arise from subsurface resource pools because the decisions of surface owners (or their licensees) are so interdependent that it is not possible for society to rely on independent but coordinated decisions. Each surface owner's decisions about where and how to extract resources has a potentially immediate and direct impact on the well-being of other surface owners and on their ability to extract wealth from the common pool. Like co-users of common property, each surface owner has an interest in the pool that cannot be easily separated from the interest of other surface owners. Unlike co-users of common property, however, with adequate technology it is generally possible to associate a particular portion of the resource pool with the surface owner, which gives common pools the attributes of private property. If the resource is to achieve its maximum social value, the coordination of decisions among surface owners must recognize subsurface resources pools as a shared resource, one that requires coordinated decision making about use of the entire pool, while recognizing the separate interest of surface owners in individualized parts of the pool.

Rather than being guided by such a theory, the common law appeared to vacillate between theories of private and common property. The private property paradigm, which was symbolized by the *ad coelum* principle, treated surface owners as owners of the portion of the pool lying beneath the surface, and was thought to apply when courts addressed leasing rights, the due process rights of surface owners, the ownership-in-place theory, and the law of trespass for slant drilling. The common property paradigm was thought to apply when dealing with issues of extraction and to be embodied in the principle of capture – the surface owner who first captures the pooled resource owns the resource. Underground pooled resources were thought to be treated as fish in a pond, available to the first successful extractor.

In fact, neither paradigm adequately captures the social problem raised by underground resource pools; nor is either consistent with how the common law courts actually treated common pool resources. Underground pooled resources fit the paradigm of shared resources, not the paradigm of private (individually owned) or common resources. Given the highly interdependent nature of the decisions of surface owners, each surface owner has the right to exploit the resource subject to the equal right of other surface owners above the pool to do the same. Equal rights to exploitation mean that the rights are shared, much like tenants in common, but each surface owner's share is proportional to the value of the pool lying underneath the surface owner's land.[23]

Not only is the shared resource paradigm the appropriate paradigm for addressing common pool resources, it is the paradigm that, by and large, common law courts intuitively followed, even though theorists, having only the private and common property paradigms to guide them, mischaracterized what courts were doing.[24] Underground subsurface pools actually posed two different problems for the common law. The first was that in the absence of good seismic technology the boundaries of the pool, and portion of the pool lying underneath various surface properties, were hidden. The hidden nature of common pool resource made regulation difficult. The other was that the resources were migratory; when resources in the pool were extracted from one part of the pool, the resource would flow to a different part of the pool. As a result, the amount of the resource under any particular surface property was subject to the decisions of those extracting the resource from a different part of the property.

The law reacted differently to these two problems, which gave the law a sense of wavering between the private property and common property paradigms. In response to the hidden nature of subsurface resource pools, the courts denied the right of one surface owner to sue another surface owner for drawing off the underground resource; courts did not have the information necessary to determine which surface owner's use of the hidden resource was adversely affecting another surface owner. The causal effects were simply too difficult to trace. On the other hand, acknowledging the migratory nature of the resources, when surface owners did things above the surface that were bound to trigger the adverse effects of resource migration, the common law developed doctrines of malicious interference, waste, and unreasonable exploitation to regulate the actions of surface owners. The hidden nature of the resources made it impossible for courts to treat the resources as private property, but the migratory nature of the resources impelled courts to create remedies that protected surface owner's rights in the common pool resources.

Within this framework, courts were applying the shared resources paradigm, with the exception that they could not, and would not, order an accounting if one surface owner took more than that owner's fair share of the pool of resources. When co-owners or co-users aboveground took more than

---

[23] The shared resources paradigm therefore combines aspects of the private property paradigm (the notion that one's right to the shared resource is ultimately tied to the ownership of the surface above the pool) and the common property paradigm (the notion that decisions of individuals with rights in the pool are highly interdependent).

[24] The details of this analysis are contained in Gerhart and Cheren (2013).

a reasonable amount of the resources – say timber or flowing water – common law courts felt comfortable making decisions about reasonable use and ordering an accounting for unreasonable use, but when the resources were hidden they could not apply the shared resources paradigm fully. On the other hand, when activities were aboveground and observable, and if their effects could be accurately predicted, courts did provide a cause of action for unreasonable use of the common pool.

The situation has changed now that seismic technology makes it possible to identify, with a reasonable degree of certainty, which portion of a pool lies beneath which surface boundary, removing the hidden nature of the resource. The hidden nature of the resource is further reduced when hydraulic fracturing is the method of extraction, because the extent and effect of horizontal drilling on the common pool can be reasonably associated with the boundaries of surface owners. Common law courts are therefore now in a position to fully implement the shared resources paradigm.

Under this paradigm, each surface owner is entitled to the proportional value of the common pool that represents that portion of the common pool under that owner's boundaries. That portion can be determined before any extraction begins, and can be subjected to an exploitation agreement between the surface owners, with judicial oversight at the behest of one of the owners to ensure that the agreement reasonably accounts for collective and individual interests. The sharing owners can then operate as a single entity, so that all decisions about extraction from the common pool are judged by their impact on maximizing the value of the pool. For this purpose, the sharing owners can make decisions by democratic voting, with each owner having votes in proportion to his or her share of the total pool, with courts giving special protection for minority voting rights and imposing reasonable decisions on minority holdouts.[25]

9.3 CONCLUSION

When more than one person owns, or has the right to use, a resource, the law functions to coordinate decisions concerning the resource so that the co-owners

---

[25] Under the current regulatory framework, many states have implemented schemes of compulsory pooling that make it impossible for a minority of owners above the pool to hold out for a greater share of the revenue from the pool. Because surface owners forced to exploit pools are guaranteed a fair share of the revenue from the pool, compulsory pooling has been upheld against claims that it is a taking without just compensation. Patterson v. Stanolind Oil & Gas Co., 182 Okla. 155, 77 P.2d 83 (1938); Superior Oil Co. v. Foote, 214 Miss. 857, 59 So. 2d 85 (1952).

or co-users make collective decisions that honor the preferences and interests of individual owners. For co-owners, the common law provides ease of exit and individual decision making that shifts to other owners the burden of acquiescing in, or objecting to, those decisions. This shared responsibility for decision making requires other-regarding decision making by each owner in order to facilitate cooperation but allows for partition when the relationship between the co-owners makes other-regarding decisions impossible. For co-users, the common law's coordinating function is more modest because in many settings the diversity of interests and bargaining costs requires a legislative allocation of rights and responsibilities. Cooperation in the context of co-ownership and co-usage reflects the difference between cooperation induced by the right to exit and cooperation that is best facilitated by restrictions on exit. When the right to use a common resource is tied to ownership of a different asset, the coordination of use rights is facilitated by ease of exit. Where the right to use a resource is independent of an underlying asset, restrictions on exit might be required to induce cooperation. Even in this setting, however, the law ought to recognize and enforce private agreements concerning the reasonable exploitation of shared resources, including the ownership of shared resources.

10 Temporal Coordination

Property law must address arrangements that divide ownership, and the responsibility for making decisions about a resource, over time. Temporal conflicts arise when a present owner seeks to control the decisions of subsequent owners by restricting the use or transfer of the property. This occurs when an owner encumbers her property with a covenant that is thought to bind subsequent owners or when, even without such a covenant, an owner transfers property to future owners with conditions on the future owner's use or transfer of the property. Property law addresses these coordination problems under the law of servitudes and under doctrines limiting restraints on alienation and use (including, under the Rule against Perpetuities, limitations on the period of uncertainty created by such conditions). In addition, the appropriate division of decision-making responsibility over time occurs when a present owner is required to take into account the well-being of future owners, which private law addresses under the doctrine of waste.

The law approaches the issue of temporal coordination with vague, generalized, and conclusory statements about dead hand control, the importance of marketability, and conditions that are "repugnant to the fee." Yet the law has trouble determining why dead hand control is sometimes too great, which restraints on alienation are impermissible, and what makes some restraints repugnant to the fee. The justifications generally given for invalidating restraints on alienation[1] illustrate the kind of issues that remain unresolved. Alienation restraints inhibit the marketability of property, but this truism begs the question of when and why marketability is important. Such restraints also concentrate control and wealth in the person imposing the restraint – which begs the issue of how we balance one owner's freedom against the next owner's lack of freedom, an issue I return to shortly. Restraints on alienation dull the

[1] Dukmenier et al. (2010) at 208–09.

initiative of the owner who is subject to the restraint, an important point, but they also enhance the initiative of the owner who imposes, and stands to gain from, the restraints.[2] Not only do these traditional justifications need to be explicated but any justification also needs to explain why restraints on transfer are sometimes unobjectionable and why the law itself sometimes prohibits the transfer of property.

Moreover, the law splinters issues of temporal coordination between the seemingly separate doctrines of servitudes, future interests, alienation, waste, and moral rights.[3] It barely notices that the law of servitudes is related to the law of future interests and does not seem to understand that the law of waste (an owner's duty to future owners) is related to both. Moral rights, perhaps because they are given so little respect in the United States, are rarely discussed with other issues of temporal coordination. And the law has a curious ambiguity about restraints on alienation. The law restrains an individual from selling her organs, but often objects if restraints are put on her sale of real property. Property theory has failed to provide an overarching theory that justifies the law's approach to temporal coordination.

As already mentioned, analysts often focus on whose freedom matters, the freedom of the owner who imposes restraints on future owners or the freedom of future owners who are subject to restraints.[4] That framework seeks to find a way of privileging one owner's freedom over another owner's freedom. On the one hand, allowing an owner to impose conditions on subsequent owners honors the first owner's decisional autonomy; it may increase the value of the property and induce investment in the property. On the other hand, conditions on transferees restrict the transferee's freedom; reduce the scope of their decisional autonomy; and may, by reducing the value of their ownership, reduce their incentive to invest in the property. As circumstances change, conditions may be increasingly oppressive and unrealistic, and the circumstances may even diverge from the circumstances contemplated by the

[2] A fourth justification seems of lesser importance. Although outlawing restraints on alienation protects creditors who expect the property to be collateral, it is not clear why the creditors cannot protect themselves by determining whether the property on which they are loaning money is subject to such a restraint. There are ways short of invalidation for protecting creditors, including recordation and full disclosure requirements.

[3] Although I will not develop here the concept of moral rights as temporal coordination, the basic outlines of the claim are clear. Moral rights bind future owners by requiring them to take into account the well-being of prior owners who were also creators of the resource in question. The right of patrimony requires future owners to attribute the resource to its creator. The right of integrity forbids future owners from modifying the resource in a way that would change its character. Another moral right requires subsequent buyers to return to the creator a portion of the increased value of the resource over time.

[4] See, e.g., Alexander (1988).

individual who imposed the conditions. This focus on comparative freedom makes the analysis into a zero sum game, pitting one individual's freedom against a subsequent owner's lack of freedom (coercion), essentially asking, but not addressing, which individual should give up his freedom for the sake of another individual.

Whose freedom matters? For formal contractarians, the freedom of the original owners and the implied assent of subsequent owners is enough to allow private ordering of rights and responsibilities over time without judicial intervention.[5] Others doubt the power of assent, especially in light of changing circumstances, to be a full expression of an individual's freedom.[6] The middle ground is held by transaction costs economists, who posit that the law's function in temporal coordination is to identify and enforce the bargain that the parties would have made if there were no transactions costs.[7] This puts contractual freedom on both sides of the equation, but does not tell us how the law ought to reconstruct the hypothetical bargain that would manifest the two freedoms. The approach in Section 3.4 of the *Restatement of Property* that the reasonableness of a restraint on alienation "is determined by weighing the utility of the restraint against the injurious consequences of enforcing the restraint" runs into the objection voiced in Chapter 6 – namely, that we would use individual hypothetical valuations to govern a choice that has important social implications.

These theoretical frameworks are unsatisfactory. They focus only on the form and not on the function of freedom. They rely on a notion of comparative freedom that is impossible to quantify, because freedoms are irreconcilable and noncomparable. They assume that one person's freedom is another person's unfreedom, and that binding an individual to a contract does not also sometimes increase that individual's freedom.

This chapter presents an overarching theory of temporal coordination that allows us to understand why and when sequential owners have responsibilities to each other. Its theme is that the responsibilities of owners to future owners reflect the imperfections of the market as a coordinating device. The law functions to make sure that the burdens and benefits that owners impose on future owners are appropriately allocated and to evaluate the conditions in light of changed circumstances. Recognizing that the law functions to distribute decision-making responsibility through time, the central idea of this chapter is to develop a theory of the relationship between sequential owners that

---

[5] Epstein (1982).
[6] Alexander (1988).
[7] Posner (1986).

understands the role of the market in protecting owner autonomy over time and that situates the role of the law in intervening when the market cannot play its coordinating role. Under this view, it is not comparative freedom that determines the allocation of rights and responsibilities through time, but the role of the market in protecting that freedom. Individuals exercise their freedom in the decisions they make in light of the possibility of transacting, and it is the transactions that provide a basis for insuring each individual's freedom. This chapter also points out why private law is inadequate to successfully coordinate decisions over time, which provides a justification for legislative intervention as a response to the deficiencies of private law and the market.

10.1 FUTURE OWNERS AND THE MARKET AS PROXY

To fully understand the crucial role of the marketability of property, it is helpful to make explicit how the law's approach to temporal coordination reflects the important function of markets in coordinating the interests of present and future owners. This is the market proxy concept.

An owner's dominion over property held in fee simple absolute is generally thought to entail few responsibilities to future owners. At one level, this reflects the absence of any identifiable future owner who would have standing in private law to enforce a right against the present owner. But at a deeper level, an owner's present dominion and lack of responsibility for the future is somewhat of a paradox. After all, an owner's decisions clearly impact future owners, making the property either more or less valuable for future owners. Why should an owner not be accountable, in private law, to even unidentified future owners for the damage the owner does to their interests?[8] It is accepted, with few exceptions, that ownership entails the right to destroy or overuse property and that plaintiffs in private law hold no warrant for second-guessing an owner's use decisions that do not injure others contemporaneously. Yet we rarely ask why the owner is given dominion to do acts that damage the future value of the property.

By and large, private law's noninterventionist stand reflects the law's understanding that the market serves as a reasonably good proxy for the interests of future owners. As long as the market accurately reflects prospective property valuations, an owner who fails to take into account those

---

[8] The question in the text suggests that standing would not be a barrier if courts would be willing to identify a proxy future owner who would have standing. As I emphasize in Section 13.2, public law functions to create causes of action for the depletion of the future value of resources when private law cannot identify the future owner or otherwise provide a plaintiff with standing.

valuations will bear the burdens of lower property values. An owner who internalizes the future decreased value of the property by suffering its market decline is led to take the interests of future owners into account when making decision about the property, even if the future owner is not herself identified and even if the owner weighs his own interests more heavily than the interests of future buyers. As long as present owners account for, and bear, the burdens they impose on future owners, they are led to socially appropriate decisions.[9]

Market institutions are ideally suited to be proxies for future owners. The market builds plasticity into any property system by allowing decisions about property use to be evaluated in light of changed circumstances. The market conserves an owner's information costs by presenting the owner with prices that serve as a summary of the information that informs an owner's use decisions and that provides the feedback needed to serve as a proxy for future owners. As markets absorb new information, valuations change to reflect future prospects, while changing valuations alter the burdens and benefits of the owner's decisions. Preserving the ability of owners to react to changed market conditions is an important way by which the market provides the discipline that requires owners to absorb the consequences of their decisions, which protects future owners. Markets require owners to be other-regarding by constantly comparing their self-regarding valuations with the valuations reflected in market prices.

Moreover, the market provides an exit strategy for owners, allowing them to cut their losses and to shift ownership to someone more willing to take on the risk of future valuations. This risk-sharing feature of markets allows coordination over time by permitting various perceptions of changing circumstances to influence decisions of owners and potential owners.

That is why a system of private property does not depend on the assumption that owners will seek to maximize the value of their property or provide an objective surplus to society over time. And that is why the law does not, as a general rule, intervene to overturn decisions that are thought objectively to decrease the property's long-run valuations. Although the property system's ability to generate wealth depends on decisions that are consistent with enhancing market valuations, a property system functions effectively over time as long as those who make decisions bear the losses that flow from those decisions, so that future owners are not burdened by them. That is why the law

---

[9] The problem of damage to the commons arises precisely because the individual using the commons does not bear all of the costs of overuse, making individual decisions subject to market discipline a poor proxy for future owners.

protects the autonomy of owners to make stupid or objectively silly decisions; the well-functioning market is punishment enough.

But the market serves its proxy function for future owners only if the market meets stringent and familiar information and internalization requirements. The law functions to police those requirements. Protecting the market mechanism is the law's way of protecting the interests of future owners and making sure that their interests are accounted for when an owner makes decisions. The general assumption that the market works well provides the law with a justification for withholding legal intervention and for allowing the market to coordinate decisions of present and future owners. But when an owner makes decisions that keep the market from adjusting the present value of property to reflect future value, or when markets otherwise fail to complete the valuations, the law is fully justified in intervening to overturn the decisions.

In other words, what is at stake in temporal coordination is not the comparative freedom of owners at different times, but the sound functioning of the market system that coordinates the exercise of that freedom. The law does not try to determine whether an owner's freedom is unduly curtailed, and it does not privilege the freedom of a present owner over a later owner, or vice versa. Rather, the law seeks to protect the market mechanism that allows each person to exercise her freedom fully informed of the potential consequences of the decisions she makes. Protecting the market mechanism protects the freedom of all individuals over time because it is the market that provides each individual with the information he needs to exercise his freedom.

Our understanding of the law's function in temporal coordination – that is, the restraints the law places on present owners on behalf of future owners – is therefore grounded on a theory of market failure – on the identification of circumstances in which the market is unable to fulfill its function as a stand-in for future owners because an owner can escape the consequences of her decisions.

The idea that markets serve as a proxy for future owners informs our theory of an owner's duty. Sequential owners, like neighboring owners, have obligations to one another that flow from the fact of ownership and from the relationship between owners when they share (over time) an interest in the same resource. This is not an extravagant notion of obligation, and it arises naturally from the relationship between sequential owners. Once we conceptualize ownership as the authority to make decisions about the property, then joint ownership over time entails joint decision making about the property over time. Sequential owners are, in a real sense, common owners (over time rather than during a period of time), and it would not surprise us that common owners have obligations to one another that are forged from their recognition of their common ownership. Because joint decisions must account for the interests of both present and future owners, if the market does not serve as an effective coordinating mechanism, owners must act as they would if they appropriately took into account the interests of others.

Accordingly, when an owner's actions either impair the proxy function of the market or when markets fail to impose the costs of decisions on an owner, an owner who fails to take into account the appropriate assignment of burdens and benefits over time is not giving equal respect to the well-being of subsequent owners. Because an owner has obligations to look out for the well-being of others when markets fail and to keep markets from failing, an owner must assign appropriate weights to his own interests in light of the interests of future owners. Equal respect for the rights of subsequent owners requires that the owner take into account the impact that her decisions will have on future owners as circumstances change.

We can reinterpret familiar property doctrines in light of the market-as-proxy concept by identifying when the market is not an effective proxy for future owners. As I develop in this chapter, this occurs under the doctrine of waste, which applies when the sequences of future owners is determined by contract or gift rather than by the market. It also occurs when the market does not serve as an appropriate coordinating mechanism. Conditions on future owners that create uncertainty as to who can negotiate to sell the property are lawful only so long as the uncertainty is reasonable in light of the grantor's objectives. The uncertainty impairs the function of the market as an effective proxy for future owners (and the Rule against Perpetuities addresses that uncertainty). Contractual restraints that enhance the value of property (and therefore support the market) are lawful until the burdens they impose on future owners are disproportionate to the benefits (in which event contractual restraints will be struck down so that the market is restored to its proxy function). Finally, restraints on transferability are lawful where the market is not an appropriate mechanism for determining the value of property, but are unlawful when the market is an appropriate coordinating mechanism and the restraints impair the ability of the market to reflect the interests of future owners.

10.2 LEGAL RESTRAINTS ON PRESENT POSSESSORS

The common law imposes almost no restrictions on an owner's decisions about how to use her property when only unspecified future owners might be adversely affected. The general assumption that the market serves as a good proxy for future owners, and the lack of standing by future owners, protects the decision-making autonomy of the owner. On the other hand, when the law intervenes to restrict decisions of present owners or possessors in order to protect future owners, it is because of a defect in the market proxy mechanism.

10.2.1 Waste

The concept of waste is important when owners have predesignated sequential rights, as is true for tenants and landlords, holders of life estates and remainder or reversionary interests, and between some sequential future interests. The doctrine of waste is necessary because once the temporal sequence of ownership is divided, by contract or gift, into present and future interests, the market cannot play its role of disciplining an owner's decisions that do not maximize the long-run value of the property. Because the sequence of present and future owners essentially replaces the market with a predetermined series of property transfers, the sequential owners treat the property as common property, making it possible for one owner to overuse the resource to the detriment of future owners. The doctrine of waste provides legal intervention to counteract that possibility.

Current theory, because it fails to model the market-proxy function, makes it difficult to understand the basis of that intervention. We can agree with Judge Posner that the goal of legal intervention is to maximize the long-run value of property,[10] but to implement that suggestion we need to know which owner's values count, and how they count, in determining long-run value. If, as we surely believe, the purpose of property law is to allow subjective value formation, the economic approach must find a way of accounting for subjective value. If the present owner wants to remove a home that a future owner cherishes, which values do we choose to determine long-run value? We can also agree with John Henry Merryman[11] that we should try to determine the intentions of the parties, by ascertaining the intention of the sequential owners (if the restriction is determined by contract) and the intention of the grantor (if the grantor determines the sequence). But intention is difficult to ascertain when we do not know whether and what the relevant parties thought about the issue at hand, and shared intention breaks down in the face of conflicting interests and from the difficulty of deciphering intention when circumstances change. Finally, we can agree with Thomas Merrill that the law should function to facilitate bargaining,[12] but that requires some standardizing assumptions

---

[10] Posner (2007) at 73–74. Posner suggests that we assess the behavior of tenants as if they were owners seeking to maximize the long-run value of the property, but this assumes that owners make predictable and uniform decisions, despite their individual projects and preferences.
[11] Professor Merryman wrote the relevant chapter of the *American Law of Property* (1952).
[12] Merrill (2011).

about how individuals value property. The default rule when individuals have a sentimental attachment to a homestead may be different from the default rule when the issue is the intensity of logging.

To implement any of these suggested approaches, we need a better model of inter-temporal decision making about resources. The central problem that the doctrine of waste addresses is the different subjective valuations of sequential owners – one owner likes income from timber and the next owner likes forests. The way to address that problem is to understand that, as in the case of interfering decisions addressed by nuisance doctrine or by joint ownership, the decision making is interdependent, which implies that each owner ought to take into account the well-being of subsequent owners. Each sequential owner makes decisions about the property knowing that she needs to take into account the legitimate interests of subsequent owners, including what she knows about a subsequent owner's subjective evaluations. A decision about the use of the property becomes unreasonable if, given the state of knowledge that a reasonable owner ought to have, the owner fails to consider appropriately the well-being of subsequent owners.[13]

In this connection, the weight given to the well-being of sequential owners depends on the nature and length of their interests over time, with decision-making authority divided to reflect their proportional ownership. An owner of a life estate may therefore not replace the home on the property in order to maximize the economic value of the property when he knows that the holders of the remainder interest want to preserve the home on the property for its subjective evaluation.[14]

By this measure, one of the landmark waste cases, *Melms v. Pabst Brewing Co.*,[15] seems to be wrongly decided, but it is the reasoning, not the result, that is mistaken. There, the corporate holder of a life estate demolished a mansion on the property because it thought that the property was worth more without the mansion. The holders of the remainder interest objected because the mansion had been their family home. The court ruled in favor of the holder of the life estate on the ground that the home impaired the objective value of the land, despite the subjective value that holders of the remainder interest put on the property. Under the reasonableness test I endorse, this decision would seem to improperly elevate the interests of the life estate holders above

---

[13] The *Restatement of Property* tries to capture this idea by providing that the tenant may make changes in the property that are "reasonably necessary in order for the tenant to use the ... property in a manner that is reasonable under all the circumstances." *Restatement (Second) of Property* § 12.2(1) (1977).
[14] Brokaw v. Fairchild, 135 Misc. 70 (N.Y. Sup. Ct. 1929).
[15] 104 Wis. 7, 79 N.W. 738 (1899).

the remainder interest holders and to ignore the long-run subjective value that should have controlled. The court's justification was that changing the property in ways that made the property objectively more valuable was permitted, despite precedent to the contrary. This interpretation would deny a central precept of property law – namely, that owners are entitled to respect for the subjective value they attach to the property.[16]

Melms is one of those cases where what the court said is less important than what the court should have said.[17] The significant fact in *Melms* is not that the life estate owners thought that they were improving the value of the land. The significant fact is that the owners thought they owned the property in fee simple. In *Melms*, the defendant's good faith and reasonable decisions shielded them from liability, even though, had the owners known they had only a life estate, they would have been liable for its destruction. The documents underlying the transfer of the land were ambiguous and the finding that the buyers of the property had only a life estate was "almost certainly wrong."[18] Under this reading of *Melms*, the case advances the theory of the modern encroachment cases, but from the opposite direction. Just as an individual is not responsible for reasonable and good faith trespasses that improve another's property, so is an individual not responsible for reasonable and good faith destruction of another's property.

When one considers the waste cases over the years, one can see a clear pattern. The holder of the present interest has an obligation to take into account, in a reasonable way, the interest of holders of future interests. That requires the holder of the present interest to maximize the long-run value of the property by appropriately balancing the burdens he imposes on future owners in light of the normal benefits of their interest, given the context of the present and future interests and what he ought to know about the subsequent owner's subjective values.[19] The reasonableness of any decision is based on several factors: the relative length, security, and depth of the interests in question;[20] what the decision maker reasonably knows or can determine about each subsequent owner's subjective valuation; and the comparative weight to be given to the various subjective valuations.

[16] Merrill (2011).
[17] This is made clear in the subsequent *Brokaw* case, which articulates the standard approach and distinguished the *Melms* case on the reasoning given in the text.
[18] *See* Merriill (2011) at 1070.
[19] For a study that emphasizes the importance of social context and understanding subjective values, see Purdy (2010) at 44–63.
[20] The security of any interest depends on the conditions under which the interest holder can lose the interest; tenants at will have less security than remaindermen whose fee is conditional, and the latter have less security than remaindermen whose interest is in fee simple absolute.

10.2.2 Destruction

The market proxy concept explains the ancient right of an owner to destroy her property. When the owner bears the costs of that destruction, the social waste of resources from destruction is internalized, and dissipated, into the owner's value. The market proxy theory also suggests that limits on the power to destroy property will arise when the owner does not bear all of the costs of that destruction. The observation that the law is increasingly limiting an owner's right to destroy property,[21] and the many instances in which legislative regulation intervenes to require preservation, recognize those instances in which the owner of property does not bear the relevant social costs of destruction.

Sometimes, the destruction of property harms existing property owners and is therefore akin to a nuisance. This is the justification for the decision in *Eyerman v. Merchantile Trust Co.*,[22] in which a court refused to enforce a testamentary direction to destroy the testator's mansion in a planned community. On one view, that decision does not so much protect the interests of future owners (in fact, the heirs of the testator wanted to uphold the direction to destroy the property) as it serves as judicial intervention to protect neighboring home owners, whose own homes would be less valuable if the testator's home was destroyed. The court found that the destruction would "carry a serious threat against the proper growth and development of the parts of the city in which the land in question is situated."[23] Under the theory developed here, the case is one in which the owner would have imposed uncompensated burdens on future owners. Because markets cannot value the worth of cultural and historical preservation, the owner and her heirs did not bear the full cost of the proposed demolition.

The law is also justified in intervening to prevent destruction when future owners are unable to protect themselves by adjusting their purchase price. If an owner pours toxic chemicals on property that are hard for future buyers to detect or evaluate, the market cannot impose a cost on the owner, and some of the burdens of the decision are borne by future owners. Information failures, such as those that occur from toxic dumping, make it impossible for the market to serve its proxy function. In other situations, markets fail because valuations made through markets underappreciate the values that are important to a society. The market may not protect values that support the provision of public goods, such as the value of cultural or habitat preservation. Because each person benefits from the public good but none can be excluded from the

---

[21] Strahilivitz (2005).
[22] 524 S.W. 2d 210 (Mo. 1975).
[23] 524 S.W. 2d at 217.

benefits, the value of the preservation cannot be determined by the market; each person may be induced to free ride on the preservation in the expectation that others will pay for it.

10.3 PRIVATE RESTRAINTS ON FUTURE OWNERS

When owners impose conditions on future owners – whether by contract or gift – the law functions to make sure that the conditions advance rather than retard the market's function as a coordinator of inter-temporal interests.[24]

10.3.1 *Conditions Identifying the Future Owner*

When a future owner is identified and is certain to take the property, the market can, in principle, function well. Those who want to purchase the property know with whom to bargain. Although the existence of named future owners, like the existence of many contemporaneous owners, will increase transaction costs, identified future owners who are certain to get the property provide a focal point that permits bargaining to occur. However, problems for market functionality occur when the identity of the future owner is uncertain, which happens when the identity of a future owner depends on conditions that may or may not occur. A gift of property that may go to Bob Jones, depending on certain conditions, makes it uncertain whether potential buyers have someone with whom to negotiate. This uncertainty clouds the market mechanism by making it unclear with whom potential purchasers should negotiate if they want to purchase the property.

Addressing this uncertainty is, of course, the function of the Rule against Perpetuities, for the Rule functions to remove uncertainty concerning future third-party owners when that uncertainty lasts unreasonably long. Although it might be more sensible to eschew a rule and restore a test of reasonableness to measure the appropriate length of uncertainty caused by conditional gifts, the function of the law in restoring the market proxy function is clear.

Given this orientation to third-party future interests, it is unclear why future interests reserved in the grantor are not also subject to the Rule against Perpetuities. After all, the question of whether and when the beneficiaries of

---

[24] For analytical purposes, the transfer of land by contract or by gift are functionally similar because each involves a kind of offer and acceptance. They differ, however, because a donee who accepts a gift is not as likely to appreciate the conditions that accompany that acceptance as conditions accepted as part of contracts. Accordingly, courts are justified in closely scrutinizing conditions put on gifts because the presumption that the conditions benefit the donee is less forceful than when the condition is bargained for.

the grantor will take the property subjects potential buyers to the same uncertainty as future interests in third parties. It is not clear why the law does not have the same concern with conditional grants to the grantor's beneficiaries that it has for conditional grants to third parties. Several reasons suggest themselves. Historically, of course, perpetual reversionary interests in the grantor were an ingrained and accepted part of feudalism; the king always had reversionary rights in the land he provided to his lords. Moreover, the grantor and his beneficiaries would have had the land in any event, so giving away some of the rights to the land but holding a reversion did not seem to upset the natural order; individuals interested in the property would have had to negotiate with the grantor's beneficiaries in any event. Finally, the grantor's beneficiaries were likely to be more easily identifiable than the beneficiaries of a contingent future interest in a third party. This reduced the costs of transactions involving future owners if the future owners did take ownership.

10.3.2 Conditions Affecting Use

The law of reciprocal promises,[25] which governs an owner's promise about how she will use her property, reflects the market proxy theory. Put succinctly, the law allows owners to impose reciprocal covenants that bind future owners when the covenants, by coordinating uses, assist the market in determining an accurate future value for the property. However, the law refuses to enforce such promises when they impede the market from appropriately valuing the property.

A major mistake in the analysis of reciprocal promises is to talk about the benefited and burdened property as if separate owners bore the benefits and burdens. In fact, an owner takes on burdens for her benefit, and the benefits of another's promise come with their associated burdens. As in all of contract law, a person takes on obligations in order to get the benefit of the counterparty's obligations. An owner who promises to use his land only for a residence of a certain type is burdened, to be sure, but that burden is offset by the benefits of reciprocal promises by other landowners. An owner who promises not to compete with a grocery store in the same shopping center is burdened, but that burden is offset by the benefits of having the grocery store attract business

---

[25] Conventionally in property law such promises are called servitudes, a confusing term that covers not only promises about how an owner will use her property but also promises by which an owner will allow another person to use her property (easements). Sometimes the term *covenants* is used for servitudes that restrict how an owner will use her property. I use the term *promise* because I wish to emphasize the commonality between long-term, relational contracts and servitudes.

to the shopping center. As a matter of expression, it is fine to talk about the burdened party, but as a matter of function, the task is always to identify what benefits flow from the burdens an owner has accepted. The topic of reciprocal promises is simply working out how the law deals with long-term contracts when circumstances change in a way that calls into question whether the contract fairly assigns burdens and benefits over time.[26]

As is now generally recognized, many reciprocal promises enhance the market's ability to serve as a proxy for future owners because they embody restrictions that future owners will value. The law must differentiate between restrictions that the market will value (reasonable restrictions) and restrictions that the market will not value (unreasonable restrictions), for this distinction allows courts to determine when the proxy function of markets is being enhanced. The law must also determine the circumstances under which the market's proxy role continues to function as the restrictions apply to new owners

Not all agreements between contemporary owners affect the value of property or the ability of the market to act as a proxy for future owners. If a developer sells a lot to purchaser A on the condition that purchaser A agree to give the developer piano lessons, the parties are not contracting to improve the ability of the market to reflect the value of the lot, and the lot is not made more valuable by that promise. The parties are simply working out the terms of the exchange between themselves, substituting piano lessons for some other valuable consideration they might have exchanged. In the parlance of property law, the promise does not touch and concern the land; it is merely a promise in gross rather than appurtenant, and the promise does not bind subsequent owners of A's property.

Other promises do help the market determine the value of the property because, when reasonable, reciprocal promises allow the market to put a future valuation on property that reflects the promises value to future buyers. Long-term contracts that bind subsequent owners allow the market to serve as a proxy for future owners by reflecting the increased future value of the property that the promises make possible. The promises are reasonable

---

[26] The *Restatement (Third) of the Law of Property (Servitudes)* has helpfully emphasized the contractual basis of these obligations and has modernized the language used to describe their legality, dropping terms such as "touch and concern" and "privity" that bore little relation to what courts were actually doing. We can further simplify the approach to reciprocal promises by understanding the way that the appropriate assignment of burdens and benefits unifies our understanding of the legality of such promises. In addition, by concentrating on the appropriate assignment of burdens and benefits in light of changed circumstances, we can see how contract principles are molded to account for the long-term nature of the obligations that must be evaluated in the light of those changing circumstances.

when the burdens that one owner undertakes are matched by the benefits of reciprocal promises by all owners, such that the burdens and benefits of the promises are appropriately divided among owners. Property law functions to ensure that the promises remain reasonable over time given the possibility of changed circumstances. If property law did not function to maintain a fair assignment of burdens and benefits over time, the contracts would impede the ability of the market to function as a proxy for future owners because markets would not be able to incorporate the true cost of the contracts into market valuations.

In order for the market to serve as a proxy for future owners as circumstances change, two requirements must be met. First, a system of running promises requires that purchasers of property be fully informed about the burdens the promises put on their property so that they can adjust the price they pay for the property to reflect those burdens. The function of the notice requirement is not, as is commonly thought, to determine whether the new owner has assented to the promises. It is, instead, to see whether the new owner was sufficiently aware of the burdens to insure that she would also get the benefits of the promises. Without adequate notice and appreciation of the burdens on the property, the buyer of property cannot make an informed decision about the value of the property and the market mechanism is disrupted. Legal intervention to relieve a property buyer of uncompensated burdens allows the market to serve as a proxy for future owners by restoring the results the market would have reached had the promises not been made.[27]

Because the focus of notice is not on the fact of assent but on the new owner'appreciation of the burdens and adjustment or the purchase price, we cannot infer assent to the burdens from the fact that the owner bought the property, even with formal notice. The focus is on assent in a functional, not a formal, sense. It is asking: Did the owner gain the benefits of the burden when the owner bought the property such that it is just to hold the new owner to the burdens associated with those benefits? After all, the function of reciprocal promise law is to make sure that those who benefit from another's commitments must also bear the burdens associated with those benefits. A subsequent owner who gets the benefits of another's commitment without suffering the burdens is acting as opportunistically as a person who asks another to accept the burdens of a commitment without the benefits.

---

[27] For the same reason, courts are fully justified in determining that an owner is under an implied covenant when the court is convinced that, in fact, the owner has benefited from the covenant under circumstance where it would be unjust to allow the person to keep the benefits of the covenant without keeping the burdens.

In addition to the question of notice, courts intervene to overturn reciprocal promises when, because of changed circumstances, the promises no longer offer an appropriate division of the burdens and benefits of the promises between the owners. As long as circumstances are consistent with the division of burdens and benefits contemplated by reciprocal promises (including ones that bind subsequent owners who, because of notice, could adjust the price they pay), the law enforces the promises because the promise is being valued by the market and the market proxy function is preserved. However, when circumstances change in a way that reduces the benefits that one or more parties get from their promise, the market no longer serves its proxy function. Potential buyers, knowing that they cannot get the benefits of the promise they have to take on when they buy the property, and finding no value in the land without the benefit, will not bid for the land, and the market's proxy function will be unfulfilled. Although courts intervene to relieve one of the parties from the burdens of his promise only upon the clearest showing of changed circumstances, when the benefits of a promise are remote, courts are justified in intervening to protect the market as a proxy for future owners by relieving an owner from her unrequited promise.

10.3.3 *Extraneous Effects (Public Policy)*

Some reciprocal promises and restraints imposed by donors are invalidated because they impose restraints that are inconsistent with market valuations and therefore with the idea that the market will serve as a proxy for future owners.

In one class of cases, courts will invalidate a restraint that affects the value of surrounding property in ways that neither the transferring owner nor the new owner will take into account. Thus, a court invalidated will provisions that barred the donee from using his property for buildings greater than three stories high or for leases of more than one year.[28] The gifted property was in the middle of a growing area in the center of the city and the inability to build on that property in a way that would suit the commercial character of the city would impair the value of surrounding property.[29] The market could not properly determine the value of that property or serve its proxy function because the restrictions disallowed uses that were important for market valuations.

---

[28] Colonial Trust Co. v. Brown, 105 Conn. 261 (1926).
[29] The court emphasized that restriction would "carry a serious threat against the proper growth and development of the parts of the city in which the lands in question are situated." 105 Conn. at 264.

Because the restrictions disabled neighbors from reaping the value of their investment in the property, the court was justified in intervening to relieve the donee from the burden of the restraints.[30]

In other instances, courts invalidate restraints because the restraints rely on factors that markets normally do not, and ought not, take into account – factors that disrupt the market proxy system because they result in skewed market valuations. Racial restrictions, although independently odious under the guarantees of the Constitution, impair the market proxy function because they ask the market to exclude valuations of those who are willing and able to pay for the property but are barred from doing so because of their race. Such restrictions, because they exclude valuations that are relevant to the market, preclude the market from serving its proxy function. The same can be said for those restrictions that are struck down on the grounds of unconscionability or duress. When a restraint results in bargaining influenced by a significant imbalance of information or alternatives, the market cannot fulfill its proxy function. If the market has to integrate values that do not truly reflect free and relatively equal bargaining, it will not serve as an accurate proxy for future owners, and owners will be able to disinvest in property without suffering the consequences of that disinvestment.

The *Restatement of Servitudes* classifies these and other invalid restrictions as covenants against public policy, although the grounds of public policy are not articulated with precision. The market proxy theory explains the invalidation of these restrictions. In general terms, market valuation that serves as a legitimate proxy for future owners takes into account matters relating to price and quality that are of interest to average future buyers, but not matters of personal preference and idiosyncratic valuation that interest only a few. Restraints that do not reflect the kind of valuation that markets are intended to account for must be struck down as against public policy because they disrupt the market proxy function.

10.3.4 *Restraints on Transfer*

The struggle to free owners from restrictions on their right to transfer was, of course, essential to allow the market to function as a proxy for future owners and to coordinate uses between present and future owners. The struggle for

---

[30] Notice that this case involved a gift, rather than a contract, and the donee was better off accepting the gift with the restraint. The restraint was thus not negotiable as between the donor and donee. Although the donee would have been better off without the restraint, he had no leverage to threaten to reject the gift. In *Eyerman* the court emphasized that destruction of the home would reduce the value of the other homes in this planned community.

supremacy of the market was in large part a struggle for an institutional way of coordinating valuations of property over time. As society developed markets to coordinate decisions about the value of resources, and as society developed rights as a means of allocating governance decisions, restraints on sale by subsequent owners concentrated control along historical lines and divorced ownership from control in a way that seemed inimical to both markets and rights.[31] The right to transfer provides the right to exit, which is important to the function of the owner as decision maker. When individual A transfers property to B, individual A transfers to B the right to make decisions about the property and forces B to accept the consequences of her decisions. The right to sell the property supports B's decision making by facilitating exit, whereas restraints on B's scope of decision making that occur because exit is foreclosed disables B's decision making in a fundamental way. Restricting the right to sell the property reduces both the benefits and the burdens of decision making. Because the new owner is not able to sell the property, the new owner loses the incentive to invest in it, and bears the burdens of the property without easily reducing those burdens by selling the property. Both the burdens and the benefits of decision making are adversely affected, and the decisions made by the new owner can hardly be expected to bear the indicia of independence that was the purpose of recognizing decision-making rights in the first place.

Transferability is especially important in light of changed circumstances. Owners must adjust to every circumstance that influences their perspective on their property – personal, environmental, social, and economic. The transferability of property allows the market to serve as a shock absorber, allowing owners to adjust to changed circumstances. Restraints on transferring the property are especially troublesome where property has more than one owner. As noted in the last chapter, exit serves the important function of inducing contemporaneous owners to cooperate. Therefore, courts are particularly vigilant when property is left to more than one person with a restriction that they may not transfer the property.

But preserving the market as a proxy for future owners is not always paramount, and restraints are upheld where there are good reasons to supplant the market. The market proxy theory explains that restraints prohibiting a future owner from transferring property are justified when the proxy role of the market ought to be subservient to other values. First, markets are not the only

---

[31] Interestingly, the development of both the trust and the corporation allowed ownership and control to be centralized in institutions that themselves divorced ownership from control, thus allowing individuals to own large accumulations of property while delegating control over the property, including when and why to sell it.

Conclusion

coordinating device between present and future owners. As we have already seen, coordination by contract often provides a good basis for coordinating uses outside the market. When contracts are reasonable, courts will uphold them.[32]

Moreover, the market-protecting function of the law is important only when the values that animate property law are subject to exchange. When society blocks exchanges, it does so because it wants values other than market values to govern allocation decisions. To keep markets from facilitating exchange, some property may not be alienated. Bodies are owned but may not be sold. An individual owns her cells but may not sell them. As Justice Mock reminded us in *Moore v. Regents of the University of California*,[33] some property may be given away but not sold (such as fish or game caught pursuant to a restricted license), and other property may be neither given away nor sold (such as licenses to practice medicine, or prescription drugs).

Blocked exchanges occur in two instances: when a society wants to inhibit an activity by inhibiting the exchanges that would make the activity profitable, and when society wants to subject the activity to decision making outside of market forces. The first reason for blocked exchanges applies to endangered species and cultural relics. The second kind of blocked exchange occurs when the market would be an inappropriate basis for allocating the resource or right because it would be a disservice to the holder of the right to subject it to exchange.

10.4 CONCLUSION

Addressing the coordination of decisions between present and future owners has been one of the most difficult issues the law has faced, for the law has not had a good understanding of the role of the market in coordinating decisions about resources across time. To be sure, the right to transfer property has been well-established, but the law's inability to understand that right in the context of the market's role in serving as a proxy for future owners has made legal intervention haphazard and episodic. In fact, legal intervention is called for when private decisions would keep the market from serving as a proxy for future owners or when the market would impose external costs unrelated to efficient

---

[32] Dodd v. Rotterman 330 Ill. 362, 161 N.E. 756 (1928) (gift to daughter who promised not to sell property was not unlawful restraint on alienation because it was intended that mother would get property back if she recovered from illness); Genet v. Florida East Coast Ry., 150 So. 2d 272 (Fla. Dist. Ct. App. 1963) (railroad's transfer of warehouse with restriction that property be used in conjunction with railroad shipping not unreasonable).

[33] 793 P. 2d 479, 510 (Cal. 1990).

allocation, and legal intervention can be withheld when the market serves as a good proxy for the interests of future owners. Within this framework, we can understand that the law intervenes to protect the market when the market cannot adequately perform its coordinating function. We also understand that when society cares about values that the market cannot capture, the law will not rely on the proxy role of the market but will block the exchanges and rely on nonmarket forms of decision making.

PART III

LEGISLATIVE REGULATION AND SOCIAL MORALITY

Part I developed a general theory to explain and justify the contours of private law applicable to various forms of property. Part II applied that theory to the most important private law issues affecting private property: exclusion, nuisance, concurrent decision making, and sequential decision making. In Part III, I inquire into the legislature's power to change the common law configuration of rights and responsibilities and examine the protections that owners have against legislative overreaching. Central to this part is a conception of the relationship between private law and public law regulation of an owner's right to make decisions about resources. We have understood private law to constrain the range of decisions that owners and nonowners make about resource use in order to coordinate resource use in a way that respects the equal freedom of each individual. Public law also constrains the decisions an owner may make, but its function is to coordinate interest of the community vis-á-vis individuals rather than interests of individuals vis-á-vis each other. The legislature and its delegates may take property and regulate the uses of property. The takings power allows the legislature to intervene when the market can no longer successfully coordinate private decisions. The power to regulate land use allows the legislature to make sure that each owner's decisions take into account a broader range of factors and appropriately reflect social interests that private law cannot address. But the core decision-making authority of owners is protected against legislative overreaching because the Constitution requires that the legislature also act in a way that respects the equal freedom of each individual. Although the legislature may impose burdens on owners in order to provide public goods, the legislature may not do so in ways that do not respect the equal freedom of individuals.

11 A Theory of Legislative Regulation

Thus far, I have examined the role of common law courts in mediating property relationships and worked out the implications of a general approach to property. We saw that private law seeks to adjust the rights and responsibilities of owners and nonowners so that (given the existing distribution of resources and the goal of equal respect for individuals) each individual bears an appropriate allocation of the burdens and benefits of decisions about resources. I portrayed this as one aspect of the social recognition concept – through the common law, the community relies on professional neutrals to assign resources to private or common use, to identify owners, and to work out the rights and responsibilities of owners in a way that is consistent with the equal freedom of each individual. I turn now to the role of public law in mediating property relationships. Here I examine the relationship between the social recognition of property rights and legislation that determines the scope of property rights by determining, through the political process, what burdens owners bear to support the well-being of the community.[1]

This part aims to develop a theory that links common law and legislative regulation of property to a common conception of equal freedom. In particular,

---

[1] Legislation can, of course, change private law by rearranging the rights and responsibilities of individuals vis-a-vis each other. Public accommodation laws, for example form private law by, among other things, rearranging the rights of nonowners against certain homeowners, landlords, and retail stores. Under the concept applied here, legislation embodies public law when it affects individual rights in the name of the interests of the community as a whole, rather than in the name of individuals as individuals. Public accommodations laws are in the community's interest, of course, but their effect is to change the private law of exclusion between owners and nonowners. Preserving wetlands is public law because the interests protected are not the interests of individuals as individuals but the interests of individuals interested in the environmental health of their community. In Chapter 13 we will see that sometimes public law, by the boundaries it draws, takes on a private law posture by affecting the relative rights of individuals and that doing so invites judicial oversight.

I seek to show how the principle of respect for the equal freedom of individuals determines the permissible scope of legislative regulation, just as it determines the assignment of burdens and benefits in private law.

11.1 SOCIAL RECOGNITION AND LEGISLATIVE REGULATION

The social recognition concept – the notion that property rights come from, and are limited by, the community – finds its strongest expression and greatest challenge in the legislative power to rearrange the private law scope of an owner's rights and responsibilities. Social recognition through the legislative process is primarily found in two sources: (1) the Takings Clause, which, by implication, gives the legislature the power to take property for public use upon the payment of just compensation; and (2) the legislature's general regulatory or police power, which gives the legislature the power to rearrange rights and responsibilities for the health, safety, and welfare of the community.[2] Both powers reflect the social recognition concept by giving the legislature the authority to rearrange the terms of the preexisting arrangement of property rights and responsibilities, changing owners or expanding or contracting the rights and responsibilities of owners and nonowners established through private law and private arrangements. What distinguishes the two forms of lawmaking is their methodology; whereas private law determines socially recognized values by asking a neutral to decide disputes between individuals, the legislature determines social values through the political process. Limitations on their lawmaking power reflect those different methodologies.

Although legislative powers embody the social recognition concept – in the sense that the legislature is empowered to recognize and limit property rights to reflect social values – the exercise of these powers challenges both the idea of rights in property and the social recognition concept itself. Legislative powers challenge the idea of rights in property because overbearing regulation could annul the concept of property and disrupt the distribution of burdens and benefits that provide the core concept of private property. We must therefore ask what rights owners have against an overreaching legislature and how we recognize when that overreaching has occurred. If, for example, the state exercises its power of eminent domain to take property for a private rather than a public purpose (even with compensation), the state could easily undermine the personal, subjective, and risk-taking values that the socially recognized

---

[2] Property is also protected by the Contracts Clause and the Equal Protection Clause, both of which are discussed in Chapter 13, where I take up constitutional limitations on government land use regulation.

system of private property was designed to foster. And if state regulation puts an undue burden on some owners, the state would upset the balance of benefits and burdens that the common law has so carefully worked out and, by doing so, would threaten the concept of property as we understand it. We must address the question asked by Joseph Singer: "How can the state both *define* property rights and be *limited* by them?"[3]

Legislative regulation also challenges the social recognition concept. If the state, through its courts and its legislature, has unlimited power to recognize rights on behalf of the community, and to change the terms of recognition, the rights of owners are contingent and unstable and the function and content of social recognition is a matter of political will rather than social construction through the rule of law. If rights are socially recognized through the act of legislation, why cannot they be socially unrecognized? If legislative power is unlimited, is the social recognition concept simply a matter of the supremacy of the legislature over the common law, or is there an aspect of social recognition that puts some regulations beyond even legislative control? The social recognition concept honors the concept of private property only if it limits state power over the rights and responsibilities of private owners.

To develop a theory of potent but limited legislative power over property, we must situate the concept of social recognition within the governmental institutions that give it content and meaning. The concept of social recognition is independent of the institutions (courts or legislatures) that implement social recognition. Social recognition arises from the interaction of individuals who make claims to resources and subject themselves to the claims of others, from the formation of social values outside of market contexts, and from recognition of the institutions that recognize claims and obligations and make them enforceable. Social recognition is neither state-centered nor legislatively-centered. It is centered on the social values that develop over time from countless interactions of individuals over claims about how resources ought to be used and over the equitable division of burdens and benefits within the society. To be sure, social recognition takes its shape and content from the way it is implemented by courts and legislatures, but courts and legislatures are themselves socially recognized (and therefore socially limited) institutions whose invocation of social values are subject to the constraints that reflect their function and functional legitimacy. That is why we cannot equate social recognition with either judicial or legislative power, and why there is a core meaning to property that limits government power over property.

---

[3] Singer (2010) at 1072 (emphasis in the original).

Two aspects of social recognition are especially important for understanding the relationships between private and public law. First, social recognition requires that the authority and legitimacy of courts and legislatures itself be socially recognized. When courts and legislatures determine the rights and responsibilities of individuals over resources, they take part in an interactive social conversation about how decisions over resources ought to be made. The assignment of rights and responsibilities that deviate from evolving social norms are likely to be overturned by courts or legislatures eventually, as the pressure to align the law with socially important norms builds. Most important, state recognition of rights and responsibilities is itself limited by social recognition of the institutional competencies of courts and legislatures, and, as we shall see, this recognition of comparative institutional competencies acts as an institutional check on governmental overreaching.

The social recognition concept suggests that the determinants of the judicial and legislative definition of property rights are the values that become socially embraced. In private law, social values evolve from the interaction of individuals over claims to rights and their rejection. In the legislative realm, social values evolve from continuing conversations about the provision of public goods that cannot be provided through private agreements and markets – goods such as environmental and historical preservation, public access to important resources, and social safety nets. To be sure, these values get applied through the political process, and are therefore subject to familiar public choice problems, but the values are nonetheless the raw materials from which the legislature molds public policy.

For these reasons, the social recognition concept does not assume that property rights come from, or are recognized by, the government, as if the government were an entity separated from the community or its norms. Although legislative recognition of rights is a form of social recognition, it is not the only form of social recognition. Property rights arise from the government only in the sense that the values generated by social forces must be implemented in common law or legislation, but property rights are grounded in, and changed in response to, the values that shape the community's recognized norms of appropriate decision making about property. And they are accepted only if the community accepts the authority and legitimacy of the institutions that give them either judicial or legislative approval.

Because social acceptance of government regulation depends on acceptance of the legitimacy of the institutions that implement social values, a theory of judicial and legislative power over property must understand the characteristics of judge-made and legislative law that support the social acceptance of their determinations. The comparative competence of the different branches of government to interpret and apply social values gives the concept of property its core meaning and stability and protects owners from overreaching regulation. Common law courts and legislatures each operate in a sphere of competence – and therefore a sphere of authority – defined by a vision of appropriate lawmaking and separation of powers. Each must stay within its competence – the courts confined by appellate and legislative review, and the legislature confined by the Constitution and judicial review. The theory developed here suggests that the scope of legitimate legislative power is determined by the values recognized by common law courts, and it understands legislative power to be legitimately exercised only within a comparative framework that respects the characteristics for which courts and legislatures are best-suited. Limitations on legislative power, like limitations on judicial power, flow not from a preset vision of the concept of property rights but from the notion that property rights can be defined only by socially recognized processes using values that the community develops through social interaction.

Because the social recognition of rights through institutional processes is the source of both the common law concept of property and the values that influence legislative regulation, it makes sense to understand legislative regulation, and its limitations, in terms of the common law concept of property, as interpreted through a theory of the relationship between common law and legislative regulation. As I developed in the first parts of the book, the common law guarantees that in interpersonal interaction each owner's interests will be protected by an appropriate assignment of the burdens and benefits of decisions about resources. This is a role for which courts are well-equipped because the disputes are resolved by ensuring the equal freedom of individuals in their dealing with each other. Private law disputes present discrete controversies capable of neutral resolution based on evidence about the interests of the individuals. By contrast, legislative regulation serves a different function; it addresses the relationship between owners as owners and the interests of the collective community (the public interest), and it is designed to ensure that owners make decisions that adequately account for community interests. The legislative process is well suited for that goal, for (unlike the common law process) it has a method of aggregating, through political processes, individual interests in both their own well-being and in the collective well-being of the community in a way that reconciles collective and individual interests.

The challenge for understanding constitutional limitations on legislative regulation is to determine what processes legitimately assign burdens to owners when the public interest, as defined by the legislative process, demands that those burdens be borne by some class of owners. The theme developed in this part of the book is that limitations on legislative regulation of property flow from the need to keep the legislative, political process from using illegitimate methodologies to assign, in the name of public interest, burdens to owners. The theory here exploits recent scholarship that understands the constitutional due process guarantee not as a substantive declaration of the values protected by the Constitution but as a limitation on the use of the legislative power to make adjudication-like decisions without appropriate protections. The separation-of-powers theory expounded by Nathan Chapman and Michael McConnell suggests that historically "Legislative acts violated due process not because they were unreasonable or in violation of higher law, but because they exercised judicial power or abrogated common law procedural protections."[4] It is no accident that cases striking down legislative regulation of land use generally involve individualistic determinations about particular owners,[5] for those are the very cases in which legislative lawmaking is most suspect and least competent. Nor is it an accident that courts generally uphold burdensome land use regulation that contains general and prospective standards,[6] for those are the ones that avoid the separation-of-powers pitfalls of adjudication-like decisions.

From this perspective, a strong parallel connects the paradigm supporting the theory of private law developed in the earlier parts of the book and the paradigm underlying the theory of legislative regulation presented in this part of the book. In private law, each decision about property must appropriately assign the burdens and benefits of the decision in light of the need to respect

---

[4] Chapman and McConnell (2012) at 1677.
[5] See Lucas v. South Carolina Coastal Council, 506 U.S.1003 (1992) (general regulation directly affected only one property on barrier reef); Nectow v. City of Cambridge, 277 U.S. 183 (1928) (residence-only restriction applied to only one property across the street from residential property); City of Monterey v. Del Monte Dunes at Monterey, Ltd., 526 U.S. 687 (1999) (particular decision denying land use is unconstitutional); Village of Willowbrook v. Olech, 528 U.S. 562 (2000) (requirement applied to one homeowner but not to similarly situated neighbors violates equal protection); Sturdy Homes, Inc., v. Township of Redford, 30 Mich. App. 53 (1971) (overturning denial of building permit because the reasons for the denial did not apply to this proposal); Lafayette Park Baptist Church v. Scott, 553 S.W.2d 856 (Miss 1977) (Board applied improper standard in determining when a demolition permit should be granted); Bowles v. United States, 31 Fed. Cl. 37 (1994) (overturning denial of permit to plaintiff that had been given to plaintiff's neighbors); Florida Rock Indus., Inc. v United States, 18 F 3d 1560 (1994) (denial of permit to mine limestone when other denied permits had been for buildings), Florida Rock Indus., Inc. v. United States, 45 Fed. Cl. 21 (1999), Loveladies Harbor, Inc. v. United States, 28 F.3d. 1171 (1994) (denial of permit to build on wetlands overturned).
[6] See, e.g., Tahoe-Sierra Preservation Council, Inc. v. Tahoe Regional Planning Agency, 535 U.S. 302 (2002); William C. Haas & Co., Inc. v. City & Cnty. of San Francisco, 605 F.2d 1117 (9th Cir. 1979) (height restrictions diminished value of property from $2 million to $100,000 but applied to entire Russian Hill area); Just v. Marinette Cnty., 56 Wis. 2d 7 (1972) (upholding, prior to *Lucas*, prohibition on filling in wetlands on ground that it would disturb the property's natural state).

the equality of all individuals. The principle of equality determines the assignment of burdens and benefits, and thereby establishes, in various contexts, the proportionality that must be maintained in interpersonal relationships. Any disruption of that proportionality must, under the commands of corrective justice, be rectified. The appropriate assignment of burdens and benefits defines the essence of property and the scope of protection it is given.

Legislative regulation performs a different function but maintains the same concept of property. The legislature functions to aggregate individual interests into a collective interest, which it does by allowing individuals to express both their interest in their own well-being and their interest in the well-being of their community. By filtering individual interests (both self-regarding and other-regarding collective interests) through a representative system that aggregates individual interests into collective interests, legislatures determine the relationship between community values and individual owners. But the legislature too is bound by the common law concept of property and the goal of equality to make sure that it makes the appropriate assignment of the burdens of providing public goods.

Just as the resolution of private disputes depends on the equality principle, the reconciliation of collective and individual values depends on a principle of proportionality that reflects the equality principle. Under the paradigm developed in this part, legislation results from a social compact between individuals and the community that allows the community to provide for public goods financed by individuals (generally through taxes). The government's goal is to maximize social surplus, but the government is subject to an equality constraint that addresses the assignment of burdens among property owners. The equality constraint serves two functions. It preserves the sense of community by ensuring that those who bear the burden of providing public goods feel that they are being treated fairly and thus enhances the social acceptance of the regulation. Second, the equality constraint is necessary to protect the integrity of the legislative process, as I will describe below.

Although the goal of legislative regulation is to maximize the social surplus, any violation of the equality constraint detracts from that goal, for the social compact, like individual interactions, requires that net maximum benefits be determined only after subtracting the losses from the unequal distribution of the burdens of providing public goods. No doubt, the assignment of burdens and benefits in private law is different from the assignment of burdens and benefits in public law, for the interests are different. Significantly, however, the assignment of burdens and benefits in both public and private law is bound by the equality principle, and each reflects the uniqueness of common law and legislative lawmaking. The goal of the legislative process is not to socialize all the burdens of regulation; the many cases in which owners bear disproportionate burdens attests to that. Nor is the goal necessarily to make sure that those who bear the burdens of regulation also get the benefits of regulation, as would be true if average reciprocity of advantage were the sole test for the validity of legislation. Rather, the goal is to distribute the burdens of providing public goods in accordance with the equality principle though processes that are fairly geared to determine the terms of equal treatment.

11.2 SUPREME COURT LIMITATIONS ON LEGISLATIVE REGULATION

The Supreme Court has been remarkably unsuccessful in crafting a constitutional vision of the relationship between owners and the government or in providing a coherent way of thinking about limitations on the legislative regulation of property.

One major source of the problem, as I have just indicated, is the failure to develop a theory of legislative regulation that will protect owners against an inappropriate assignment of the burdens of community benefit. Another source of the problem, I believe, is the failure to grasp the distinct functions of the two powers the government exercises over property – the takings power and general regulatory or police power – and the failure to understand limitations on those functions in terms of the functions themselves. There is a fundamental difference between government action that impairs the right to exclude (which eminent domain protects) and government action that impairs the right to use property (which, I will show, is protected by a different application of the equality principle). Indeed, the Supreme Court has taken a step toward recognizing that distinction by noting that "The text of the Fifth Amendment itself provides a basis for drawing a distinction between physical takings and regulatory takings."[7] That distinction, I maintain, is between regulations that take away the right to exclude and those that affect only the right to use property.

Although the Supreme Court has recognized the distinction between physical takings and regulatory takings, it has not yet recognized what that distinction means for the way we think about the relationship between the government and private owners. Instead of drawing on the distinction to craft constitutional restrictions that reflect the different functions of legislative regulation, the Supreme Court has made up, almost by accident, a hybrid

---

[7] Tahoe-Sierra Preservation Council, Inc. v. Tahoe Regional Planning Agency, 535 U.S. 302, 321 (2002).

doctrine – the doctrine of regulatory takings – that wrongfully equates the government's obligation to compensate owners for nullifying the right to exclude with limitations on state regulation of the right to use property. The result is a mishmash of restrictions on governmental regulation under the Equal Protection Clause, the Due Process Clause, and the Takings Clause that are incoherent and unworkable. Anyone spending even a little time reading lower court opinions governing land use regulation recognizes that there is no intelligible approach for addressing government regulations of how owners use their property.

To be sure, the Supreme Court needs to recognize a doctrine that prohibits the legislature from doing an end run around the Takings Clause by enacting, without the required compensation, regulations that are equivalent to the power of eminent domain.[8] But this principle requires that we determine which government regulations, because they are "equivalent" to the use of eminent domain, trigger requirements of public use and just compensation. One cannot make the appropriate equivalency argument without specifying the function of the eminent domain power, and it is by no means clear that the eminent domain power functions to protect owners against the diminution of value of their property from land use regulations. As I will argue below, restrictions on land use, even those that severely reduce the value of property, are not equivalent to the power of eminent domain and do not justify the doctrine of regulatory taking on an equivalency ground.

I argue that the Takings Clause restricts the legislature's right to impair, through regulation, an owner's right to exclude because impairing the right to exclude is equivalent to the use of eminent domain. The Takings Clause prohibits the legislature from doing an end run around the eminent domain power, and thereby avoiding its limitations, when the legislature, by regulation, takes away the right to exclude. This is the function of cases prohibiting, without compensation, regulations that result in the "permanent physical occupation" of property. These cases protect the Takings Clause because, by taking away the right to exclude, physical occupation is equivalent to eminent domain. I also argue that limitations on the legislative power to regulate land use decisions cannot stem from the Takings Clause because reducing the value of property

---

[8] Dana and Merrill (2002) at 4. *See also*, Lucas v. South Carolina Coastal Council, 505 U.S. 1003, 1014 (1992) (Justice Scalia: "if the protection against physical appropriate of private property was to be meaningfully enforced, the government's power to redefine the range of interests included in the ownership of property was necessarily constrained by constitutional limits)" and First English Evangelical Lutheran Church of Glendale v. Los Angeles Cnty, 482 U.S. 304 (1987) (repeating equivalency argument in reviewing land use regulation that was later found not to be a taking).

is not equivalent to the use of eminent domain in a relevant and meaningful sense. In the view presented here, limitations on land use regulation stem not from the Takings Clause but from the equality principle, which restricts legislative power to make judgments in particularized cases. As I will argue in Chapter 13, the legislature and its delegates are required by the equality principle to make rules of general applicability and prospective effect, and may not make individualized determinations that do not meet the equality principle. The source of these restrictions is not the Takings Clause, but other constitutional limitations on legislature power, including the Equal Protection Clause, the Contracts Clause, and the Due Process Clause (in its nonsubstantive form).

To be sure, government regulation of land use is sometimes unconstitutional, and because unconstitutional government regulation can give rise to a suit for damages, impermissible regulation sometimes supports a damage suit against the government.[9] But this is not, I will demonstrate, because the government action is a taking. It is because the legislature has impermissibly assigned burdens to an owner and has therefore deprived the owner of the essence of property: an assessment of burdens and benefits that meets the equality principle. My claim is that cases in which courts have invalidated land use regulation (as opposed to regulation that takes away the right to exclude) reveal a consistent pattern: in each case, the regulation of land use employs an impermissible process to assign burdens to owners or impermissibly asks a particular owner to bear burdens that should have been borne by a general class of owners. These restrictions exceed the legislative power because the legislative process is bound by the same equality principle that shapes private law regulation.

My primary concern here is in understanding limitations on government power over property to be a reflection of the concept of ownership developed in this book – namely, that ownership guarantees the appropriate assignment of the burden of decisions about property. As is already clear, I see no room for doctrine that would invalidate a land use regulation simply because it has "gone too far" in reducing the value of the property (unless it has taken away the owner's right to exclude); I would therefore retire the regulatory takings doctrine insofar as it turns on a diminution-of-value test. This is not, of course, the first effort to come to grips with the regulatory takings muddle;[10] and the

---

[9] City of Monterey v. Del Monte Dunes at Monterey Ltd., 526 U.S. 687 (1999).
[10] The word "muddle" is from Rose (1984) at 561. Among the works that collect descriptions of the muddle are Heller (1999) at 1202. The attack on the regulatory takings doctrine comes from Byrne (1995). A potent argument that regulatory takings are inconsistent with the original constitutional scheme is in Treanor (1985).

huge literature of justification – largely unsuccessful[11] – is itself a testament to the incoherence of the doctrine. Never have so many able minds tried so hard,[12] with so little success, to provide content to an idea that, when properly understood, is vacuous. We should dispel the regulatory takings mirage so that we can make room for a meaningful and coherent theory of the limitations on legislative land use regulation.

In view of the vast literature criticizing the regulatory takings doctrine, I will emphasize only the points most salient to the themes of this book. Then, in the following two chapters, I construct a coherent theory of the relationship between ownership and the legislative function, focusing separately on the Takings Clause (Chapter 12) and the constitutional limitations on the regulation of land use (Chapter 13).

I challenge the central idea of the regulatory takings doctrine – that the regulation of land use that goes "too far" in reducing the value of property requires the state to compensate the owner.[13] To be clear, there is much that is sometimes swept under the regulatory takings rug that I do not challenge. As I have said, if the regulation takes away the owner's right to exclude (which occurs when the government effects a permanent physical occupation), the regulation has gone "too far," but that is not because the regulation has reduced the value of the property. That is because the right to exclude is what the Takings Clause is designed to protect; if the right to exclude is impaired by a physical occupation, the regulation has gone too far and the owner's property has been taken.[14] A regulation that leaves unaffected an owner's right to exclude but regulates the owner's right to use the property is not a taking and ought never be subjected to the just compensation requirement of the Takings

---

[11] Radin (1993) at 146 ("The sight of such a pervasive and central field in apparent disarray has enticed many able theorists, but their critical commentary has been more convincing than their efforts to reconstruct.").

[12] The literature is huge. Major citations are collected in Dukeminier et al. (2010) at 1189–95. Richard Epstein's views on the topic are predetermined by his assertion that rights exist naturally and that the state functions to protect them. Epstein (1985).

[13] The idea that a regulation may go "too far" can be traced to Justice Holmes's opinion in Pennsylvania Coal Co. v. Mahon, 260 U.S. 393 (1922). I show later on in this chapter why the case need not be read to support the regulatory takings doctrine.

[14] Readers familiar with the regulatory takings doctrine will observe that I am interpreting one of the per se categories of the regulatory takings doctrine – the category of permanent physical possession – as an actual taking subject to the Takings Clause. That is because the cases in which the state has occasioned a permanent physical occupation are ones in which the state has taken away the right to exclude. For reasons advanced in the text, these are not regulatory takings but actual takings, and are distinct from regulations that control the right to use property. Under this reading, we do not have to define property rights other than the right to exclude in order to understand when a taking has occurred.

Clause (even if the government is required to pay compensation for a constitutional violation). Property is protected against takings and deprivations. The former applies when the state has taken the owner's right to exclude; it requires compensation. The latter applies when land values are lowered (a deprivation), is protected by due process, and requires compensation only when statutes authorize compensation for constitutional violations.[15] Further, when an owner retains the right to exclude, no regulation takes away the total economic value of the property, for an owner with the right to exclude has the right to transfer, and transfer is the protector of value.

That is not to say that every time the government impairs the right to exclude there is a taking. As we saw in Chapter 7, the right to exclude is itself limited at common law if the burdens and benefits tip in favor of access, and the takings concept exempts a number of government acts of appropriation or destruction, including the destruction of property to fight a raging fire, the destruction of property by police or the military when a necessary part of their duties, and forfeitures of property used in a crime.[16] Because these exemptions from the Takings Clause do not implicate the notion that a regulation has gone too far, I do not discuss them here.

I also do not challenge (or discuss) the exactions cases, which limit the government's power to exact compensation from the owner as the price of doing something the owner would otherwise be allowed to do. These cases do not reduce the value of property as such, and the Supreme Court has put them on a different analytical footing from the regulatory takings doctrine.[17] Finally, I do not challenge cases in which the government has been held responsible for its torts, for it is worthwhile to distinguish the government's responsibility for its own activity from the government's responsibility when it regulates land usage. When the state engages in activity – such as determining flight patterns, delivering the mail, and deciding how to use *its* property – it is responsible for the wrongs it commits in the activity decisions it makes and must provide

---

[15] The Supreme Court, in Loretto v. Teleprompter Manhattan CATV Corp., 458 U.S. 419 (1982), recognized the difference by comparing two wartime mining cases. In United States v. Pewee Coal Co., 341 U.S. 114 (1951) the Court unanimously held that taking over and operating a coal mine because of a labor stoppage was a taking. In United States v. Central Eureka Mining Co., 357 U.S. 155 (1958), the Court held that shutting down a mine to divert equipment and manpower to other uses was not a taking. The former case was a taking of the right to exclude; the latter only deprived the owner of the right to use his land. Only the former action required just compensation.

[16] Dana and Merrill (2002) at 110–20, Fennell (2012) at 67–71, and Levmore (1990).

[17] City of Monterey v. Del Monte Dunes at Monterey, Ltd., 526 U.S. 687, 703 (1999) (the rough proportionality test "was not designed to address, and is not readily applicable to, the much different question arising where, as here, the landowner's challenge is based not on excessive exactions but on denial of development").

compensation to those it injures. Paying compensation is not, however, the just compensation of the Takings Clause. The state pays compensation for its wrongful activities for the same reason that private parties pay compensation for their wrongful activities – the party injured by a wrong is entitled to compensation under tort and property law. When the government compensates a property owner for the government's torts, it does so not because it has taken the property in any constitutional sense, but because when the government has waived sovereign immunity it has agreed to compensate others for the wrongs it commits.[18] These are instances of liability for a governmental activity, not liability for regulating a private owner's activity.[19]

I make several points about the regulatory takings doctrine that advance the themes of this book. In Section 11.2.1 I explain the functional and conceptual distinction between government regulation of the right to exclude and government regulation of the right to use property. Here I show why keeping the two functions distinct is important to the concept of property. In the next section, Section 11.2.2, I show how the failure to grasp this distinction results in a mistaken understanding about property rights, property values, and the government's role in protecting the value of property. This supports the point, made by others, that the regulatory takings doctrine embodies a form of substantive due process that is as objectionable as the doctrine of the *Lochner* era. Finally, in Section 11.2.3, I argue that the regulatory takings doctrine is based on a mistaken reading of Justice Holmes's opinion in *Pennsylvania Co. v. Mahon*.[20] Going "too far" can take away the right to exclude (and therefore be a taking), as it did in *Mahon*, even if it comes in the form of a land use regulation; however, given the facts of that case, going "too far" provides no general limitation on land use regulation.

11.2.1 The Functional Distinction between Takings and Use Restrictions

My basic claim is straightforward: the Takings Clause and the Due Process Clause are conceptually, operationally, and functionally independent of each

---

[18] The mistake is of old lineage. In 1888, John Lewis wrote as if the harm from a governmental nuisance were a taking (Lewis (1888) at 45). In fact, it is a simple tort.
[19] In other words, the Takings Clause ought not to be interpreted to require compensation for government torts because torts are not takings and just compensation is not necessary to provide compensation. Once the government waves sovereign immunity, the tort system imposes liability. This tort-based theory explains some of the early cases that look like forerunners of the regulatory takings doctrine. Muhlker v. New York & Harlem Railroad Co., 197 U.S. 544 (1905) (awarding nearby residents the damages for harm caused by elevated railway; decided, however, as contract or due process case).
[20] 206 U.S. 393 (1922).

other.[21] They operate in different spheres of influence, with different functions, and with different justificatory structures that limit government power. To be sure, some state regulations are takings and ought to be treated as such under the Takings Clause (requiring the state to meet the just compensation and public use requirements). Those are the regulations that the Supreme Court classifies as "permanent physical invasions." They are takings because they take away the owner's right to exclude.[22] However, regulations governing how an owner uses her land, under the theory developed here, are not takings and should never be analyzed under the Takings Clause (except when, as in *Mahon*, they take the right to exclude). They are deprivations of property, to be sure, but the justification for exercising regulatory power is different from the justification for exercising the takings (eminent domain) power, and the limitations on the regulatory powers are different. Moreover, an owner deprived of property without due process is entitled to have the deprivation annulled, and the government ought not be allowed to buy its way out of violations of the equality principle in land use regulations.[23]

[21] The effect of this point is to restore the understanding of nineteenth-century law, as exemplified in Chief Justice Lemuel Shaw's opinion in Commonwealth v. Alger, 7 Cush. 53, 84–85 (1851). There, Judge Shaw upheld the power of the legislature to limit the extension of privately-owned wharfs in Boston's harbor, even if the wharf was on the owner's property. There, he said:
> We think it is settled principle, growing out of the nature of well-ordered civil society, that every holder of property, however absolute and unqualified his title, holds it under the implied liability that his use of it may be so regulated, that it shall not be injurious to the equal enjoyment of others having an equal right to the enjoyment of their property, nor injurious to the rights of the community. Rights of property, like all other social and conventional rights, are subject to such reasonable limitations in their enjoyment, as shall prevent them from being injurious, and to such reasonable restraints and regulations established by law as the legislature, under the governing and controlling power vested in them by the constitution, may think necessary and convenient. This is very different from the power of eminent domain – the right of the state to take and appropriate private property whenever the public exigency requires it, which can be done only on the condition of providing a reasonable compensation therefore.

This original understanding has not been lost on modern commentators. *See, e.g.*, Graglia (2002) (a taking was understood to occur only when government seized or caused the physical occupancy of property) and Treanor (1985).

[22] The regulatory takings doctrine once encompassed two kinds of regulations: regulations that authorize or require a physical occupation of the owner's property, and regulations that regulate the use of an owner's property. Although regulatory takings doctrine once put regulations that result in physical occupation in a special per se category, the Supreme Court changed that approach in Tahoe-Sierra Preservation Council, Inc. v. Tahoe Regional Planning Agency, 535 U.S. 302 (2002) and now recognizes that regulations that require or approve of a permanent physical occupation are takings, not regulatory takings, where just compensation and public use requirements are in force. All other regulations – those affecting the use of land but not the right to exclude – are addressed under the regulatory takings doctrine.

[23] Admittedly, violations of constitutional rights can give rise to a suit for damages under 42 U.S.C.A. § 1983, which provides for civil rights suits seeking damages for deprivation of

Superficially, there is logic to the assertion, which the regulatory takings doctrine advances, that the just compensation requirement ought to depend on the value of the property taken. If the state takes title to an owner's land, the property has no value to the owner. Similarly, if a legislative regulation forbids uses that would otherwise give the property value, it looks, by its effect, to be an equivalent state action. But the analogy between takings and land use regulations rises or falls on the question of what dimensions of property ought to determine equivalency, and it implicitly (and wrongly) assumes that a property's value is relevant to the legality of both eminent domain and land use regulations. But the analogy overlooks the crucial distinction between taking the right to exclude and regulating the right to use property. The state's eminent domain power does not turn on the property's value (even though just compensation returns some of the value to the owner); it depends on taking away the right to exclude. Land use regulation that does not take away the right to exclude reduces the property's value but leaves the right to transfer the property interest intact.

Significantly, the two forms of regulation stand in different relationship to the market. Eminent domain supersedes the market; land use regulation influences values in the market but does not supersede the market. Eminent domain allows the government to act when the market cannot effectively coordinate the decisions of private owners, a point I will develop in the next chapter. Land use regulation allows the government to require an individual owner to reflect collective values in her decisions.

As I will elaborate in the next chapter, the Takings Clause applies when the state impairs an owner's right to exclude, and the Takings Clause authorizes a taking when an owner's right to exclude effectively impairs the market's ability to coordinate decisions of private owners. This is no paradox. The right to

constitutional rights under color of state law, including rights arising under the Due Process Clause. That damage remedy under the Due Process Clause, does not, however, vitiate a claim that the violation ought to be enjoined. Significantly, in cases of permanent physical invasion, those that are indeed "takings" rather than regulatory takings, courts traditionally ordered compensation under the eminent domain power. Damages were traditionally denied for regulatory takings that involved land use restrictions, and courts instead relied on declaratory or injunctive relief. This required the government to either bring the regulation into conformity with the Constitution or to take the property by eminent domain. Dukeminier et al., (2010) at 1167. Injunctions against government land use regulation were routinely entered in many cases where the government was not expected to use its eminent domain power to take the property. See, e.g., Nectow v. City of Cambridge, 277 U.S. 183 (1928). The injunctions were issued against invalid land use regulations and courts expected the government to remove the offending regulation. The fact that the government could use its eminent domain power as an alternate way of achieving its goals does not take away from the fact that the landowner was able to get the offending regulation modified; eminent domain did not purchase the right to have an unconstitutional regulation; it purchased the property.

exclude makes markets work, for without the right to exclude individuals who want the resource would take, rather than purchase, the resource. The market system that is enabled by the right to exclude performs the valuable function of coordinating decisions between owners, and the coordination function depends on the right to exclude. Yet sometimes the market is unable to coordinate private decisions because market failures and holdouts impair the coordinating function. The Takings Clause allows government intervention to play the coordinating role that markets normally play, and it does so by mimicking the market. Under the Takings Clause, the government purchases the right to exclude so that it can perform functions that markets cannot perform because of market failures.

But the right to exclude does not depend on the value of the property. An owner's right to protect, and receive protection, against trespass does not depend on showing that the trespass has or will lower the value of the property. Even a person with valueless property maintains the right to exclude, and an owner has the right to exclude even if a trespass would not damage the property or lower its value.[24] Exclusion is not about value protection, even though exclusion can protect value. As I developed in Chapter 7, exclusion is about protecting a right not a value – the right not to benefit others without compensation; taking that right away is a taking. Moreover, whether there is a taking does not depend on the diminished value of the property. Taking an easement may take very little value from the owner but it is still a taking because the state has taken the right to exclude. Moreover, because the owner of property receives just compensation the government exercise of power under the Takings Clause does not take the value of the property. Although just compensation does not compensate the owner for her subjective valuation of the property, the idea of the eminent domain power is, as I have said, to mimic the value that the market would provide the owner if markets were functioning well.

By contrast, regulations affecting the use of property are not justified by the need to coordinate decisions of different owners. They represent not a failure of the market to coordinate decisions but a failure of individual decision makers to take collective values into account. Land use regulations affect the level of return that markets provide, but generally do not affect the right to exclude. A decrease in the value of the property does not impair the right to exclude. Even in *Lucas v. South Carolina Coastal Council*,[25] where the regulation

[24] *See, e.g.*, Jacque v. Steenberg Homes, Inc., 563 N.W.2d. 154 (Wis. 1997).
[25] Lucas v. South Carolina Coastal Council, 505 U.S. 1003 (1992).

was found to have rendered the property of no economic value to the owner (because of his contemplated use of the property), the owner retained the right to sell the property to someone for whom it had value (a point made in the dissenting opinion). To be sure, use restrictions impair the marketability of the property for the forbidden uses, but that does not keep the market from performing its coordination function; the market continues to coordinate uses among owners for the non-forbidden uses. The justification for regulating land use is not that markets are unable to perform their coordinating function; it is that individual owners do not account for all the information that is relevant to the social value of the property.

In a point I will amplify below, the suggestion that regulation of the use of property could be a taking because it goes "too far" suggests that the state ought to act as the guarantor of the value of property. That is precisely what the common law refuses to do. The benefits of ownership in terms of the possibility of increased value are matched by the burdens of ownership in terms of the risk of decreased value, and to set up constitutional limits on decreases in value when the burdens meet the equality principle is to upset the balance of burdens and benefits that were so carefully worked out at the common law.

In light of this foundational difference between takings and regulations, the oft-repeated statements that regulating land use can be the functional equivalent of a taking are simply wrong. Those who argue that the use of eminent domain takes away the property's value and that land use regulation can take away the property's value have not thought through the analogy. The regulatory takings doctrine is asking the wrong question. It asks: "When, as a matter of political theory, should the state be required to pay compensation to an owner adversely affected by government action?"[26] That is an interesting question, but it is not a constitutional one, for the Constitution has already answered it. Under the Constitution, the compensation requirement is triggered by a taking; the compensation requirement does not define a taking. The constitutional question is: "When has a taking occurred?," and it is circular to say that a taking is defined by the obligations that follow once a taking is found.

The regulatory takings doctrine also undercuts the idea of procedural, separation-of-powers due process. The relevant question under due process is: Should the state be allowed to act in this way? Those challenging a regulation that is overbearing want the regulation overturned; they do not want

---

[26] The mistake has been made by some of our finest minds. See, e.g, Michelman 1967) at 1165 ("Taking is, of course, constitutional law's expression for any sort of public injury for which the Constitution requires payment of compensation.").

compensation.[27] The regulatory takings doctrine suggests that the state can act arbitrarily as long as it compensates those affected by its arbitrary action. When owners find regulation to be too oppressive, they do not want compensation; they want the state to be told to stop. Analyzing regulation under "regulatory takings" doctrine does just the opposite: it gives the state a license to be oppressive as long as the state compensates the oppressed. The problem of arbitrary regulation is not that it takes property. The problem is that it violates a sense of the proper relationship between the community and the owner. To allow the state to buy its way out of that sense of propriety is perverse. If the regulation imposes a burden that violates the equality principle, that burden ought not be addressed by compensating the owner. Just compensation does not reflect an owner's personal attachment to property and it is precisely that attachment that ought to be protected from state overreaching.[28] The law ought to address the burden on the owner by telling the state that it cannot do what it wanted to do in the way it wanted to do it.

Given the differences between impairing the right to exclude and impairing the right to use, it is not surprising that the Constitution requires compensation every time the legislature takes away the right to exclude but not when the legislature takes away the right to use property through general and prospective rules about land use. The right to exclude must always be purchased; that is the essence of property – an individual cannot take what is not his. Eminent domain power, and its regulatory equivalents, function to rearrange ownership patterns when the market cannot supply public goods; compensation performs the market-mimicking function of ensuring that the owner is compensated for having taken the risks of ownership. But the right to use property is highly contingent because it depends on the character of the property and the uses made by neighbors. Over a broad range of non-nuisance circumstances, the right to use property may be impaired without compensation because owners accept the risk that natural or man-made changes will impair the value of the property under circumstances in which compensation may not be required. Only when the legislature violates the equality principle in assigning the burdens of land use regulation is the owner entitled to complain about the regulation.

---

[27] This is true even if the owner can get compensation under Section 1983 for the time that the deprivation occurred. That is compensation for a constitutional violation that causes injury. Its availability does not substitute for an order enjoining the offending government action.

[28] It is not a paradox that the Constitution fails to protect subjective value under the Takings Clause but does so under the Due Process Clause. Under the Takings Clause, the government cannot distinguish between subjective value and holdout value. Wanting to protect one (subjective value) but not the other (holdout value), but unable to separate them, it protects neither. See Alexander and Peñalever (2012). This conclusion is warranted despite impressive academic work seeking ways of separating an individual's holdout value and subject value.

11.2.2 A Question of Value

Indeed, the regulatory takings doctrine is pernicious precisely because it asserts that a function of the state is to protect the value of property rather than to protect the right to seek value from property.

Land use legislation adjusts the burdens and benefits of ownership to account for a broad range of factors that connect individual ownership to the interests of the community – factors that cannot be accounted for under the common law. As long as land use regulation appropriately assigns the burdens of achieving a public good, it does not "take" anything; it simply redefines the scope of decision making that society has entrusted to the individual owner as part of a socially recognized attribute of ownership. If the regulation works a deprivation, it deprives the owner of the fair distribution of burdens to which the owner is entitled under the terms of social recognition, not because the owner has, by the restriction, lost value in its property. Private owners hold their ownership subject to the fair assignment of burdens and benefits and are protected against their unfair assignment, but the Constitution ought not be construed to require compensation simply because land use regulation has reduced the value of property. It is the unequal reduction in property value, not the reduction in property value, that is protected by the Constitution.

Not only is there nothing to compensate owners for when the state regulates land use (because nothing was taken), the suggestion that just compensation might be required fundamentally misconstrues the relationship between the community and the owner. The regulatory taking doctrine suggests that the state's role is to relieve owners of some of their burdens of ownership rather than to identify the burdens that are appropriately imposed to deliver public goods. To see this distinction, consider *Miller v. Schoene*.[29] There, the state had to choose between two classes of property owners: preserving stands of ornamental red cedar trees that were infected with a rust disease or saving nearby apple orchards, to which the disease could easily spread. In upholding the legislative choice to sacrifice the cedar trees, Justice Stone said:

> The state was under the necessity of making a choice between the preservation of one class of property and that of the other wherever both existed in close proximity. It would have been none the less a choice if, instead of enacting the present statute, the state, by doing nothing, had permitted serious injury to the apple orchards within its borders to go unchecked. When forced to such a choice the state does not exceed its constitutional powers by deciding upon the destruction of one class of property in order to save

[29] 276 U.S. 272 (1928).

another which, in the judgment of the legislature is of greater value. It will not do to say that the case is merely one of conflict of two private interests and that the misfortune of apple growers may not be shifted to cedar owners by ordering the destruction of their property; for it is obvious that there may be, and that there is, a preponderate public concern in the preservation of one interest over the other.[30]

The case was decided under the Due Process Clause, not the regulatory takings doctrine, but it illustrates why the regulatory takings doctrine is misguided. To even ask whether this literal taking of the cedar trees was a taking that required just compensation is to show the ugly underbelly of the regulatory takings doctrine. The regulatory takings question asks whether the state is required to protect property owners from the ravages of disease. It is clear that disease "took" the trees, not the state, and that the state, not being implicated in the infestation, did no more than act in the public interest in light of the need to make a choice. The notion of regulatory takings implies that the state would, in some circumstances, insure against the burdens of ownership.[31] The state may well want to provide a safety net for owners, but the Constitution does not require it.

In other words, the regulatory takings doctrine plays fast and loose with the concept of causation. If there is no social problem to be addressed (that is, if there is no legitimate end of state action) the subject matter ought not be regulated by the state at all. But if there is a social problem to be addressed, it is the social problem that causes the diminished value of the property, not the regulation itself.[32] Behind many regulatory takings cases one can see that the state has not caused the loss; natural forces have. The cedar rust caused he harm in *Miller v. Schoene*, natural erosion caused the harm in *Lucas v. South Carolina Coastal Council*,[33] and fire destroyed the property in *First English*

---

[30] 276 U.S. at 279.

[31] I honor the notion of James Buchanan that the state may make a mistake, but not the related notion that if the state is required to compensate the loser in this battle, it will automatically choose the least costly option and thus avoid a mistake. See Buchanan (1972). The price of avoiding a governmental mistake is, as Justice Stone recognized, to paralyze the government from acting at all.

[32] One might attempt to distinguish between causes that are attributable to the state (where the regulatory takings doctrine would apply) and causes that are attributable to non-state sources (where the regulatory takings doctrine would not apply), but I do not think that is possible. The state acts because of a perceived need that attracts sufficient attention from a majority of legislators. The perceived need, and not the legislature, is the cause of the decreased value. If the perceived need is an illegitimate end of government, the legislation on that basis ought to be struck down under the Due Process Clause.

[33] 505 U.S. 1003 (1992).

Evangelical Lutheran Church v. County of Los Angeles.[34] Government ought not be required by the Constitution to act as a guarantor against such losses.

The regulatory takings doctrine is, in effect, the perpetuation of substantive due process of the *Lochner* variety. The heart of *Lochner's* substantive due process – namely, that the Constitution protects the value of some assets over the value of others – forms the central premise of the regulatory takings doctrine. Having gotten rid of economic due process in one form, the Supreme Court ought not smuggle it back into the Constitution in the form of the regulatory takings doctrine. Owners ought not be protected, as a constitutional requirement, from the risks of ownership. Under the principles of social recognition outlined in this book, owners take their ownership subject to changing circumstances that affect the value of their ownership, including changing social perceptions about the value of resources in various contexts. Their investment-backed expectations, having been formed against a backdrop of potential regulation, ought not be guaranteed by a doctrine that focuses on the fact of their loss rather than the way the loss was assigned to them by the government.

This is not to say, of course, that owners are not protected against inappropriate legislative regulation of their property. It is simply to say that what triggers that protection is not the fact that they have suffered a loss in the value of their property, but the way the legislature has assigned the loss to them and not to others, the topic addressed in Chapter 13.

11.2.3 *Misunderstanding* Mahon

The regulatory takings doctrine is generally traced to Justice Holmes's misunderstood 1922 opinion in *Pennsylvania Coal Co. v. Mahon*.[35] There the legislature forbid the mining of anthracite coal in a way that would cause a subsidence of, among other things, any structure that was used as a human habitation, except where one person owned both the surface and the mineral rights and posed no danger to neighbors. This regulation was said to have gone "too far" and the government was required to justly compensate the owners of

---

[34] 482 U.S. 304 (1987).
[35] 260 U.S. 393 (1922). Careful scholars point to earlier origins of the regulatory takings doctrine. Brauneis (1996). John Ely points out that the regulatory takings doctrine can be traced to late nineteenth-century writings, and in particular to dictum in Justice Holmes's opinion in Bent v. Emery, 137 Mass. 495, 496 (1899) ("It would be open to argument at least that an owner might be stripped of his rights so far as to amount to a taking without any physical interference with the land.") Ely (2012) at 164. *See also*, Hudson Water Co. v. McCarter, 209 U.S. 349, 355 (1908) (Holmes, J.) (if limiting height of building makes lot "wholly useless," compensation would be required).

the coal if they wanted to maintain the regulation. Despite scholarly doubts about *Mahon* as a takings case,[36] the notion has not been put to rest.

The opinion serves as a Rohrsarch test for how to read a judicial opinion; how we read the case depends on what property we think was taken. The traditional reading is to think that the legislation took property (coal). If coal was taken, the opinion is properly read as one of the origins of the regulatory takings doctrine; when Justice Holmes wrote that the regulation went "too far," he must have meant that the regulation took too much coal. The language of the opinion then can be read as the wellspring of the regulatory takings doctrine. On the other hand, this is a somewhat strange reading, especially coming from Justice Holmes. Certainly the amount of coal taken was small, both absolutely and as a percentage of the total coal that was taken, and many other land use cases, both before and after *Mahon*, have allowed far greater deprivations without requiring compensation.[37]

On the other hand, the opinion reads much differently if it is understood, as I think it should be, that it was not the coal that the government took but the contract to mine the coal despite the danger of subsidence to the owners of the surface rights.[38] Significantly, the legislation at issue undid contracts in which homeowners and governmental entities had bought the surface rights from the coal companies on the express condition that they would have no claim against the coal companies for subsidence; the coal companies bought both the mineral rights and the right to cause subsidence by extracting the minerals (the so-called third estate).[39] The surface owners had effectively sold the subsidence rights to the coal company in return for a lower price. Even

---

[36] Brauneis (1996). Rose (1984), at note 22, recognizes that *Mahon* "fits more logically under this [Contract Clause] rubric" but reads the opinion as a takings case, relying on Holmes's statement that "the extent of the taking is great" 260 U.S. at 414–415. However, the next sentence of the opinion returns to the contract theme: "[The legislation] purports to abolish what is recognized in Pennsylvania as an estate in land – a very valuable estate – and what is declared by the Court below to be a contract hitherto binding on the parties." *Id*. Felix Frankfurter, writing just a year after *Mahon*, viewed the case to have been about the impairment of contracts. See Frankfurter (1923) at 937. Under the view presented here, as is discussed in the text, taking the right to exclude that has been bargained for is both a taking and an impairment of contracts.

[37] See, e.g., Mugler v. Kansas, 123 U.S. 623 (1887); Hadacheck v. Sebastian, 239 U.S. 394 (1915), and Penn Cent. Transp. Co., v. New York City, 438 U.S. 104 (1978).

[38] See, e.g., Rose (1984) at 571 ("To require that the company support the surface reverses the original bargain and seems improper and unfair."); Michelman (1967) (referring to demoralization costs of taking bargained-for property rights). Carol Rose's comprehensive analysis of the welfare implications of such bargains also provides the rationale for holding that such contracts ought not be enforced, and thus support the Supreme Court's later overruling of *Mahon*, even understood as a Contracts Clause case, in *Keystone Bitumious Coal Ass'n v. Benedictis*, 480 U.S. 470 (1987).

[39] Rose (1984) at 563.

more significantly, because some of the buyers were government entities, the government was in the position of selling the right to risk subsidence and then passing legislation to recover, without cost, the right that it had just sold. What was taken was not the physical property of coal but the contractual property that represented how surface owners and coal companies had allocated the risks of subsidence.

That the case ought to be understood as an unlawful interference with contract seemed clear to Holmes. This is "the case of a single private house," not of a nuisance to the public – a fact of significance in contract, where rights are divided between two parties, but not in property, where in rem rights are divided between an owner and the rest of the world. Because the statute did not apply when a person owned both the surface and the mineral rights, the legislature could not have been concerned with a generalized problem of subsidence, only with a problem that arises when surface and mineral rights are divided (which is done by contract). And this legislation could not be "justified as a matter of personal safety" because that "could be provided for by notice." The buyers of property, having bought the risk of subsidence, had no protectable interest in their structure but only in their safety, which they could protect by being notified when subsidence might be a risk.

The case was decided under the contract and due process provisions.[40] Even those passages of the opinion that speak most directly to eminent domain power are couched in contractual terms. The state could have taken both the surface and subsidence rights by condemnation when it condemned the surface property, but it would have had to pay for them. The state bought the surface rights, and it ought not be able to get the subsidence rights without payment. "If in any case [state] representatives have been so short sighted as to acquire only surface rights without the right of support, we see no more authority for supplying the latter without compensation than there was for taking the right of way in the first place and refusing to pay for it because the public wanted it very much." Eminent domain was relevant not because this was a case of the taking of physical property but because the government is not allowed to take contractual rights through legislation that it refused to take though condemnation or through the open market. The legislation went "too far" because, by taking the contract rights the coal company had paid for, the government had taken away the coal company's right to exclude (by giving control of that supporting coal back to the surface owners), which is the essence of a taking. And the opinion concludes with the contract rationale: "so far as private persons or communities have seen fit to take the risk of acquiring only surface rights, we

[40] Brauneis (1996).

cannot see that the fact that their risk has become a danger warrants the giving to them greater rights than they bought."

To be sure, in *Mahon* Holmes expressed expansive views about the need to limit state power when rights are taken, but those expansive views, in the context of the taking of contract rights, boil down to the proposition that the state may not interfere with contracts that divide risks between private parties without compensating those whose contract rights were taken. Under this analysis, it appears that Holmes's reference to regulation that "goes too far" had to do with the subject matter of the regulation (the contract rights) rather than with the impact of the regulation on property values. Significantly, when the state takes a contract right, it takes the right to exclude, for a contract creates exclusion rights as between the parties. The taking of a contract right is therefore a taking under the Takings Clause and requires just compensation. The *Mahon* opinion did not find in the Takings Clause an implied limitation on legislative regulation of property use; it was a statement that taking away an individual's existing contractual rights without compensation is impermissible because it takes away the right to exclude that contract rights give.

11.3 CONCLUSION

This chapter has outlined a framework for thinking about the relationship between common law and legislative regulation of property. Social recognition exists independently of the courts and legislative bodies that determine how social recognition will be implemented in law. Yet social recognition also embodies recognition of the appropriate institutional setting through which courts and legislatures determine rights with respect to resources. Both social recognition of rights and social recognition of the institutional setting for implementing rights are grounded in the principle of equal freedom, and the principle of equal freedom limits legislative regulation of rights. In thinking about the relationship between ownership and government, it is important to recognize the distinct and separate functions of the government's two sources of power: the power to take property and the power to regulate property. The takings power allows the government to take an owner's right to exclude, but it may be wielded only for a public purpose and with just compensation. The power to regulate land use allows the government to impose burdens on owners in order to provide public goods, but it may be wielded only if the government respects the principle of equal freedom by allowing processes that ought to be used when the government makes particularized determinations and only if the government equitably assigns both benefits and burdens among affected owners.

Conclusion

Based on the distinction between exclusion and use, I have argued that the regulatory takings doctrine ought to be retired because it is a mistaken attempt to protect property values rather than property relationships. In the next two chapters, I reconstruct a meaningful way of understanding government power over property and its limitations.

12 The Takings Power

12.1 INTRODUCTION

Under the eminent domain power impliedly authorized by the Fifth Amendment, the state (on behalf of the community) exercises the power to reorganize property rights established through private law, private arrangements, and the market. This power allows the state to replace the existing owner/decision makers with new owner/decision makers, provided that the taking is for a *public use* and that the state pays the owner *just compensation*.[1] The power of eminent domain existed at common law and has a venerable lineage; many uses of eminent domain are uncontroversial and well-regarded. The use of eminent domain for public goods – to build interstate highways, to establish public parks, and to expand airports – is an accepted state function for which eminent domain, and the coercive, nonmarket power that it authorizes, is well-suited. For these kinds of uses, eminent domain produces little controversy: the uses are acknowledged to be public uses, and the just compensation requirement relieves the owner whose property is taken from some of the burdens of providing public benefits.

Yet the power of eminent domain is now of intense public controversy, for two reasons. First, as the state has expanded its role in society, it has used its coercive power for an ever-broader range of activities. Second, the doctrine of regulatory takings, even if errant, has suggested that the power to take property is an implied limitation on legislative regulation of the use of property, thus thrusting the idea of just compensation into every dispute over the scope of

---

[1] It is worth noting that the just compensation requirement was originally imposed by common law, which authorized state takings and imposed the requirement of just compensation. This confirms that common law judges understood the importance of maintaining a balance between burdens and benefits as the core value of property. For comprehensive reviews of the takings power, see Bell (2009) and Treanor (1985).

Introduction

legislative regulation. As a result, property theory must address when a taking occurs and the uses of the taking power that will be considered to be nonpublic uses that are beyond the power of government. Understanding the function of, and limitations on, state taking of property is central to restoring a coherent view of the relationship between the government and private owners.

In the last chapter I registered objections to the regulatory takings doctrine. Just compensation is not, structurally or analytically, a general limitation on state power; it is a condition for the government to exercise its takings power. The constitutional issue is not: "When must the state compensate an owner for harm?"; the issue is: "Has a taking occurred?" To be sure, when compensation is required, the state will not go forward if it cannot afford to compensate owners. Nor will it go forward if it believes that the costs of the taking, including the just compensation required by the Constitution, outweigh the benefits. But that provides a political, not a legal, limitation on state power. The takings power is a conditional privilege of the state, with just compensation the condition for the state to exercise the privilege. The only unqualified limitation on the takings power is the public use limitation. If the state puts the property to a use that is not a public use, the state may not exercise its taking power, even if it is willing to pay just compensation. The state may not buy its way out of the public use requirement.[2]

Under this reading, the operative words of the Takings Clause are *taking* and *public use*. The question of what is a taking and what is a public use are related in important ways. The word *taking* connotes an act the state may undertake, whereas the words *public use* limit the circumstances under which the state may undertake that act. To provide a unified theory of takings, we ought to be able to understand both the concept of a taking and the concept of public use as flowing from a theory of state power that is both granted and limited by the takings power. That is the theory developed here. Whether

---

[2] It is possible to read the public use requirement not as a limitation on the use of eminent domain but simply as a declaration of when compensation must be paid; under this reading, the clause would say nothing about taking for private use. See Fennell (2012). The Supreme Court does not treat the public use requirement that way; instead the Court treats it as an implied limitation on the use of eminent domain power. The analysis of the public use concept in the text suggests that the Takings Clause ought to be read as authorizing eminent domain for a public use but not for a private use. The alternative interpretation, that the use of eminent domain for private use is a violation of due process, is supported by the historical understanding of due process (see Chapman and McConnell (2012) at 1758–59) and has been recently endorsed by noted scholars (Fennell, 2012) and Peñalver and Strahelivitz (2012) at 327; indeed, it seems to be a Chicago School concern. See Coniston Corp. v. Vill. of Hoffman Estates, 844 F. 2d 461 (7th Cir. 1988 (Judge Posner). The textual analysis is complicated, of course, by the fact that the Constitution assumes, but does not authorize, the power of eminent domain.

there is a taking depends on the character of the state act, not on the value of property that was taken.[3] The state has the power to replace market forces when, because of market failures, the market cannot successfully coordinate decisions of disparate users; the power is limited to that circumstance, for any other use of eminent domain is not a public use. The rationale for exercising the power of eminent domain also limits that power. Just compensation is a market-mimicking device, intended to replicate the results the market would have reached in the absence of a market failure and the possibility of holdouts. The just-compensation requirement balances the burdens and benefits of state decisions by making sure that the owner does not bear an objectively unfair share of the burdens of the public benefit of property-rights acquisition.

Current interpretations of the public use requirement focus on the purpose or ends of state taking or distinguish between ends and means. The Supreme Court takes the former tack by asking whether the taking is for use by the public or for the public benefit. Under this approach, the Court asks whether the takings power may be used, for example, to restore blighted property or redistribute property, or for economic development. This approach joins the takings power with the police and regulatory power. Although this approach is consistent with the regulatory takings doctrine (because it assumes that the takings power and legislative regulatory power over land use are interchangeable), it effectively eviscerates the public use limitation by equating the takings power with regulatory power.[4] This, in turn, transforms the public use limitation into a political rather than a federal legal question.[5] The concept of economic development as a public use has no legal meaning; it simply summarizes a conclusion about when the state may act. Even the Supreme

---

[3] The Court in Lorretto v. Teleprompter Manhattan CATV Corp. said that "the 'character of the government action' not only is an important factor in resolving whether the action works as a taking but also is determinative," 458 U.S. 419, 426 (1982), citing language from Penn Cent. Transp. Co. v. City of New York, 438 U.S. 104, 124 (1978). As pointed out in the last chapter, a taking is not defined by the amount of the taking or by the decreased value of the property affected by it. Some takings include quite low amounts of compensation; a utility easement, for example, takes property but does not take much property, and therefore does not provide the owner with much compensation. The just compensation requirement follows from a taking; it does not create a taking by signaling any threshold amount of decreased value that makes state action a taking.

[4] Inherent in my critique of the regulatory takings doctrine is the question of why the Constitution would specially enumerate the takings power if the takings power is coexistent with general regulatory or police power. If a public use is anything that the state lawfully may do, the Takings Clause provides neither independent significance nor a distinction between police and regulatory power and the takings power.

[5] Indeed, many commentators believe that the judicial philosophy behind *Kelo* was the federalism-based desire to let states control their use of the eminent domain power. *Kelo* itself supports that reading; *see* 545 U.S. at 482–83.

Introduction

Court's attempt to surround the concept of economic development with procedural prerequisites (by asking whether the plan is comprehensive, deliberate, and transparent) fails to explain what economic development is or why it justifies coerced transfers under the Takings Clause.

Because the ends-focus of the Supreme Court's takings jurisprudence does not meaningfully limit state power,[6] commentators seeking to understand public use have concentrated on reading into the Takings Clause substantive limitations on the ends of the state. For Frank Michelman, public use implies a check on state power that would make sure that the benefits of state action clearly outweigh the costs, including "demoralization costs."[7] This approach is foreign to the Supreme Court jurisprudence, of course, and it is hard to make operational. Which costs count and how do we calibrate the exchange between costs and benefits? More important, how does one account for the use of coercion rather than consent (that is, the means of taking) in any cost-benefit analysis? At the other extreme, Richard Epstein suggests an ends test that would confine public use to property used by the public (including common carrier property) and pure public goods.[8] But the concept of pure public goods is neither self-defining nor a constitutional one. That concept too does not track the means authorized by the takings power. Buying property for schools, army recruiting stations, and fire stations would, by most reckoning, meet the tests of pure public goods, but such uses would involve purchases that could be made through the market rather than through coercion. Eric Claeys bases a similar conclusion limiting public use on a theory of natural law, but he does not define the ends he endorses independently of the rights that he believes come from natural law.[9]

Trying to find meaningful limits on the takings power by focusing on the permissible ends of the state is a dead end because the Constitution seems not to limit the ends of state power.

On the other hand, scholars such as Thomas Merrill and Alexander Bell focus on the means authorized by the Takings Clause – that is, the state's use of coercion rather than consent to assemble the property it needs to achieve

---

[6] Indeed, the Supreme Court has never struck down the state exercise of eminent domain power on the ground that its use was not a "public use." See, e.g., Sager (1980) at 383 ("Courts have suggested that if the ultimate purpose behind the taking is a matter subject to legislative control, the finding of a public use is almost inevitable."). The Court has struck down state action that takes from individual A and gives to individual B, but historically has done so on due process grounds. See Chapman and McConnell (2012). It has also struck down the state use of eminent domain on due process grounds. Cincinnati v. Vester, 281 U.S. 439, 448 (1930).
[7] Michelman (1967).
[8] Epstein (1985).
[9] Claeys (2004).

its ends.[10] Under this approach, the relevant question is: Given the ends the state seeks to achieve, why should the state be authorized to use coercion rather than consent (market purchases) to achieve those ends? The universal response to this question is that the state needs the coercive power to overcome the holdout problem – the fact that owners, when they know they are dealing with the state, will seek a premium when they can predict that the value of their property will go up the longer they refuse to sell it.[11] The analysis explains the acquisition of property for railroads, utilities, and mills, but not the use of the takings power for the redistribution of property or the elimination of neighborhood blight.

The mistake of this means-based analysis is to try to separate the ends and means of the state. In fact, the ends and means of the state, being two sides of the same coin, are inseparable. The end of the state is to help society accomplish what cannot be accomplished through the market, and the factors that contribute to market failure are the same factors that require coercive rather than cooperative means for acquiring property. The market is not an end in itself but an institutional arrangement that serves society's needs. Legislative regulation, including the taking power, is an alternative institutional arrangement, with different means of aggregating individual interests – one designed to address social issues the market cannot address. The state takes over when markets fail and the state either corrects the failure (while allowing decisions to be made through the market) or supplants the market by taking private property and creating an ownership pattern that is not infected with market failure.

When markets fail to such a degree that the state must intervene to replace one set of owners with another, the conditions of market failure are the conditions that make consensual acquisition of property unworkable. Using eminent domain to support the construction of railroads was not the means to the end of faster transportation: providing faster transportation was the function that only the state, and not the market, could provide because acquiring the right-of-way would have been too expensive without the state's eminent domain power. Neither the private railroad corporation nor coercive land acquisition were ends in themselves; they were both means to the end that resulted in the development of the chartered corporation and the use of eminent domain

[10] Bell (2009) at 529 and Merrill (1986).
[11] The holdout problem comes with various names, including strategic bargaining and the property assembly problem. It includes several variations on the basic holdout problem, including the problem of bilateral monopoly and of information asymmetry (because private land assembly is made easier when the buyer but not the seller has information about the intended use of the property).

to do what the market alone (that is, consensual transactions) could not have done.

Under the theory developed here, the state's eminent domain power recognizes that the market cannot always successfully coordinate private decisions about property use; it authorizes the state to overcome these market failures by taking property and rearranging patterns of ownership in ways that the market could not. The state's means – the use of coercive power with market-based compensation – is the end of the state and a necessary adjunct to a system of private property. Understanding the function of eminent domain in the context of the market's inability to coordinate successfully the decisions of private owners provides a coherent and normatively attractive way of understanding the limits on state power imposed by the concepts of public use and taking.

As I will now show, the public use and taking concepts work together to reflect a theory of the role of state when markets inadequately coordinate private property decisions.

12.2 PUBLIC USE

We must start by understanding the takings power in light of often unspoken assumptions about the relationship between markets and private property.

A system of private property assumes that private decisions about the use of resources will be coordinated through the market. Under this compelling assumption, decision-making authority is dispersed yet coordinated. Individual decisions about how property is used promote autonomy and individual responsibility; they promote the creation of subjective values and subjective wealth, which has great expressive importance. Decisions about land use are not subject to judicial review or state intervention unless, and to the extent that, the decisions impose an actionable harm on others. At the same time, individual decisions are coordinated in ways that increase the value of property. Markets serve as an effective coordinating device because markets provide both incentives to invest in resources and information about the value that others place on the resources. Markets allow owners to make decisions with knowledge of how others view their property, and to stick with their subjective valuations, adjust their use, or transfer their ownership to someone who values the property more. Well-functioning markets, in other words, address the tragedy of the anticommons – situations in which rights are too fragmented and splintered to allow resources to be put to valuable uses. They allow owners to assemble diffuse property rights into more valuable patterns. Property assembly for useful projects would, in a world of no transactions costs, be frictionless; in the real world it is generally not difficult, in large part because the law shapes itself to reduce the transactions costs of the property assembly.[12]

Not only do pluralistic, atomistic decisions about patterns of use conserve information costs and induce change in response to new opportunities, but markets influence individual decision making in ways that generally increase the values of resources. External benefits of one owner's investment in property induce other owners to make better use of their property; building a resort or shopping mall yields spillover benefits that induce other owners to make decisions that take advantage of the increased value of new uses. Businesses tend to congregate in areas where prior investments allow others to benefit from new investments as they share infrastructure and social capital. As long as the external benefits of an owner's land use decisions exceed the external costs, the value of patterns of independent decisions about property use decisions will go up.

Even when markets fail, the state has a variety of ways, short of its eminent domain power, to supplement markets in order to coordinate decisions among various private owners, as the prior chapters of this book have shown. Social norms impose informal constraints on individual decision making. Nuisance law rules out certain detrimental social costs. Zoning and other land use regulations constrain private decision making and facilitate coordinated patterns of decision making among owners. Regulation allows the community to influence individual decision making in ways that achieve nonmarket goals. Under a broad range of circumstances, markets and regulation allow private and atomistic decisions to be coordinated reasonably well.

This vision of private property, with a wide scope of land use decision making coordinated though the market and land use regulation, is embodied in a bedrock principle, embraced under both the Due Process Clause and the Takings Clause, and endorsed by all of the current Supreme Court justices – namely, that the state may not take property from owner A and give it to owner B.[13] This principle embodies the central idea of property: namely, that over a broad range of decisions the community must respect the decisions made by owners and may not intervene to reverse those decisions just because, in the judgment of the community, there may be a higher or more efficient use

---

[12] See, e.g., Kelly (2006); Kronman (1978).
[13] Synsbuty's Case, 1 Kirby 444 (Conn. 1785) (conflicting land grants by legislature decided in favor of first grantee), Bowman v. Middleton, 1 S.C.L. (1 Bay) 252 (1792) (same); Wilkinson v. Leland, 27 U.S. Pet. 627, 658 (1829); Trustees of the Univ. of North Carolina v. Foy, 5 N.C. (1 Mur.) 58 (1805); Taylor v. Porter, 4 Hill 140 (N.Y. Sup Ct. 1843) (invalidating statute that authorized an official to divest landholder of land and vest it in the applicant for a private road, even with compensation).

for the property. The fact that individual decisions do not comport with some vision of the public interest is no basis for replacing one owner/decision maker with another.[14] The justification for eminent domain must be something other than reviewing the social value of the decisions of individual owners.

Yet, we know that eminent domain is used to change the identity of owners from one individual or group of individuals to a different individual or group of individuals, and this requires some basis for distinguishing a permissible from an impermissible taking from A and giving to B. If the state can take land for economic redevelopment, as the Supreme Court has held, why cannot the state take the land from owner A and give it to owner B in the name of economic redevelopment? Our challenge is to find a meaning for the public use requirement that enables the state to assemble property in the public interest while at the same time disabling the state from substituting its judgment for the decisions made by individual owners.

We therefore start our analysis of public use in the same place that most observers do. When we say that a taking is for a public use we are not saying that an owner's decisions are themselves being second-guessed by the state, or even that they are *capable of* being second-guessed by the state. Mrs. Kelo's decision to stay in her home, even as her neighborhood changed, provides no justification, by itself, for intervening through the Takings Clause to replace her as decision maker of the property. No public interest can justify overriding her decision on its own terms.

However, market failure often keeps markets from effectively coordinating private decisions. Some aspects of market failure are well-known, but I believe the concept is broader than is commonly understood. As all theories of market failure recognize, markets do not provide public goods, such as parks, missile sites, or sewer facilities, whereas eminent domain is an ideal tool through which the state provides such public goods. In addition, as is well-known, even well-regulated markets do not work well when resource acquisition requires the coordinated cooperation of many landowners, especially where each

---

[14] In other words, the state has no warrant for telling an owner how best to use her land, or for second-guessing the owner's decision to use the property for farmland rather than for development. We expect, and even celebrate, cornfields in the middle of residential developments. Even if a farmer's decision not to use her land for development is, from some perspective, inefficient, we uphold the decision because the community recognizes private property so that property can reflect an owner's values. As it is true in the competitive sphere, the state ought not to be in the business of picking winners and losers among resource owners or making judgments that are best left to individuals in the context of well-functioning markets. The social recognition that particular resources ought to be delegated to private owners was made precisely to enable owners to make unreviewable decisions, ones that reflect their individuality and preferences and are free from majoritarian constraint.

owner has an effective veto power over the project. If the value of projected land use requires the assent of a large number of owners, each owner will have an incentive to hold out for a higher price, knowing that her rights are made more valuable as other owners transfer their rights. Faced with the prospect of holdouts, the market may fail to coordinate uses in a way that allows the state to move property to a higher social value.

These well-known justifications for the state's use of eminent domain, however, are but examples of a broader principle. The state's eminent domain power is justified within a system of private property in order to solve coordination problems that cannot be addressed by the market supplemented by land use regulation. The state's eminent domain power allows the state to acquire property rights when market failures make it impossible for markets to coordinate effectively the decisions of private owners, and when coerced transfers are necessary because the holdout problem would otherwise make property acquisition unduly expensive. This justification serves to anchor our understanding of the public use requirement. The state may exercise its eminent domain power if, but only if, it can show a market failure of the kind that cannot be addressed by well-regulated markets.

Market failures that justify the use of eminent domain occur when the coordinating mechanisms of the market have broken down; it extends beyond the holdout problem. In particular, market coordination between private decision makers sometimes breaks down because private decisions are interdependent in a way that imposes only negative costs on other decision makers or on society, so that private decisions cannot be socially coordinated through well-regulated markets. Under these circumstances, it would be fruitless to trust the decisions of individual decision makers because the decisions would be made under circumstances where the coordinating mechanisms of the well-regulated market do not give decision makers an opportunity to make decisions that meet even the owner's interests. When decisions become negatively interdependent, no decision maker is capable of making decisions that deserve community respect.

When these conditions occur, the assumptions supporting the social recognition of private property no longer apply and the community can no longer rely on the coordinating mechanism of the well-regulated market to induce coordinated decisions that are socially useful. Intervention under the Takings Clause to change the dynamic of interdependent negative decisions is a public use because it essentially restores ownership to productive independent decisions coordinated through the market.

In the next section, I will demonstrate that the hallmark of a taking is the state's usurpation of the owner's right to exclude. This demonstration

Public Use

is consistent with the market failure theory of public use that I advance. As already noted, the right to exclude allows markets to function by protecting property from private appropriation; those who want access to the property must purchase the property. Because the taking power is designed to address market failures and mimic the results of well-functioning markets, it is natural that the essence of a taking is the usurpation of the owner's right to exclude. Without acquiring the right to exclude, the state cannot rearrange ownership patterns in a way that restores the coordinating function of well-regulated markets.

Consider the two public use cases that played such a prominent role in *Kelo*. One, *Hawaii Housing Authority v. Midkiff*,[15] addressed the highly concentrated land ownership in Hawaii, a legacy of the history of conquest and historical acquisition. The Supreme Court justified the taking of land for redistribution by the need to eliminate the "social and economic evils of a land oligopoly." In the context of the theory developed here, what is important is not the "social and economic evils" as an undesirable end. That is too open-ended a goal to put meaningful limitations on the takings power. What is important is the breakdown of the coordinating effect of the market. What mattered was not the effects of oligopoly, but the coordination problems of interdependent decisions that brought about those effects. When ownership is highly concentrated, individual decision making is replaced by collective decision making because each owner knows that if she lowers her prices she will gain nothing (because others would lower their prices too). She also knows that if she does not lower her prices, no other owner would have an incentive to do so (for they know that she would also react with lower prices). Under those circumstances, the state is justified in changing the structure of ownership to eliminate this form of collective decision making and yield the kind of coordinated, independent decisions that the market is designed to produce. The state was not reviewing the decisions made by individual owners; rather the state recognized that because of ownership concentration the normal coordinating mechanisms of the market had broken down.[16] The only way to restore those coordinating mechanisms was to reduce the concentration in ownership; this restoration of property and the market to their rightful function was a public use.

More broadly, our system of private property assumes that decentralized and individual decisions about resources, when coordinated through well-

---

[15] 467 U.S. 229 (1984).
[16] It will be recalled from our discussion in Chapter 4 that markets embody an implicit fairness norm that disallows monopoly profits unless those profits can be justified by the incentive effect they give. The use of eminent domain in the *Midkiff* case enforced that fairness norm, one well embedded in our social understanding of markets.

functioning markets, lead to the appropriate outcome for the community. Property is an input into other goods, and decentralized and individual decision making means that no person who needs the resource will have to pay more than the cost of providing the resource. However, when owners are so few that they can raise their prices above competitive levels, the property system is not functioning as anticipated and the state is justified in intervening and re-delegating decision-making authority (in this instance redistributing the property to a larger number of private owners) so that the dynamics of property decision making are changed. Importantly, what was crucial to the decision in *Midkiff* was not that owners made individual decisions that were in themselves antisocial; it was that the structure of ownership made it difficult for individual decision makers to make any decision but an anti-social one.[17]

In the other opinion that played a significant role in *Kelo*, the coordination problem inherent in dispersed and uncoordinated systems of private property drove prices down rather than up. In the Washington, DC redevelopment case, *Berman v. Parker*,[18] individual property owners had let the value of their property decrease so much that their houses were only marginally habitable. The coordination problem involved the social cost of systematic disinvestment; an owner who lets his property deteriorate adversely affects his neighbor's incentive to invest in her property. When underinvestment cascades, the incentive to invest goes down, rather than up, as the external effect of underinvestment by each owner spreads throughout the neighborhood. In the absence of any enforceable duty to make investments in property (which is the kind of obligation that private law finds it difficult to create), the pattern of individual decision making ruins a neighborhood. The only antidote is to change the structure of decision making, which requires the state to change the identity of the owners and the nature of the investment climate. The state was not questioning or second-guessing the decisions of individual owners as much as it was intervening to recognize that the coordinating mechanisms of the market had broken down. Such intervention is a public use because eminent domain overcame the market's coordination failures.[19]

---

[17] Ironically, in *Midkiff* the problem was too much coordination between owners – coordination that effectively replaces the market system with a system of managed prices. But that is the point: our system of private property wants individualized but coordinated decisions so that it gets the benefits of the property system without the costs of a poorly coordinated system. The concentration of ownership in Hawaii provided the burdens of concentrated ownership with none of the benefits of dispersed and individual decisions.

[18] 348 U.S. 26 (1954).

[19] The *Kelo* Court also relied on Ruckelshaus v. Monsanto Co., 467 U.S. 986 (1984), where the government required disclosure of trade secrets in order to overcome barriers to market competition.

This analysis suggests what was missing in *Kelo*: a rationale for intervening in the market to disrupt patterns of interdependent decisions that cannot produce positive, coordinated results. Under this reading, it is not the fact of redevelopment that justifies the use of eminent domain, and the label of "redevelopment" cannot be used as a pretext for taking property from one person and giving it to another. Instead, in order to show that the taking is a public use, the state must demonstrate that the coordinating mechanisms of the well-regulated market have so broken down that the pattern of individual decision making must be replaced to restore a situation in which individual decisions are well-coordinated through the market.

Under this standard, how might we understand whether the pattern of coordinated decision making in *Kelo* was so dysfunctional that decision making by individual owners could no longer be positively coordinated to restore property values in the downtown area after the naval facility closed? Significantly, the City of New London was in competition with suburban Connecticut for a new Pfizer research facility. Land acquisition costs were far cheaper in the suburbs than in the city because land could be bought in bigger parcels in the suburbs; negotiations with one person would be cheaper than negotiations with many people. Potential sellers in the suburbs who found out about Pfizer's interest would have no incentive to hold their property off the market in order to get a higher price (because other large tracts of land provided Pfizer with good alternatives).

In downtown New London, the possibility that market decisions would preserve the value of property or induce new investment was disappearing. Not only did potential locations in the city offer fewer amenities then the suburbs, but land acquisition costs to support the investment in required amenities would require negotiations with many owners. Under these circumstances, once property owners knew that Pfizer and the city needed to assemble a large parcel of land, they had an incentive to hold out and seek a higher price than the market would otherwise offer. Because Pfizer's investment was conditioned on the assembly of land with a far greater footprint than Pfizer needed, and because no property would be of value if the city acquired only some pieces of the needed land, every owner would have an incentive to hold out for a price that reflected the value of the entire development around the Pfizer facility. The coordinating mechanisms that usually facilitate large land acquisitions for projects such as this had broken down, just as they would have if the railroads had not had the power of eminent domain.

In other words, the dynamic behind the public use in *Kelo* is much like the dynamic of the public use in other eminent domain cases. There is reason to think that the redevelopment was in the city's interest, but the existing pattern of land ownership and use would not allow the market to produce the desired result. The possibility of holdouts always reduces investment, shifting investment to areas where holdout problems can be minimized. If the investment was worth making, then using the Takings Clause to overcome the holdout problems that would otherwise make the investment impossible presented a situation in which changing ownership patterns would be a public use. Assembly of a right-of-way for the railroad and one for downtown development both need state power to intervene in patterns of ownership that would otherwise block the investment.

Under this reading, when applied to economic redevelopment, the public use requirement does not relate to how the property is used before and after the taking. There is no possibility of taking property from A and giving it to B on the pretext that A's use was not in the public interest. Rather, before the state takes property it must show that decision making concerning the property is negatively interdependent in the sense the each owner's decisions interact with the decisions of other owners in a way that makes it clear that the market can no longer coordinate effectively the decisions of various owners.[20]

12.3 WHAT IS A TAKING?

Although the state normally exercises its takings power in an eminent domain proceeding, sometimes the state issues regulations about what individuals must do on their land that, although not formally invoking the eminent domain procedure, are themselves a taking because they function identically to eminent domain proceedings. It is important to recognize when this occurs, for then the public use and just compensation requirements apply.

Like the concept of public use, the concept of a taking reflects the centrality of the right to exclude in allowing the market to coordinate decisions about land use. A prerequisite to market coordination of private decisions is that private owners have the right to exclude others. Without the right to exclude, the market does not function. When the market is not serving its coordinating function and needs to be replaced with another method of coordinating decisions about resources (which is the function of the takings power), it is the

---

[20] Under this analysis, the Takings Clause ought not be read to justify the state in using the eminent domain power when it could easily buy the property on the market, even if the purchase is for a state use. If the state wants to build a fire station, it can go on the market and buy the property it needs. It is one of many purchasers who face many potential sellers, and no bargaining impediment or holdout problem would preclude the state's business. It ought to be required to use market mechanisms rather than condemnation proceedings because doing so is more efficient and less error prone. In fact, the government usually buys property it needs in the market when holdout problems do not make land acquisition unduly expensive. See Merrill (1986).

right to exclude that must be taken because taking the right to exclude allows the state to coordinate uses in a way that mimics a well-functioning market.

Accordingly, regulations that take away the right to exclude are takings, even if the state has not affected ownership rights through eminent domain proceedings. These regulations are takings because they serve the same function, with the same effect and characteristics, as the state's use of its eminent domain power. Although regulations of this type are, in a sense, a "regulatory taking" (because the state acts by regulation and not by eminent domain), they are more accurately described as an "eminent domain regulation" because the state acts through a regulation that, like an eminent domain proceeding, takes away the right to exclude. They ought to be (and are) treated as takings.[21] Without this classification, the state could enact a regulation that each owner of land along a certain route should set aside land for a railroad or for an irrigation project and thereby evade the just compensation and public use requirements under the Takings Clause

The cases involving "eminent domain regulations" are relatively easy to identify. They are the ones that the Supreme Court now classifies as permanent physical invasions. That description, however, is not quite apt, for it is not the physical invasion that makes the act a taking;[22] it is the usurpation of the right to exclude that results from the permanent physical invasion.[23] Thus,

[21] Under the current regulatory takings typology, these cases were once thought of as a per se category of the broader category of "regulatory takings" – that is, regulations that are too severe to be tolerated. That typology missed the point; those regulations should be categorized as takings not because of their severity, but because they take away an owner's right to exclude. The Supreme Court has now recognized the "permanent physical occupation" cases as a species of takings, not regulatory takings. See Tahoe-Sierra Preservation Council, Inc., v. Tahoe Regional Planning Agency, 535 U.S. 302 (2002).

[22] The idea that all government-required or authorized permanent physical invasions are a taking is unworkable. The state often requires an owner to accept a physical invasion of the owner's property without the invasion being considered a taking. The state authorizes physical invasions by requiring owners to install safety equipment; to allow the exercise of free speech rights; to avoid unjust discrimination; and to regulate relationships between, say, landlords and tenant, mortgagors and mortgagees, and lawyers and their clients. These and many other cases are not takings because they do not take away a lawful right to exclude and are not therefore tantamount to eminent domain. Courts must therefore determine the scope of the right to exclude in order to determine whether to characterize an invasion as a permanent physical invasion, or, in the terms used here, as a taking of the right to exclude.

[23] An important distinction is between cases defining the scope of the right to exclude (which are not takings) and cases in which the state takes away the right to exclude that would exist at common law (which are takings). The boundary is determined by the common law scope of the right to exclude, as developed in Chapter 7. A court can determine that an owner has no right to exclude because a nonowner has a privilege to enter the property; defining the circumstances in which an owner must take into account the well-being of others does not take away the right to exclude. This distinction explains cases in which privileged permanent physical occupation is held not to be a taking. See, e.g., Pruneyard Shopping Ctr. v. Robins, 447 U.S. 74

where the state requires apartment owners to allow a cable company to attach its cable to their buildings in order to reach tenants, the state is creating easements for cables that are akin to the state's use of its eminent domain power to acquire rights-of-way for railroads.[24] The state has taken the right to exclude because the holdout problem would make it impossible to coordinate land use for cable technology. Whether the state moves by eminent domain or regulation is irrelevant to whether this is a taking.[25]

Similarly, where the state authorized a canal company to build a dam that would flood the plaintiff's land, the state was using its eminent domain power to remove the owner's right to exclude others.[26] The fact that the state did this by authorizing the private conduct rather than by giving the private party the power of eminent domain (as it had in similar cases in the past), does not make it any less a taking. Finally, in *Kaiser Aetna v. United States*,[27] the state claimed a navigable servitude over a privately developed channel between the ocean (public domain land) and a private body of water that the defendant investor had made useful by dredging the channel. As in the other physical invasion cases, the servitude claimed by the state would abolish the defendant's right to exclude. Although there was no particular problem of land assembly in that case, the state took, without privilege, the very thing – the right to exclude – that defines a taking.

12.4 CONCLUSION

The state's takings power allows the state to intervene when markets fail to coordinate effectively the decisions of private owners. Such market failures

---

(1980) (limiting the right to exclude from a shopping center that was open to the public), Heart of Atlanta Motel, Inc. v. United States, 379 U.S. 241 (1964) (limiting the right to exclude on the basis of race), and Block v. Hirsh, 256 U.S. 135 (1921) (limiting the right to charge a higher price on rent-controlled property).

[24] Loretto v. Teleprompter Manhattan CATV Co., 458 U.S. 419 (1982). *See also*, Preseault v. United States, 100 F. 3d 831 (Fed. Cir. 1996) (authorizing bike and recreational trail on former site of a railroad easement is unlawful physical occupation).

[25] To a similar effect is *Glosemeyer v. United States*, 45 Fed Cl. 771 (2000) (abandoned railroad right-of-way that extinguished prior easement requires the state to pay compensation if it wants to create a bike path on the old railroad).

[26] Pumpelly v. Green Bay Co., 80 U.S. 166 (1872).

[27] 444 U.S. 164 (1979). *See also*, Golden Gate Hotel Assoc. v. City and Cnty. of San Francisco, 836 F. Supp. 707 (N.D. Cal. 1993), *vacated and remanded to consider whether the claim was barred by the statute of limitations*, 18 F. 3d 1482 (9th Cir. 1994) (enjoining city ordinance that prohibited conversion of residential hotels to other kinds of hotels because, among other reasons, the ordinance took away the right to exclude). Significantly, the Court has distinguished between limitations on the right to exclude, which may not be taken without just compensation, and limitations on the right to transfer, which may. *See* Andrus v. Secretary of the Interior Allard, 444 U.S. 51 (1979) (upholding prohibition on selling parts of birds).

Conclusion

occur when decisions are so interdependent that no present owner or prospective purchaser can put the property to effective use or when markets lead to unearned rewards. The Takings Clause allows the government to identify new ownership arrangements for the property so that the market better serves its coordination function. Doing so is a public use because the public depends on the well-regulated market to facilitate and coordinate decisions of private owners. But the owners of property so taken must be compensated at rates that mimic the market because government is taking the right to exclude, and the right to exclude, once defined, must be purchased.

13 Legislative Regulation and Assigning Burdens

Thus far, I have argued that legislative regulation that takes away an owner's right to exclude is subject to the Takings Clause, whether the state proceeds by eminent domain or by regulation. I have also argued that legislative regulation of an owner's use of her property that does not impair the right to exclude is never subject to the Takings Clause requirements of the Constitution (although it may subject the government to damages for violation of a constitutional right). In this chapter, I argue that limitations on legislative regulation of land use come from the Due Process Clause (persons may not be deprived of property without due process) and the Equal Protection Clause, and that these restrictions limit legislative overreaching when the legislature or its delegate determines how to assign the burdens of regulation that is deemed to be in the public interest.

13.1 INTRODUCTION

The central thesis in this chapter is that the legislature is bound by the equality principle, just as common law courts are bound, and that the equality principle requires that owners be treated equally, such that the necessary burdens of providing public goods through land use regulation are distributed in a way that avoids arbitrary determinations or individualized burdens. When the legislature regulates by general and prospective law, it meets the equal treatment principle as long as the categories it creates bear a reasonable relationship to the ends it seeks to achieve. But when the legislature or its delegate make individualized determinations uniquely affecting one or a small number of landowners, the legislature, by making individualized decisions, is acting like a common law court and the legislature's decisions are then subject to judicial review to ensure that judicial-like procedures have been followed and that the burdens of regulation have been equitably assigned. In this way, restrictions

Introduction

on legislative regulation of land use preserve the separation of powers between common law courts and the legislature by allowing judges, rather than legislatures, to determine whether individualized determinations have been made with sufficient sensitivity to the principle of equality. This form of judicial review of individualized decisions is necessary to protect the integrity of the legislative process and the separate and distinct powers of the legislative and judicial branches.

I start with the idea that legislative regulation is different in scope but not different in kind from common law regulation.[1] Common law and legislative regulation are two means of assigning the burdens and benefits of decisions about property. Like common law regulation, legislative regulation honors the right of owners to make decisions, the central attribute of ownership. Like common law regulation, legislative regulation operates by influencing the decisions that owners make. And, I contend, like common law regulation, legislatures regulate the use of property when they perceive that the burdens and benefits of resource use are out of line because the owner ought to take into account the burdens that his decisions would otherwise unjustifiably impose on other individuals or on the community as a whole.

Moreover, both common law and legislative regulation, to be considered just, must meet the requirements of equal freedom. Like the common law, which is required to choose outcomes that respect the equal freedom of individuals when individuals interact, the legislature must follow the principle of equal freedom that gives the rule of law its moral force, weighing the interests of each individual in a way that gives equal respect to those interests (even if it cannot give each interest dominant weight). As I will develop here, the principle of equality animates the due process concept and restrains legislatures in the way they go about assigning the burdens of the regulations they enact. In short, common law and legislative regulation serve the same function and ends, and follow the same moral requirements.

Despite that basic similarity, legislative regulation and common law regulation are different in scope because they use different methods of achieving their ends in the context of the principle of equality. Common law regulation asks a judge to compare interpersonal well-being against a standard of equal respect for individuals. Accordingly, common law regulation is confined to particular

---

[1] I use the term "common law regulation" literally, to reflect the fact that the common law regulates relations between individuals. By using that term, I do not mean to imply that common law judges act as public law regulators or take into account considerations external to the private law applicable to the dispute. As the text makes clear, common law regulation proceeds on the basis of internal factors that determine the proper relationship between the parties in the dispute and those similarly situated.

disputes brought by individuals against each other, where the parties represent the relevant interests and bring to the court the information relevant to resolving the dispute, and where the court's role is to assess past acts against a standard of ideal decision making to determine the parties' rights and responsibilities.[2] Common law regulation moves from the particular to the general, and is confined by concepts of duty, causation, and harm that determine responsibility under the private law. Legislative regulation makes law by aggregating interests through the political process and defines the relevant interests not by evaluating the interests of individuals vis-à-vis each other, but by examining the interests of individuals as they attach to classes of interests, where an individual's identity with a coalition of interests (as defined by each individual) becomes the input into lawmaking. Moreover, legislative regulation has access to a wider range of information sources than the common law, and can assign responsibility without the common law strictures of causation and past harm.

The respective institutional methods of lawmaking simultaneously empower and limit the two branches of government. As we will see, courts are aware of, and respect, their institutional capabilities and limitations under the common law, and due process and other constitutional restrictions channel the process of common law lawmaking to keep it from spilling into roles that exceed judicial competence in dispute resolution. The scope of common law regulation is necessarily limited by the common law's means of lawmaking. At the same time, limitations that reflect common law regulation provide the justification for legislative regulation. Legislative regulation is designed to expand the range of considerations that owners and nonowners must take into account when making decisions about resources so that rights and responsibilities reflect not just the correlative relationship between individuals that the common law accounts for, but also the relationship between individuals and the aggregate preferences of individuals acting as members of a community.[3] Legislative regulation is designed to represent a broader range of interests than is possible under common law regulation, over a wider time horizon, and to account for a community's heterogeneity of interests. The inherent limitations of common law lawmaking provide the justification for the government to deprive someone of her property *with* due process.

---

[2] As the court said in Boomer v. Atlantic Cement Co., 26 N.Y. 2d. 219, 222 (Ct. App. N.Y. 1970): "It is a rare exercise of judicial power to use a decision in private litigation as a purposeful mechanism to achieve direct public objectives greatly beyond the rights and interests before the court."

[3] This is what the Supreme Court had in mind when it said that "the great office of statutes is to remedy defects in the common law as they are developed, and to adopt it to the changes of time and circumstances." Munn v. Illinois, 94 U.S. 113, 134 (1877).

Introduction

However, just as common law courts respect the limitations on their lawmaking power that reflect their methodology, legislatures must respect the limitations on their lawmaking power that reflect the legislative methodology. We would not expect a common law court to declare, at the behest of a single environmental advocate, that several acres of land must be set aside as a wetland; doctrines of standing and the concept of harm to the individual limit the common law and the kinds of interests that it can vindicate.[4] Similarly, we would not expect the legislature to determine, in an individualized dispute, that individual A has adversely possessed individual B's land. Common law courts do not normally make decisions that require an aggregation of interests among heterogeneous individuals, and legislatures do not normally decide individualized disputes. In general, common law courts make particularized decisions imposing consequences for past harms based on disputes between individuals, whereas legislatures make generalized decisions about aggregative interests that have prospective application.

The Due Process Clause, grounded in norms of appropriate lawmaking, serves to make sure that common law and legislative regulation employ methods appropriate to their legitimate function as they apply the equality principle in making law. This vision of due process puts no substantive limitations on legislative power. It does not privilege the rights of owners, or the value that owners might get from their property, over the collective interests in the environmental impact of an owner's land use decisions. But due process does serve to protect property rights (and the opportunity to find value in property) by ensuring that the burdens of decisions about resources are determined by appropriate processes, taking into account the institutional competencies and infirmities of common law and legislative lawmaking. The limits on common law and legislative regulation ensure that owners and other individuals are treated equally in the process that affects their rights; it is a process, not a substantive, limitation. In particular, as I argue in this chapter, legislative power is restricted by the requirement that when imposing burdens on owners, the legislature and its delegates must follow general and prospective rules, avoiding ad hoc, individualized determinations, and fairly dividing legislative burdens among owners similarly situated.

I proceed by elaborating, in Section 13.2, the relationship between common law and legislative regulation. I point out the limitations on common law regulation that are derived from the common law methodology, and I show how legislative regulation is itself necessary because of the range of social issues that cannot be addressed through common law regulation. Under this view,

[4] See, e.g., Ginsberg and Weiss (1980–81).

legislative regulation is justified by the need for an institutional mechanism for resolving conflicting aggregate interests that cannot be deployed through the common law system. In Section 13.3, I then develop a theory of the limitations on legislative land use regulation that protects property owners against deprivations without due process or equal protection by requiring the legislature to assign appropriately the burdens of regulation under the principle of equality.

13.2 THE SCOPE OF COMMON LAW AND LEGISLATIVE REGULATION

The common law confines itself to issues of interpersonal responsibility, claims that one person has been wronged by another. Its lawmaking methods are appropriate to that function. The common law is at its best when disputes involve clear harm to identified individuals from identified sources attributable to other individuals, and where the range of interests and information that must be taken into account is narrow and well-represented by the parties to the dispute. The genius of the common law system is that each litigant represents the interests of each other individual similarly situated, and each brings relevant interests and information before the court. The resolution therefore does not depend on the aggregation of individual interests into a collective interest. Individuals not similarly situated, or holding different views about the value of those interests, are protected because they are able to argue that their different situation justifies a different disposition of their interests in a different case. The focus on interpersonal responsibility invokes concepts of duty, causation, and harm that confine the scope of common law regulation.

The private law of property has the characteristics just described: disputes between owners and those who want access to the property, disputes between neighbors, disputes between rival claimants to a resource, and disputes between contemporaneous or temporal co-owners of a resource. In each of these instances, individuals representing carefully defined and restricted interests ask the court to assign entitlements and determine the scope of an entitlement's protection in order to adjust the responsibilities of individuals to each other.

Beyond these kinds of disputes, private law leaves unaddressed a large number of relevant issues concerning the appropriate scope of decision making about resources. Common law judges know that the limits of their lawmaking competency restrict the kinds of issues they may address. The history of property and other law is littered with instances in which the common law has refused to provide a remedy because judges, not having the tools appropriate for resolving disputes, either let the loss lie where it falls or, to the same effect, defer to legislatures to address the dispute.[5] It is instructive to reflect on the limits of common law regulation and the role of legislative regulation in addressing the burdens and benefits of decisions about property that the common law leaves unattended.

Consider first the requirements of duty, causation, and harm that characterize interpersonal responsibility and constrict the scope of common law regulation. As we examined in Chapter 5, the no-duty concept at work in private law limits the common law's reach. In the absence of a preexisting relationship of the kind we identified there, common law judges are reluctant to create a claim that would divert one individual's energy in order to benefit another individual. Legislatures, on the other hand, will impose the duty of rescue when they feel competent to recognize a collective value that justifies the imposition of a burden on one person for the harm that another would otherwise suffer. Good Samaritan statutes, for example, although infrequently adopted, represent a legislative expansion of the common law concept of duty that common law courts would not be comfortable taking.

One setting in which the no-duty concept restricts common law regulation occurs when individuals are able to confer reciprocal benefits on each other. The adage "do no harm" generally does well in a common law setting that involves neighbors who are disputing something that one is thought to have done to the other. The adage is broad enough to cover situations of misfeasance and nonfeasance in which one owner affirmatively harms another by emitting smoke (misfeasance) or by failing to support adjacent property (nonfeasance). But what if two neighbors would be better off if they jointly took action that would improve the value of both properties?[6] Say that adjacent coal mines could reduce the risk of flooding if they left a column of coal between their mines, or that two neighbors could reduce costs if they invested in a party wall that would support structures on both properties. These are cases of

---

[5] See, e.g., Moore v. Regents of the Univ. of Cal., 51 Cal. 3d 120 (1990) (leaving it to the legislature to determine whether scientific users of cells should be required to compensate person from whom cells were extracted; issue involves complex policy issues about notice and amount of compensation); Int'l News Serv. v. Associated Press, 248 U.S. 215 (1918) (Justice Brandeis dissenting: only legislature can balance the need for access to news (in light of foreign censorship) against the disincentive that comes when the defendant appropriates news from East Coast sources and sends it to the West Coast).

[6] See, e.g., Plymouth Coal Co. v. Pennsylvania, 232 U.S. 531 (1914) (legislature may require pillar of coal to be left at line between adjoining coal properties to protect workers in each mine from hazards in the adjacent mine). Cases such as this gave rise to the notion that regulation that imposes burdens that provide reciprocal advantages for owners (so that each was burdened and benefited reciprocally) do not constitute a regulatory taking of property.

reciprocal inaction where cooperative action would be beneficial. The interference is not in what the neighbors have jointly done (as in nuisance) but in what the neighbors have jointly failed to do. In an ideal world, the neighbors could coordinate their decisions to avoid such inaction and jointly improve the value of their property, but bargaining impediments, including holdout problems and different valuations of the proposed action, are likely to impede their bargaining. Moreover, no private law claim would arise; it is not possible for a plaintiff to sue a neighbor for failing to benefit her by declining to share the burden of, for example, a party wall or of a protective column of coal. If the plaintiff does nothing, how can the plaintiff complain; if the plaintiff makes the investment, what does the plaintiff have to complain about?[7] Under these circumstances, legislative regulation to impose reciprocal affirmative obligations serves as a form of regulation that avoids the nuisance of mutual nonaction and fills an uncomfortable gap in common law regulation.

Because the common law addresses interpersonal responsibility, its causal requirements are strict. Although courts have relaxed, to a small degree, the burden of proving causation by adopting market share theory and other doctrines of shared responsibility, many claims that would be meritorious without the causal requirement go unaddressed by the common law. Common law courts routinely withhold judicial intervention when causation cannot be proven with the required certainty or when multiple sources of harm make it difficult to assign responsibility to an individual source.

Finally, the harm requirement of interpersonal responsibility limits the reach of the common law. It is understood that the common law is reactive, whereas legislation can be proactive; zoning and nuisance address the same social problem from two different directions. Although the common law may provide a remedy for prospective harms, it generally does so against a background of past wrongful conduct. The harm requirement also means that individuals who suffer small harms may have insufficient incentives to sue (where class actions are not appropriate), even though collective injury would justify legal intervention. In many settings, the harm to individuals would be too diffuse, too evanescent, or too varied to justify a private suit or remedy. Most important, the harm that the common law addresses is harm to an individual as an individual and not the harm to an individual's sense of what is right

---

[7] Reciprocal inaction would be a good basis for invoking the doctrine of unjust enrichment; one owner could make the investment and then seek payment of a proportion of the investment from the benefited neighbor. But if the investing owner also benefits from the investment, the required contribution from the neighbor is unclear, and owners might be reluctant to make the investment and claim their reward if the doctrine of unjust enrichment does not promise them a fair and assured return.

for the community. Trees and endangered species do not have standing, and neither do individuals whose only interest in the trees or endangered species stems from their understanding of what is good for the community and for themselves as a member of the community.

The common law system is limited to protected interests that are personal in the sense that they affect an individual acting as an individual, and not an individual reflecting the values of the community. The common law protects interests that an individual has in how he or she will be treated by other individuals, and does not encompass interests that an individual has as a member of the community or an individual's beliefs about what makes a community healthy. This is appropriate, for interests other than an individual's right to equal treatment by other individuals raise issues of aggregating and evaluating preferences and beliefs that common law judges are not methodologically equipped to undertake. Common law regulation is constricted in the range of interests and information it can account for because those interests (and associated information about them) must be personal interests. Only in that way can the court be assured that the interests before it truly represent those of other similarly interested individuals in a way that allows a judge to make decisions in particular cases that can be generalized, for the outcome of a particular dispute binds only people with similar interests.

Even when the requirements of duty, causation, and harm are met, the common law on occasion refuses to intervene to vindicate one individual's right to better treatment by another individual when it feels that social norms have not advanced to accept such rights.[8] The common law's refusal to adopt a more robust antidiscrimination limitation on the right to exclude is an example. The pragmatism of common law judges sometimes means that the common law follows rather than leads public opinion, and judges sometimes defer to the legislature, and its method of aggregating interests across diverse populations, to determine when the time is right to expand individual rights.

If decision-making power over resources were confined only by the kind of interpersonal claims made through the common law, the law would ignore a wide range of relevant and important interests. In addition to interests that affect individuals as individuals, individuals have interests as a member of the community that take into account their vision of what is good for the community over the long run. Individuals care about how land use decisions affect other individuals and the community of individuals, both present and future; they care about the future of their environment and the sustainability of the ecological system. Without legislative regulation, those interests would not be

---

[8] *See generally*, Singer (1996).

accounted for by the legal system. Just as individuals are limited in their ability to resolve disputes with other individuals through bargaining, negotiations between the community and an owner over the scope of the owner's responsibilities are limited by barriers to bargaining. Just as the idea of private ownership is conditioned on a private law system of dispute resolution that can fairly distribute the un-privatized social costs of decisions about resources, the idea of private property depends on a mechanism for assigning social costs that are not assigned through private law.

Legislative regulation therefore addresses social costs that have a broader footprint than the ones the common law addresses. Public law picks up where the common law left off by examining the burdens and benefits of decisions about resources when a larger, more heterogeneous range of interests and empirics is taken into account. Legislative regulation can therefore take into account harms that are highly individualistic, varied, or community oriented. Landmark or wetlands preservation laws, for example, involve a conflict between present and future generations and an intra-generational conflict between those who find preservation to be worthwhile and those who do not. Because trees, endangered species, and future generations do not have standing, those with an interest in trees, endangered species, and future generations can use the legislative outlet to express their interests. The resolution of disputes over these kinds of interests requires consideration of both the harm to the owners and the benefits to a widely diffuse and heterogeneous population (over time) and are best dealt with in the aggregation process that only legislative regulation can provide. Other legislative regulation responds to situations in which the risk of future harm is of unspecified dimension, and where the common law cannot address the situation because the adversarial system lacks important information. It is one thing to adjudicate disputes about smoke coming from a factory (which is difficult enough) and quite another to adjudicate disputes over which species are endangered and who should take the steps necessary to preserve them.

The central competency of legislatures is to aggregate interests and values over a wide spectrum, which allows legislative regulation to assign responsibility for present and future harm in a way that would not be possible under the common law. But even legislative regulation is limited in what property interests it can affect because, under the principle of separation of powers, the legislature may not adjudicate disputes of the kind that are more wisely and deftly treated by common law adjudication and must defer to judicial judgments when making decisions that have individualized impact. Respect for the lawmaking function of the common law and the limits of legislative competency give the concept of due process its power to restrain the kinds of burdens that the legislature might otherwise impose in the name of collective benefit.

13.3 LIMITATIONS ON LEGISLATIVE REGULATION

I have argued that legislative regulation is justified by the need to fill regulatory gaps that are created because judges, recognizing the inherent limitations of common law regulation, decline to intervene in important disputes about property, even when considerations of community well-being would call for intervention. I have also argued that legislative regulation deploys lawmaking methodologies that are socially recognized as a legitimate method for aggregating individual belief systems in order to define collective well-being. Here, I argue that to sustain the legitimacy of its lawmaking methodology, and the separation of powers between judicial and legislative lawmaking, legislative lawmaking is properly restricted by the methodologies of common law lawmaking when it makes individualized decisions that either assign burdens to particular owners or determine which particular owners ought to be in the class that bears the burdens of providing public goods.

Legislatures are constrained by considerations of appropriate process to respect the limits of their lawmaking authority and to follow processes that legitimize particularized decisions when assigning the burdens of ownership. When legislative regulation requires adjudication-like determinations, legislatures must provide the protections normally accorded to individualized determinations, and they subject themselves to judicial review when they do not. Accordingly, when the legislature follows methodologies of preference aggregation over which they have comparative advantage, their actions are generally immune from judicial review, but when legislatures act through adjudication-like process to make judicial-like determinations, they are subject to the same limitations that judges have imposed on themselves. Legislative regulation harnesses a lawmaking process that relies on the aggregation of disparate views of many individuals, some of whom express self-regarding interests and others of whom express broader, other-regarding interests. Those other-regarding interests take into account the interests of the community rather than just the interests of other individuals qua individuals. Legislative regulation is therefore well suited for aggregating interests when some individuals would be adversely affected by the regulation and other individuals feel that the regulation would benefit, or uphold the values of, the community. That is what gives legislative regulation its scope and breadth.

But the aggregation method at the heart of legislative lawmaking also constrains the legislative process by suggesting that legislation follow the important principles of prospectivity, generality, and equality. The first principle prohibits the legislature from making laws addressing past controversies and imposing penalties for conduct that was lawful when it was undertaken. This principle separates the legislative function from the common law function by recognizing the procedural illegitimacy of addressing past harms by asking a community of individuals to vote on who should pay whom for what.[9] How strange it would be if the legislature were asked to determine which of two automobile drivers was responsible for an accident. The legislative process takes past events as data points but does not intervene on the basis of those events to impose penalties for violating individual-specific rights and responsibilities.

The principle of generality also recognizes that legislatures, while relying on past events to shape rights and responsibilities, do not intervene in particularized disputes. The principle of generality not only avoids intervention in specific disputes between individuals, it also means that the legislature is not invading the domain of the judiciary by legislating with such specificity that it disables the judiciary from interpreting the legislation when applying it to specific circumstances. Again, a legislature's method of lawmaking does not lend itself to resolving particularized disputes, and legislative respect for the domain and concept of the common law's individualized adjudication suggests that particularized decisions made in the context of enforcing legislative regulation ought to reflect the process worked out over centuries to determine what process is due for particularized decisions.

The idea that legislative regulation must be prospective and general has been a consistent constitutional theme.[10] Indeed, the principle that the government may not take property from A and give it to B — which is now closely associated with the public use question under the Takings Clause[11] — was originally adopted as a limitation on legislative power under the Due Process Clause. When the legislature attempts to take property from A and give it to B it is adjudicating specific claims based on past events, violating the principles of prospectivity and generality that mark the separation of powers between legislative and common law. That violates due process.

[9] To be sure, the common law process relies upon juries to interpret and apply local norms, but jury discretion is carefully circumscribed to reduce the jury's lawmaking power.
[10] Chapman and McConnell (2012) at 1755–61
[11] Kelo v. City of New London Conn., 545 U.S. 469 (2005) (Justice Stevens affirms that "it has long been accepted that the sovereign may not take the property of A for the sole purpose of transferring it to another private party B, even though A is paid just compensation").

Finally, the principle of equality, embodied in the notion that legislation may not be "arbitrary," requires the legislature to draw regulatory boundaries in a way that recognizes and adjusts to real differences and similarities between and among individuals, and it subjects legislation to judicial review when the process becomes fine grained in its determinations or makes decisions of individualized application. The general edict to treat like persons alike and unlike persons unlike is especially pertinent when determining who among several landowners ought to bear the burdens of providing public goods.[12]

Within this framework, due process, in its procedural manifestations, serves to limit land use regulation when the legislative process leads, as it often does, to particularized decisions. Limitations take various forms: the requirement that particularized decisions be made according to standards rationally related to the legislative ends, the requirement that benefits provided to some owners be provided to others similarly situated, and the requirement that burdens assigned to some owners be assigned to others similarly situated. The cases that purport to find regulatory takings seem to be better explained as cases involving arbitrary legislation.

The notion that particularized decisions must be made according to standards, and that standards be the ones embodied in general legislation, is well-known. Several "regulatory takings" cases embody that idea. Notable among them, of course, is *City of Monterey v. Del Monte Dunes at Monterey, Ltd.*[13] The jury determined that there was a regulatory taking because, following a "tortuous and protracted"[14] series of hearings over a number of years, there remained "no permissible or beneficial use of the property."[15] But the infirmity in the case was not that the owner was unable to develop his property as he wanted, but that he faced vacuous[16] and shifting standards at the behest of a political body (the city council) that ignored the recommendations of the city planners and operated without the kind of protections that are due when particularized decisions are made. The jury instructions allowed the jury to punish the city not for taking the property but for taking the promise of a fair process that impaired the owner's inability to develop the property. Other

---

[12] The principle of equality, for example, explains why the Supreme Court has held that an owner who buys property after a land use regulation is passed is not, for that reason, disabled from challenging the regulation. Palazzolo v. Rhode Island, 533 U.S. 606 (2001). Although the regulation may be beyond reproach when passed, it may become unreasonable through the "passage of time" (*id.* at 627), which requires attention to the application of the regulation to changing circumstances.

[13] 526 U.S. 687 (1999).

[14] 526 U.S. at 706.

[15] 526 U.S. at 700.

[16] 28 F. 3d 1171 (Fed Cir. 1994).

cases decided under the rubric of "regulatory taking" involve a failure to follow the general standards given in the legislation.[17]

It is not surprising that the concept of due process includes the concept of equal treatment in individualized determinations. The common law finds legitimacy in the concept of precedent, which applies the equality principle by positing the obligation to follow or distinguish prior decisions. Legislative regulation of land use is therefore constrained by both the Equal Protection Clause[18] and the Due Process Clause to ensure that owners in like situations are treated alike. Some cases that are decided as regulatory takings cases are better understood as due process cases.[19] It is equally true that particularized determinations must treat different owners differently. This may explain the result in *Florida Rock Industries v. United States*.[20] There, the Court of Claims required compensation when the Army Corps. of Engineers declined to issue a permit to mine limestone on wetlands property purchased for that purpose. Although the case was decided on the ground that the owner had a right to mine limestone and that the right was a protectable and separable property right under Florida law (making the regulation a total deprivation of the right to the economic value of the limestone), the case might be understood in a different way. The Army Corps of Engineers had denied other owners of the same wetlands the right to develop their surface property, apparently without having to pay compensation. The owner in *Florida Rock*, by contrast, was not trying to develop the surface property but to mine the subsurface property. Although doing so would disturb the wetland, the effect on the wetland was different in kind and degree from the effect of surface development, a fact emphasized by the court when it discussed whether the mining would be a common law nuisance,[21] Perhaps, therefore, the lesson of *Rock Industries* is

---

[17] Lafayette Park Baptist Church v. Scott, 553 S.W. 2d 856 (Mo. 1977) (historic preservation legislation must be interpreted to require both structural and economic feasibility to deny permit to destruct; otherwise is it confiscatory and not rationally related to its legitimate end).

[18] Vill. of Willowbrook v. Olech, 528 U.S.562 (2000).

[19] Bowles v. United States, 31 Fed. Cl. 37, 46 (1994) (although decided as "total deprivation" case, "All [the owner] wanted to do was the same exact use as his surrounding neighbors; build a home in the surrounding neighborhood"). Of course, the principle of equality also requires that in making individualized determinations, owners who are not like the regulated owners should not be subject to the regulation. See e.g., Sturdy Homes, Inc. v. Township of Bedford, 30 Mich. App. 53 (1971) (owner whose property was not in flood area and had never been flooded may not be denied a building permit under zoning ordinance aimed at risk of flooding).

[20] 18 F 3d. 1560 (Fed Cir 1994), on remand, Florida Rock Industries v. United States, 45 Fed. Cl. 21 (1999). A finding of a regulatory takings that seems not to fit the analysis here is *Loveladies Harbor, Inc. v. United States*, 28 F. 3d 1171 (Fed Cir. 1994).

[21] 45 Fed. Cl. at 29–30 (testimony about minimal and temporary pollution from mining). In addition, the record showed that landowners in the vicinity had been allowed to operate rock quarries. *Id.*

that mining permits are sufficiently different from permits for surface development to require a different kind of particularized decision when the owner seeks the right to develop.

The principle of equality also explains *Nectow v. City of Cambridge*,[22] a case involving a due process challenge to a zoning regulation that zoned as residential a lot on the industrial side of a street that served as a border between industrial and residential neighborhoods. The Supreme Court invalidated the regulation, adopting the finding of a special master that "no practical use can be made of the land in question for residential purposes" and that the health and safety of the neighbors "will not be promoted" by the regulation. On its face, the case seems to hold that a regulation that yields no public benefit but imposes substantial private burdens violates due process, which appears to turn on a substantive review of the net social benefits of the regulation.

Under the analysis advocated here, however, the case is better understood as violating the principle of equality. The zoning board apparently wanted to protect the residential neighborhood from the industrial neighborhood, requiring that a portion of the property on the industrialized side contain only a residence (its historical use). The effect of course, was to distinguish one lot on the industrial side of the street from all the other lots on that side. If the state wanted to extend the residential neighborhood to the industrial side of the street, it should have done that for all owners of property on the industrial side. Even though the dividing line, Brookline Avenue, was being widened and a residence on the industrial side of the street would provide an additional partial buffer to separate industrial and residential uses, to impose the burden on only one owner and exempt similarly situated owners is impermissible.

Just as particularized decisions about land use must take into account equal benefits for owners who are similarly situated, the particularized decisions of the legislative process must incorporate equal burdens for similarly situated owners. This principle protects the legislative process against the undue imposition of burdens on some owners that ought to be imposed on owners more generally. Policing this requirement is important to the integrity of the legislative process.[23]

Legislative lawmaking depends on coalition building that identifies a confluence of overlapping interests that can gain majority assent. Individuals with various interests and perspectives join coalitions that seek enough allies, and overcome dissenting voices, to support legislative intervention. In this context, there is a danger that the legislative process will result in coalitions that

---

[22] 277 U.S. 183 (1928).
[23] The idea that judicial review legitimately protects the integrity of the legislative process is developed in other contexts in Ely (1980).

concentrate the impact of the burdens of legislation on some individuals in order to induce other individuals to join the majority, interventionist coalition. This is the danger of legislative coalition busting: one way of building interventionist coalitions is to exempt some individuals from legislation in order to neutralize their opposition to it.

Accordingly, legislatures ought not be allowed to legislate in a way that imposes the burdens of regulation on some individuals, or on some group of individuals, in order to neutralize the opposition of other individuals who are, functionally and by their self-regarding interests, in an identical position. Nor should legislatures impose burdens on one owner for the benefit of other particularized owners. In this respect, the legislature's obligation to respect the judicial function reflects a potential failure of the legislative process. The decision to impose burdens on some owners and to exempt other, similarly situated, owners from those burdens is akin to a judicial decision, for it addresses an intramural dispute between specific owners over who should be burdened and who should be exempt from burdens. When deciding in particular contexts how to distribute the burdens of regulation, legislatures are making a decision about the well-being of specified individuals vis-à-vis each other, which is a judicial, not a legislative function; their determination ought, for that reason, to be subject to judicial review.

In other words, the need for judicial oversight of the legislative process is clear, for the legislative process is abused if it is used to put together coalitions in favor of regulations by concentrating the burdens of regulation on fewer and fewer individuals from among those similarly situated.[24] Legislation considers not only the relationship between individuals and the collective, but also disputes between individuals, some of whom will bear the burdens imposed by the legislation and some of whom seek to be relieved of those burdens. The legislative process must fairly distribute those burdens and ought not relieve some individuals of their fair share of the burdens in order to secure the legislation's passage.

---

[24] In this respect, judicial oversight of the legislative process not only protects the separation of powers inherent in a system that values judge-made law and legislation for their respective strengths, it also plays to the particular strength of judges in defining the impermissible, unrepresentative contours of the legislative process. Although John Hart Ely was writing about judicial review of legislation affecting the rights of racial and ethnic minorities, his theory of judicial review is equally relevant to legislation that, by focusing on a subset of similarly situated owners, refuses "to recognize commonalities of interest, and thereby denying that minority the protection afforded other groups by a representative system." Ely (1980) at 103. Significantly, Ely's description of the virtues of judicial (rather than democratic) oversight highlights the comparative advantage that judges have in making judgments about unequal treatment in the legislative process. Id.

The danger of improper legislative line drawing is especially significant in land use regulation. When the legislative process contemplates preserving wetlands, for example, it must draw lines that define the scope of the regulation by determining which owners bear the burdens of the regulation and what burdens they carry. We can think of this as involving two operations. The legislature must determine which classes of individuals ought to be included (and which excluded) from the regulation, and the legislature may also determine which members of a class of individuals ought to be included. Presumably, the legislature performs the first operation by determining the characteristics of the wetlands that are important to the legislative goals and imposing burdens on owners of those wetlands but not others. It is appropriate for the legislature to exclude a class of owners from the regulation on the ground that including them would impose burdens without offsetting benefits. Yet the pro-interventionist forces in the legislature will also be tempted to reduce opposition to the legislation by relieving some wetland owners of the burdens of the regulation in order to reduce opposition to the legislation. When that occurs within a class of wetland owners who are similarly situated it is impermissible because the legislature has abused its own process by building coalitions that do not fairly measure the social costs and benefits of the intervention, and because it has inequitably distributed the burdens of regulatory impact.[25]

The distinction between determining the scope of regulation by examining its net social costs and determining the scope of regulation by examining its impact on individual members of a class accounts for the two-part test that makes up the due process standard. The means–ends standard suggests that as long as the legislature, in its judgment, finds that the aggregate benefits of the regulation exceed the aggregate burdens, the legislative judgment is valid under the Due Process Clause. The requirement that the government must show a rational relationship between the regulation and a legitimate government goal implements the concept of burdens and benefits that is at the heart of the concept of property. Owners exercise dominion over their property subject to burdens that a community recognizes as producing offsetting social benefits.

But due process also requires that regulation be nonarbitrary, and this imposes the requirement that the scope of the regulation not fall disproportionally on some owners who are similarly situated with owners who escape the burden of the regulation. The check of due process ensures that the lines

---

[25] The point is not that burdens on some owners are necessarily increased because other owners are relieved of burdens. The point is that owners justifiably resent carrying burdens that their neighbors do not carry.

are not drawn for political purposes or drawn so rigidly that some owners suffer burdens that ought, in fairness, to be distributed among a wider range of owners. Under this reading, courts are empowered to determine when the legislature has drawn arbitrary lines between burdened and unburdened owners because that determination involves the rights of individual owners against each other, which functionally is a judicial determination.[26] Legislative regulation that depends on such coalition-busting ought not be allowed because it does not fairly measure the aggregate costs and benefits of the regulation. Arbitrarily excluding some of the costs of regulation (by excluding some of those who would bear those costs if like owners were treated alike), cannot attain the kind of aggregate assessment of burdens and benefits that the legislative process is designed to provide. It also improperly asks some owner to bear burdens that ought, under the principle of equality, to be borne by a wider range of owners.

The proposal advanced here does not violate the oft-cited principle that an owner subject to regulation may not complain because the regulation did not have a broader scope or did not encompass all the individuals who might have been subject to it. Drawing the boundaries between those who bear the burdens of regulation and those who are exempt from the burdens involves two separate operations. Legislative regulation must decide whether the burdens that would be imposed if the boundary were drawn more broadly yield offsetting benefits – it must determine the characteristics of the class of individuals subject to the regulation. It is in that sense that an owner burdened by a regulation may not complain that the legislature stopped at one point rather than another when drawing boundaries. If that argument were accepted, legislative regulation would quickly unravel, for the judiciary cannot possibly assemble the information and replicate the process for drawing that line. That form of line drawing is a discretionary matter subject to judicial review under only the lenient means–ends standard.

But that is a different matter from drawing the boundaries in one place and then unfairly excluding some owners who are so similarly situated that they ought, under the principle of equality, to be included. That is a justiciable matter because it involves a contest between members of that class, and an adversely affected owner ought to be allowed to argue that her burdens of regulation were wrongfully imposed because other owners benefited by being

---

[26] When upholding land use restrictions – even those that have a severe impact on property values – courts often emphasize that the adversely affected owner was not singled out by the regulation. See, e.g., William C. Haas & Co., Inc. v. City & Cnty. of San Francisco, Cal., 605 F.2d 1117 (9th Cir. 1979) (height restrictions diminished value of property from $2 million to $100,000 but applied to entire Russian Hill area).

exempt from the burdens. Adversely affected owners ought to be allowed to show that they are being asked to bear burdens that ought, in fairness, to be borne by a larger class of individuals.

To be sure, the principle that like individuals ought to be treated alike is not an easy one to apply. It requires a judgment about which similarities between individual owners are relevant to the legislative goal, and a judgment about whether the legislature has honored those similarities in the means that it has chosen. This is not, however, an abstract inquiry, for it is rooted in the question of whether the legislature has fairly treated individuals in their relationship with other individuals. It can be determined by asking whether the legislative scheme provides evidence that the legislature has distributed the burdens of the regulation in a way that are best explained by the desire to build interventionist coalitions. Because the relevant inquiry is rooted in the question of whether one individual is bearing burdens that ought to be shared by another individual – that is, the distribution of burdens and benefits between individuals – it is the kind of inquiry that judges are accustomed to making. The inquiry would put meaningful limitations on government regulation by focusing on the central concept of property at common law – namely, that owners, under the principle of equality, are entitled to an appropriate distribution of the burdens and benefits of decisions about resources.[27]

This idea that legislation must allocate the burdens of regulation in a non-arbitrary way is reflected in Supreme Court regulatory jurisprudence. The Court's insistence that the regulatory scheme be comprehensive is a check on the completeness and thoughtfulness of the regulatory process. Under a comprehensive scheme, it is unlikely that decisions determining who should bear the burden of regulation will be ad hoc, arbitrary, or coalition-busting, for regulation is comprehensive only when the relevant interests, and therefore the technical borders of regulation, are well-identified. Moreover, the special scrutiny that the Court requires when property has been rendered valueless serves as a convenient and accurate way of identifying regulations that ought to be examined closely, for it signals the possibility that the legislature has imposed burdens on some owners when the same objectives might be achieved with burdens spread more widely. When one owner's property is rendered valueless while other owners are exempt for the burden of achieving the community's goal, the possibility of arbitrary regulation seems especially significant.

---

[27] Several land use cases that are normally thought of as substantive due process cases can be better understood on the basis of the separation-of-powers analysis given in this chapter. Pennell v. City of San Jose, 485 U.S. 1 (1977); Village of Arlington Heights v. Metro. Hous. Dev. Corp., 429 U.S. 252 (1977),

Lucas v. South Carolina Coastal Council[28] illustrates the kind of analysis I am advocating.[29] There, the South Carolina Coastal Council was addressing the problem of beach erosion on a barrier island protecting the coast of South Carolina, a problem that affected owners of beachfront property subject to the erosion, and, if the barrier island eroded away, owners of property on the mainland. Two facts are significant. First, the Coastal Council had two options for addressing the problem. The one the Coastal Council chose was to require new construction to be set back from the water sufficiently to not disrupt the natural shifting of the sands. This had the effect of making coastal lots unavailable for new residential building. The Coastal Council's other option was to require each landowner to build a barrier in front of his property to keep the sand from eroding, an option that would obviously affect each landowner, whether the property was developed or not. Most of the property subject to erosion contained residences built in front of the setback line. Under the regulation, owners of these residences would be required to build behind the setback line if their home were destroyed (say by fire or hurricane), but were not required to bear any other expense to address the erosion problem. The plaintiff bought the only property on the beach that was not developed and therefore owned the only property directly affected by the regulation.

Applying the regulatory takings doctrine, the Supreme Court held that a regulation that eliminates the economic value of the property is a taking that requires just compensation. Although the Court in subsequent cases modified the extreme implications of that holding by, for example, allowing a "temporary" moratorium on all development around Lake Tahoe,[30] the test itself is suspect, for it is not clear how one might distinguish between different uses of the property in a way that would allow one to determine whether the owner has been deprived of the property's total economic value.[31] As I argued previously, as long as the owner has the right to exclude, the owner has the right to transfer the property. As long as the right to transfer is not impaired, the property has transfer (and therefore economic) value, even if not for the uses contemplated by the owner. For this reason, many find the *Lucas* test, especially as modified by *Lake Tahoe*, to insignificantly restrict legislative regulation.

[28] 309 S.Ct. 424 (1992).
[29] *See also*, E. Enters. v. Apfel, 524 U.S. 498, 537 (2008) (plurality opinion) (invalidating a legislative remedy that "singles out certain employers to bear a burden that is substantial in amount, based on the employers' conduct far in the past, and unrelated to any commitment that the employers made or to any injury they caused …").
[30] Tahoe-Sierra Preservation Council, Inc. v. Tahoe Regional Planning Agency, 535 U.S. 302 (2002).
[31] The problem is an extension of the denominator problem – the problem of not knowing what percentage of the property was taken without knowing what property goes into the denominator of the equation. The Court has not successfully addressed that question. *See, e.g.*, Palazzolo v. Rhode Island, 533 U.S. 606 (2001).

Limitations on Legislative Regulation 309

The regulatory takings doctrine got in the way of a more appropriate understanding of *Lucas*. The South Carolina Coastal Council created a class of one where, given the option of asking each owner to construct an erosion barrier, there could have been a larger class, burdening the Lucas property for the benefit of the neighboring property, which was similarly situated. To be sure, on its face, the regulation looks as if it treated like owners alike. The regulation applied to all landowners who were undertaking new residential construction on the island barrier, whether the new construction replaced an existing residence or created a new residence on formerly vacant property. Yet the immediate impact of the regulation was on only one landowner (because the other landowners had built their homes before the regulation was passed), and the government's goal (to control beach erosion) might have been achieved by imposing costs on all those who had residences on the beach. The choice to impose a cost on Lucas's property rather than on the property of all of his neighbors was a choice to burden one homeowner for the benefit of other homeowners.

In addition, it is clear, in retrospect, that the choice to impose all the costs of preventing erosion on the Lucas property was a coalition-busting move rather than the least-expensive way of achieving a lawful government goal. Existing homeowners did not oppose the regulation because the regulation's only effect on them occurred if their home was destroyed, so its "bite" was hypothetical only. Their opposition to the setback regulation must therefore have been tepid, leaving Lucas as the only owner with enough interest in the question to oppose the regulation. The regulators had evidently shaped the regulation to minimize opposition to it rather than to deal with the problem by fairly balancing the burdens and benefits of their solution to the problem. That conclusion is fortified by the story's dénouement: as Vicki Been has shown, soon after the regulation was passed, Hurricane Hugo destroyed many of the homes on the barrier island, and their owners were then required to comply with the setback regulation when rebuilding. The Coastal Council, faced with their opposition, then repealed the setback provision and resorted to a different means of addressing the erosion problem.[32]

Lucas involved legislative boundary drawing that required a class of one to carry the burdens of the regulation. It would be a mistake, however, to assume that every class of burdened owners that contains only one individual would, for that reason, be unlawful; a class of one could be the source of an appropriate regulatory boundary if no other owners were similarly situated. This was the circumstance in cases such as *Hadacheck v. Sebastian*,[33] where the

---

[32] Been (2009) in Korngold and Morriss (2009).
[33] 239 U.S. 394 (1915). *See also*, Goldblatt v Hempstead, 369 U.S. 590 (1962) (regulation barring continued operation of an existing sand and gravel pit was upheld to protect public safety).

regulation banning the manufacture of bricks, although general and prospective, applied to the only brick maker in the city. It was upheld for the same reason that a single common law nuisance case is allowed to adjudicate the rights of a single defendant – namely, that burdens may be imposed on one person to provide benefits to a group of people as long as all of those who contribute to the harm are asked to contribute fairly to the resolution of the harm. The legislature is not disabled from adjudicating as a common law court would; its disability is in making judgments in individual cases in ways that a common law court would not undertake.

In short, the manifold problems of the regulatory takings doctrine are unnecessary to protect property owners and, by subjecting to litigation many cases in which there is no legitimate claim of government overreaching, they unnecessarily increase the cost of providing public goods. The Due Process Clause contains respect for property rights that limits government overreaching on procedural grounds, and its use would allow courts to focus on what really matters in land use regulation –namely, whether the legislature has followed the equality principle when determining the burdens of providing public goods.

13.4 CONCLUSION

The protection of private property from legislative regulation depends on the concept of property developed at the common law, which provides our understanding of the nature of property that is constitutionally protected. This chapter has carried forward the concept of property revealed in this book – namely, that property guarantees owners an appropriate division of the burdens and benefits of decisions about their resource under the equality principle. That concept neither guarantees that the property will have value nor does it guarantee freedom from government regulation. Ownership is taken subject to land use regulations when the legislature finds that the social benefits of regulation exceed the social costs. But ownership does guarantee that when regulating land uses the legislature will fairly assign the burdens of regulation and will not subvert the legislative and judicial functions by making particularized decisions without the process due under the common law or by unfairly exempting some owners from regulation that ought to be borne by other owners. The benefits of ownership can be offset by the social costs of various uses of the resource that is owned, but the owner is guaranteed that the burdens of regulation will be carried by all those who are similarly situated; the Due Process Clause prohibits the legislature from acting otherwise.

14 The Promise of Unity

My goal in this book – to suggest the outlines of a unified theory of property law – requires that we reorient our understanding of property law in several important respects. It may be helpful to summarize the main ways in which the theory developed here challenges the reader to rethink the idea of property.

One important reorientation is to shift the focus of property theory from a theory of private property to one of property as resource management, including both private and non-private forms of management. This supports the unification theme by pointing out that all property – whether private or otherwise – responds to the social need to determine who makes decisions about resources and how those decisions ought to be made. Private property is one possible response to that question, but not the only response. Because the theory here views property to be a response to the single social question that all societies face, the theory is both universal and contextual. The theory is universal because it sees property regimes to have grown from a response to a universal question, and it allows us to trace any property system back to its roots in the social system that responds to that single question. The theory is contextual because it has provided the framework that allows us to discern how the social context has influenced the development of the property system in response to the social issue that property law addresses.

The assimilation of theories of private and non-private property requires us to reorient the way we think about ownership, but not our concept of property. All forms of property require an individual, a group of individuals, or an entity to be responsible for making decisions about the resource involved, and all forms of property constrain those decisions so that decisions serve the function that a particular society proscribes for a system of property. The concept of property continues to be about dominion over resources, but the theory now encompasses dominion by individuals, by collections of individuals, and by the state, whereas the concept of dominion distinguishes between dominion over the right to exclude and dominion over the right to use property.

This conception of property does challenge our idea of ownership, for ownership is generally equated with private ownership, whereas in the theory here ownership can take on a different, and variegated, coloration. We do not usually speak of *owning* common or state property, nor do we speak of tenants as owners. Owners of common property do not have the same set of rights as owners of private property; in particular they do not have the crucial right to transfer the property and therefore do not have the right to realize the gains (or suffer the losses) of the value of property. They are owners only in the limited sense of having the right to use property and, when the commons is not an open commons, to be part of a group that has the right to exclude those not authorized to use the property. It seems jarring, at first, to say that an individual owns the highway, a public park, the fire station, or the apartment she leases.

One option is to restrict the concept of ownership so that it applies only to those who can realize the gains and losses in the value of a resource. To do so separates the concept of ownership from the concept of property this book advocates. That leaves no word to describe the rights of individuals who have interests in property other than the right to gain or lose from changes in market value. To be sure, we call individuals who have rights with respect to other forms of property either *users* or *possessors* of the property, which aptly describes those with rights to common, state, or leased property. But the concepts of *use* and *possession* do not connote rights and, in fact, connote the absence of rights because they create political and social distance between owners and users.

It would be beneficial to change our conception of ownership. An alternative meaning of ownership would connote some measure of control over, and connection to, a resource. It would therefore create a bond between an individual and the resources subject to the individual's decision making and control. If we confine the idea of ownership to owners of private property, we constrict the relationship between individuals and a society's resources and suggest that owners of private property have special status, in terms of their control over, and connections with, resources that separates them from other individuals. By contrast, if we expand the idea of ownership to include common, state, and leased property, we emphasize the connection between individuals and a society's resources. If individuals understood that as members of a relevant community they in some sense "own" the highway, the park, the fire station, and the apartment they rent, we would reduce the political distance between individuals and the community of individuals.

In real ways, the owners of common, state, or leased property have control over and connection to the resources they use or possess. Individuals "own" the highways and have the right to use them, subject to the equal right of all other authorized users to also use the highways. A user of the highways can exclude others by getting to a place where it would be unreasonable for another user to expect to be. Individuals "own" the fire station in the limited, but real, sense that they participate in the political process that shapes decisions about the fire station. Certainly, local participation in decisions about where to put prisons, highways, and other state facilities suggests that such control is not ephemeral. And tenants have control over many aspects of the resources they lease. Indeed, the tenant's rights revolution of the past half century suggests that tenants have a status greater than users and possessors and a measure of control over, and connection with, the resource that reflects aspects of traditional ownership. Viewing ownership as control and connection rather than the right to market gains and losses shifts our focus from property as the holder of value to property as the reflection of things individuals value.

Another fundamental reorientation required by the theory here is to shift our analytical focus from what owners *do* with their property — that is, from the traditional rights to exclude, use, transfer, and so on — to a focus on what decisions an owner makes given the nature of her ownership interests, and on the authorized scope of her decisions. This reorientation does not deny that the law evaluates human behavior; it simply suggests that when evaluating human behavior the law is asking whether an ideal decision maker would have behaved in a certain way, and compares an individual's behavior with the behavior of that idea decision maker. This decision-centric focus not only unifies property theory across various forms of property (for, as I have said, all forms of property require a decision maker), but it also unifies legal theory by defining the unit of analysis around which theory can develop. This, in turn, allows the idea of an individual as decision maker in a social setting to be used to integrate ideas drawn from various social sciences in a way that unifies our understanding of the nature and morality of the cooperation that is the foundation of any system of property.

The decision-centric focus of the theory defended in this book suggests that individual decisions are the mediating force that allows a property system to function. The law functions to evaluate and influence individual decisions against those of an ideal decision maker to ensure that they are consistent with the values that a society uses when it determines which ownership claims to recognize and how those claims ought to be constrained. The law is both corrective and instructive. An individual who causes harm when not mimicking the decisions of an ideal decision maker is required to correct the harm. The concept of the ideal decision maker, and its applications, instructs individuals about how they ought to behave. Importantly, the concept of the ideal decision maker is congruent with the way people think about how they ought to act. Under the decision-centric approach, the law erects no artificial rules or doctrines that create distance between the way the law expects individuals to think about their behavior and the way individuals normally think about their behavior.

The decision-centric focus is also an integrating device, invoking game theory as the model through which we can understand the interdependence of decisions. Because game theory is the branch of the social sciences that focuses directly on how an individual's decision interacts with the decisions of other individuals, the decision-centric focus of the theory here links legal theory with game theory and its behavioral assumptions. This advances the unification goal because game theory is an integrating, not a divisive, methodology. Game theory does not assume that the individuals or institutions of the law have a preset goal, and it does not depend on a theory of human behavior that is exclusively cultural, social, psychological, or economically rational. Game theory makes its assumptions clear (and therefore subjects them to evaluation), makes the relevant causal connections explicit, and can account for both rational self-interested decisions and decisions that reflect emotional responses.

Because game theory models the boundary between cooperation and conflict, it is ideal for understanding the continuing evolution of property systems. The theory here suggests that property systems evolve at the boundary between cooperation and conflict because a claim of ownership or dominion is an invitation to either conflict or cooperation. When claims of dominion over a resource are accepted within a society, the claims evolve into rights; when the claims are rejected by a society, they must be renegotiated or settled by conflict. As societies mature, claims are modulated because individuals form accurate expectations about which claims will be accepted and which rejected. As the boundary between the acceptance and rejection of claims becomes well-defined and recognized, the form that conflict over claims takes can itself be modulated and subjected to institutional conflict resolution without the need for violence.

Significantly, the evolutionary theory suggested by the substitutability of cooperation and conflict is agnostic about starting points; it applies equally to property systems arising from the state of nature and to property systems that evolve from a preexisting political hierarchy. In the pre-political state of nature, property systems evolve from claims and the rejection or recognition of those claims by others; the political framework (including the development of markets and states to protect the rights that are recognized) are responses to the property system. Where property systems arise from, and after, a political system, the stability of the property system depends on recognition of the legitimacy of the political system and the rights that it gives. Human history can be told as the evolution of governments that tried to control individuals by controlling their access to resources, and the evolution of democracy and markets largely reflects the evolution of ideas about resource governance.

The theory here is agnostic about starting points because the theory suggests that cooperation depends on the creation of shared belief systems, and shared belief systems can form around claims to resources, whether those claims are made by individuals or by the state. Indeed, an individual claiming all the resources of the state, and therefore the right to govern by controlling access to resources, can do so (without coercion) only so long as the individuals subject to that control share beliefs about the legitimacy of that exercise of power. Once those shared beliefs disappear, evolution and revolution are in the wings.

Shared beliefs are important because cooperation requires that one individual be able to predict how other individuals will act in a given context. If an individual does not have the belief that others share his beliefs, it will be hard to make cooperative moves because the risk of opportunism will be high. The concept of shared beliefs is itself an integrating device, for all theories of cooperation depend on a method by which individuals can be assured that they share beliefs with other individuals. Whether theories of cooperation depend on ideas about trust, or repeat games, or communication, or social sanctions, or any of a number of other coordinating devices, a theory of cooperation is, at bottom, a theory of how communities form beliefs about shared beliefs.

The evolution of cooperation depends on the formation of shared beliefs but not on any particular beliefs; the shape and content of the shared beliefs depends on the interaction of individuals and the values that guide that interaction. Accordingly, the evolutionary theory presented here allows us to account for social and cultural factors that influence the formation of shared beliefs. We can then examine any social system and determine what shared beliefs matter, isolating the kind of shared beliefs that individuals accept and those that they reject. In a society that embraces hierarchy, shared beliefs may well be formed by the statements of a tribal leader. In a society where power is more highly dispersed, shared beliefs arise from constant interaction between individuals that, in effect, negotiate the contours of the beliefs.

Individual beliefs about shared beliefs drive the decisions that individuals make and are therefore integrated into the decision-centric concept espoused here. It is possible to identify the kind of shared beliefs that are important to cooperation. Because shared beliefs that support cooperation are a form of exchange, the theory here has advanced a general theory of exchange that posits two different kinds of shared beliefs that make cooperation possible – shared beliefs about what makes each person in the exchange better off and shared beliefs about the appropriate divisions of the gains of exchange. Although much economic analysis subsumes both kinds of shared beliefs under the single label of welfare maximization, when we disaggregate the two kinds of beliefs, we have a richer understanding of the kinds of shared beliefs that support cooperation. The theory here is therefore consistent with the understanding from game theory and behavioral economics that cooperation depends on a selection from multiple efficient points of the efficient point that will support cooperation, where welfare maximization is understood not as a discrete point but as a choice between different outcomes that divide the gains from efficiency outcomes in different ways. By forming belief systems that account for both increasing welfare and dividing welfare in ways acceptable to the community, the theory here shows how societies develop concepts of efficiency and fairness that support cooperation.

The decision-centric focus of the theory here allows one final integrative possibility. Under the theory presented here, we understand the decisions a person makes to involve two separate processes. The first is to decide how to decide – that is, to determine a methodology of decision making that is appropriate to the context being considered. The second process is to make the decision, following the appropriate methodology, to a reasoned conclusion. The first process is categorical, for that is what the ideal decision maker will do when decisions implicate the well-being of other individuals. The second process is contingent, for it means the decision maker must apply the appropriate methodology in a particular context to reason toward a decision that takes into account the consequences that are relevant to the methodology of the ideal decision maker. The decision-centric approach therefore integrates the deontic and the consequential.

References

Acheson, James M., *Lobster Gangs of Maine* (Yale University Press 1998).
Ackerman, Bruce, *Private Property and the Constitution* (Yale University Press 1977).
Adler, Jonathan H., Legal Obstacles to Private Ordering in Marine Fisheries, 8 *Roger Williams U. L. Rev.* 9 (2002).
Aleinikoff, Alexander T., Constitutional Law in the Age of Balancing, 96 *Yale L.J.* 943 (1987).
Alexander, Gregory S., Freedom, Coercion, and the Law of Servitudes, 73 *Cornell L.R.* 883 (1988).
  Commodity and Propriety (University of Chicago Press 1997).
  The Social-Obligation Norm in American Property Law, 94 *Cornell L. Rev.* 745, 747 (2009).
Alexander, Gregory & Eduardo Peñalver, Properties of Community, 10 *Theoretical Inq. L.* 127, *available at* http://www.bepress.com/til/default/vol 10/iss2/art6 (2009).
  An Introduction to Property Theory (Cambridge University Press 2012).
Alexander, R. D., *The Biology of Moral Systems* (Transaction Publishers 1987).
Anderson, Terry L. & Peter Hill, Cowboys and Contracts, 31 *J. Legal Stud.* 489 (2002).
Aristotle, *Nicomachean Ethics*, Book 5, sec 4 at 120–23 (Martin Ostwald, trans; Bobbs-Merrill Co., 1962).
Aristotle, *Politics*, Book 2, Part 3 (Benjamin Jowett trans., Dover Publications 2000).
Ayres, Ian & Eric Talley, Solomonic Bargaining: Dividing a Legal Entitlement to Facilitate Coasean Trade, 104 *Yale L J.* 1027 (1995).
Bagchi, Aditi, Distributive Injustice and Private Law, 60 *Hastings L.J.* 105 (2008).
Baker, Edwin C., The Ideology of the Economic Analysis of Law, 5 *Phil. & Pub. Aff.* (1975).
  Starting Points in Economic Analysis of Law, 8 *Hofstra L. Rev.* 939 (1980).
Banner, Stuart, Transitions between Property Regimes, 31 *J. Legal Stud.* S359 (2002).
  Who Owns the Sky?: The Struggle to Control Airspace from the Wright Brothers On (Harvard University Press 2008).
  American Property: A History of How, Why and What We Own (Harvard University Press 2011).
Baron, Jonathan, *Morality and Rational Choice* (Kluwer Academic Press 1993).

Been, Vicki L., Lucas v. The Green Machine: Using the Takings Clause to Promote More Efficient Regulation, in Gerald Korngold & Andrew Morriss, eds., *Property Stories* 221 (Foundation Press 2009).
Bell, Abraham, Private Takings, 76 *U. Chi. L. Rev.* 517 (2009).
Binmore, Kenneth, *Natural Justice* (Cambridge University Press 2005).
Birks, Peter, Unjust Enrichment and Wrongful Enrichment, 79 *Tex. L. Rev.* 1767 (2001).
Blackstone, William, *Commentaries on the Laws of England*, Book 2 (1765–69) (University of Chicago Press 1979).
Bowles, Samuel, *Microeconomic Behavior, Institutions, and Evolution* 43 (Princeton University Press 2004).
Bowles, Samuel & Sandra Ponania-Reyes, Economic Incentives and Social Preferences: Substitutes or Complements? 50 *J. Econ. Lit.* 368 (2012).
Brauneis, Robert, The Foundation of Our "Regulatory Takings" Jurisprudence: The Myth and Meaning of Justice Holmes's Opinion in *Pennsylvania Coal Co., v. Mahon*, 106 *Yale L.J.* 632 (1996).
Brudner, Alan, *The Unity of the Common Law* (University of California Press 1995).
Byrne, Peter J., Ten Arguments for the Abolition of the Regulatory Takings Doctrine, 22 *Ecology L.Q.* 89 (1995).
Buchanan, James, Politics, Property, and the Law: An Alternative Interpretation of Miller et. al. v. Schoene, 15 *J.L.& Econ.* 439 (1972)
Calabresi, Guido & Douglas Melamed, Property Rules, Liability Rules, and Inalienability: One View of the Cathedral, 85 *Harv. L. Rev.* 1089 (1972).
Cane, P., *Responsibility in Law and Morality* (Hart Publishing, 2002).
Chapman, Nathan S. & Michael W. McConnell, Due Process as Separation of Powers, 121 *Yale L.J.* 1672 (2012).
Claeys, Eric R., Public-Use Limitations and Natural Property Rights, 2004 *Mich. St. L. Rev.* 877 (2004).
  Property 101: Is Property a Thing or a Bundle? 32 *Seattle U. L. Rev.* 617 (2009).
  Exclusion and Exclusivity, 53 *Ariz. L. Rev.* 9 (2011).
Coase, Ronald, The Problem of Social Cost, *J.L. & Econ.* 1 (1960).
  The Firm, the Market, and the Law (University of Chicago Press, 1990).
Cohen, Felix S., Transcendental Nonsense and the Functional Approach, 35 *Colum. L. Rev.* 809 (1935).
Coleman, Jules L., *Risks and Wrongs* (Cambridge University Press 1992).
  Corrective Justice and Property Rights, in Ellen Paul et al. eds., *Property Rights* 131 (Cambridge University Press 1994).
  The Practice of Principle (Oxford University Press 2001).
Coleman, Jules L. & Jody Kraus, Rethinking the Theory of Legal Rights, 95 *Yale L. J.* 1335 (1986).
Craswell, Richard, Passing on the Cost of Legal Rules: Efficiency and Distribution in Buyer-Seller Relationships, 43 *Stan L. Rev.* 361 (1991).
Dagan, Hanoch, Exclusion and Inclusion in Property, *in Property and Institutions* 37 (Oxford University Press 2011).
Dagan, Hanoch & Michael A. Heller, The Liberal Commons, 110 *Yale L.J.* 549 (2001).
  Conflicts in Property, 6 *Theoretical Inq. L.* 37 (2005).

Dana, David A. & Thomas W. Merrill, *Property Takings* (Foundation Press 2002).
Dawkins, Richard, *The Selfish Gene* (Oxford University Press 1976).
Deigh, John, *An Introduction to Ethics* (Cambridge University Press 2010).
Demsetz, Harold, Toward a Theory of Property Rights, 57 *Am. Econ. Rev.* 347 (1967).
Dobris, Joel C., Boomer: Twenty Years Later; An Introduction with Some Footnotes about "Theory", 54 *Alb L. Rev.* 171 (1989–90).
Dorfman, Avihay, Private Ownership, 16 *Legal Theory* 1 (2010).
  Property and Collective Undertaking: The Principle of Numerus Clausus, 61 *U. Toronto L.J.* 467 (2011).
Dow, George Francis, *Whale Ships and Whaling* (Dover Publications 1985).
Dukeminier, Jesse, James Krier, Gregory Alexander & Michael Schill, *Property* (Aspen Publishers 7th ed. 2010).
Dworkin, Ronald, *Justice for Hedgehogs* 273 (Belknap Press 2011).
Economic Journal Watch, *Property, A Bundle of Rights?* Vol. 8, Issue 3 (Sept. 2011) *available at* econjwatch.org/issues/volume-8-issue-3-September 2011.
Edgeworth, Francis, *Papers Relating to Political Economy I* (Thoemmes Press 1925).
Eggertsson, Thrainn, Open Access versus Common Property, *in* Terry L. Anderson & Fred S. McChesney eds., *Property Rights: Cooperation, Conflict, and Law* 74 (Princeton University Press 2003).
Ellickson, Robert C., Alternatives to Zoning: Covenants, Nuisance Rules, and Fines as Land Use Controls, 40 *U. Chi. L. Rev.* 681 (1973).
  A Hypothesis of Wealth-Maximizing Norms: Evidence from the Whaling Industry, 5 *J.L. Econ. & Org.* 83 (1989).
  Order without Law: How Neighbors Settle Disputes (Harvard University Press 1991).
Ely, James W., Jr., Two Cheers for Justice O'Conner, 1 *Brigham-Kanner Prop. Rts. Conf. J.* 149, 164 (2012).
Ely, John Hart, *Democracy and Distrust: A Theory of Judicial Review* (Harvard University Press 1980).
Epstein, Richard A., Notice and Freedom of Contract in the Law of Servitudes, 55 *S. Cal. L. Rev.* 1353 (1982).
  Takings, Private Property, and the Power of Eminent Domain (Harvard University Press 1985).
  Property Rights, State of Nature Theory, and Environmental Protection, 4 *N.Y.U. J. L. & Liberty* 1 (2009).
Farber, Daniel A. & Philip P. Frickey, *Law and Public Choice* (University of Chicago Press 1991).
Fee, John E. Of Parcel and Property, *in* Thomas E. Roberts ed., *Taking Sides on Taking Issues: Public and Private Perspectives* 101 (American Bar Association 2002).
Fehr, Ernst, Oliver Hart & Christian Zehnder, Contracts as Reference Points – Experimental Evidence, 101 *Am. Econ. Rev.* 493 (2011).
Fennell, Lee Anne, Ostrom's Law: Property Rights in the Commons, 5 *Int. J. Commons* 9 (2011), *available at* http://www.thecommonsjournal.org.
  Picturing Takings, 88 *Notre Dame L. Rev.* 57 (2012)
  The Problem of Resource Access, 126 *Harv. L. Rev.* 1471 (2013).
Field, Barry C., The Evolution of Property Rights, 42 *Kyklos* 319 (1989).
Fitzpatrick, Daniel, Evolution and Chaos in Property Rights Systems: The Third World Tragedy of Contested Access, 115 *Yale L. J.* 996 (2006).

Frank, Jerome, *Law and the Modern Mind* (Brentano's Publishers 1930).
Frankfurter, Felix, Twenty Years of Mr. Justice Holmes' Constitutional Opinions, 36 *Harv. L. Rev.* 909 (1923).
Freyfogle, Eric, The Last Right to Roam, *in On Private Property: Finding Common Ground on the Ownership of Land* 29 (Beacon Press 2007).
Fukuyama, Francis, *Trust: The Social Virtues and the Creation of Prosperity* (Simon & Schuster 1995).
Fuller, Lon L., *The Morality of the Law* (Yale University Press 1964).
   The Forms and Limits of Adjudication, 92 *Harv. L. Rev.* 353 (1978).
Gerhart, Peter M., The Death of Strict Liability, 56 *Buff. L. Rev.* 245 (2008).
   Tort Law and Social Morality (Cambridge University Press 2010).
   Nuisance as a Strict Liability Offense (working paper on file with the author, 2011).
Gerhart, Peter M. & Robert D. Cheren, The Shared Ownership Theory of Subsurface Resource Pools, 63 *Case W. Res. L. Rev.* 1040 (2013).
Ginsberg, William R. & Lois Weiss, Common Law Liability for Toxic Torts: A Phantom Remedy, 9 *Hofstra L. Rev.* 859 (1980–81).
Gintis, Herbert, *The Bounds of Reason* (Princeton University Press 2009).
Goldberg, John C. P., Introduction: Pragmatism and Private Law, 125 *Harv. L. Rev.* 1640 (2012).
Grady, Mark F. & Michael T. McGuire, The Theory of the Origin of Natural Law, 8 *J. Contemp. Legal Issues* 87 (1997).
Graglia, Lino, The Rehnquist Court and Economic Rights, *in* Martin H. Belsky ed., *The Rehnquist Court: A Retrospective* 116 (Oxford University Press 2002).
Grey, Thomas C., The Disintegration of Property, *in* J. Roland Pennock & John W. Chapman eds., *Nomos XXII: Property* 69 (New York University Press 1980).
Grief, Avner, *Institutions and the Path to the Modern Economy: Lessons from Medieval Trade* (Cambridge University Press 2006).
Grotius, Hugo, *The Freedom of the Seas* (Oxford University Press, 1916).
Guth, Werner & Reinhard Tietz, Ultimatum Bargaining Behavior: A Survey and Comparison of Experimental Results, 11 *J. Econ. Psychol.* 417 (1990).
Guth, Werner, R. Schmittberger & B. Schwarze, An Experimental Analysis of Ultimatum Bargaining, 3 *J. Econ. Behav. & Org.* 367 (1982).
Hardin, Garrett, The Tragedy of the Commons, 162 *Science* 1243 (1968).
Harris, Jim, *Property and Justice* (Oxford University Press 1996).
Harsany, John C. & Reinhard Selten, *A General Theory of Equilibrium Selection in Games* (Cambridge University Press 1988).
Hart, H. L. A., *The Concept of Law* (Oxford University Press 1961).
Hart, Henry M. & Albert Sacks, *The Legal Process* (William Eskridge Jr. & Philip P. Frickey eds., 1st ed., Foundation Press 1994).
Hegel, George, *Philosophy of Right* (T.M. Knox trans., Clarendon Press 1942)
Heller, Michael A., The Tragedy of the Anticommons: Property in the Transition from Marx to Markets, 111 *Harv. L. Rev.* 621 (1998).
   The Boundaries of Private Property, 108 *Yale L.J.* 1163 (1999).
   Three Faces of Property, 79 *Or. L. Rev.* 417 (2000).
   The Dynamic Analytics of Property Law, 2 *Theoretical Inq. L.* 79, 80 (2001).
   Common Interest Developments at the Crossroads of Legal Theory, 37 *Urb. Law.* 329 (2005).

The Rose Theorem? 18 *Yale J.L. & Human.* 29 (2006).
The Gridlock Economy: How Too Much Ownership Wrecks Markets, Stops Innovation, and Costs Lives (Basic Books 2008).
Heller, Michael A. & James E. Krier, Deterrence and Distribution in the Law of Takings, 112 *Harv. L. Rev.* 997 (1999).
Hirschleifer, Jack, Evolutionary Models in Economics and Law: Cooperation versus Conflict Strategies, 4 *Res. L. & Econ.* 1 (1982).
Hirschman, Albert O., *Exit, Voice, and Loyalty: Responses to Decline in Firms, Organizations, and States* (Princeton University Press 1970).
Hobbes, Thomas, *Leviathan* (C. B McPherson ed., Penguin Books 1968).
Holmes, Oliver Wendell, The Path of the Law, *in Collected Papers* 167, 184 (Harvard University Press 1920).
Honore, A. M., Ownership, *in Making Law Bind: Essays Legal and Philosophical* 161 (Oxford University Press 1987).
Horkheimer, Max & Theodor W. Adorno, *Dialectic of Enlightenment* (John Cumming trans., Seabury Press 1972).
Hume, David, *A Treatise of Human Nature* (David Fate Norton & Mary J. Norton, eds., Oxford University Press 2000).
Hunt, E. K., Property and Prophets: The Evolution of Economic Institutions and Ideologies (7th ed. M.E. Sharpe 2003).
Hunt, Lester H., An Argument against a Legal Duty to Rescue, 26 *Soc. Phil.* 16, 18–20 (1959).
Jones, Richard H., *Mysticism and Morality: A New Look at Old Questions* (Lexington Books 2004).
Jordan, Cora, *Neighbor Law: Fences, Trees, Boundaries & Noise* (4th ed. Nola 2001).
Kahneman, Daniel, *Thinking, Fast and Slow* (Farrar, Strauss, and Giroux 2011).
Kant, Immanuel, *Groundwork on the Metaphysics of Morals* 428 (Cambridge University Press 1785).
Kant, Immanuel, *Kant's Critique of Practical Reason and Other Works on the Theory of Ethics*, (Thomas Kingsmill Abbott ed., 4th revised edition, Kongmans, Green and Co. 1889).
Kant, Immanuel, *The Metaphysics of Morals* (1797) (Mary Gregor ed. & trans., Cambridge University Press 1996).
Kaplow, Louis & Steven Shavell, Property Rules versus Liability Rules: An Economic Analysis, 109 *Harv. L. Rev.* 715 (1996).
Fairness versus Welfare (Harvard University Press 2002).
Katz, Larissa, Exclusion and Exclusivity in Property Law, 68 *U. Toronto L. J.* 276 (2008).
Katz, Larissa, Red Tape and Gridlock, 23 *Can. J.L. & Jurisprudence* 99 (2010).
Katz, Larissa, The Regulative Function of Property Rights, *Econ Journal Watch* 236 (2011), *available at* http://papers.ssrn.com/sol3/papers.cfm?abstract_id=1957115.
Keating, Gregory, Nuisance Law as a Strict Liability Wrong, 4 *J. Tort L.* 1 (2012).
Kelly, Daniel B., The "Public Use" Requirement in Eminent Domain Law: A Rationale Based on Secret Purchases, 92 *Cornell L. Rev.* 1 (2006).
Kelman, Mark, Consumption Theory, Production Theory, and Ideology in the Coase Theorem, 52 *Cal. L. Rev.* 669 (1979).

Kennedy, Duncan, The Structure of Blackstone's Commentaries, 28 *Buff. L. Rev.* 205 (1979).
　Cost-Benefit Analysis of Entitlement Problems: A Critique, 33 *Stan. L. Rev.* 387 (1981).
Kettles, Gregory W., Regulating Vending in the Sidewalk Commons, 77 *Temp. L.Rev.* 1 (2004).
Komesar, Neil K., *Imperfect Alternatives: Choosing Institutions in Law, Economics, and Public Policy* (University of Chicago Press 1994).
　Law's Limits: The Rule of Law and the Supply and Demand of Rights (Cambridge University Press 2001).
Kordana, Kevin A. & David H. Tabachnick, On Belling the Cat: Rawls and Tort as Corrective Justice, 92 *Va. L. Rev.* 1279 (2006).
Korngold, Gerald & Andrew Morriss, eds., *Property Stories* (Foundation Press 2009).
Krier, James E., The Tragedy of the Commons, Part Two, 15 *Harv. J.L. & Pub. Pol'y* 325 (1992).
　Evolutionary Theory and the Origin of Property Rights, 95 *Cornell L. Rev.* 139 (2009).
Krier, James E. & Stewart J. Schwab, Property Rules and Liability Rules: The Cathedral in Another Light, 70 *N.Y.U. L. Rev.* 440 (1995).
Kronman, Anthony, Mistake, Disclosure, Information, and the Law of Contracts, 7 *J. Legal Stud.* 1 (1978).
Landes, William M. & Richard A. Posner, Salvors, Finders, Good Samaritans, and Other Rescuers: An Economic Study of Law and Altruism, 7 *J. Legal Stud.* 83 (1978).
Lessig, Lawrence, Re-Crafting the Public Domain, 18 *Yale J.L. & Human.* 56 (2006).
Levmore, Saul, Two Stories about the Evolution of Property Rights, 31 *J. Legal Stud.* S421 (2002).
　Just Compensation and Just Politics, 22 *Conn. L.Rev.* 285 (1990)
Levy, Ken, Killing, Letting Die, and the Case for Mildly Punishing Bad Samaritanism, 44 *Ga. L. Rev.* 607 (2010).
Lewis, John, *A Treatise on the Law of Eminent Domain in the United States* (Callaghan & Co.1888).
Libecap, Gary D., Economic Variables and the Development of the Law: The Case of Western Mineral Rights, 38 *J. Econ. Hist.* 338 (1978).
Libecap, Gary D. & James L. Smith, The Economic Regulation of Petroleum Property Rights in the United States, 31 *J. Legal Stud.* 589 (2002).
Lipkin, Robert Justin, Beyond Good Samaritans and Moral Monsters: An Individualistic Justification of the General Legal Duty to Rescue, 31 *UCLA L. Rev.* 252 (1993).
Lisker, Marc R., Regulatory Takings and Denominator Problem, 27 *Rutgers L J.* 663 (1996).
Lucy, William, *Philosophy of Private Law* (Oxford University Press 2007).
Madison, James, *The Federalist No. 78*(Clinton Rossiter ed., New American Library 1961).
Malloy, Robin Paul, *Law and Market Economy: Reinterpreting the Values of Law and Economics* (Cambridge University Press 2000).

Law in a Market Context: An Introduction to Market Concepts in Legal Reasoning (Cambridge University Press, 2004).
Malloy, Robin Paul & M. Diamond, eds., *The Public Nature of Private Property* (Ashgate Publishing 2011).
Mandeville, Bernard, *The Fable of the Bees: Private Vices, Public Benefits* (Clarendon Press 1924).
Massey, Calvin, *Property Law: Principles, Problems, and Cases* (West Publishing Co. 2011).
McFadden, Patrick, The Balancing Test, 29 *B. C. L. Rev.* 585 (1988).
McKean, Margaret A., Success on the Commons: A Comparative Examination of Institutions of Common Property Resource Management, 4 *J. Theoretical Pol.* 247, 261–62 (1992).
Merrill, Thomas W., Property Rules, Liability Rules, and Adverse Possession, 79 *Nw. U. L. Rev.* 1122 (1984–85).
   Trespass, Nuisance, and the Costs of Determining Property Rights, 14 *J. Legal Stud.* 13 (1985).
   The Economics of Public Use, 72 *Cornell L. Rev.* 61 (1986).
   Property and the Right to Exclude, 77 *Neb. L. Rev.* 730 (1998).
   Introduction: The Demsetz Thesis and the Evolution of Property Rights, 31 *J Legal Stud.* 331 (2002).
   Melms v. Pabst Brewing Co. and the Doctrine of Waste in American Property Law, 94 *Marq. L. Rev.* 1055 (2011).
   Property as Modularity, 125 *Harv. L. Rev.* 151 (2012).
Merrill, Thomas W. & Henry E. Smith, Optimal Standardization in the Law of Property: The Numerus Clausus Principle, 110 *Yale L.J.* 1 (2000).
   What Happened to Property in Law and Economics? 111 *Yale L.J.* 357 (2001).
   Property: Principles and Policies (Foundation Press 2007).
   The Morality of Property, 48 *Wm. & Mary L. Rev.* 1849, 1850 (2007).
   Making Coasean Property More Coasean 54 *J.L. & Econ.* (forthcoming), available at http://papers.ssrn.com/sol3/papers.cfm?abstract_id=1758846 (August 2013).
   Smith, Introduction to United States Property Law (Oxford University Press 2010).
Merryman, John Henry, Waste, *in* A. James Casner ed., *American Law of Property* §20.11 n.1 (1952).
Mesterton-Gibbons, Michael & Eldridge S. Adams, Landmarks in Territory Partitioning, 161 *Am. Naturalist* 685 (2003).
Michelman, Frank, Property, Utility and Fairness: Comments on the Ethical Foundations of "Just Compensation" Law, 80 *Harv. L. Rev.* 1165 (1967).
Michelman, Frank, Ethics, Economics, and the Law of Property, *in* J. Roland Pennock & John W. Chapman, eds., *Ethics, Economics, and the Law* 3 (New York University Press 1982)
Mitchell, Gregory & Philip Tetlock, An Empirical Inquiry Into the Relationship of Corrective and Distributive Justice, 3 *J. Empirical Legal Stud.* (2006).
Moore, Michael, *Placing Blame: A General Theory of the Criminal Law* (Oxford University Press 1997).
Nance, Dale, Legal Theory and the Pivotal Role of the Concept of Coercion, 57 *U. Colo. L. Rev.* 1 (1985).
   The Weights of Evidence, 5 *Episteme* 267 (2008).

Guidance Rules and Enforcement Rules: A Better View of the Cathedral, 83 *Va. L. Rev.* 837 (1997).
North, Douglass C., *Institutions, Institutional Change, and Economic Performance* (Cambridge University Press 1990).
North, Douglass C., Barry Weingast & Jim Wallis, *Violence and Social Orders: A Conceptual Framework for Interpreting Recorded Human History* (Cambridge University Press 2009).
Nozick, Robert, *Anarchy, State, and Utopia* (Basic Books 1974).
Ostrom, Elinor, *Governing the Commons: The Evolution of Institutions for Collective Action* (Cambridge University Press 1990).
  Private and Common Property Rights, *in* Boudewijn Bouckaert & Gerrit Geest eds., *Encyclopedia of Law and Economics* 332 (2000).
  Beyond Markets and States: Polycentric Governance of Complex Economic Systems, 100 *Am. Econ. Rev.* 641 (2010).
  Collective Action and the Evolution of Social Norms, 14 *J. Econ. Persp.* 137 (2011).
Ostrom, Elinor & Thomas Dietz, eds., *The Drama of the Commons* (National Academies Press 2002).
Parfit, Derek, *On What Matters* (Oxford University Press 2011).
Parchomovsky, Gideon & Alex Stein, Reconceptualizing Trespass 103 *Nw. L. Rev.* 1823 (2009).
Paul, Ellen Frankel, Fred D. Miller Jr. & Jeffrey Paul, *Property Rights* (Cambridge University Press 1994).
Peñalver, Eduardo M. & Sonia K. Katyal, *Property Outlaws: How Squatters, Pirates and Protesters Improve the Law of Ownership* (Yale University Press 2010).
Peñalver, Eduardo & Lior Strahilevitz, Judicial Takings or Due Process? 97 *Cornell L. Rev.* 305 (2012).
Penner, J. E., The "Bundle of Rights" Picture of Property, 43 *UCLA L. Rev.* 711 (1996).
  The Idea of Property in Law (Oxford University Press 1997).
  Ownership, Co-Ownership, and the Justification of Property Rights, *in* Timothy Endicott, Joshua Getzler & Edwin Peel eds., *Properties of Law: Essays in Honour of Jim Harris* 166, (Oxford University Press 2006).
Perry, Stephen, On the Relationship between Corrective and Distributive Justice, *in* Jeremy Horder ed., *Oxford Essays in Jurisprudence* (Oxford University Press 2000).
Posner, Richard, A Theory of Negligence, 1 *J. Legal Stud.* 29 (1972).
  Some Uses and Abuses of Economics in Law, 46 *U. Chi. L. Rev.* 281 (1979).
  Economic Analysis of Law (Aspen Publishers 3d ed. 1986).
  Economic Analysis of Law (Aspen Publishers 6th ed. 2003).
  Economic Analysis of Law (Aspen Publishers 7th ed. 2007).
  Economic Analysis of Law (Aspen Publishers 8th ed. 2011).
Purdy, Jedediah, *The Meaning of Property: Freedom, Community, and the Legal Imagination* (Yale University Press 2010).
Radin, Margaret Jane, Property and Personhood, 34 *Stan. L. Rev.* 957 (1982).
  Reinterpreting Property (University of Chicago Press 1993).
Rawls, John, *A Theory of Justice* (Harvard University Press 1971).
  Justice as Fairness: A Restatement (Erin Kelly ed., Belknap Press 2001).

Reichman, Toward a Unified Concept of Servitudes, 55 *S. Cal. L. Rev.* 1179 (1982).
Restatement (First) of Property (1936).
   (Second) of Property (1977).
   (Second) of Torts (1977).
Ripstein, Arthur, *Equality, Responsibility, and the Law* (Cambridge University Press 1999).
   Three Duties to Rescue: Civil, Moral, and Criminal, 19 *Law & Phil.* 751 (2000).
   Private Order and Public Justice: Kant and Rawls, 92 *Va. L. Rev.* 1391 (2006).
   Force and Freedom: Kant's Legal and Political Philosophy (Harvard University Press 2009).
Rose, Carol M., Mahon Reconstructed: Why the Takings Issue Is Still a Muddle, 57 *S. Cal. L. Rev.* 561 (1984).
   The Comedy of the Commons: Custom, Commerce, and Inherently Public Property, 53 *U. Chi. L. Rev.* 711 (1986).
   The Liberal Conceptions of Property: Cross Currents in the Jurisprudence of Takings, 88 *Colum. L. Rev.* 1667 (1988).
   Property as Storytelling: Perspectives from Game Theory, Narrative Theory, Feminist Theory, 2 *Yale J.L. & Human.* 37 (1990).
   Property and Persuasion: Essays on the History, Theory, and Rhetoric of Ownership (Westview Press 1994).
   The Several Futures of Property: Of Cyberspace and Folk Tales, Emission Trades and Ecosystems, 83 *Minn. L. Rev.* 129 (1998).
   Psychologies of Property (and Why Property Is Not a Hawk–Dove Game), in J. E. Penner & Henry E. Smith eds., *The Handbook of the Philosophy of Property Law* (Oxford University Press 2013).
Rubin, Edward L., The New Legal Process, The Synthesis of Discourse, and the Microanalysis of Institutions, 109 *Harv. L. Rev.* 1393 (1996).
Sager, Lawrence G., Property Rights and the Constitution, XXII *Nomos* 376 (1980).
Sandel, Michael, *Justice: What's The Right Thing To Do*, (Farrar, Straus, and Giroux 2009).
Scanlon, Thomas M., *What We Owe Each Other* (Harvard University Press 1998).
Schlatter, Richard Bulger, *Private Property: The History of an Idea* (Russell & Russell 1973).
Schorr, David B., Appropriation as Agrarianism: Distributive Justice in the Creation of Property Rights, 32 *Ecology L.Q.* 3 (2005).
Schwartz, Alan & Robert E. Scott, Contract Theory and the Limits of Contract Law, 113 *Yale L.J.* 541 (2003).
Shavell, Steven, *Foundations of Economic Analysis of Law* (Harvard University Press 2004).
Simon, William H., Social-Republican Property, 38 *UCLA L. Rev.* 1335 (1991).
Simpson, A. W. Brian, *A History of Land Law* (2d ed. Oxford University Press 1986).
   Coase v. Pigou Reexamined, 25 *J. Legal Stud.* 53 (1996).
Simpson, A. W. Brian, The Story of *Sturges v. Bridgman*: The Resolution of Land Use Disputes Between Neighbors, *in* Gerald Korngold & Andrew P. Morriss eds., *Property Stories* 11 (Foundation Press 2009).
Singer, Joseph William, The Reliance Interest in Property, 40 *Stan. L. Rev.* 611, 678 (1988).

No Right to Exclude: Public Accommodations and Private Property, 90 *Nw. L. Rev.*1283 (1996).
The Edges of the Field: Lessons on the Obligations of Ownership (Beacon Press 2000).
Entitlement, The Paradoxes of Property (Yale University Press 2000).
After the Flood: Equality & Humanity in Property Regimes, 52 *Loy. L. Rev.* 243 (2006).
Democratic Estates: Property Law in a Free and Democratic Society, 94 *Cornell L. Rev.* 1009 (2009).
Normative Methods for Lawyers, 56 *UCLA L. Rev.* 899 (2009).
Property Law (Aspen Publishing 2010).
Original Acquisition of Property: From Conquest and Possession to Democracy and Equal Opportunity, 86 *Ind. L J.* 763 (2011a).
The Anti-Apartheid Principle in American Property Law, 1 *Ala. C.R. & C.L. L. Rev.* 91 (2011b).
Singleton, Sara & Michael Taylor, Common Property, Collective Action and Community, 4 *J. Theoretical Pol.* 309, 311 (1992).
Smith, Adam, *The Theory of Moral Sentiments* (1759) (Oxford University Press 2008).
Smith, Henry E., Exclusion versus Governance: Two Strategies for Delineating Property Rights, 31 *J. Legal Stud.* 453, 453–57 (2002).
The Language of Property: Form, Context, and Audience, 55 *Stan. L. Rev.* 1105 (2003).
Exclusion and Property Rules in the Law of Nuisance, 90 *Va. L. Rev.* 965 (2004).
Property and Property Rules, 79 *N.Y.U. L. Rev.* 1719 (2004).
Mind the Gap: The Indirect Relation between Ends and Means in American Property Law, 94 *Cornell L. Rev.* 959, 964 (2009).
Property as the Law of Things, 125 *Harv. L. Rev.* 1691 (2012).
Smith, Stephen A., *Contract Theory* (Oxford University Press 2004).
Smith, Vernon, Microeconomic Systems as an Experimental Science, 72 *Am. Econ. Rev.* 923 (1982).
Smith, Vernon & Arlington W. Williams, Experimental Market Economics, *Scientific American* 116 (Dec. 1992).
Stein, Gregory M., Takings in the 21st Century: Reasonable Investment-Backed Expectations after Palazzolo and Tahoe-Sierra, 69 *Tenn. L. Rev.* 891 (2002).
Stout, Lynn A., Social Norms and Other-Regarding Preferences, *in* John N. Drobak ed., *Norms and the Law* 13 (Cambridge University Press 2006).
Strahilevitz, Lior, The Right to Destroy, 114 *Yale. L. J.* 781 (2005).
Sugden, Robert, Conventions, *in* Peter Newman ed., *The New Palgrave Dictionary of Economics and Law* 453 (Palgrave Macmillan 1998).
The Economics of Rights, Cooperation, and Welfare (Palgrave Macmillan 2004).
Taylor, Michael, *Community, Anarchy, and Liberty* (Cambridge University Press 1982).
Treanor, William M., The Origins and Original Significance of the Just Compensation Clause of the Fifth Amendment, 94 *Yale L. J.* 694 (1985).
Underkuffler, Laura S., *The Idea of Property: Its Meaning and Power* (Oxford University Press 2003).
Property as Constitutional Myth: Utilities and Dangers, 92 *Cornell L. Rev.* 1239 (2007).

Unger, Roberto M., The Critical Legal Studies Movement, 96 *Harv. L. Rev.* 561 (1983).
Vermeule, Adrian, The Invisible Hand in Legal and Political Theory, 96 *Va. L. Rev.* 1417 (2010).
Wagner, Wendy, Administrative Law, Filter Failure, and Information Capture, 59 *Duke L.J.* 1321 (2010).
Waldron, Jeremy, What Is Private Property? 5 *Oxford J. Legal Stud.* 313, 327 (1985).
  The Right to Private Property (Clarendon Press 1988).
  On the Road: Good Samaritans and Compelling Duties, 40 *Santa Clara L. Rev.* 1053 (2000).
Walt, Stephen M., Eliminating Corrective Justice, 92 *Va. L. Rev.* 1311 (2006).
Weinrib, Ernest J., The Case for a Duty to Rescue, 90 *Yale L.J.* 247 (1980).
  The Idea of Private Law (Harvard University Press 1995).
  Corrective Justice in a Nutshell, 52 *Toronto L.J.* 349 (2002).
Wenar, Leif, The Concept of Property and the Takings Clause, 97 *Colum. L. Rev.* 1923 (1997).
Wiener, Jonathan B., What Begat Property, 43 *Hist. Pol. Econ.* 353 (2011).
Wilkinson III, J. Harvie, The Dual Lives of Rights: The Rhetoric and Practice of Rights in America, 98 *Calif. L. Rev.* 277 (2010).
Wyman, Katrina, From Fur to Fish: Reconsidering the Evolution of Private Property, 80 *N.Y.U. L. Rev.* 117 (2005).
Yeager, Daniel B., A Radical Community of Aid: A Rejoinder to Opponents of Affirmative Duties to Help Strangers, 71 *Wash. U. L.Q.* 1 (1993).
Zipursky, Benjamin C., Palsgraf, Punitive Damages, and Preemption, 125 *Harv. L. Rev.* 1757 (2012).

Index

alienation, 244
altruism
   distinguished from other-regarding, 114
anticommons
   described, 39
   and well-functioning markets, 279

belief systems
   as important for cooperation, 78
   and institutions, 83
   and tragedy of commons, 220
   and value formation, 84
Bell, Alexander, 277
Berman v. Parker, 284
Boomer v. Atlantic Cement, 140
bundle of sticks metaphor. *See* theories of property
burdens and benefits
   and alienation, 244
   as defining property, 130
   and due process, 302–10
   generally, 55–59
   and land use regulation, 255
   as a unifying theory, 130

Categorical Imperative
   and finding a maxim, 124
   and universality, 125
Chapman, Nathan, 254
City of Monterey v. Del Monte Dunes at Monterey, Ltd., 301
Claeys, Eric, 277
Coase Theorem. *See* Coase, Ronald
Coase, Ronald, 31, 32, 33, 186, 187, 204

Coleman, Jules, 24
common interest communities
   and decision making, 65
common law
   and causal requirements, 296
   characteristics of, 294
   compared with legislation, 294–99
   and harm requirement, 296
common pool resources. *See* common property: shared resources
common property
   and co-owners, 214
   and co-users, 218
   and Elinor Ostrom's ideas, 219
   shared resources, 213, 225
comparative institutional analysis, 38–41. *See also* institutional analysis
condominiums. *See* common interest communities
cooperation
   and belief systems, 84
   and co-owners, 217
   and co-users, 219
   and exit, 213, 220
   and fable of exchange, 89–91
   and individual decisions, 67
   and invisible hand theories, 86
   and the liberal commons, 222
   and other regarding behavior, 114
   and reciprocal benefits, 295
   and severance, 218
cooperatives. *See* common interest communities
corrective justice, 22–26
   and communitarian theory, 36

Demsetz, Harold
    and private property, 96
distributive justice
    and communitarian theory, 36
    relationship to corrective justice, 22–26
Due Process Clause
    and burdens and benefits, 310
    and limits on legislation, 310
    as policing lawmaking process, 293
    and regulatory takings, 266
    and separation of powers, 254, 293
    and takings, 300
duty
    and the categorical imperative, 124
    in contracts, property and tort, 27
    and the duty to repair, 133
    generally, 115–23
    implied by decisions to use, 168
    implied by purchase, 173
    as limitation on right to exclude, 166
    and limits of common law, 295
    and no duty, 116, 295
    no duty principle
        source of right to exclude, 163
    and nuisance, 196
    and right to exclude, 260
    and temporal coordination, 232
Dworkin, Ronald
    and the duty to rescue, 117
    equality principle, 20

eminent domain. *See* Takings Clause
Epstein, Richard, 277
equality
    and assent, 229
    and burdens and benefits, 131
    and due process, 302
    and fault, 143–49
    and freedoms, 228
    and land use regulation, 255, 290
    the principle, 20
essentialist theories. *See* theories of property
evolution of property rights, 34, 75, 98
    and belief systems, 84
    and common property, 219
    generally, 92–96
    and invisible hand theories, 75, 79
    and social recognition, 48–51
    and statist theories, 75, 80, 100
exclusion, 261. *See also* duty; right to exclude

exit. *See* cooperation
externality, 32, 33, 189

Fifth Amendment. *See* Takings Clause; Due Process Clause
First English Evangelical Lutheran Church v. County of Los Angeles., 269
Florida Rock Industries v. United States, 302
Fontainebleau, 209
Foster v. Preston Mills Co, 202
future interests
    and the market, 230–33
    and Rule Against Perpetuities, 238
    and uncertainty, 238

Hand formula, 28, 29, 110
Hawaii Housing Authority v. Midkiff, 283

information cost theory, 41–44
    and the right to exclude, 178
institutional analysis, 37
    and belief systems, 83

Jacque v. Steenberg Homes Inc, 182

Kaiser Aetna v. United States, 288
Kant, Immanuel
    and the Categorical Imperative, 124
    equality principle, 20
Komasar, Neil, 38
Krier, James, 74

land use regulation
    and burdens and benefits, 255
    as distinct from takings, 256
    and equality, 255, 290
    and right to exclude, 264
law and economics, 28–31
legislation
    and abuse of process, 304
    central competencies, 298
    compared with common law, 294–99
    due process limitations, 299–310
Lochner, 269
Lucas v. South Carolina Coastal Council, 264, 268, 308

markets
    and blocked exchanges, 245
    as coordinating devices, 244
    and property destruction, 237

Index

as proxy for future owners, 230–33
and public use, 280
and right to exclude, 263, 286
and servitudes, 239
McConnell, Michael, 254
Merrill, Thomas, 42, 161, 234, 277
Merryman, John Henry, 234
Michelman, Frank, 277
Miller v. Schoene, 267
Moore v. Regents of the University of California, 51, 245
moral rights
as problem of temporal coordination, 228

necessity
and the right to exclude, 175
Nectow v. City of Cambridge, 303
norms
as developed through cooperation, 87
and the division of gains, 91
and entitlements, 207
nuisance
and duty, 196
generally, 185–211
and insignificant harms, 206

obligations. *See* duty
Ostrom, Elinor, 219
other regarding behavior
and altruism, 114
and cooperation, 114
and co-owners, 215
generally, 54–55
and the rational person, 113
and waste, 235
owner as decision maker
and alienation, 244
co-owners, 212
co-users, 212
and eminent domain, 274
as essentialist theory, 64
generally, 47–48
as mediating device, 67–69
and motive, 71
and owner rights, 62
shared resources, 213
as unifying device, 313
and waste, 235
ownership
meaning of, 311

Pareto efficiency
and indeterminate outcomes, 77
and perfect competition, 86
Parfit, Derek
and veil of ignorance, 154
Pennsylvania Coal Co. v. Mahon, 269
permanent physical occupation. *See* Takings Clause
Posner, Richard, 234
possession
and rights of co-owners, 216
private law
and decision making, 71
distinguished from public law, 47
and public law, 252
public law
and decision making, 72
and private law, 252
public use, 279
current theories, 276–79

reasonable person
and decision making, 68
and the duty to investigate, 181
and duty to repair, 132
and the equality principle, 149
and Hand formula, 28
and Kant, 124
and location decisions, 193
and other-regarding decisions, 122, 123
and strict liability, 140
as unifying ideal, 139
regulatory takings
and diminished value, 263
distinguished from permanent physical occupations, 287
and due process clause, 266
and exactions, 260
generally, 257
and government torts, 260
as guarantor of value, 267
and just compensation, 275
and *Lochner*, 269
and *Mahon*, 269
to protect Takings Clause, 257
remedies
in exclusion cases, 179
Restatement of Servitudes, 243
right to destroy
and future interests, 237
as nuisance, 237

right to exclude
  distinguished from right to use, 263
  and duty, 166
  and eminent domain, 283
  generally, 161–84
  and land use regulation, 264
  and *Mahon*, 270
  and markets, 263
  and necessity, 175
  and no duty principle, 163
  and remedies, 179
  and Takings Clause, 286–88
rights theories
  inadequate as behavior theories, 62
  and land use regulation, 250
  underspecified limitations, 5
  underspecified origins, 14
Ripstein, Arthur
  and the no duty principle, 119
Rule Against Perpetuities. *See* future interests

Scanlon, Thomas
  and veil of ignorance, 154
separation of powers
  and due process, 254
servitudes
  generally, 239–43
  and markets, 239
severance
  and cooperation, 218
Shaprio, Scott, 74
Smith, Adam
  and veil of ignorance, 154
Smith, Henry, 42, 161
social recognition
  basic idea, 81
  and Demsetz theory, 98
  generally, 48–53
  by judges, 51
  and legislation, 250
  by legislatures, 53
  and markets, 107

strict liability
  as unworkable concept, 134
Sturges v. Bridgman, 204

Takings Clause
  current theories, 276–79
  distinct from land use regulation, 256
  and eminent domain regulations, 287
  and market failure, 279–82
  permanent physical occupations, 287–88
  protecting right to exclude, 257
  and right to exclude, 259, 286–88
  and value of property, 276
theories of property
  bundle of sticks theories, 38
  communitarian theories, 35
  and constrained decision making, 66
  essentialist theories, 38, 64, 66
    owner as decision maker, 47–48
  invisible hand theories, 75
  libertarian theories, 34, 229
  possession, 77
  statist theories, 35
tragedy of the commons. *See* cooperation; common property
transactions cost economics, 31

unjust enrichment
  and the fault principle, 137

veil of ignorance, 21, 24, 29, 56, 110, 133, 155, 157, 210
  generally, 154–57
  and nuisance, 208
Vincent v. Lake Erie Steamship Co., 134, 139, 196, 207

waste, 234
wealth maximization
  and the assignment of entitlements, 150
  as indeterminate, 6, 76